COLLECTIVE COURAGE

JESSICA GORDON NEMBHARD

COLLECTIVE COURAGE

A HISTORY OF
AFRICAN AMERICAN
COOPERATIVE
ECONOMIC THOUGHT
AND PRACTICE

THE PENNSYLVANIA STATE UNIVERSITY PRESS

UNIVERSITY PARK, PENNSYLVANIA

Library of Congress Cataloging-in-Publication Data

Gordon Nembhard, Jessica, 1956– , author.
Collective courage : a history of African American cooperative
economic thought and practice / Jessica Gordon Nembhard.
          p.   cm
Summary: "Chronicles the achievements and
challenges of African American collective economic action
and social entrepreneurship in the struggle for civil rights
and economic equality"—Provided by publisher. Includes
bibliographical references and index.
ISBN 978-0-271-06216-7 (cloth : alk. paper)
ISBN 978-0-271-06217-4 (pbk : alk. paper)
1. African Americans—Economic conditions.
2. Cooperative societies—United States—History.
3. Cooperation—United States—History.
I. Title.

E185.8.G674   2014
330.90089'96073—dc23
2013042173

Contents

Acknowledgments

This has been more than a ten-year project and has taken up much of my academic career. Therefore, almost everyone in my life has had to hear about the book or wait on me while I reedited or submitted yet another version. Most of the public presentations I have made have been about the book, so many audiences have listened patiently as I talked about the project. Many people have expressed kind interest in this book, and I've received several offers of book parties. So there are many people to thank. If I have forgotten anyone, please blame it on aging and overwork, and not on intentional oversight. This has been a cooperative effort.

Heartfelt thanks—for faith and friendship and for always believing that the book would be finished and would be great—go out to many people in my life, especially the following:

J. JEROME HUGHES ("How can I help to make sure the book gets done?")—for myriad small and large gestures and tasks, free research assistance, and editorial advice.

DOMINIC MOULDEN—for moral support and for reading the entire manuscript at least once!

AJOWA NZINGA IFATEYO—for always providing information and insight, support, and especially ideas for promotion and dissemination.

CURTIS HAYNES—for inspiring me to ask the question, for eternal intellectual inquiry, and for modeling the praxis.

MOUSSA WALKER FOSTER—for faith, genuine interest, research, and editing.

TOM PIERSON—for adding my interests to yours and always sharing your great research.

MELINDA CHATEAUVERT—for indescribable generosity in sharing personal research that provided essential historical perspective on the Ladies' Auxiliary.

CLYDE WOODS—for incredible insights, wisdom, and historical perspective, and for introducing me to the cooperative side of Fannie Lou Hamer.

FAYE WILLIAMS—for always asking about the book and reminding me of my priorities.

I am indebted to my family and friends for their spiritual support and inspiration. My parents, Drs. Susan E. G. Gordon and Edmund W. Gordon, have always supported me in every way possible and continuously believed in me—their love and wisdom have been indispensable. My children are my inspiration and my purpose. Additional friends have enriched the book and my life in countless ways: Rosemarie Maldonado, Audrey Gillette, Rubie Coles, ShepsaraAmenamm Berry, Tania Abdulahad, Mary Helen Washington, Elsa Barkley Brown, Rosemary Ndubuizu, Tanya Mitchell Lander, Khalil Tian Shahyd, Valerie O. Pang, Bob Stone, Christina Clamp, Gary Dymski, Sonia Pichardo, Michael Johnson and the members of the Grassroots Economic Organizing Collective, and the members of Organizing Neighborhood Equity DC.

I am grateful to my research assistants: T. J. Learman, who was there at the beginning and found some of the original information from Crisis magazine and other publications, Christelle Onwu, Dwayne Pattison, Chryl Laird, Charlotte Otabor, Morgan Diamond, Nigel Greaves, Laura Blackwood, and Mike McGuire (who read through all the FSC annual reports).

In-kind support and generous information also came from the Federation of Southern Cooperatives/Land Assistance Fund: John Zippert, Ajamu Nangwaya, Ralph Paige, George Howell, Heather Gray, Jerry Pennick, Melbah Smith, and Myra Bryant.

Financial and academic support was generously provided by the University of Saskatchewan Centre for the Study of Co-operatives and its director, Lou Hammond Ketilson (with support from CURA and SHHRC grants from the Canadian government); the Howard University Economics Department and the Center on Race and Wealth (and their directors, Rodney Green, Charles Betsey, and William Spriggs), which provided several research grants and a research assistant (with Ford Foundation grants to the Center on Race and Wealth); a PSC-CUNY 2012–13 research grant and the PSC union contract, which includes course buyouts, at City University of New York (through John Jay College); the John Jay College Provost's Office (through the Research Foundation of CUNY) for research support; the Africana Studies Department

at John Jay College, CUNY, and its chair, C. Jama Adams; the African American Studies Department at the University of Maryland, College Park, and its
director at the time, Sharon Harley; the Democracy Collaborative at the University of Maryland, College Park; and the University of Wisconsin Center for
Cooperatives in Madison (USDA research grant).

Many thanks to Sandy Thatcher, my first editor at Pennsylvania State University Press, for always believing me when I promised to meet a deadline,
and for maintaining his enthusiasm. Thanks to Kendra Boileau for seeing it
through to the end and to Robert Turchick and the rest of the editorial staff at
Penn State Press. Thanks to my anonymous reviewers. In addition, thanks to
the many, many others who have shared information, provided study tours,
showed interest, asked about the book, or invited me to speak about the subject, including Carlos Perez de Alejo, Nicole Marín Baena, Melissa Hoover, Ed
Whitfield, and the National Cooperative Business Association, the Canadian
Association for the Study of Co-operatives, the Association of Cooperative
Educators, the U.S. Federation of Worker Cooperatives, the Eastern Confer-
ence for Workplace Democracy, the Association for the Study of African-
American Life and History, the African American Credit Union Association,
and the National Economic Association. Also many thanks to Thomas Wil-
son, Emmanuel Briggs, William Darity, Margaret Sims, Ann Reynolds, Ann
Hoyt, Roger Herman, Jackie Smith, Lawrence Gyot, Jonie Eisenberg, Linda
Leaks, Stu Schneider, Heather McCulloch, and Erin Rice. Special thanks to
James Stewart and Patrick Mason for the example of their pioneering work
and their strong support.

Many thanks to the Bancroft Library, University of California, Berkeley,
for permission to refer to selections from the manuscript collection BANC
MSS 72/132 in the C. L. Dellums Papers. Many thanks also to the Chicago
History Museum for permission to refer to selections from the Brotherhood
of Sleeping Car Porters manuscript collection. Many thanks to the Library of
Congress for access to the Brotherhood of Sleeping Car Porters archives and
Nannie Helen Burroughs Papers; to the Chicago Historical Society for access
to the Brotherhood of Sleeping Car Porters archives; and to the Schomburg
Center for Research in Black Culture, New York Public Library, for access to
the Ella Baker Papers. For access to the Fannie Lou Hamer Collections, thanks
to the Tougaloo College Civil Rights Collection T/012, Mississippi Department of Archives and History, Jackson; and the Amistad Research Center,
Tulane University. Thanks to the University of Wisconsin Center for Cooperatives for permission to reprint Table I.1.

Because this book has been so long in the making, I have carved many
articles, book chapters, working papers, and oral presentations out of early
drafts of the manuscript, including Gordon Nembhard 2000a, 2002a, 2002b,

2004a, 2004b, 2005, 2006a, 2006b, 2008a, 2008b, 2008c, 2008d, 2010, 2011; Gordon Nembhard and Haynes 2002; and Haynes and Gordon Nembhard 1999. In particular, I acknowledge the permission of the *Review of International Co-operation* (Gordon Nembhard 2004b) to reprint table 9.1 and portions of the early version of the case study of the Federation of Southern Cooperatives/Land Assistance Fund in chapter 9; and of Palgrave Macmillan to reprint table 1 (included in revised form as table 10.1 in this volume) and content in Gordon Nembhard 2006a.

A Continuous and Hidden History of
Economic Defense and Collective Well-Being

Courage: Every great movement started as we have started. Do not feel discouraged
because in our few months of life we have not rivaled some long established Co-
Operative venture. Each successful Co-Operative enterprise has taken much time and
energy and sacrifice to establish. Nothing worth accomplishing is ever achieved without WORK.
—BAKER (1931D, 2)

No race can be said to be another's equal that can not or will not protect its own interest. This new order can be brought about once the Negro acknowledges the wisdom in
uniting his forces and pooling his funds for the common good of all. Other races have
gained great wealth and great power by following this simple rule and it is hoped some
day that the Negro will do the same.
—WILSON (1942C, 1—2)

We can by consumers and producers co-operation, . . . establish a progressively self-
supporting economy that will weld the majority of our people into an impregnable,
economic phalanx.
—DU BOIS (1933B, 1237)

We have a chance here to teach industrial and cultural democracy to a world that bit-
terly needs it.
—DU BOIS (1940, 715)

African Americans have a long, rich history of cooperative ownership, especially in reaction to market failures and economic racial discrimination.
However, it has often been a hidden history and one obstructed by White
supremacist violence. When there is a narrative, the history is told as one of
failure. The challenges have been tremendous, and have often been seen as
insurmountable. The successes are often anecdotal and isolated, little understood, and even less documented—particularly as part of an economic
development strategy and a larger economic independence movement. My
research suggests that African Americans, as well as other people of color

and low-income people, have benefitted greatly from cooperative ownership and democratic economic participation throughout the history of the United States, much like their counterparts around the world. This book documents these practices and experiences, as well as the various philosophies behind the strategy of cooperative ownership among African Americans.

Considering the broad aspects of cooperative economic development in African American communities over the past two centuries, my research shows that cooperative economic thought was integral to many major African American leaders and thinkers throughout history. These include known figures such as W. E. B. Du Bois, A. Philip Randolph, Marcus Garvey, E. Franklin Frazier, Nannie Helen Burroughs, George Schuyler, Ella Jo Baker, Dorothy Height, Fannie Lou Hamer, and John Lewis, as well as lesser-known figures such as Halena Wilson, Jacob Reddix, W. C. Matney, Charles Prejean, Estelle Witherspoon, Ralph Paige, and Linda Leaks; and organizations such as the Young Negroes' Co-operative League, the North Carolina Council for Credit Unions and Associates, and the Federation of Southern Cooperatives/ Land Assistance Fund. This study attempts to show how these individuals and organizations contributed to the development and philosophy of the African American co-op movement. I consider the various organizations' agendas and strategies over time, as well as the kinds of impact cooperative practices have had on Black communities. There are lessons to be learned from the history of cooperative economic models that can be applied to future discussions about community economic development in communities of color.

What Is a Cooperative?

Cooperatives are companies owned by the people who use their services. These member-owners form the company for a particular purpose: to satisfy an economic or social need, to provide a quality good or service (one that the market is not adequately providing) at an affordable price, or to create an economic structure to engage in needed production or facilitate more equal distribution to compensate for a market failure. The International Co-operative Alliance (ICA), a nongovernmental trade association founded in 1895 to represent and serve cooperatives worldwide, defines a cooperative as "an autonomous association of persons united voluntarily to meet their common economic, social, and cultural needs and aspirations through a jointly-owned and democratically-controlled enterprise" (ICA 2012b). Cooperatives range across the globe from small-scale to multi-million-dollar businesses. There are more than one billion members of cooperatives throughout the world

(ICA 2012a).[1] According to the ICA, in 1994 the United Nations estimated that "the livelihood of nearly 3 billion people, or half of the world's population, was made secure by co-operative enterprise" (2012a)—and the cooperative movement has continued to grow since then. Moreover, the United Nations designated the year 2012 "the international year of cooperatives," with the theme "cooperative enterprises build a better world" (UN 2011), recognizing the viability of the model in addition to its widespread use. Although they were not a well-publicized economic structure before 2012, cooperatives are a significant force in the world economy. Building on the successful year of cooperatives, the ICA and UN have now declared the following ten years to be the international decade of cooperatives.

Cooperatives are classified into three major categories, depending on the relationship between the member-owners and the co-op's purpose: consumer-owned, producer-owned, or worker-owned (or some combination of the three).[2] Consumers come together and form a buying club or cooperative retail store in order to pool their money to buy in bulk the kinds of goods and services they want, and the quality they want, at an affordable price. Consumers establish a grocery cooperative, for example, if fresh produce and natural and vegetarian foods are not supplied elsewhere or are very costly. Consumers also come together to buy electricity, financial services (as in a credit union), environmentally friendly fuels, pharmaceuticals, or child care, for example. Cooperative retail enterprises such as natural-food grocery stores and rural electric and energy cooperatives, together with credit unions, are the most common and successful examples of consumer cooperatives. Credit unions offer financial services and loans to a specific group of members (affiliated with a union, a workplace, or a church, for example) or to underserved communities, and keep financial resources circulating in the community. Housing co-ops expand home or apartment ownership to more people, addressing both financing and maintenance issues, and often build in long-term affordability.

Producers also form cooperatives to jointly purchase supplies and equipment or to jointly process and market their goods. Here again, cooperative economics facilitates the pooling of resources to supply producers or to help produce or enhance their product, to standardize procedures and prices, to increase the selling price, or to decrease the costs of distribution, advertising, and sales. Agriculture marketing and craft cooperatives are the most common form of producers' cooperatives.

Workers form cooperatives so as to jointly own and manage a business themselves, to stabilize employment, make policy, and share the profits. Worker cooperatives are often established to save a company that is being sold off, abandoned, or closed down, or to start a company that exemplifies workplace democracy and collective management. Worker-owned businesses offer economic security, income and wealth generation, and democratic economic participation to employees, as well as provide communities with meaningful and decent jobs and promote environmental sustainability.

Cooperative businesses must operate democratically, according to a set of principles that include open membership, equal voting rights for each member regardless of how much is invested, returns based on use, continuous education, and concern for the community.[3] According to the ICA, "cooperatives are based on the values of self-help, self-responsibility, democracy, equality, equity and solidarity" (ICA 2012b), as well as accountability and transparency. Cooperatives operate on a "double bottom line"—paying attention not just to good business practices and producing a surplus but also to good functioning of the association and to member and community participation (democratic participation) and well-being (Fairbairn 2003; Spear 2000). Because many cooperatives also address sustainability (both economic and environmental), they are often seen as addressing a "triple bottom line": economic (business), social (mutuality and participation), and ecological sustainability. Fairbairn argues, however, that making distinctions between social and economic sustainability is reductionist because it suggests trade-offs instead of synergies. A more integrated approach recognizes that "social and economic functions come together" and that economic activities achieve social goals (Fairbairn 2003, 4). This is not an either/or relationship in which one goal has priority over others.

Comparisons with Other Business Forms

The co-op participation structure and its mission or purpose are the major ways in which cooperatives differ from other businesses. Like all businesses, "all types of co-operatives have to cover costs with revenues raised in a competitive context" (Fairbairn 2003, 5). Cooperative enterprises, however, modify capitalist principles by limiting the amount of dividends earned, limiting voting power, and limiting the number of shares any one member may own (Emelianoff 1995, 83). In cooperative enterprises, the three major interests of any business—ownership, control, and beneficiary—are all "vested directly in the hands of the user" (ICA 2007). Cooperatives are organizations of buyers and sellers and consumers and owners—not one or the other.[4] This combination solves the general economic problem of overproduction and business uncertainty, eliminating the middle man and reducing costs, according to Warbasse (1918). The University of Wisconsin Center for Cooperatives

(2012) provides a chart that explains the major purpose, membership/owner-ship requirements, and tax liability differences between cooperatives and other corporations and legal business structures (see table I.1). A co-op's purpose is to meet member needs, not just to earn a return on investment (the purpose of a traditional corporation). Profits, or what co-ops call sur-plus, are distributed to members in proportion to use, with a limited return on capital in general in cooperatives, a departure from the practice of corpo-rations, where profits are distributed according to stock ownership (in pro-portion to investment). Tax liability is also different. Under U.S. law, members pay income tax on "qualified profit distributions based on patronage," and the cooperative pays taxes on unallocated surplus and nonqualified profits (University of Wisconsin Center for Cooperatives 2012). Owners of C corpo-rations (the stockholders) pay taxes on their dividends and capital gains from the sale of stock, while the corporation pays taxes on profits. Stockholders of S corporations pay individual-rate taxes on their profit share and their capi-tal gains.

Table I.1 provides more details about differences and comparisons with other business structures. For specific details about how cooperatives com-pare with employee-owned businesses, table I.2 compares cooperatives, par-ticularly worker cooperatives, with employee stock-ownership plan (ESOP) companies. Under worker-cooperative-ownership structures, the employee-owners vote for the board of directors, which sometimes consists of all the employee-owners. In worker cooperatives, labor rents capital instead of cap-ital renting labor, which allows the "new assets and liabilities created in pro-duction" to accrue to the residual claimants (workers) (Ellerman 1990, 207). In worker cooperatives, "the relationship between the worker and the firm is membership, an economic version of 'citizenship,' not employment"—the employment relationship is abolished (206). In ESOP structures, ownership is still determined by traditional corporate stock ownership—with voice and profits determined by how much stock is owned—and the proportion of stock ownership allocated to employees is determined by the actual plan that cre-ated the ESOP. ESOP companies democratize some of the stock ownership by distributing stock to employees and thus giving them some level of participa-tion in profit distribution and overall governance. But unless the company is 100 percent employee owned, the ownership of stock does not translate into employee control over decisions and work rules. ESOP structure does not necessarily change any of the major economic relationships or institute workplace democracy. An ESOP is basically a retirement plan that distributes stock ownership to employees as a major component of the retirement account. ESOP employees receive a return on their investment and any share

TABLE I.1 Cooperative vs. corporation comparison

	Cooperative corporation	Unincorporated cooperative association	Corporation (C or S)	Limited liability company (LLC)	Partnership	Proprietorship	Nonprofit
Who are the owners?	Members (individuals or entities).*	Members (individuals or entities); may include both patron and investor classes.	One or more shareholders (individuals or entities). S Corp. limited to 100 shareholders.	One or more individuals who are members.	At least two individuals or entities.	Individual.	No ownership.
What are membership requirements?	Determined by bylaws. Usually one share/fee. May include other requirements.	Determined by bylaws.	One share of stock, with rights and privileges attached to it determined by the articles of incorporation, bylaws, shareholder agreement, and applicable law.	At discretion of LLC members.	At discretion of partners.	At discretion of owner.	Membership fee may be required to participate.
What is the business purpose?	To meet member needs for goods or services; earn return on member investment.	To meet member needs for goods or services; earn return on member investment.	To earn a return on owner investment.	To earn a return on owner investment; provide employment for members.	To provide employment for partners and a return on partners' investments.	To provide employment for owner and a return on owner's investment.	To provide services or information.
How is the business financed?	Stock/shares to members and/or outside investors; retained profits.	Stock/shares to patron and investor members; retained profits.	Sale of stock; retained profits.	LLC member investments; retained profits.	Partner investments; retained profits.	Proprietor's investment; retained profits.	Grants, individual contributions/donations, fees for services.

Who receives profits?	Members in proportion to use; preferred shareholders in proportion to investment, up to 8%.	Patron members in proportion to use; patron and investment members in proportion to investment.	Shareholders in proportion to investment.	LLC members in proportion to investment, or by agreement.	Partners in proportion to investment, or by agreement.	Proprietor.	Retained within the organization.
Who pays income taxes on profit?	Members on qualified profit distributions based on patronage;** co-op pays on nonqualified and unallocated profits; co-op receives credit and passes through tax liability when nonqualified allocated profits redeemed to members.	Members pay individual rate, or can elect to be taxed as cooperative corporation.	C Corp. pays on profits; shareholders pay individual capital gains rates on dividends; S Corp. stockholders pay individual rate on profit share and capital gains.	LLC members pay individual rate, or can elect to be taxed as a corporation.	Partners pay individual rate.	Proprietor pays individual rate.	Not applicable: tax exempt.
What is owner's legal liability?	Limited to member's investment.	Limited to member's investment.	Limited to shareholder's investment.	Limited to member's investment.	Unlimited for general partners, limited to investment of limited partners.	Unlimited for proprietor.	Limited to assets of the organization.

Source: University of Wisconsin Center for Cooperatives 2012. Reprinted with permission from the University of Wisconsin Center for Cooperatives, 2012.

Note: There may be exceptions to what is summarized here. See state business statutes and/or consult an attorney for further information.

*Preferred–stock shareholders may include nonmembers and may vote on certain issues such as dissolution. As a group, preferred–stock shareholders do not set policy; only members can vote for directors.

**Members of personal consumer co-ops do not pay taxes on patronage refunds that follow certain IRS guidelines.

TABLE 1.2 Comparison of cooperative businesses (worker co-ops) with employee stock ownership programs

	Worker co-op	ESOP	Other employee ownership mechanism
Who are the owners?	Employees; sometimes nonvoting preferred-stock owners.	One or more shareholders (individuals or entities). Some proportion of employees (can be 100% or less) through trustee; employee stock held in trust (defined contribution pension plan).	Nonemployees and employees with some stock options in partnership, sub-S Corp., nonqualified stock purchase plans, incentive stock options.
What is the business purpose?	To meet member needs for stable high-quality jobs; have control over their own work; jointly market their services; earn return on member investment. For local employee control over investment and disinvestment.	Employee trustee retirement plan; to earn a return for retirement on owner investment. Local employee control over investment and disinvestment (depending on percent employee owned).	To earn a return on owner investment and provide some profit sharing with employees.
How is the business financed?	Stock/shares to members, and/or outside investors (social investment); sometimes earn grants for social mission; retained profits/surplus. Equity capital challenges.	Sale of stock: equity investors (partnerships with private investors and/or loans to employees); retained profits. Equity capital challenges if 100% employee-owned.	Sale of stock: equity investors; retained profits.
Who votes for and serves on the board of directors?	Worker-owners (one person, one vote). Employees under democratic governance and self-determination.	Owners, managers, employees (proportion depends on the ESOP agreement and percent employee ownership) (one share, one vote). Employee governance not guaranteed and depends on percent ownership.	Based on stock ownership (one share, one vote).
Who receives the profits/surplus or net income?	Worker-owners in proportion to use (patronage) and contributed capital at time of annual distribution; preferred stockholders in proportion to investment.	Based on share of stock ownership: for employees, dividends per share retained in retirement account distributed upon exit from the company/retirement; penalty for early distribution.	Based on share of stock ownership, dividends per share.

Who pays income taxes?	Worker-owners on salaries and on qualified profit/surplus distributions based on patronage (when distributed to member accounts); co-op pays on nonqualified and unallocated profits. Fewer tax advantages than ESOPs, co-op status (subchapter T of the Internal Revenue Code), but no taxes to pay on exit. Not tax exempt.	Many exemptions from taxes on the corporation, lenders, selling shareholder/original owner, and ESOP participation; benefits for retiring employee-owners (also employee-owners pay taxes upon exit or retirement, i.e., when distributed). Private investors also have tax advantage on exit. Not tax exempt.	Fewer or no tax advantages. Not tax exempt.
Incorporation/ charter jurisdiction?	State, with applicable federal requirements under tax law; less legally complicated than ESOP.	Federal; more federal regulation (through ERISA) than co-ops.	Federal.

Sources: Based on information in Olson 1993 and Britton and Stewart 2001, adapted by author.

of the profits upon exit from the company, which usually occurs at retire-ment, rather than during their employment or in proportion to their use, as in a cooperative.

Owners of corporations are stockholders, and their power derives from the amount of stock they own (their proportion of the investment). Co-op members are the owners, determined by the enterprise's bylaws and the fact that they have invested at all in the co-op (no matter how much or how little). Co-op members all have equal voting power ("one person, one vote"), and their influence on the cooperative depends on their participation in and use of the cooperative. Surplus distribution is decided jointly and shared rela-tively equally. These differences in structure and procedure provide cooper-atives with different mechanisms and unique functioning for conducting business—and they often give cooperatives an advantage over other types of businesses.

Cooperatives are not just economic enterprises; they are also relatively homogeneous associations of people who have come together to address a common need or want, which "reduces to a minimum potential frictions and suspicions within the aggregate" (Emelianoff 1995, 250). Traditional neo-classical economics lacks a theory of democratic or social enterprise, because "the firm is seen as a technologically specified black-box or, from the institu-tional viewpoint, as a piece of property, a capital asset—not a community of work qualifying for democracy" (Ellerman 1990, 207; see also Fairbairn 2003). Emelianoff (1995) tried to apply pure neoclassical economic theory to the theory of cooperation, and while he could describe what cooperatives are, he had trouble categorizing them as economic enterprises because of their social aspects and their function for use rather than for profit. Emelianoff seemed more comfortable categorizing cooperatives as some kind of not-for-profit organization without an economic basis, i.e., not a business. Fair-bairn (2003, 3) notes that business leaders, policymakers, and mainstream economists view cooperatives as burdened and marginal and as more likely to fail because they are expected to do more (i.e., they are hindered by the expectations of and obligations to their members), but they cannot raise cap-ital from markets in the same way as other business corporations. Spear (2000, 510) turns this notion on its head and expresses the concern that for-profit businesses, in their quest for excessive profits, exploit situations to provide inferior products and services. Spear observes that asymmetrical information and lack of opportunity to monitor quality create a failure in the ordinary contractual processes so that exploitation can occur. This gives not-for-profit enterprises an advantage as companies that can build and depend on trust, reciprocity, and transparency.

Emelianoff (1995) had no theory of the social enterprise when he wrote about the economic theory of cooperation in 1948. Later in the twentieth century, as scholars developed theories of not-for-profit enterprises, social entrepreneurship, the social economy, and the solidarity economy, there was a better understanding of cooperatives as economic enterprises with unique strengths. Today we have a much better understanding of not-for-profits and of organizations that operate economically and within some kind of market using monetary exchange, but where making a profit is not the primary purpose. Spear, for example, explains that demand-side theories of contract failure and excessive market power help to explain how state and market failures lead consumers and workers to search for alternatives that base economic exchanges more on trust and transparency (2000, 510). In addition, supply-side theories that focus on agency and the dynamics of institutional choice (508–9) contribute an understanding of social entrepreneurship and historical legacies to the understanding of cooperative effectiveness and efficiencies.

The Cooperative "Advantage"

Spear sums up the current understanding of the economic and social advantages of cooperatives: the associative nature of cooperatives and their tight connections with community "provide a uniquely favourable basis for the utilization of social capital, its reproduction and accumulation." This attracts nontraditional resources, reduces costs of ownership, provides "a network of [reciprocal and] trust relationships which reduce asymmetric information and opportunistic behavior," and allows "more efficient economic exchanges and activities" (2000, 519). Cooperatives address market failure, asymmetric information, distrust of opportunism, excessive market power, and barriers to entry.

As early as the 1920s there was clearly a growing concept of cooperatives as economic entities that solve economic problems in different ways than conventional for-profit businesses. For example, the director of the Division of Foods and Markets of the New York Department of Farms and Markets argued that "there is scarcely a duty connected with the marketing work that we cannot accomplish more effectively by the path of organization of cooperative enterprises than we can through any means of governmental control or governmental direction that did not involve cooperative effort" (Jones 1920, 51). He also argued that cooperative organization was the best way "to accomplish standardization, uniform packing and more economical methods of shipping" in the private sector, and to change distribution conditions: "if you have a consumers' organization that is distributing foodstuffs solely for use, you can change the physical facilities and change the methods of doing business and approach your whole problem from the standpoint of rendering the most efficient and economical service to the people" (53). The chair of the Committee on Cooperative Organizations of the Division of Foods and Markets also noted that cooperatives allow "uniformity of shipments." In addition, the committee emphasized the role of cooperatives in facilitating "needed market reforms," writing that the cooperative organization "often increases the price to the producer and lowers it to the consumer by eliminating abnormal profits, wastes and losses between the two"; "enables the grower to understand commodities and discuss them in the same terms with the purchaser"; "makes possible better business methods in dealing with the buyer, transportation companies, etc."; and disseminates "valuable information to help prevent losses in business" (White 1920, 29–30).

Others have studied the social purpose of cooperatives. Also writing in 1920, Ruby Green Smith noted the "loyalty to collective action that shall result in the greatest good to the greatest number" (1920, 16). Bristow Adams observed that "successful cooperation means the ability to work so that the other fellow can work with you" (1920, 48). The president of the Cooperative League of the USA, James P. Warbasse, noted that "the fundamental principle of cooperation is the principle of democracy" (Warbasse 1920, 26). These early twentieth-century views of cooperative enterprises anticipate Vanek's (1971) notion of active participation, Ellerman's (1990) concept of universal membership, and Fairbairn's theory of interlocking and multidimensional relationships between members and the co-op: "a co-operative has powerful advantages because of its integrated, flexible and dynamic relationship with its members" (2003, 26).

How are these notions of business and democracy connected? Can there be an effective and efficient business that is also a social enterprise operating on the principles of democracy and equality? Cooperative economic theory gives us an understanding of communities of work (Ellerman 1990) and associations of people engaged in common economic activity that "aggregate the market power of people" (Birchall and Ketilson 2009, 10). Cooperatives are understood more and more for their unique contribution to economic development, particularly community-based economic development. Cooperative economic development is experiencing success in urban as well as rural areas around the world, developing—and surviving—as a response to market failure and economic marginalization (see Fairbairn et al. 1991). Cooperatives address such issues as community control in the face of transnational corporate concentration and expansion; the pooling of resources and profit sharing in communities where capital is scarce and incomes low; and increased productivity and improved working conditions in industries where work conditions may be poor and wages and benefits usually low (Gordon Nembhard 2008c). Cooperatives "aggregate the market power of people who on their own could achieve little or nothing, and in so doing they provide ways out of poverty and powerlessness" (Birchall and Ketilson 2009, 10). Spear contends that "co-operatives have a greater social efficiency by generating positive externalities, and through their social benefits of empowerment, community links, etc." (2000, 522).

The United Nations (UN) and the International Labour Organisation (ILO) recognized the potential of cooperative enterprises for economic development and poverty reduction at the beginning of the twenty-first century (ILO 2002; Birchall 2003). During the UN's 2005 Year of Micro-Credit, the ICA highlighted the role that cooperative enterprises have played for more than a century in providing microfinance and supporting microenterprise throughout the world. The ICA claimed that "cooperatives are amongst the most successful micro-finance institutions" (ICA 2005, 1) at the International Day of Co-operatives on July 2, 2005, when it launched the campaign "Microfinance is our business: Co-operating out of poverty." The UN explains that its designation of 2012 as "the International Year of Cooperatives is intended to raise public awareness of the invaluable contributions of cooperative enterprises to poverty reduction, employment generation and social integration. The Year will also highlight the strengths of the cooperative business model as an alternative means of doing business and furthering socioeconomic development" (UN 2011).

People in every country and throughout history have used cooperative economics as a development strategy. Cooperatives—particularly worker-owned cooperative businesses—are examples of democratic economic institutions that provide a mechanism for pooling resources, increasing benefits, and sharing profits. In addition, those of us who study cooperative business development find that it solves many problems created by market failure, economic discrimination, and underdevelopment. Haynes and Nembhard suggest that "many who worry about the survival of our cities recognize that collaboration and cooperation are and will continue to be critical elements in any strategy of community revitalization" (1999, 65). Fairbairn et al. elaborate: "For decades, co-operatives in market economies have arisen where there are market deficiencies—imperfect competition, excessive concentrations of power, and unmet needs. They have arisen, too, where the costs of adjustment to economic change have threatened to destroy communities, where local people needed power to control the pace and direction of change in order to preserve what they valued. Look for the market deficiencies, look for the costs of change—look for the need—and find the niche where a co-op may thrive" (1991, 1).

Cooperative businesses are group-centered, need-based, and asset-building local development models based on the pooling of resources, democratic economic participation, and profit sharing. They are locally controlled, internally driven democratic institutions that promote group learning, economic interdependence, consolidation of resources, development of assets, and protection of people and the environment. Cooperatives stabilize their communities—increasing economic activity, creating good jobs, increasing benefits and wages, and encouraging civic participation. Community-based cooperatively owned enterprises are characterized by greater community input and participation in the planning, development, and governance of commercially viable, socially responsible businesses. Cooperatives provide a mechanism for low-resource people with few traditional opportunities to create new economic opportunities for themselves and their co-workers and neighbors.

Evidence suggests that cooperatives increase productivity and create value, particularly those owned and controlled by employees. Levine and Tyson, for example, surveyed the research and found that "both participation and ownership have positive effects on productivity" (1990, 202). Vanek (1971) similarly emphasizes the importance of and efficiencies gained from active participation (in ownership, which leads to participation in control and management) and equitable income sharing. Levine and Tyson summarize the research and conclude that cooperatives create superior working conditions. Spear finds that worker co-ops are more flexible than traditional companies, and have "less inflation and less unemployment in downturns which produces a positive macroeconomic effect" (2000, 522). Logue and Yates have found more recently that worker cooperatives and employee-owned firms have survival rates that equal or surpass those of conventional firms, and produce a combination of conventional and nontraditional economic returns. They "place more emphasis on job security for employee-members and employees' family members, pay competitive wages (or slightly better than their sector), provide additional variable income through profit-sharing, dividends or bonuses, and offer better fringe benefits" (2005, ix). In addition, cooperatives often support community programs and facilities such as schools and health clinics. Cooperatives tend to promote increased civic engagement (see, for example, Gordon Nembhard 2000, 2002, 2004b; Gordon Nembhard and Blasingame 2002, 2006), helping to empower communities to create new economic structures and infrastructure that meet their myriad needs, based on their particularities and experiences. Small, democratically governed cooperatives in particular, whose members are often low-income, work to broaden and democratize business and home ownership, and allow members to pool resources and skills to enable them to be owners and to achieve economies of scale and higher efficiencies.

Birchall and Ketilson (2009) document both the resilience of the cooperative business model and the ways that cooperatives and credit unions have weathered financial and economic crises over the past hundred years or more. Cooperative business ownership, cooperative financial institutions, and co-op housing have been solutions to past economic challenges, such as debt peonage under Jim Crow, and lack of food, affordable housing, and financial services during the Great Depression; and they can solve current and continuing economic challenges such as the redevelopment of the Gulf Coast after Hurricane Katrina and recovery after the housing crisis of 2007–9 and the current "Great Recession."[5]

In the twentieth century there was a growing recognition of the benefits of cooperatives, even for African Americans. In 1918, writing in the *Crisis* for an African American audience, Warbasse observed, "The fact that he [the Negro] is the most exploited of all people, that the government discriminates against him, and that he pays more for what he buys than does the white citizen should open his eyes to the possibility of co-operation" (1918, 224). Du Bois argued that cooperatives would provide the economic opportunities denied to African Americans, and would allow Blacks to serve the common good rather than be slaves to market forces (Du Bois 1933b).[6] Similarly, George S. Schuyler contended early in his career that cooperative economics would "save the race" (Schuyler 1930b, n.d.). A. Philip Randolph connected the consumers' cooperative movement to the labor movement (Randolph 1918; Wilson and Randolph 1938). Halena Wilson (1952) urged her fellow members of the Ladies' Auxiliary to the Brotherhood of Sleeping Car Porters to seriously consider the "mutual profit and common benefit" of cooperative ownership. By 1992 Jeremiah Cotton was rationalizing that since Blacks suffer common material conditions ("if each black person's material well-being is dependent on that of all other blacks"), they should exercise "community cooperation" (1992, 24). This book explores the cooperative thought of these and other Black leaders, chronicles their cooperative practices, and provides context for their cooperative economic ideas and strategies.

Is There an African American Cooperative Tradition?

When I began this project fifteen years ago, my colleague Curtis Haynes Jr. and I had been exploring how theories of cooperative economic development and Black self-help could address late twentieth- and early twenty-first-century urban redevelopment or revitalization. We made the case that what we called Du Bois's theory of racial cooperative economic development,[7] combined with Hogan's theory of Black self-help and the model of Mondragon Cooperative Corporation among the Basque people in northern Spain,[8] made a compelling case for public policy that fostered and supported cooperative economic development in Black urban communities (Haynes and Gordon Nembhard 1999; Gordon Nembhard and Haynes, 2002, 2003). It seemed reasonable to us that combining the thought of two important African American activist scholars with successful practice among another subaltern group would provide a straightforward prescription for economic revival in U.S. inner cities. Before the Haynes and Gordon Nembhard article in 1999, contemporary Black political economy rarely included an analysis of cooperative economics; and, to date, neither the delineation of a theory of Black cooperative economic development nor an in-depth analysis of the strategy and its accomplishments and benefits has been accomplished.

Haynes and I have also identified the elements of the Mondragon Cooperative Corporation in northern Spain that are replicable and illustrate networked cooperative economic development (Gordon Nembhard and Haynes 2002, 2003). We identified elements such as solidarity, worker sovereignty, clustering, leadership development, and education as essential to understanding cooperatives as a group economy strategy. I examine these concepts more fully in part III of this volume.

While presenting the general theory that cooperatives are an important strategy for economic development for African Americans and discussing our analysis with others, two major questions arose: have Black folk ever practiced cooperative economics? And why would resources be allocated for this? I became very curious about the first question, and as I began to talk more about cooperatives as a strategy for Black community economic development, more and more people told me that Black people do not participate in co-ops. So I set out to determine whether, and how much, African Americans have been involved in cooperative economics, and why African American memories and histories do not include cooperative practices or address cooperative strategy. In the wake of the UN celebration of cooperatives in 2012, this book offers a history of African American cooperative economic development that documents significant Black involvement in the cooperative movement. It is my hope that it will help us to understand the challenges and celebrate the successes of African American cooperative activity.

Methodology

Seeking to understand African Americans' connection to cooperatives, I began by rereading Haynes's theoretical analysis of Du Bois's cooperative economic thought (Haynes 1993, 1994, 1999) and then reread Du Bois himself on the subject (Du Bois 1907, 1933b, 1933c, 1935b, 1940). After 1907, Du Bois rarely wrote about specific Black co-op practices, but his 1907 study, *Economic Cooperation Among Negro Americans*, provided a brief outline of a history of cooperative activity among Blacks and was full of examples. His 1940 autobiography and his speeches of the 1930s discussed the promise of cooperative economic practice and why it was important. Since Du Bois was also a founding editor of the NAACP's magazine the *Crisis*, I thought that that would be a good place to look for references to twentieth-century African American cooperatives. Indeed, the *Crisis* published twelve articles between 1914 and 1944 about African American–owned cooperatives. Other Black publications—the *Black World*, the *Messenger*, and *Phylon*—contained several more. The stories in the *Crisis* and these other periodicals led me to archives of Ella Jo Baker, executive director of the Young Negroes' Co-operative League in the early 1930s, where I found more information about African American–owned cooperatives. I also looked at the papers of Nannie Helen Burroughs and Fannie Lou Hamer, and the several archives housing the papers of A. Philip Randolph and the Brotherhood of Sleeping Car Porters and its Ladies' Auxiliary. I discovered the Federation of Southern Cooperatives/Land Assistance Fund and started attending its meetings and conferences, exploring its archives, and learning more about the Black rural cooperative economic movement. The Federation of Southern Cooperatives is the only existing organization of African American cooperatives (see chapter 9).

As my research progressed and I began to cast a wider net, discussing my findings with colleagues and seeking new leads, more and more people approached me with information about cooperatives they had heard of or that their families had been involved in. In what I can only describe as a snowball effect, friends, acquaintances, and other scholars referred me to others who knew about the Black co-op movement, offered to share material, or even wanted to help with my research. I also began reading the memoirs of Black activists for references to co-ops or cooperative economic strategies, which also proved to be quite fruitful. While I rarely found enough information to re-create the complete history of any one cooperative business, I found references and information about many African American–owned cooperatives— more than I had expected to find—that revealed a picture of cooperative ownership as an important economic strategy for African Americans. Once I started, it was impossible to stop. Each new discovery led to two or three more.

In addition, whenever I talked about my research, I met African Americans who suddenly recovered a memory or made a family connection to a cooperative, or discovered a connection with something they were trying to accomplish. During presentations and workshops on my research, faces would light up and memories of cooperative efforts would surface. More and more people approached me to say that they had suddenly realized that their parents, aunts, uncles, or grandparents had been involved in a cooperative venture, and that they now saw its significance in a new light. People from all over the country have sent me information and offers to help; even more people have asked me for information. This is a subject that not only resonates with people but never stops expanding. I finally had to establish some firm parameters for this volume, because otherwise I would never have finished it!

I connected the rich archival research I was undertaking with the economic analyses I was conducting about cooperative ownership and economic development. I read DeMarco 1974 and 1983, Stewart 1984, Shipp 1996 and 2000, Cotton 1992, Tabb 1970, Handy 1993, and Woods 1998 and 2007. Some of these works gave me ideas about alternative economic development theories and strategies; others provided more specific information about Black cooperative economic development. I was interested in cooperative economic development as a community economic development strategy, and my focus was on how cooperatives help subaltern populations gain economic independence, especially in the face of racial segregation, racial discrimination, and market failure. My colleague Melbah Smith told me early on that many of the urban challenges that could be solved by cooperatives were similar to the rural challenges, and so I broadened my focus to include community economic development rather than just urban revitalization. I made connections with Canadian scholars who study cooperatives as part of community economic development and as part of social and solidarity economies. I began to focus on worker-owned cooperatives and engaged in participatory action research in the U.S. worker co-op and larger cooperative movements. As a specialist in racial wealth inequality, I also began exploring ways in which cooperative ownership, particularly in worker cooperatives, is a strategy for community-based asset building, and I began to develop a concept of community wealth based on cooperative ownership and community assets.

The result is a book that focuses less on situating Black cooperative economics within one theory of Black political economy (as Haynes and I first attempted to do in our 1999 paper) and more on analyzing it as a theory and practice of economic development within a broad tradition of populism and economic justice.

Collective Courage is a historical study based largely on primary sources (newspaper, magazine, and journal articles; co-ops' articles of incorporation, annual meeting minutes, newsletters, budgets, and income statements; and cooperators' letters and papers, memoirs, and biographies). This study is also informed by scholarly secondary sources and relies on economic analysis of quantitative and qualitative data, theoretical analysis, and applied theory using historical and present-day case studies and applying modern theories to understand the effectiveness of particular practices and strategies. In addition, I provide some analysis of balance sheets, budgets, and stock values.

While my archival research proved it impossible to uncover full case-study narratives of most of the African American cooperative enterprises and organizations from the past, I was able to collect many case-study "snapshots" of cooperative activity among African Americans to illustrate the successes and challenges of Black cooperative enterprises. Much of this information comes from newspaper and journal articles about specific cooperatives, memoirs of cooperative developers, and archives of cooperative organizations and their directors.

In addition, I engaged in applied participatory community-based research. As a part of the U.S. cooperative movement and the African American cooperative movement, I have studied cooperative enterprises and economics in the United States and Canada, and have participated in developing cooperative organizations and conferences to promote cooperative education and development. These organizations bring co-op members and supporters together to exchange best practices, provide education and training, organize and participate in co-op study tours, promote cooperative development, and network. This has allowed me to meet with many people (practitioners and scholars) in the cooperative movements in the United States and Canada, to learn from their presentations, talk with their members, and visit some of their cooperatives. I am particularly involved in the growing U.S. worker cooperative movement, and I now specialize in worker cooperatives. My participatory community-based research involves co-op members, co-op leaders, and co-op developers who articulate social, cultural, and political as well as economic impacts, and identifies relevant indicators to measure traditional and nontraditional outcomes of cooperative ownership. In addition to gathering information from workshops, presentations, and conferences, I used existing case studies and annual reports to assess the impact and benefits of co-ops and to understand their mission and history. I also conducted informal interviews and conversations, particularly during my own work-shops. I am a member of several cooperative research organizations and research efforts in the United States and internationally. All of these con-tacts and the access to this information have helped to inform this study.

This story of African American cooperative economic activity is told partly in chronological order and partly thematically. Themes such as economic independence, economic protection and stabilization in the face of discrimi-nation and violence, women's roles, education and training, youth involve-ment, and community economic development are interwoven into a linear treatment of the development of African American cooperatives in the nine-teenth and twentieth centuries. This is the first book-length work to connect the dots of African American cooperative endeavors.

A note on terminology. I use the terms *African American* and *Black* inter-changeably, although I understand that there are nuanced differences between the two terms and how they are used. I also capitalize the word *Black* when I use it as a racial category. I use the word *cooperative*, no hyphen (as opposed to the short form, *co-op*, always hyphenated), except when quoting or refer-ring to organizations that use the hyphen, as some of the cooperatives dis-cussed in this book do, especially until the 1940s.

Organization of the Book

This book is divided into three parts. Part I, "Early African American Coop-erative Roots," covers collective benevolence, grassroots economic organiz-ing, cooperative agriculture, and union cooperative ownership through the early twentieth century. The specific, deliberate development (or attempts at development) of Rochdale cooperatives among African Americans is the subject of part II, "Deliberative Cooperative Economic Development," which covers Black co-op federations and agency-driven co-op development from about 1917 to 1975. Part III, "Twentieth-Century Practices, Twenty-First-Century Solutions," consists of two chapters that pull this history together and attempt to provide a guide for pursuing cooperative development in the twenty-first century.

Chapter 1, "Early Black Economic Cooperation: Intentional Communities, Communes, and Mutual Aid," analyzes the mutual-aid movement among African Americans and the development of communal societies. The mutual-aid movement involved a large proportion of the Black community and con-tinued for centuries. I chronicle the myriad Black mutual-aid societies that sprang up during and after enslavement and examine their accomplishments, effectiveness, and the special role of African American women in founding and running them. Examples include the Independent Order of Saint Luke (Maryland and Virginia), the National Ex-Slave Mutual Relief, Bounty and Pension Association (Tennessee), founded by African American women, and the Free African Society (Pennsylvania). These early forms of collective ownership, buying in bulk, and charitable service were the precursors of mutual insurance companies, social service agencies, and joint-stock companies. They were also often the basis of early Black intentional communities. DeFilippis (2004) credits the Black "organized communities" of the nineteenth century as one of the most significant roots of the modern community-control movement. Chapter 1 thus highlights important elements of the early Black self-help communal settlements and intentional communities, both before and after the Civil War, that were often inspired by or part of the European and U.S. utopian commune movement. The contributions to this movement of African American abolitionists such as Sojourner Truth, David Ruggles, and Frederick Douglass are also noted.

Chapter 2, "From Economic Independence to Political Advocacy: Cooperation and the Nineteenth-Century Black Populist Movement," focuses on African American involvement in early populist movements for grassroots empowerment, particularly in rural areas of the United States after the Civil War. This chapter discusses the struggle for agricultural independence from sharecropping through cooperative ownership and African American economic solidarity, for example, in the Colored Farmers' National Alliance and Co-operative Union. The American populist movement was highly segregated. This chapter looks at African Americans' struggle to have a voice in that movement, to have their issues addressed, and to create agricultural, marketing, and industrial cooperatives through populist organizations and unions (such as the Knights of Labor and the Cooperative Workers of America) during the late nineteenth century.

Mutual insurance companies were the earliest cooperative-like incorporated businesses in the United States for both Blacks and Whites.[9] The Grand United Order of the True Reformers (Richmond, Virginia) and the Independent Order of Saint Luke (Richmond, Virginia) are examples of African American fraternal and mutual-aid societies that created mutual insurance companies. Their mutual insurance companies, such as North Carolina Mutual (Raleigh), stores, and banks are discussed in chapter 3, "Expanding the Tradition: Early African American–Owned 'Cooperative' Businesses." In addition, starting in the late nineteenth century, African Americans organized cooperatively owned and democratically governed enterprises that followed the "Rochdale Principles of Cooperation," first set out by the Rochdale

Society of Equitable Pioneers in Rochdale, England, in 1844 and adopted by the International Co-operative Alliance in 1895. Hope (1940) refers to these as Rochdale cooperatives, and I follow his tradition. The first such cooperatives were farm co-ops and cooperative marketing boards, consumer cooperative grocery stores, cooperative schools, and credit unions. The Mercantile Cooperative Company (Ruthville, Virginia) is the earliest detailed example I found of an African American Rochdale cooperative. Black capitalism was a strategy of racial economic solidarity and cooperation, as was Negro joint-stock ownership. This chapter looks at the businesses of the Universal Negro Improvement Association and Marcus Garvey's back-to-Africa movement in New York; the Chesapeake Marine Railway and Dry Dock Company and the Lexington Savings Bank in Baltimore; and the Coleman Manufacturing Company in Concord, North Carolina.

Chapter 4, "Strategy, Advocacy, and Practice: Black Study Circles and Co-op Education on the Front Lines," begins part II of this volume. This chapter documents the strategic importance of education to cooperative development and the sustainability of cooperatives. The study-circle strategy used by most African Americans in the early stages of starting a cooperative is highlighted, along with the importance of self-education as an economic resource in cooperatives. The Negro Cooperative Guild, though short-lived, was an early example of the deliberate use of a national study circle to inspire Black cooperative business development around the country. The variety of ways in which Black co-ops educate their members and communities, particularly about cooperative economics, democratic participation, and business development, are identified, with a focus on the education program of the Consumers' Cooperative Trading Company in Gary, Indiana, and the Ladies' Auxiliary to the Brotherhood of Sleeping Car Porters.

The Young Negroes' Co-operative League is the focus of chapter 5. The 1930s were an active time for cooperative development for both Blacks and Whites. The YNCL, founded in December 1930 by twenty-five or thirty African American youths in response to a call by George Schuyler (Schuyler 1930b, 1932, n.d.), first published in the *Pittsburgh Courier*, was strong in five cities by the early 1930s. Several cooperatives were developed through the league. The leadership of both Schuyler and Ella Baker (the league's executive director) was significant for different reasons, which are explored in this chapter.

In the 1930s, scholars and activists alike advocated the cooperative way and experimenting with co-op development. Chapter 6, "Out of Necessity: The Great Depression and 'Consumers' Cooperation Among Negroes,'" explores the accomplishments of African American cooperatives during the

Great Depression. This part of the history begins with the Colored Merchants Association of the National Negro Business League in 1927. Black involvement with the trade union movement also included support for and establishment of consumer cooperatives in particular. Du Bois and the YNCL were joined by A. Philip Randolph, writing in the *Black Worker*, in advocating consumer cooperatives among African Americans. I document the range of existing cooperatives in the 1930s and '40s, from YNCL-inspired co-ops in New York City, to the Consumers' Cooperative Trading Company in Gary, the Red Circle Cooperative in Richmond, and the Aberdeen Gardens Association in Hampton, to the People's Consumer Cooperative in Chicago and the Modern Co-op Grocery Store in Harlem.

Chapter 7, "Continuing the Legacy: Nannie Helen Burroughs, Halena Wilson, and the Role of Black Women," highlights the role of women in the cooperative movement, with a focus on Halena Wilson and the Ladies' Auxiliary to the Brotherhood of Sleeping Car Porters, and Nannie Helen Burroughs and Cooperative Industries in Washington, D.C. Women's roles in Black cooperative development have been strong throughout history, much like their role in the Black mutual-aid movement of the nineteenth century. In addition to early efforts by Black women, Estelle Witherspoon of Alabama (the Freedom Quilting Bee) and Fannie Lou Hamer of Mississippi (Freedom Farm) were leaders of the cooperative movement in their communities in the 1960s and 1970s. The BSCP's Ladies' Auxiliary and its international president, Halena Wilson, promoted consumers' cooperation. That case study provides many insights into the Black cooperative movement, its strengths and challenges, its champions, and its relationships to organized labor and the broader cooperative movement in the United States.

There are also rural examples of African American cooperative development in the early twentieth century. Many small farmers, particularly National Farmers Union members, turned to radical action during the Depression years. The activities of the National Federation of Colored Farmers are chronicled in chapter 8, "Black Rural Cooperative Activity in the Early to Mid-Twentieth Century." The chapter also examines the organization of the Eastern Carolina Council as well as the North Carolina Council for Credit Unions and Associates.

Founded in 1967, the Federation of Southern Cooperatives has supported cooperative economic development as a way to support and sustain Black farmer ownership and control, the economic viability of farm businesses (especially small, sustainable, and organic farming), and stewardship of African American land and natural resources in rural low-income communities. The early story of the FSC is also the history of the Southwest

Alabama Farmers' Cooperative Association and the Southern Cooperative Development Fund. After merging with the Land Emergency Fund, the organization became the Federation of Southern Cooperatives/Land Assistance Fund. The FSC/LAF is a network of rural cooperatives, credit unions, and state associations of cooperatives and cooperative development centers in the southern United States. Chapter 9, "The Federation of Southern Cooperatives: The Legacy Lives On," begins part III of this book and includes examples of cooperatives in the federation such as the Freedom Quilting Bee and the North Bolivar County Farm Cooperative. The organization has an important reach throughout the South, is the heart of the present-day African American cooperative movement, and is connected to the larger U.S. cooperative movement.

Cooperation is a deliberate and necessary expansion of in-group solidarity and cohesion. Chapter 10, "Economic Solidarity in the African American Cooperative Movement: Connections, Cohesiveness, and Leadership Development," traces group solidarity in African American cooperatives through civil rights activities, worker solidarity and leadership development in general, and women's and youth leadership in particular. Cooperative economic development is also a strategy to engage youths of color in school and community economic development. I analyze programs that involve African American students in community economic development and cooperative business development, such as Food from the 'Hood, and Toxic Soil Busters. While not yet fully achieved, the history of African American cooperative ownership demonstrates that Black Americans have been successful in creating and maintaining collective and cooperatively owned enterprises that not only provided economic stability but also developed many types of human and social capital and economic independence.

The Larger Project

This book is just the beginning of a theoretical analysis of African American cooperative economic development. I focus here on the first part of this journey—finding and documenting Black-owned co-ops in the United States and understanding their achievements and challenges, as well as the philosophy and strategy that African Americans used to foster and develop co-ops. I examine the big picture of co-op movements among African Americans and their organizations and leaders. I focus on the national organizations, the philosophy and strategy behind cooperative economic development, and its broad impacts. I show that cooperative economic thought was integral to

most of the major African American leaders, thinkers, and organizations of
the past two centuries.

In researching this book, I learned that almost all African American leaders were involved in Black co-ops in some manner: they either promoted or
engaged in the practice of cooperative ownership, particularly in their early
careers or as part of their vision for a prosperous future without discrimination. In many ways, this cooperative history is also a retelling of African
American history in general—a reconstructing of African American history
through the lens of the Black cooperative movement. Many of the players are
the same. Many of the great African American thinkers, movers, and shakers
were also leaders in the Black cooperative movement. That part of their history and thought, however, has been mostly left out, ignored until now. Adding the cooperative movement revitalizes the telling of the African American
experience and increases our understanding of African American agency and
political economic organizing. This study answers the question of whether
African Americans have a cooperative tradition with a resounding *yes*.

Economic participation in cooperatives increases the capacity to engage in
civic and political participation and leadership development. Cooperatives
also increase women's economic participation, control over resources, and
economic stability, with important implications. Cooperatives were used
heavily during the Great Depression, contributing to community revitalization and saving struggling communities. In fact, the 1930s appear to mark the
height of African American cooperative economic activity in the United
States. With unemployment and poverty high, and services curtailed or
unavailable, African Americans struggled to feed their families. They chose
cooperative economics as a solution. Throughout history, especially in trying
times, African Americans chose cooperation and often had good results. The
current Great Recession has been the second-worst economic crisis in U.S.
history. These are times in which many Black communities exist under conditions of high unemployment, deep poverty, and homelessness. Many who
had assets were stripped of them. The cooperative solution is one that has
addressed these same conditions throughout history. Cooperative ownership
helps address the challenges of capitalism, marginalization in labor, capital,
and product markets, and the lack of adequate, affordable, quality services.
Current conditions require alternative strategies. Cooperatives are again a
solution.

Part One

EARLY AFRICAN AMERICAN COOPERATIVE ROOTS

Consequently we find that the spirit of revolt which tried to co-operate by means of insurrection led to widespread organization for the rescue of fugitive slaves among Negroes themselves, and developed before the war in the North and during and after the war in the South, into various co-operative efforts toward economic emancipation and land buying. Gradually these efforts led to co-operative business, building and loan associations and trade unions.
—DU BOIS (1907, 26)

Early African American cooperative roots include collective benevolence, grassroots economic organizing, and cooperative agriculture. Part I of this book provides examples of many of the efforts at grassroots economic organizing and collective ownership among African Americans, starting from enslavement and focusing on the nineteenth and early twentieth centuries. Included in part I are efforts of African Americans to buy their own freedom collectively or escape enslavement collectively, as well as highlights of the Black mutual-aid movement, the Black utopian communities movement, early activities of Black trade unionists (particularly in the South), and early Black-owned businesses (particularly mutual insurance companies and joint-stock companies). These efforts illuminate the perseverance of African Americans in finding alternative economic strategies to promote economic stability and economic independence in the face of fierce competition, racial discrimination, and White supremacist violence and sabotage.

The first chapter reviews the history of Black cooperative communities and communes, and focuses on the history of African American mutual-aid and beneficial societies. Black cooperative agriculture and the Colored Farmers' National Alliance and Co-operative Union form the basis of chapter 2, about cooperatives and the African American populist movement. Much of this history is fraught with examples of efforts at collective economic action that were thwarted by racial discrimination, White supremacist sabotage, and violence. Such efforts to undermine African American cooperative development persisted throughout the centuries (Du Bois 1907; Woods 1998).

Part I ends with a discussion of early African American–owned businesses that were at least jointly owned and often collectively or democratically governed, some according to the Rochdale principles, codified in Europe in 1895. Chapter 3 also includes a discussion of the economic ventures of the Universal Negro Improvement Association in the United States and Marcus Garvey's interest in economic democracy. It remains difficult to distinguish formal cooperative businesses from Du Bois's descriptions of joint economic ownership in his two early books, as well as in the discussion of the Universal Negro Improvement Association's joint-stock businesses. I discuss both cases as examples of economic cooperation and solidarity. Where possible, I mention specifically which examples in this chapter intentionally follow Rochdale principles of cooperative business ownership.

What we learn from this history is that economic cooperation was natural and continuous in the Black community of the United States. There were periods of rapid and successful cooperative effort and periods of relative dormancy, though there seems to be no period in U.S. history where African Americans were not involved in economic cooperation of some type.

Lessons Learned from Early Cooperative Efforts

Many different kinds of cooperative ventures have been tried in the Black community. A few of them are featured in part I. What do we learn from these early collective economic efforts, which led to the development and ownership of cooperative businesses, often based on the Rochdale principles, among African Americans? The lessons can be summarized as follows:

- In every period of American history, African Americans pooled resources to solve personal, family, social, political, and economic challenges. They often addressed freedom, health, child development, education, burial, employment, and investment in cooperative ventures in ways that leveraged and maximized returns and reduced risks.
- African Americans formed distinct, purposive, and formal (as well as informal) organizations through which to coordinate and channel collective action and joint ownership. Many of these were stable collective organizations that lasted for decades.

- African Americans used existing connections and affiliations—religious, fraternal, geographical, and political—to develop new organizations or promote new missions. These existing networks provided the sense of trust and solidarity that often helped solidify the new effort. Racial solidarity, for example, became a major resource for these and future Black organizations and businesses.
- African American women played significant roles, held leadership positions, and often formed their own organizations throughout these periods and across almost every kind of organization. As founders and main participants in many mutual-aid societies, women were instrumental in organizational development, fund-raising, day-to-day coordination, and networking for cooperatives as well as other organizations.
- These activities developed among diverse groups and in diverse settings: in urban and rural areas among farmers, landholders, sharecroppers, day laborers, domestic workers, industrial workers, and the unemployed, as well as small business owners and professionals. Geography had little impact on depressing the cooperative spirit and seemed not to stand in the way of collective economic activity. Similarly, while some organizations were class based and exclusive, many more began as grassroots self-help movements, open to all—and were sometimes all the stronger because multiple classes were represented. In addition, these collective activities took place among ideologies of both racial separation and integration. Some of the stronger efforts were racially integrated; some equally effective organizations were strictly segregated by race.
- Many of these organizations spun off additional organizations and more formal businesses. Statewide, regional, and national federations and networks often developed around these local movements. Mutual insurance companies grew out of mutual-aid societies, and Black-owned banks developed from insurance companies.
- These organizations used meetings, conventions, newsletters, and newspapers to provide information, promote dialogue, and connect members to one another.
- Many if not all of these efforts were targeted for destruction by White supremacists, unsympathetic (often fearful) Whites, and/or White economic competitors (the plantation bloc and/or corporatists). White competitors used slander, violence, murder, physical destruction, and economic sabotage. They burned down the offices, farms, and houses owned by these organizations or their members. They shot and lynched leaders, members, and their families. They accused Black leaders of mail fraud and treason, jailed them, and initiated federal indictments. They denied loans to fledgling

businesses. They established their own businesses to undercut and outcompete the Black products and services. They even passed laws to outlaw the activities in which Black organizations and collectives were engaged.

- African Americans involved in collective economic activities often found that they needed also to engage in political activity to enact public policies or counteract White blocs and racially discriminatory legislation. In addition, African Americans often found it necessary to engage in collective economic practices in order to achieve or maintain the independence they needed to assert themselves politically.

- Lessons learned from the African American–owned businesses that were formal cooperative ventures include the need for education and training of members, leaders, and managers; stable and adequate capitalization and clientele; the building of trust and solidarity among members; and support from the community.

1

EARLY BLACK ECONOMIC COOPERATION

Intentional Communities, Communes, and Mutual Aid

This tendency toward mutual helpfulness appeared even among the slaves. Wherever Negroes had their own churches benevolence developed as the handmaiden of religion. They looked out for the sick, provided them nourishment which the common fare of the plantation did not afford, and often nursed and treated such patients until they were reestablished in health. Free Negroes of the South were well known for their mutual helpfulness.
—WOODSON (1929, 202)

The history of community control in the United States has several different components, but in terms of providing the roots for the emergence of community ownership, the most important of these is the history of black "organized communities" of the nineteenth century.
—DEFILIPPIS (2004, 38)

The history of African American cooperative economic activity begins with solidarity and collective action (economic and social) in the face of oppression, racial violence, discrimination, and sometimes betrayal. Even though separated from their clans and nations in Africa, enslaved as well as the few free African Americans continued African practices during the antebellum period—cooperating economically to till small garden plots to provide more variety and a healthier diet for their families. For two centuries they did not earn a regular wage or even own their own bodies, but they often saved what money they could and pooled their savings to help buy their own and one another's freedom (especially among family members and spouses) (Du Bois 1907; Douglass 1882). Free African Americans pooled their resources to purchase operating farms toward the end of and immediately after the Civil War, in order to own land and make a living (Du Bois 1907; Jones 1985). Freedmen and enslaved alike formed mutual-aid, burial, and beneficial societies, pooling their dues to take care of their sick, look after widows and children, and bury their dead. These mutual-aid societies were often organized and led by women (Jones 1985) and connected to religious institutions (Du Bois 1898, 1907; Weare 1993). Blacks often formed their own intentional communities to work together for mutual benefit. Some consisted of free Blacks, but many were organized by groups of fugitives from enslavement. Sometimes White benefactors created Black communities to paternalistically help African Americans learn how to be good citizens. Finally, some White intentional communities welcomed a few Blacks to integrate their communities. This chapter provides an overview of all these of precursors to formal cooperatives among African Americans.

Early African American cooperative economic action took many forms: mutual-aid and beneficial societies, mutual insurance organizations, fraternal organizations and secret societies, buying clubs, joint-stock ownership among African Americans, and collective farming. W. E. B. Du Bois, in *Some Efforts of American Negroes for Their Own Social Betterment* (1898) and *Economic Co-operation Among Negro Americans* (1907), documents myriad examples of economic cooperation. In his early work on the subject at the turn of the century, Du Bois used the term "cooperative business" loosely, even though he was familiar with the growing cooperative economics movement in Europe and the United States and corresponded with its leaders. The president of the Co-operative League of America (CLUSA), J. P. Warbasse, wrote an article in Du Bois's *Crisis* magazine in 1918. Du Bois's correspondence with Warbasse (DuBois 1925; Warbasse 1925) also indicates that Du Bois knew about the Co-operative League of America,[1] and therefore eventually understood the formal definition of a cooperative business. CLUSA did not, however, form until 1916, so that in 1898 and 1907, when Du Bois first wrote about cooperative efforts among Blacks, it is conceivable that formal, well-developed definitions of cooperative economics and cooperative businesses had not yet become standard in the United States. On the other hand, Du Bois studied in Europe in the 1890s, and the International Co-operative Alliance was established there in 1895, so he may have had some familiarity with the formal definition of cooperative businesses that was developing during that time. That said, his intention in these early studies appears to be to document the variety of ways in which African Americans shared the costs, risks, and benefits of economic activity that helped Black families and communities, and to illustrate joint Black business and economic successes. Later in his career, Du Bois proposed Rochdale cooperative organizations as an important economic strategy for African Americans, and in 1918 he organized the Negro Cooperative Guild (see chapter 4) to promote Black cooperative economic development.

Collective Resistance

Africans in the Americas and African Americans have showed throughout history their willingness and ability to organize themselves in order to survive enslavement and poverty. They have organized myriad strategies of emancipation, including buying their freedom, work slowdowns, the creation of escape paths, and the formation of separate communities. Du Bois (1898) notes the importance of collective resistance and organization for resistance and escape. The Underground Railroad was also a type of economic and social cooperation. The Underground Railroad has been much described and researched, so I will only mention here that Du Bois and others wrote about the ways in which the design and implementation of escape routes throughout the United States and into Canada were examples of high-level social and economic cooperation and collaboration among African Americans and between Blacks and Whites. The Underground Railroad system also linked independent Black communities to one another and connected fugitives from slavery to Black and White support systems.

Curl similarly notes the ways in which mutual aid and cooperation for survival "both among slaves and among servants were almost universal"(1980, 4). While their cooperative networks were mostly invisible to masters, African Americans used them as channels for organized resistance. In addition, the communal settlements and villages organized by fugitives from enslavement were used "as bases for guerrilla raids on the slavers. These 'maroon' outlaw communes, many with both Black and Indian members, appeared wherever slavery spread" (Curl 1980, 4). Like Du Bois, Curl notes that religious gatherings were also mutual-aid gatherings and often served as planning meetings for revolts and escapes. For Du Bois, religious camaraderie was the basis for African American economic cooperation, and churches, secret societies, and mutual-aid societies among enslaved and free alike created the beginnings of economic cooperation. In terms of official organization, mutual-aid societies actually predate independent African American churches (Hine, Hine, and Harrold 2010), but not Black religious activity. However, more important than what came first are the many ways in which African Americans used cooperation to survive enslavement, gain freedom, and advance economically.

Black Communities or Communes and Utopian Ideals

Runaways from enslavement formed their own communities where they eluded or fought off bounty hunters, took on the identity of Maroons, and lived collective existences in relative isolation. Du Bois notes that the African American "spirit of revolt" used cooperation in the form of insurrection to establish "widespread organization for the rescue of fugitive slaves." This in turn developed, in both the North and the South, into "various co-operative efforts toward economic emancipation and land buying," and those efforts led to cooperative businesses, building-and-loan associations, and trade unions (1907, 26).

In addition, abolitionists and abolitionist societies deliberately established Negro-organized communities and communes to house freed African Americans and to teach them how to live as free people, earn a living and an education, and run their own communities. They raised money and often managed these communal farms. These communities created spaces of isolation and independence from racism, used mutual aid and assistance, and pooled Black and White resources until African Americans could manage on their own. While not exactly centers of Black self-help (because African Americans were so dependent on White benefactors), they are early examples of African American communalism. Such communities were scattered throughout the American Midwest—in Michigan, Indiana, Ohio, and Wisconsin—and southern Ontario, Canada (DeFilippis 2004, 38; Pease and Pease 1963). The first communities were recorded in 1830 and were gone by the end of the Civil War, with emancipation. Weare (1993) notes that Negro-led societies were organized only after White groups refused to allow Black leaders to join them.

While most of the successful communes were located in Canada, some took root in the United States. The Wilberforce Colony in Ontario was nearly self-sustaining in 1831. Black inhabitants owned their own sawmill and one hundred head of cattle, as well as pigs and horses. They had a system of schools for their children that were so successful that neighboring Whites sent their own children there (Pease and Pease 1963, 50). However, the families remained poor, their homes were tiny and not well kept up, and they spent time and money on "endless controversies and lawsuits with their U.S. agent" (51). The Dawn Settlement near Dresden, Ontario, another Black community, developed around the British-American Institute. Josiah Henson, a fugitive from enslavement in the United States, was one of the founders and an early leader. Founded in 1837, the first tract of land, of two hundred acres, was bought in 1841 (64). In December 1842 the manual-labor school opened. The community developed to serve the school and operated "formally, and informally, as a co-operative unit in maintaining it" (65). By the early 1850s roughly five hundred African Americans/Canadians owned about fifteen hundred acres, separate from the three hundred acres belonging to the institute. Inhabitants raised corn, wheat, oats, and tobacco, and operated a sawmill, a gristmill, a rope factory, and a brickyard.

The Northampton Association of Education and Industry

The Northampton Association of Education and Industry (NAEI) was a utopian community and short-lived integrated commune in western Massachusetts. Among its inhabitants were Sojourner Truth, a washerwoman, formerly enslaved, who became an outspoken abolitionist and feminist, famous for her "Ain't I a Woman" speech, and David Ruggles, an African American printer and leader of the Underground Railroad, and an advocate of hydrotherapy (by 1845 he had established a water-cure hospital in the area, one of the first in the country). The NAEI was established in 1842 in the town of Florence (outside Northampton) as an intentional utopian community by abolitionists and social reformers (Historic Northampton n.d.). They established a community around a communally owned and operated silk mill. Milling of silk was chosen in part because the "equal and classless" silkworm is a symbol of democracy. The NAEI was a predominantly White organization that believed in the possibility of a socially, politically, and economically egalitarian society. It operated as an economic commune, and education was an integral component of the collective's aim to create a democratic and socially responsible society. The founders felt that everyone could do any job and encouraged members to learn silk milling, housekeeping, and social justice work "by doing"—by engaging in the work together, fostering active participation by all, and creating an egalitarian work environment. Members worked and studied together six days a week. On Sunday morning they worshipped, and Sunday afternoons were set aside for free discussions and debates about world issues as well as commune policies (Collaborative for Educational Services 2009b).

Three or four African Americans were associated with the NAEI. The abolitionists Sojourner Truth, Frederick Douglass, and David Ruggles were active participants and the most famous of the NAEI's Black members. The association accepted (harbored) fugitives from enslavement as part of its abolitionist and social justice mission (Collaborative for Educational Services 2009a).

Frederick Douglass was a fugitive from enslavement, an abolitionist, a newspaper editor, and a shipbuilder by trade who became an advisor to presidents and the first African American recorder of deeds in the District of Columbia after the Civil War. Although Douglass started his association with the NAEI at its beginnings in 1842, and would stop there on his way to giving abolitionist lectures in New England, he never lived there. Douglass visited several times, engaged in debates there, and gave speeches at the commune. He wrote about his experience with the NAEI in 1895, noting that its goals were to "change and improve conditions of human existence; to liberate mankind from the bondage of time-worn custom; to curb and fix limits to individual selfishness; to diffuse wealth among the lowly; to banish poverty; to harmonize conflicting interests, and to promote the happiness of mankind generally" (1895, 129). Douglass was struck by the sense of liberty and equality he felt among the group: "The place and the people struck me as the most democratic I had ever met. It was a place to extinguish all aristocratic pretensions. There was no high, no low, no masters, no servants, no white, and no black. I, however, felt myself in very high society" (130). The NAEI was the only place Douglass had ever been in the United States where he felt that his color was not used against him. "My impressions of the Community," he wrote, "are not only the impressions of a stranger, but those of a fugitive slave to whom at that time even Massachusetts opposed a harsh and repellant side. The cordial reception I met with at Florence, was, therefore, much enhanced by its contrast with many other places in that commonwealth. Here, at least, neither my color nor my condition was counted against me" (130). Douglass also mentioned meeting David Ruggles and Sojourner Truth there, and noted how well the community treated and protected them.

Sojourner Truth joined the NAEI in 1843 and lived there for about two years. It was there that she met William Lloyd Garrison, Douglass, and Wendell Phillips, and afterward became an abolitionist and women's rights activist and speaker. The commune elected Truth head of laundry, where she supervised White members of the collective, an unheard-of arrangement at the time (Collaborative for Educational Services 2009b). Truth recalled that the NAEI, more than anywhere else she had ever lived, provided "equality of feeling," "liberty of thought and speech," and "largeness of soul" (Historic Northampton n.d.), in spite of difficult living conditions. Truth described her first thoughts about the NAEI:

> She did not fall in love at first sight with the Northampton Association, for she arrived there at a time when appearances did not correspond with the ideas of associationists, as they had been spread out in their writings; for their phalanx was a factory, and they were wanting in means to carry out their ideas of beauty and elegance, as they would have done in different circumstances. But she thought she would make an effort to tarry with them one night, though that seemed to her no

desirable affair. But as soon as she saw that accomplished, literary and refined persons were living in that plain and simple manner, and submitting to the labors and privations incident to such an infant institution, she said, "Well, if these can live here, *I* can." Afterwards, she gradually became pleased with, and attached to, the place and the people, as well she might; for it must have been no small thing to have found a home in a "Community composed of some of the choicest spirits of the age," where all was characterised by an equality of feeling, a liberty of thought and speech, and a largeness of soul, she could not have before met with, to the same extent, in any of her wanderings. (Truth 1850, "Another Camp Meeting")

The commune did not last, and Truth's feelings of contentment and security there wore off as well.

When we first saw her, she was working with a hearty good will; saying she would not be induced to take regular wages, believing, as once before, that now Providence had provided her with a never-failing fount, from which her every want might be perpetually supplied through her mortal life. In this, she had calculated too fast. For the Associationists found, that, taking every thing into consideration, they would find it most expedient to act individually; and again, the subject of this sketch found her dreams unreal, and herself flung back upon her own resources for the supply of her needs. (Ibid.)

Over its four and a half years of existence, more than two hundred people joined the commune. Largely because they could not operate the silk mill at a profit, the community disbanded in 1846 (Collaborative for Educational Services 2009c). According to Truth and her biographer, however, the NAEI also failed because individualism corrupted the communal spirit. All members, including the African American members, moved on, but they recalled the experiment fondly, though also with disappointment.

Black communes or independent communities, such as Nashoba Commune in Tennessee and the Combahee River Colony of Black women in South Carolina, experienced both success and failure.

The Nashoba Commune

The Nashoba Commune was planned as an organized Negro community that practiced communitarianism in Tennessee in 1825. Founder Frances Wright, an early women's suffragist and an admirer of New Harmony, the Owenite utopian community in Indiana, planned to buy fifty to a hundred enslaved African Americans, set them up in a community, divide their time between manual work and academic study, train them for freedom, and provide for their colonization outside the United States (Pease and Pease 1963; Curl 1980).[2] All African American members were responsible for paying their own way, purchasing their own freedom, and paying the cost of eventual colonization. Slave owners were to be compensated, and the money invested in the community was to be paid back. According to Curl, "While Owen's concept strove toward the liberation of all people from wage-slavery, Wright tried to apply the concept to chattel-slavery. She considered it one last hope for the liberation of black people short of violent insurrection" (1980, 11).

Wright bought three hundred acres near Memphis. Once established, the Nashoba Commune actually became an interracial community of free persons—enslaved people were no longer invited to join unless they were original inhabitants and their masters moved with them. Sometimes called a cooperative and sometimes a commune, the community struggled socially and politically for three years. African Americans were not allowed to hold leadership positions. Local racists also harassed the community (Curl 1980, 11). In 1828, when Wright returned from convalescence in Europe, the community was suffering from the national economic depression, as well as mismanagement. In 1829 Nashoba members could not pay their mortgages and disbanded. Wright sent the original African American inhabitants whom she was responsible for, including the enslaved members whom she still owned, to freedom in Haiti (Pease and Pease 1963, 36–37). According to Curl, Wright then became active in the New York Workingmen's Party, "giving up the socialist community strategy as impracticable at the time" (1980, 11).

The Combahee River Colony

The Combahee River Colony had a much different beginning and purpose. The colony was located in a remote area where African Americans established their own settlements and remained relatively self-sufficient and semiautonomous: the Gullah/Geechee communities in the South Carolina and Georgia Sea Islands. The Combahee River Colony in South Carolina consisted of several hundred African American women during the Civil War whose men had gone to join the Union Army. They occupied abandoned farmland where they "grew crops and cared for one another" (Jones 1985, 52). They refused to work for Whites and were proud of their handicrafts and cotton crop, as well as their independence. The community became relatively well known as an example of Black women's independence, perseverance, and collective spirit.

Fit to Be Free

Pease and Pease describe these "organized Negro communities"—"designed to prove that the Negro was fit to be a free man"—as "impressive undertakings," both in the goals set and "in the dedication, zeal, and vision of those who devoted themselves to" them (1963, 160). They were political and economic havens for escaped enslaved people and impoverished freedmen, operating under ideals of Jeffersonian agrarianism and, later, urban-industrial entrepreneurship. These communities provided academic and vocational education, as well as citizenship and political training for moral and spiritual improvement and leadership development. Although collective in practice, the ideals promoted most by the White organizers (and many of the Black leaders) were the ultimate achievement of middle-class culture, individualism, and capitalist development. Individuals and their families did benefit. During the time they lived there, and while the communities were successful, members were able to make a living collectively, to provide themselves and their children with a good education and other training, and often to own their own land. While the examples show that there were benefits from and positive aspects of these communities, they were also based largely on paternalistic relationships between White benefactor-managers and Black residents. These communities suffered many hardships, missteps, frauds, and failures. Pease and Pease observe that "often settlements looked less like co-operative community enterprises than like isolated reservations" (1963, 162). The goal was to create gentleman farmers out of ex-enslaved people, to have them work the soil to improve their character. Most of these communities succeeded in training Blacks to adjust to and integrate into White society, but not in changing White attitudes, making systemic changes, or even operating in separate utopian societies. The Combahee River Colony stands out as one of the few that had genuine strong African American leadership and were largely autonomous of White oversight. Pease and Pease conclude pessimistically that "the results were, on the whole, . . . tragically inconsequential" (160).

Nevertheless, these experiments in communal living provided training in and collective memory of democratic communities and attempts at cooperative economics among African Americans. Some of the communities, especially those organized by African Americans for their own independence, such as the Combahee River Colony, were much more separatist in desire and collective in practice. DeFilippis notes that some socialist communes were radical:

> While the black communes emerged in the 1830s and were explicitly geared toward reproducing agrarian and mercantile capitalism in black communities, there was a parallel and yet completely different history of nineteenth-century communes and collectives that were oriented toward exactly the opposite goal—creating places outside the constraints and structures of the emergent industrial capitalist world of wage slavery and employment-based production. These "utopian" communities were attempts at local-scale communism, and they were largely divided between secular and religious communes, although there was a good deal of overlap. (2004, 39)[3]

Although none of the Owenite communes were predominantly African American—most had no Black members at all (because Blacks and Whites were not supposed to live together)—an exception was the Northampton Association of Education and Industry. As noted above, the NAEI invited interracial membership and allowed Black leadership. The Nashoba Commune was supposed to be, first, a predominantly Black utopian society (or at least training ground), and, second, an integrated utopian society whose purpose was to provide opportunities for African Americans to learn communal living while earning enough to buy their freedom and passage to Haiti or Liberia. Unlike the NAEI, Nashoba was not particularly egalitarian and did not encourage Black leadership. While not particularly successful, Nashoba lasted longer than some of Owen's White socialist utopian communes. Nonetheless, according to DeFilippis, the history of nineteenth-century Black "organized communities" provides the "roots for the emergence of community ownership" and community control in the United States (2004, 38).

Mutual-Aid and Beneficial Societies

Collective practice and leadership among independent African Americans was more evident in the more prevalent and very successful African American mutual-aid and beneficial societies. The majority of early African American cooperative economic activity revolved around benevolent societies, beneficial societies, mutual-aid societies, and, more formally and more commonly, mutual insurance companies. Many of these societies were integrally connected with religious institutions or people with the same religious affiliation, and they established educational, health, social welfare, moral, and economic services for their members. Chief among the activities was care for widows and children, the elderly, and the poor, and provision of burial services.[4] Woodson describes a "tendency toward mutual helpfulness" among the enslaved and notes that free Negroes in the South "were well known for their mutual helpfulness." In addition, "wherever Negroes had their own churches benevolence developed as the handmaiden of religion" (1929, 202).

The purpose of these mutual-aid societies was to "provide people with the basic needs of everyday life—clothing, shelter, and emotional and physical sustenance" (Jones 1985, 127). In addition to social welfare functions, many of the societies promoted temperance and other middle-class and Christian values; but they also protected fugitives and free African Americans from kidnappers (Hine, Hine, and Harrold 2010, 116). Berry notes that "African Americans had long been in the habit of forming mutual assistance associations, providing help when government refused to help. For African Americans, such mediating institutions historically provided the only available social assistance" (2005, 61). Similarly, Weare contends that mutual aid was a "pragmatic response to social and economic needs. In many cases autonomous Negro societies were organized only after Black leaders were rebuffed when they sought to join existing white groups" (1993, 8).

According to Hine, Hine and Harrold, "the earliest Black community institutions were mutual aid societies" (2010, 116). Du Bois notes their large numbers and wide ramifications by 1907 (1907, 93). Berry calls mutual aid "one component of the broad effort at community care among African Americans, which included secret societies, homes for children, old-age homes, and a flexible family system for individuals throughout the life cycle" (2005, 64). In addition, Black Freemason societies united Black men regionally and were a major social movement in the late eighteenth and early nineteenth centuries (Hine, Hine, and Harrold 2010, 117). Fraternities and secret societies were equally plentiful and influential. Woodson observes that "while they were secret in procedure and benevolent in purpose these fraternal agencies offered unusual opportunities for community effort, the promotion of racial consciousness, and the development of leadership" (1929, 205).

Most scholars of this era (Berry 2005; Weare 1993; Pollard 1980; Woodson 1929; Du Bois 1898 and 1907, for example) note the connection between mutual aid and religious activity. As Du Bois observed:

> Of the 236 efforts and institutions reported in this inquiry [about practical insurance and benevolence], seventy-nine are churches. Next in importance to churches come the Negro secret societies. . . . Of the

organizations reported ninety-two were secret societies—some, branches or imitations of great white societies, some original Negro inventions. . . . There are, however, many Negro organizations whose sole object is to aid and reform. First among these come the beneficial societies. . . . These beneficial organizations have spread until to-day there are many thousands of them in the United States. They are mutual benefit associations and are usually connected with churches. Of such societies twenty-six are returned in this report. (1898, 4–5)

Interestingly, the first independent Black church in the United States, the African Methodist Episcopal (AME) Church, was established by the leaders of the second African American mutual-aid society in the country, the Free African Society in Philadelphia. The first official mutual-aid society was organized in Newport, Rhode Island, in 1780 (Hine, Hine and Harrold 2010), followed by the Free African Society (often erroneously believed to be the first), established by Richard Allen and Absalom Jones in 1787. Allen and Jones also founded the AME Church in Philadelphia in 1816. Six years earlier, the first African American insurance company, African Insurance Company, was established in Philadelphia (Du Bois 1907, 98). The Negro convention movement also began in Philadelphia, in 1830, and was an important stimulus to the growth of beneficial societies across the nation (Pollard 1980, 231). Here we see the interconnectedness in one city between the different forms of society and help, and between the various institutions that provided them with solidarity and support.

Black mutual-aid and beneficial societies spread rapidly in the early 1800s, especially in the North and in urban areas (Jones 1985, 126; Weare 1993). Although more common in the North, many southern cities, such as New Orleans, Charleston (Berry 2005), and Richmond (Weare 1993), also had these societies. By 1830 there were more than a hundred mutual-aid societies in Philadelphia alone, and about thirty in Baltimore. In 1855, 9,762 African Americans were members of 108 Black mutual-aid societies in Philadelphia (Hine, Hine, and Harrold 2010, 183). Du Bois (1907) focused much of his research on the various societies in Baltimore.

Du Bois (1898, 19) described the business methods of beneficial societies. A group of people who know each other through their neighborhood or church or other organization join an organization to provide a service or set of services. They agree to pay an initial fee to join and a weekly or monthly fee to keep the common fund operating. A specified portion is paid to any member who needs the service, whether he or she is sick and needs a doctor, hospitalization, an income while convalescing, or needs to be buried or needs food or clothing. Sometimes other members donate their services instead of, or in addition to, funds from the organization's treasury. Some societies hire their own doctor or nurse to attend to members' health needs (Berkeley 1985). According to Pollard, these societies paid death benefits of between $10 and $20, and sick benefits from $1 to $3, each on premiums of 25 cents on average (1980, 231). Weare similarly records that premiums ranged from 25 to 37 cents per month and that benefits ranged from $1.50 to $3 per week for sickness and $10 to $20 for death claims (1993, 9). Many families belonged to two or more aid societies in order to increase their sick benefits.

Although the first mutual-aid societies were male only or dominated by men, by the 1790s women had established their own mutual-aid and benefi-cial societies (Berkeley 1985; Jones 1985; Lerner 1974; Boylan 1984). Berkeley contends that "black women were often in the vanguard in founding and sustaining autonomous organizations designed specifically to improve social conditions within their respective communities. . . . In creating autonomous institutions to solve the problems caused by inadequate health care services, substandard housing, economic deprivation, and segregated schools, black women served notice that they felt a special responsibility to provide social welfare programs for their communities" (1985, 184). Black women estab-lished day nurseries, orphanages, homes for the aged and infirm, hospitals, cemeteries, night schools, and scholarship funds (Berkeley 1985; Jones 1985; Lerner 1974). They pooled "meager resources," sponsored fund-raisers, solicited voluntary contributions (Berkeley 1985, 85), and used modest dues that even the "poorest women managed to contribute" to meet vital social welfare needs (Jones 1985). Women's mutual-aid societies proliferated and were sometimes more numerous than all-male or men-oriented ones, and became influential in the Black community throughout the 1800s and into the 1900s. "In 1793 Philadelphia's Female Benevolent Society of St. Thomas took over the welfare functions of the city's Free African Society" (Hine, Hine, and Harrold 2010, 116). This was one of the first female societies among Afri-can Americans. Other Black women's societies in Philadelphia included the Benevolent Daughters, the Daughters of Africa, and the American Female Bond Benevolent Society. In Petersburg, Virginia, half of the mutual-aid societies were exclusively female, such as the Sisters of Friendship, Sisters of Charity, and Ladies Union (Jones 1985, 126).

Mutual-aid, benevolent, self-improvement, and fraternal organizations also proliferated after the Civil War (Hine, Hine, and Harrold 2010, 183). Berry explains that after emancipation, African Americans sought to pool their resources and work together in order to survive (2005, 102). Those who were free before the Civil War provided the only economic base the African

American community had immediately after emancipation. The mutual-aid societies provided a structure for their collective efforts.[5] Petersburg, Virginia, had twenty-two different voluntary societies in 1898 (Jones 1985). The Workers' Mutual Aid Association in Virginia, for example, was organized in 1894. In 1898 it had twelve stockholders and two salaried officers, 10,053 members, an annual income of $3,600, and property worth $550 (Du Bois 1898). It paid sick and death benefits totaling $1,700 during that year (20). The Cotton Jammers and Longshoremen's Association No. 2 of Galveston, Texas, was more than a trade union, according to Du Bois. It invested $1,000 in tools. Members and "different gangs at work" paid dues to the organization, and the association paid sick and death benefits (26).

By 1898, 15 percent of Black men and 52 percent of Black women in New York City belonged to a mutual-aid society, even though nationally the number of mutual-aid societies was beginning to decline (Du Bois 1898, 19). If New York City is typical, women were overwhelmingly members of mutual-aid societies at the end of the nineteenth century. And although there were fewer aid organizations by the beginning of the twentieth century, the record shows that many remained strong and effective. It is important to note that while the federal Freedmen's Bureau engaged in similar efforts to help newly freed African Americans during the first Reconstruction era, this did not prevent African Americans from organizing on their own and continuing to provide aid through local (and sometimes regional) Black-owned and Black-controlled organizations.

The Ex-Slave Mutual Relief, Bounty and Pension Association

Mary Frances Berry, in her biography of Callie House, describes the dual purpose of the Ex-Slave Mutual Relief, Bounty and Pension Association, founded in 1896 in Tennessee. The primary purpose was to pressure legislators to enact legislation to establish pensions for ex-slaves. Its secondary purpose was to provide aid and relief to members in need. The mutual-aid function operated continuously, even after the pension movement declined, kept the organization solvent, and helped to protect it from prosecution for mail fraud (as a lobbying organization, the association was accused of accepting unlawful payments through the mail). Even after giving up the pension legislation mission by 1916, the association remained a mutual-aid society, some of the chapters continuing mutual-aid activities until 1931 (Berry 2005). Berry's biography provides a comprehensive account of the organization's operations, members' political activities, and the importance of the association's mission to provide economic and social welfare safety nets.

The National Ex-Slave Mutual Relief, Bounty and Pension Association took on what was "essentially a poor people's movement" (Berry 2005, 51), demanding pensions for the formerly enslaved to compensate for years of unpaid labor. The association also provided medical and burial assistance. In addition, it offered a democratic structure in which local people had control and a voice, "at a time when blacks were practically disfranchised or on the verge of becoming so throughout the South" (51–52). The association emphasized self-help, and local chapters were required to use part of their dues for sick benefits and the burial of members (61). Many of the founders and charter members of the association already had experience in a mutual-aid society. Lead organizer Callie House "emphasized the need for local mutual benefit activities as the linchpin of their solidarity" (94). Members paid an initial fee of 25 cents, plus 20 cents per month in dues. Local organizations paid $2.50 for a charter. Also, if needed, the association could collect "extraordinary" collections of 5 cents per member to defray unusual expenses.

Maggie Lena Walker and the Independent Order of Saint Luke

Elsa Barkley Brown explores the role of Maggie Lena Walker and other women in the development and expansion of the Independent Order of Saint Luke, which was failing when Walker became grand secretary in 1899. The Independent Order of Saint Luke began as a women's sickness and death mutual-benefit association in Maryland in 1867. The organization accepted men starting in the 1880s, when it expanded to New York and Virginia (Barkley Brown 1989, 616). When Walker took over, a majority of the board of directors were also women. They became politically active in their communities and served as role models for other women and girls. Walker "insisted that organization and expansion of women's roles economically and politically were essential ingredients without which the community, the race, and even black men could not achieve their full potential" (621). Women members argued that their community could not be developed fully by men alone, and that Black women had to be integral to the process (629). Walker also institutionalized a notion of family that encompassed everyone who worked within the organization (619), which helped to cement community ties.

Walker built up the Richmond branch of the Order of Saint Luke, which later became the organization's headquarters, adding a department store and a bank (the Saint Luke Penny Savings Bank) in 1903; the purpose of the bank was to provide loans to the community. The Saint Luke Penny Savings Bank also owned six hundred homes by 1920. By 1929 it had bought up all the other Black-owned banks in Richmond and became the Consolidated Bank and

Trust Company, the board of which was chaired by Walker. "By 1924, the Independent Order of Saint Luke had 50,000 members, 1500 local chapters, a staff of 50 working in its Richmond headquarters and assets of almost $400,000" (Bois 1998).

In terms of Walker's leadership and perspective on Black women and collective action, Barkley Brown writes:

> Undergirding all of their work was a belief in the possibilities inherent in the collective struggle of black women in particular and of the black community in general. Walker argued that the only way in which black women would be able "to avoid the traps and snares of life" would be to "band themselves together, organize, . . . put their mites together, put their hands and their brains together and make work and business for themselves." The idea of collective economic development was not a new idea for these women, many of whom were instrumental in establishing the Woman's Union, a female insurance company founded in 1898. . . . The institutionalization of this notion of family cemented the community. (618–19)

Barkley Brown makes several important points about how collective economic activity came naturally to the Black women leaders of Saint Luke's, because they had been involved in other organizing and economic development activity. The women also recognized that men needed to work together with them. This created a strong institution that expanded economically, socially, and politically.

Major Contributions of Mutual-Aid Societies

In addition to providing assistance to members, mutual-aid and beneficial societies also taught members many skills, both individually and collectively. Du Bois (1907) lists four major contributions: they encouraged economic cooperation, inspired self- and group confidence, consolidated small amounts of capital, and taught business methods. These important skills were transferable to other spheres of life, and set the stage for future collective economic activities. There are many examples throughout this volume of African American women and men who were first involved in mutual aid and then became involved in more formal cooperative businesses. Halena Wilson, the president of the Ladies' Auxiliary to the Brotherhood of Sleeping Car Porters and a co-op developer, started out as the leader of a mutual-aid society, for example (see chapters 4 and 7). Charles Prejean, the former executive director of the Federation of Southern Cooperatives, another example, notes that many of the early activists in Black southern cooperative economic efforts in the 1950s and '60s had first been members of community-level benevolent organizations. This experience "brought to [cooperative economic efforts] some skills that were very useful to the organization" (Prejean 1992, 15). Some mutual-aid organizations transitioned into formal businesses, particularly mutual insurance companies, which were the earliest of the formal cooperatives.

2

FROM ECONOMIC INDEPENDENCE TO POLITICAL ADVOCACY

Cooperation and the Nineteenth-Century Black Populist Movement

Generation after generation, ethnic and class alliances arose in the [Delta] region with the aim of expanding social and economic democracy, only to be ignored, dismissed, and defeated. These defeats were followed by arrogant attempts to purge such heroic movements from both historical texts and popular memory. Yet even in defeat these movements transformed the policies of the plantation bloc and informed daily life, community-building activities, and subsequent movements.
—WOODS (1998, 4)

The story of the African American cooperative movement in the United States is also a story of unionization, organized labor's early efforts at cooperative development, and populism. The Cooperative Workers of America and the Knights of Labor, integrated unions operating in the South, supported small farmers, laborers, and the grassroots Black rural sector (Ali 2003, 44–45). The Colored Farmers' National Alliance and Co-operative Union continued their legacy, challenging White supremacy and establishing cooperatives in a hostile environment. In the late nineteenth century, the cooperative movement was part of the populist movement for the rights of small farmers and laborers, working for political power, economic survival, and control over production.

The Knights of Labor

According to Steve Leikin, the Knights of Labor (KOL) was the American organization that came closest to replicating the experience of European cooperative movements, starting immediately after the Civil War years, an era in which the American Federation of Labor specifically rejected cooperatives as a strategy of labor reform (1999, 2). The cooperative movement in the United States was not closely aligned with organized labor, as in Europe, although there were exceptions, including advocacy, on the part of some labor unions, for worker, consumer, and producer cooperatives, such as cooperatively owned mills, factories, craft production, and retail stores. In 1836, for example, the National Trades Union, after prolonged struggles with employers, recommended cooperation as a solution to strikes and the dilution of craft skills (6), sponsoring about eighteen production cooperatives; and in the 1840s, the associationist movement produced twenty-two industrial cooperatives (Curl 2009, 4). Cooperative ideals revived in the 1860s, immediately after the Civil War.

Rochdale cooperatives had emerged by 1863 and began to attract supporters within the American labor movement.[1] Hundreds of cooperatives had been launched in the United States by the early 1870s (Curl 2009; see also Leikin 1999). The Iron Molders union, for example, organized cooperative foundries in Troy, New York, and Cincinnati, Ohio, in 1866. The National Labor Union (NLU), the first national union federation in the country, "threw all its weight behind the cooperative movement" in the late 1860s, in addition to promoting the eight-hour day, rights for women, and Black and White labor solidarity (Curl 2009, 65). The NLU advocated that all states should pass cooperative incorporation laws, and organized more than 180 production cooperatives between the late 1860s and the 1870s. The Sovereigns of Industry, a "reform organization" of industrial workers (1874–79), began advocating for cooperative stores in its more than three hundred local chapters across the Northeast and midwestern and central United States (Leikin 1999, 9; Curl 2009, 80–81). A decade later, the Knights of Labor supplanted the Sovereigns of Industry and operated cooperatives from their local chapters. By the 1880s, 334 worker cooperatives had been organized in the United States.[2] Two hundred were part of a chain of industrial cooperatives organized by the Knights of Labor between 1886 and 1888 (Curl 2009, 4). The KOL envisioned widespread adoption of economic democracy and the development of a "cooperative commonwealth." Leikin notes that at least five hundred cooperative workshops and factories opened in the twenty-five years following the Civil War (1999, 10). KOL cooperatives were concentrated in the East and Midwest. Most were mines, foundries, mills, and factories making barrels, clothes, shoes, and soap, but KOL cooperatives also included printers, laundries, furniture makers, potters, and lumberjacks (Curl 2009, 92). In Virginia, KOL locals organized a cooperative building, a soap factory, and an underwear factory (Rachleff 2012). Products made in KOL cooperatives carried the KOL label. African American members of the KOL operated a cooperative cotton gin in Stewart's Station, Alabama, and built cooperative villages near Birmingham (Curl 2009, 101).

The KOL achieved its greatest victory in 1885, when it won union representation against the Union Pacific Railroad. At its height, the KOL was the largest labor organization in the world, with almost one million members (Curl 2009, 4, 102). It was also one of the few racially integrated unions. According to Sidney Kessler, "tens of thousands of Negroes" who had never been in the labor movement before joined the KOL in the 1880s. In 1886 there were an estimated sixty thousand African Americans in the Knights of Labor, although some estimate that by 1887 there were closer to ninety or ninety-five thousand. "More than any other union of the eighteen eighties, the Knights of Labor realized that the self-interest of its white members was in the organization of Negro Labor" (Kessler 1952, 272, 275).

An example of the way in which Blacks and Whites worked together in the KOL can be seen in Richmond, Virginia, where small KOL locals began forming in 1881 on the basis of workplace, trade, neighborhood, or fraternal or mutual-aid ties. White and Black workers organized separate locals, and in 1884 and early 1885 established local district assemblies, which combined the small locals. Twelve African American locals organized District Assembly 92; six weeks later, in March 1885, eleven White locals organized District Assembly 84. District Assembly 92 had more than five hundred members and was the first African American KOL district assembly in the United States, according to Rachleff (2012). An integrated KOL campaign in Richmond organized the Workingmen's Reform Party, which won control of the municipal government in 1886, electing Black candidates. This new administration in Richmond proceeded to build a new city hall with a racially integrated, unionized local workforce. This was actually a biracial coalition of men and women laborers, with Black and White members organizing separately for a linked campaign with shared goals (Rachleff 2012, 34). As significant as the integrated coalition was, the gender equality was equally remarkable, especially given that women could not vote. Women participated in the KOL's campaigns and boycotts (often as leaders), and in the cooperatives as workers and consumers.

A major issue for the Richmond Knights of Labor was the construction of the new city hall—the old one had been burned down by the Confederate government as it abandoned Richmond in April 1865. In the early 1880s, the reigning conservative White city government solicited bids for the reconstruction of the building. In 1885 the KOL submitted a petition requesting that the hall be built with local materials by local workers employed directly by the city, who would be paid union wages and work eight-hour days. The petition also specified that all jobs, skilled as well as unskilled, should "be open to the employment of 'colored' workers" (Rachleff 2012, 35). This was of particular concern because the city had been contracting with workers from the Virginia State Penitentiary and using convict labor. KOL coopers in Virginia were skilled workers and among the most racially integrated of the trades. In the early 1880s the penitentiary housed a mechanized barrel factory within its walls and used convicts to make the barrels. This had a large negative impact on the local Black and White coopers, and the two KOL district assemblies in Virginia mounted a campaign to close the factory. Rachleff notes that not only was the strategy—boycotts, petitions, and electing KOL members to city government—successful, but it also transformed "their labor organization into a political and social movement" (35). Richmond Blacks, for example, convened a statewide Black political convention in October 1885, calling for an end to convict labor and a suspension of support for the Republican Party if it did not agree to this plan.

The Role of Women in Early Union Co-ops

The early union cooperatives were often relatively conservative politically and limited the rights and mobility of women and unskilled workers in their operation and decision making (Leikin 1999, 16). As women entered the labor movement, they began to challenge the gender bias of established cooperative values. Curl notes that co-op women attempted to incorporate "feminine" ideals of mutual aid and volunteerism as central to their cooperative visions (2009, 17). Black women, who had a long and impressive history in the mutual-aid movement, pursued the same goal, and brought time-honored strategies and skills to African American cooperatives. In 1886, Leonora Barry was elected head of the new department of women's work at the KOL convention (101). Barry was the first female professional labor organizer in U.S. history, and supported the KOL's vision of cooperative development.[3] Women members of the KOL set up cooperative garment factories in Chicago, St. Louis, and Indianapolis.

The Legacy of the Knights of Labor

The Knights of Labor connected workplace issues and labor rights with local, state, and federal policies, and was active in politics and mutual aid as well as economic development. The KOL connected and built upon earlier activities and organizations, and encouraged and promoted women's and African American involvement. Black members were known for their militancy, and were eventually forced underground in the face of antiunion and racist intimidation and violence (Ali 2003). Many militant White members also went underground in the face of violent opposition from conservatives and the corporate sector (Curl 2009). After the famous Haymarket strike of 1886 in Chicago, the decline of the Knights of Labor was felt most strongly among the cooperatives. As Curl observes, "The entire economic system came down hard on the Knight cooperatives: railroads refused to haul their products; manufacturers refused to sell them needed machinery; wholesalers refused them raw materials and supplies; banks wouldn't lend" (2009, 106). Most of the cooperatives were forced to close by the end of 1888. The Knights of Labor led a movement that tore through the country, mostly the South. It had a significant impact but then went underground and resurfaced in other forms.

The Cooperative Workers of America

In South Carolina, the Cooperative Workers of America (CWA) built on the foundation laid by the Knights of Labor. Hiram F. Hoover (or Hover), a former KOL member in North Carolina, was president and chief organizer of the CWA. Much of the leadership of the CWA in South Carolina was African American. Most were landless farm laborers with large families. The Hoover movement was strongest where cotton was important and the Black population was highest. Here again, women were admitted with equal status to men (Ali 2003, 62; Baker 1999, 284, 270).

The CWA focused on starting cooperative stores and a free cooperative school system, and addressed issues of wages, work conditions, and electoral reform. The organization's goal was to strengthen the position of workers, especially Black workers, by decreasing their dependence on the credit system. The CWA used Black organizers (though Hoover was White) and connected the movement to Black Baptist and Methodist churches, union leagues, Black fraternal orders, and other mutual-benefit societies that continued after Reconstruction and often met in secret for protection. As with other African American movements, a strong connection to mutual-benefit societies was important (Ali 2003, 63; Baker 1999, 284, 264).

Locals assembled in clubs, where they studied the organization's constitution. The initiation fee was fifty-five cents, and for another dollar a member could contribute to the establishment of a cooperative store "where all the members could trade and buy at wholesale rates" (Baker 1999, 264). One noted CWA attempt to establish a cooperative store was unsuccessful because of lack of funds, a shortage of time, and insufficient membership (Ali 2003, 64; Baker 1999, 285). The CWA advanced a progressive platform that included repeal of the poll tax and of all unjust laws against labor, weekly wage guarantees, and "implementation of a free cooperative school system" (Ali 2003, 65). According to Ali, White attempts at infiltration of the

CWA failed, but "terroristic suppression" was successful in many areas, especially after rumors of a strike. Also, differences within the Black community led to the organization's demise after a vigilante attack in the CWA stronghold of Fairview, South Carolina, in early July 1887 (Baker 1999, 279, 282, 283, 285).

The Populist Movement

The populist movement developed out of the experiences—including the failures—of the early unions and the growing National Farmers Alliance in the late 1880s, as well as other grassroots farmers' movements such as the Patrons of Husbandry, better known as the Grange, in the 1870s. In 1887, the three-million-strong Farmers Alliance opened its first cooperative, intended to be part of a network of organized agricultural cooperatives in an extensive cooperative economic system (Curl 2009, 5). The Farmers Alliance in South Carolina, for example, arrived in that state "only a few months after the demise of the CWA [in 1887, and] also centered its efforts on cooperation. The Farmers' Alliance, however, 'whose members were primarily landowning farmers,' had far more resources upon which to draw than did the rural, black day-laborers who made up the bulk of the membership of the CWA" (Baker 1999, 280). In the face of rising costs, falling prices, and rural isolation, White and Black farmers in the South in the late 1880s were joining farmers' fraternal organizations such as the Grange, the Agricultural Wheels, state farmers' unions, and the Southern Farmers' Alliance. The Southern Farmers' Alliance emerged as the most significant agricultural organization in the South, but it did not accept Negro membership and at best promoted separate Black chapters (Reynolds 2002). African Americans formed their own organization, the Colored Farmers' National Alliance and Co-operative Union (CFNACU), which worked with the Southern Farmers' Alliance but remained a separate organization.

There were disparate Black agrarian groups before the CFNACU, such as the Colored Farmers Association in Texas (mid-1870s), the Colored Grange of Tennessee (1880), and the Negro Alliance of Arkansas (1882) (Ali 2003). The Mississippi Union Leagues were also "hatcheries of radical economic experiments" (Woods 2007, 55). The Colored Agricultural Wheels expressed Black populism in the mid-1880s. "Colored Wheels were non-partisan agrarian groups that focused on economic cooperation while pressing for economic and political reforms," according to Ali, and by the late 1880s were spreading in Alabama and Tennessee as well as Arkansas (2003, 45).

According to Berry, in the 1880s, depressed economic conditions for poor farmers led them to join radical agrarian organizations (2005, 26–27). Radicals preached solidarity for poor Black and White farmers. The Populist Party tried to protect African Americans to ensure the equal application of voting procedures in 1892. Democrats forced African Americans who worked for them to vote Democratic and used riots and murder to maintain political power. "The Populists feared that they would not always be able to control African Americans if they were permitted to behave as allies and not subordinates, and they also feared Democratic control of black voters and efforts to disfranchise poor whites. Poor whites, the planter class, and industrialists joined together in forcing African Americans out of the political arena in the 1890s" (Berry 2005, 27). Similarly, Ali observes that "the inherent conflict between the poor African American agrarian base of black Populism (drawn from the approximately 92% of the rural southern black population that was virtually landless) and the relatively affluent white leadership of the Populist movement would continue into the early 1890s" (2003, 56–57). Violence and intimidation were frequently used to suppress the growth of Black populism, as the movement spearheaded plantation strikes.

Woods describes this period as one in which African Americans wanted to dismantle the plantation regime, establish self-governing communities, and become landowners, both individually and collectively. By the 1880s, a mass movement of Blacks and Whites had arisen under the populist banner. Populists identified northern industrial capitalists and southern plantation monopolists as "enemies of cooperatively based community development" (Woods 1998, 7). African Americans pushed their community-development agenda by building schools, establishing new towns, buying land, and protesting the denial of civil and human rights, even though they were essentially voteless and increasingly segregated. "Out of necessity," Woods observes, "many of those who remained in the South focused again on the land and labor reform agenda by organizing rural unions to end peonage, to improve wages, and to end the thievery associated with year-end settlements" (9).

This is the context in which the Colored Farmers' National Alliance and Co-operative Union matured and operated. It tried to promote political action among African Americans to ensure economic opportunity and stability (Ali 2003). "Dominated by small land-owners, this movement engaged in independent party politics while simultaneously building an economic infrastructure for a new society" (Woods 1998, 8).

The Black populist movement was heavily influenced by the attempts of racially integrated unions to develop a cooperative commonwealth in the late nineteenth century. The CFNACU pulled together elements of the Black populist movement in the 1880s and '90s. The colored alliances also continued the cooperative development that the Knights of Labor began. From the beginning, the CFNACU presented itself as a mutual-benefit organization devoted to improving the lives of Black farmers and agrarian laborers through education and economic cooperation. Its members became as militant as the Knights of Labor and led "some of the most ambitious strikes and boycotts," which made Black populism "even more of a threat to the establishment" (Ali 2003, 61n107).

The Colored Farmers' National Alliance and Co-operative Union

As the earlier populist organizations disbanded and went underground, the CFNACU began to pull together grassroots efforts and form a network of regional and national organizations. Like the mutual-aid societies, many were connected with and relied on churches (Ali 2003, 70). The first Negro alliance was organized in Arkansas in 1882 (76n3). Members of local chapters shared agricultural techniques and innovations and coordinated cooperative efforts for planting and harvesting (77). Similarly, in Macon, Georgia, at a meeting of 350 African Americans, a Reverend Love offered a resolution to form "cooperative associations, cooperative farms, and storehouses."[4]

Officially founded by J. J. Shuffer, H. L. Spencer, and R. M. Humphrey in 1886 in Houston County, Texas, the CFNACU spread to establish chapters in every state in the South (Curl 2009, 111; Holmes n.d.). In March 1888, the alliance held its first national meeting in Lovelady, Texas (Humphrey 1891; Miller 1972; Spriggs 1979; Ali 2003). The CFNACU consolidated several Black-focused agrarian organizations in the South—the Colored Agricultural Wheels, the Knights of Labor, the Cooperative Workers of America, and the Florida Farmers Union[5]—into a regional coalition. "The focus of these early groups was on relief through collectivizing resources, and collective bargaining through boycotts and strikes" (Ali 2005, 5). By 1891 the CFNACU boasted a membership of more than one million (Ali 2003), though, according to Curl, the alliance "had one and a quarter million members, making it the largest-ever organization of black Americans, most of them sharecroppers and tenant farmers" (2009, 111). Most accounts, however, suggest that the total was closer to four or five hundred thousand members (Holmes 1973). In any case, the CFNACU was indisputably the largest African American organization of its time. While its local leaders were Black, the state and regional organizers were largely White, headed by the White founder

Reverend Humphrey, who was general superintendent. Whites were able to organize openly in places where Blacks would be physically attacked (Curl 2009, 112).

The CFNACU was a self-help organization that encouraged members to work hard and sacrifice to uplift themselves. Some state chapters raised money to keep Black public schools open for longer terms, founded academies, and solicited funds to help the sick and disabled. In many ways, the CFNACU was another mutual-aid society. But it was also formed to increase Black political participation, and it advocated a political agenda. It often mirrored its White counterpart, the Southern Farmers' Alliance (a branch of the National Farmers Alliance and Industrial Union, referred to as the Southern Alliance), in terms of philosophy and program, supporting most of the same policies (Holmes 1973). For example, in 1890 the CFNACU supported the Southern Alliance's subtreasury plan, hoping that it would provide low-interest loans for farmers and high prices for agricultural produce (Holmes 1973, 269; Reynolds 2002; Ali 2003). The CFNACU also supported policies that the Southern Alliance did not, such as the Lodge election bill to provide federal protection to safeguard voting rights in the South, and the 1891 cotton pickers' strike.

While some Black members owned small farms, many were sharecroppers and field hands on White plantations. The CFNACU urged members to improve their farming methods and learn new techniques, purchase their own land and homes, and improve their education (Holmes 1973, 268). It promoted collectivizing resources (Ali 2005). "Before being violently suppressed, the Colored Farmers' Alliance advocated the expansion of land ownership and the creation of cooperative stores designed to pool African American resources while boycotting stores owned by planters or allied merchants and commissaries" (Woods 1998, 8). Branches established exchanges (cooperative stores/warehouses and credit outlets) in the ports of Norfolk, Charleston, Mobile, New Orleans, and Houston where members could buy goods at reduced prices and borrow money from the organization to buy land and equipment or pay off a loan (Ali 2003, 89; Holmes 1973 and n.d.). In some areas, the CFNACU shared an exchange with the Southern Alliance, although these were tenuous collaborations and often short-lived. The CFNACU communicated through branch newspapers to provide information about discriminatory legislation, monopolies and their effects on African Americans, and the latest initiatives of the organization, such as cooperative exchange projects, lobbying efforts, credit programs, and cost-saving measures (Ali 2003, 80–81). The organization sustained almost continuous opposition to its very existence from the White plantation bloc and even from Southern Alliance members.

The Leflore Massacre

"The troubles in Leflore County sprang largely from the attempts by blacks to improve themselves financially" (Holmes 1973, 268). In Leflore County, Mississippi, the CFNACU shared an exchange with the White Southern Alliance. One Oliver Cromwell began organizing chapters of the CFNACU in Leflore County in 1889. Holmes credits Cromwell with persuading Blacks to stop trading with local merchants and use the Farmers' Alliance cooperative store in the nearby town of Durant. White Leflore County merchants were losing Black business (and debt) and began to try to undermine Cromwell and the CFNACU. They defamed Cromwell, threatened him, and started rumors that he had embezzled CFNACU funds. The CFNACU men rallied to defend him. The White citizens were fearful of a rebellion and requested that the governor send troops to protect them. While the rest of the account is confused and contradictory, the governor did send three companies of troops, and local armed Whites patrolled the county. It appears that local militias or posses massacred at least twenty-five Blacks. Accounts, including Black newspaper accounts, reported as many as a hundred African Americans murdered. While CFNACU men rallied, most accounts agree that they had little ammunition; no Whites were killed. The incident was not actually well publicized at the time. Neither state nor county officials took any action in response to the mass killings. "The killings in Laflore County illustrate a condition then widespread in the South" (Holmes 1973, 274).

The episode helps to explain "why the Colored Alliance was such a short-lived movement" (Holmes 1973; see also Holmes 1975 and n.d.). After the massacre, White planters held a meeting declaring that the CFNACU had overstepped its bounds. They notified the editor of the *Colored Farmers' Alliance Advocate* that distribution of the newspaper to its subscribers in the county would be halted and that and any attempt to distribute the newspaper in Leflore County would be dealt with harshly. The plantation bloc leaders also ordered the cooperative store, the Durant Commercial Company, to "desist from selling goods or loaning money to the Colored Alliance or to any of its members" (Holmes 1973, 274), although it was still allowed to serve the White members of the Southern Alliance. Many of the CFNACU leaders had fled by this time if they hadn't been killed, and the Colored Farmers' National Alliance and Co-operative Union in Leflore County collapsed.

By 1896, all branches of the CFNACU nationwide had dissolved, although other organizations, including the Knights of Labor, continued their work (Reynolds 2002; Ali 2003).

Shift in Focus to Politics

The White and Black populist movements had similar purposes but often used different strategies. African American populists supported White programs when it served their interest, such as patronizing Southern Alliance cooperative stores and lobbying for the same legislation (Ali 2003, 120; Holmes 1973), but they pursued their own policies and actions when it did not. White alliance members tolerated Black support but were intolerant of the organization when it diverged from White aims and control. As Holmes puts it, "As long as the Colored Alliance supported the programs of the Southern Alliance, many whites tolerated its existence. But when it tried to solve problems that contributed directly to the plight of Southern blacks [bettering their economic conditions and lessening their dependence on whites], it conflicted with the economic and racial policies of the white South" (1973, 274).

Many of the CFNACU's economic efforts were failures, and so members turned to politics. Increasing debt, lack of capital, declining crop prices, and poor wages hurt their members in particular. Also, as with earlier co-op efforts, members of these organizations usually engaged in economic activities, particularly the cooperatives, while on strike, unemployed, or experiencing economic difficulties. Resources were therefore scarce. Running businesses of any kind under these conditions was difficult. In addition, Ali notes that tactical failures, the inability to sustain cooperative stores, and limits to lobbying for agrarian reforms "convinced increasing numbers of black Populist leaders of the need to enter the political arena directly" (2003, 117). While the CFNACU "began as a strictly 'non-partisan' mutual benefit association focused on economic cooperation, it developed into one of the most radical organizations of the era, carrying out boycotts and strikes and ultimately helping to create an independent political party, the People's Party" (81). When efforts to make economic change were thwarted, the CFNACU changed strategies, applying pressure on political candidates. Between 1890 and 1892 there was talk of forming a third national political party. Black and White southerners affiliated with the alliances held a series of meetings with other activists from labor, agrarian, and reform organizations ("including the northern-established Knights of Labor, which de facto became a black organization as it spread into the South") to discuss the issue (Ali 2005, 6). By 1892 they had formed the national People's Party, with state-based independent parties in coalition with White independents.

Thwarted Dreams

Like the Knights of Labor, the Cooperative Workers of America, and other farmers' alliances, whose vision of establishing cooperatives and exchanges was not realized, the CFNACU and its cooperative ventures were short-lived.[6] At its height, the CFNACU, learning in part from the mutual-aid movement as well as the various Black populist and organized labor movements, used collective action, cooperative economics, economic solidarity, and political action to strengthen the position of Black farmers and farmworkers, form strategies for sustainable farming, and advocate for economic and political rights. All of the Black populist efforts (like the White ones) were targeted by White employers, banks, and railway owners, who sanctioned White vigilan- tes. Early Black cooperators suffered physical violence—even death—as well as economic sabotage. At the same time, even the unsuccessful campaigns provided invaluable lessons about economic and political organizing at the grassroots level. Both the frustrations and the small victories associated with these efforts would be remembered, and the vision of a cooperative society would continue to surround the Black civil rights and liberation movements.

3

EXPANDING THE TRADITION

Early African American–Owned "Cooperative" Businesses

Even rural communities that lacked the almost total isolation of the Sea Islands possessed a strong commitment to corporatism and a concomitant scorn for the hoarding
of private possessions. . . . It is clear that these patterns of behavior were determined
as much by economic necessity as by cultural "choice." If black household members
pooled their energies to make a good crop, and if communities collectively provided
for their own welfare, then poverty and oppression ruled out most of the alternative
strategies. Individualism was a luxury that sharecroppers simply could not afford.
—JONES (1985, 101–2)

More importantly, the Commission [the 1961 Civil Rights Commission] failed to recognize the degree to which community cooperation during the early years of the
twentieth century helped move local farmers away from economic dependence on
whites. Actuated by a strong sense of community, residents of Charles City County
developed a diverse agricultural economy that included very few tenant farmers. With
little need or desire to depend on white factory and landowners, between 1900 and
1930 black farmers achieved a level of economic independence that later aided in the
struggle for political rights and racial justice.
—CRAIG (1987, 133–34)

Cooperative businesses among African Americans developed slowly—often
evolving from mutual-aid societies to mutual insurance companies and from
joint-stock companies to Rochdale cooperatives—as African Americans became more sophisticated and experienced in cooperative ownership. W. E. B.
Du Bois's 1907 study in some ways lumps all efforts at economic cooperation
together. In this chapter, I examine these businesses from the 1880s to the
early 1900s for elements of cooperative economic principles and practices
and as examples of the evolution into formal cooperative businesses. During
this era, most of these businesses were urban enterprises engaged more in
offering services and retail sales than in the production of goods. In addition,
in the nineteenth century, the concept of Black capitalism was a strategy of

---

This chapter incorporates heavy revisions of Gordon Nembhard 2004a and 2006a.

racial economic solidarity and cooperation, as was Negro joint-stock ownership (for example, the Chesapeake Marine Railway shipyard in Baltimore, the
Coleman Manufacturing Company in Concord, North Carolina, and the Universal Negro Improvement Association's Black Star Line and Negro Factories
Corporation). Mutual insurance companies were the earliest formal cooperative businesses among Blacks and Whites in the United States. As noted earlier, starting in the late nineteenth century, African Americans also organized
official cooperative businesses that followed the European "Rochdale Principles of Cooperation."[1] Other early official cooperatives were farm cooperatives and cooperative marketing boards, consumer cooperative grocery stores,
cooperative schools, and credit unions.

Mutual Insurance Companies

Some of the successful mutual-aid societies developed into insurance companies when they formalized as businesses. As some societies became more
sophisticated and substituted a board of directors for general member control, they became insurance companies (Du Bois 1898, 18). In the 1880s,
many Blacks had joined White insurance companies but discovered that they
received fewer monetary benefits for the same service, even though they paid
the same premium (or higher). This inspired Blacks to establish their own
insurance companies that would not defraud or discriminate against African
American clients (Du Bois 1907, 98). Many southern states then passed laws
protecting White insurance companies.

One of the largest Black mutual insurance companies was the Grand
United Order of the True Reformers, which grew to have branches throughout the South and East. It owned "considerable real estate and conduct[ed] a
banking and annual premium insurance business at Richmond," according
to Du Bois (1898, 20). Organized in Richmond, Virginia, in 1881, it began with
one hundred members and capital of $150. By 1901, with more than fifty
thousand members, the society paid out $606,000 in death claims and
$1,500,000 in sick claims. The True Reformers held more than $223,500 in
assets. In addition, the organization boasted of having 2,678 lodges (totaling
a hundred thousand members) and had paid out $979,440.55 in claims; and
the Rosebud children's department served more than thirty thousand children (Du Bois 1907, 101–2). Woodson also highlights the fact that the True
Reformers added death insurance to burial insurance so that families would
have something to live on after the death of a family member, especially a
breadwinner (1929, 209–10).

The organization also supported a savings bank founded in 1887, the Reformers Mercantile and Industrial Association (a chain of stores with annual business of more than $100,000), a weekly newspaper, a 150-room hotel, a home for the elderly, a building-and-loan association, and a real estate department (Du Bois 1907, 103). The True Reformers bank enhanced its reputation in 1893, during the financial panic, by paying all claims made on it (Woodson 1929, 210). Other banks in Richmond did not.

The Independent Order of Saint Luke (discussed in chapter 1) developed along similar lines. It rapidly became more than a mutual-aid society and included a successful insurance company and bank. Under Maggie Lena Walker's direction, "this order with more experience and better trained workers than those of others overcame the difficulties which worked the undoing of the True Reformers. The Independent Order of St. Luke still carries on its insurance work, operates a printing plant, publishes a newspaper, and conducts a bank" (Woodson 1929, 211; for more details on the Order of Saint Luke, see Barkley Brown 1989).

The North Carolina Mutual Insurance Company was the largest of the state-based, locally owned insurance companies until World War I. It was established in 1903 out of the mutual-aid movement. At its first annual meeting in 1904, at the Colored State Fair in Raleigh, the company's agents "testified to the powers of racial cooperation" and offered resolutions at sessions open to the public to promote the message of racial solidarity (Weare 1993, 86). It became the largest Negro insurance company in the world (118). The company's standing was so strong that it qualified as a legal reserve company in 1912–13 with loans from Fidelity Bank in Duke (a White bank that must have believed in its solvency and reliability in order to back those loans) (94). North Carolina Mutual was very involved in the Black community and "formed the heart of a black political economy in Durham" and beyond (182–83; see also Woodson 1929). In 1927, North Carolina Mutual's president, Charles Clinton Spaulding, worked with the federal government on what would become President Hoover's "black capitalism" initiative (Weare 1993, 147–48). That same year, Spaulding started the "Durham stock taking and fact finding" conferences. The first conference was attended by well-known African American scholars and leaders, among them W. E. B. Du Bois; R. R. Moton, the president of Tuskegee University; Mordecai Johnson, the president of Howard University; and Asa Philip Randolph, editor of the *Messenger* and founder of the Brotherhood of Sleeping Car Porters. Weare notes that "Randolph, like Du Bois, recognized that the Mutual spirit stood for race cooperation at least as much as individual entrepreneurship" (152). Spaulding was also influential in the National Negro Business League and took over its leadership after the death of Booker T. Washington, its founder and first president (for more about the NNBL, see chapter 4).

Weare assesses the significance of the North Carolina Mutual Insurance Company. Every success it had was seen as a racial success: buying a policy meant "double protection"—life insurance and Negro employment (96). White rejection actually brought more customers (98), so that, in a way, the company thrived on Black economic marginalization. North Carolina Mutual "stood as an expression of Afro-American thought centering on the doctrine of self-help and racial solidarity" (95). These are some of the same attitudes held by members of African American cooperatives in the twentieth century.

Du Bois's critique of the insurance company model suggests that some of the businesses were conducted in an "unscientific" way, using "speculation and dishonesty" and depending on lapsed policies for profits (1907, 108–9). On the other hand, they yielded one of the strongest business models (and models of mutual economic cooperation) of Black economic development.[2] In addition, Weare notes that Negro banks "sprang almost involuntarily from Negro insurance companies" (119), continuing the progress of economic development started by mutual-aid societies.

Early African American–Owned "Cooperative" (or Joint-Stock) Businesses

The Chesapeake Marine Railway and Dry Dock Company, the Coleman Manufacturing Company, and the Lexington Savings Bank were early joint-stock companies that may have been cooperatives; they were definitely collectively owned. Marcus Garvey and the Universal Negro Improvement Association also made use of the joint-stock ownership model to develop Black businesses.

The Chesapeake Marine Railway and Dry Dock Company

Between 1865 and 1883, African American caulkers and stevedores owned their own company with the help of prominent African Americans in Baltimore, Maryland. According to Du Bois, the Chesapeake Marine Railway and Dry Dock Company was organized in part to combat the growing demand among White laborers in Maryland that all free Blacks be fired from the shipyards and leave the state or "get a master." Baltimore had become famous for its caulking, but it was the Black caulkers who "were the most proficient in the state" (Du Bois 1907, 152–53). Shipyard owners were not willing to reduce their Black workforce until White mobs attacked Black caulkers and stevedores on their way home, and White carpenters boycotted shipyards that hired African American caulkers. At that point, a group of Black men decided that they needed to own their own shipyard, to protect and secure jobs for Blacks.

The jointly owned business, which Du Bois (1907) called a cooperative, was quite successful. The Chesapeake Marine Railway Company bought a shipyard—encompassing the property that included the spot where Frederick Douglass describes sitting on a cellar door studying a stolen spelling book to teach himself how to read. According to Du Bois, the founders of the company raised $40,000 by selling eight thousand shares at $5 per share. They paid off their $30,000 mortgage in five years and employed between one and two hundred Black and White caulkers and stevedores per year. In the sixth year of operation, the company paid stock dividends to members totaling $14,000. In the seventh year, it paid dividends of 10 percent, and for four years after that paid dividends of between 4 and 10 percent per year. Therefore, we know that for at least six years the company was profitable enough to pay dividends. The company went out of business in its eighteenth year, in part because of repair problems, changes in the industry, and management issues, but also because of "the refusal of the owners of the ground to release the yard to the colored company except at an enormous rate of increase" (Du Bois 1907, 153). The ground rent was doubled. The cooperative went out of business soon after.[3]

The significance of this joint-stock company is manifold. The success of the Chesapeake Marine Railway and Dry Dock Company showed that African Americans could successfully use joint ownership in the face of racial oppression and ostracism, particularly to save jobs, create jobs, and accumulate wealth. It showed that African Americans could run a substantial industrial enterprise at a profit. The company also changed the nature of industrial relations in the state of Maryland. Du Bois observes that even after Chesapeake's demise, "the organization of the ship company saved the colored caulkers, for they are now members of the white caulker's union. The failure of the whites in driving out the colored caulkers put an end to their efforts to drive colored labor out of other fields. And although the company failed, it must surely have been an object lesson to the whites as well as to the blacks of the power and capability of the colored people in their industrial development" (1907, 153). Du Bois reminds us that even if the shipyard went out of business after eighteen years, much was accomplished, particularly in terms of job creation, profit distribution, civil rights, unionization, and the overall security of the livelihoods and reputation of Black stevedores and caulkers in Maryland.

Coleman Manufacturing Company

The Coleman Manufacturing Company of Concord, North Carolina, was incorporated in 1897 with $50,000 of capital stock. According to a letter from W. C. Coleman published by Du Bois (1898, 26), Coleman Manufacturing was "a co-operative stock company of colored men who propose to build and operate a cotton mill in the interest of the race." Many of the stockholders were influential Black businessmen and White citizens around Concord, North Carolina. After raising the first $50,000, they offered the second $50,000 at $100 per share (payable in installments of 10 percent). The company produced between forty and fifty thousand bricks a day and planned to begin bricklaying for the mill that would employ three to four hundred people. It planned ultimately to establish (on its own or with others) a boardinghouse, truck farm, livery stable, and dairy, according to Coleman's letter. The White-owned *Concord Times* enthusiastically reported on March 10, 1898, that

> the [Coleman cotton] mill is to have from 7,000 to 10,000 spindles and from 100 to 250 looms, and, by their charter, will be allowed to spin, weave, manufacture, finish and sell warps, yarns, cloth, prints or other fabrics made of cotton, wool or other material. They own at present, in connection with the plant, about 100 acres of land on the main line of the Southern Railway and near the site of the mill. The mill and machinery with all the fixtures complete will represent an outlay of nearly $66,000, and will give employment to a number of hands. (Du Bois 1898, 26–27)

The newspaper projected that the cotton mill would be a successful Negro business. Calling the new board of directors "some of the highest lights of the Negro race," the *Concord Times* also noted that it was "the only cotton mill in the world owned, conducted and operated by the Negro race" (27). In the twentieth century, a few cooperative sewing factories owned by African American women in North Carolina would also be successful and important businesses in their communities. Coleman foreshadows these later developments.

The Lexington Savings Bank

The Lexington Savings Bank, in Baltimore, was incorporated in 1895 with $10,000 of capital stock raised by Black leaders in Baltimore (Maryland State Archives 1998). The bank's president, Everett Waring, was a graduate of Howard University School of Law and reportedly admired Capital Savings

Bank in Washington, D.C. According to the Maryland Archives summary, Waring planned to gain as much of the Black savings in Baltimore as possible. Prominent African Americans in Baltimore—businessmen, lawyers, ministers, elected officials—were charter members and stockholders. Depositors came mostly from the Black working class: the bank "was supported entirely by colored people . . . and catered entirely to the poorer classes" (*Baltimore Morning Herald*, news clipping, ibid.). Several hundred people held deposits in the bank by 1896, and all celebrated the success of its first year.

In the second year there was a major scandal, from which the bank did not recover. This is another example of an attempt to pool Black resources and jointly own a business that would provide needed services to the Black community. It is also an example of mismanagement and apparent lack of transparency and adequate oversight. There are many examples of both throughout the history of African Americans. The failures, especially of Black banks, also feed the collective Black memory of distrust of and aversion to business ownership, which in the twentieth century has limited the willingness of many African Americans to become involved in Black-owned business ventures. The devastating failure, after the Panic of 1873, of the Freedman's Savings and Trust Company (signed into law along with the Freedmen's Bureau at the beginning of Reconstruction) in 1874 (Hine, Hine, and Harrold 2010),[4] and the failure of Marcus Garvey's Universal Negro Improvement Association business ventures in the early 1900s (see below), also contributed to Black ambivalence and often aversion to business ownership and investment in Black-owned banks. However, there remain many other examples of successful ventures and of people willing to give joint ownership a chance, as we will see in chapter 4.

Marcus Garvey and the Universal Negro Improvement Association

Shipp (1996) and Martin (1976) report that Marcus Garvey and the Universal Negro Improvement Association had a model of cooperative economic development. Shipp writes, "Marcus Garvey's Universal Negro Improvement Association (UNIA) produced an alternative cooperative model for Black community development that has also been utilized by other groups including the Nation of Islam and many Black religious denominations. It shares many characteristics with the Mondragon. Although never fully realized, Garvey's strategy envisioned the collective economic advancement of African peoples throughout the world" (1996, 86).[5] Similarly, Martin contends that

Garvey had a "grand design" to link all the UNIA businesses into a "world-wide system of Pan-African economic cooperation."

> Garvey's attempts to establish economic self-reliance went beyond cooperative business enterprises, for UNIA branches acted as mutual aid friendly societies for the payment of death and other minor benefits to members. In rural areas among poor communities, this aspect of the organization's operations assumed greater importance. Local divisions also were required to maintain a charitable fund "for the purpose of assisting distressed members or needy individuals of the race," a fund for "loans of honor" to active members, and an employment bureau to assist members seeking work. (1976, 35–36)

Martin also lists the ways in which the UNIA businesses operated cooperatively. He observes that one manager engaged in cooperative buying for all the stores and restaurants of the Negro Factories Corporation (34). In Colón, Panama, the UNIA ran a cooperative bakery, and in Kingston, Jamaica, the African Communities League Peoples Co-operative Bank sold shares only to UNIA members (35). For Garvey, economic self-reliance was primary, according to Martin. Successful political action required an independent economic base. Blacks needed to be independent producers, not just consumers. Many businesses and assets should be jointly owned by all UNIA members. In the case of the Black Star Line Steamship Corporation, Garvey claimed that "the ships that are owned by this corporation are the property of the Negro race."[6] Everyone was an owner.

The Universal Negro Improvement Association was originally organized in Jamaica in 1914 as a mutual-benefit society—a "Universal Confraternity among the race"—with a mission to establish educational institutions and improve conditions for Blacks everywhere (Martin 1976, 6). It was incorporated in New York in 1918. At its height, the UNIA was the largest African American political organization in the early twentieth century (Hine, Hine, and Harrold 2010, 452). Interestingly, the Colored Farmers' National Alliance and Co-operative Union was the largest Black organization a decade or two earlier. Here again, while at first the Black cooperative movement seems to have been small and inconsequential as well as little acknowledged, it has actually played a part in many of the major movements for Black liberation in the United States. The UNIA's Negro Factories Corporation was a joint-stock holding company for two uniform assembly factories, a laundry, a printing plant, three restaurants, and three grocery stores (Shipp 1996).[7] The Black Star Line was a joint-stock company that handled international shipping; it purchased three ships altogether in the early 1920s but could not maintain them enough to use them for transport (Hine, Hine, and Harrold 2010, 454; Martin 1976). Garvey was indicted for mail fraud for soliciting (selling shares and asking for contributions) through the mail, and the businesses went bankrupt.[8] Between 1920 and 1924, however, UNIA businesses employed as many as a thousand employees. Stock certificates for both the Black Star Line and the Negro Factories Corporation sold for $5 per share. Individual member investors could buy up to two hundred shares in the Black Star Line. The UNIA newspaper, the *Negro World*, posted advertisements for stock in these businesses and published articles describing the progress of the businesses. In promotional documents such as Garvey's article in the issue of May 24, 1924, Garvey pushed for all members to invest in the Black Cross Navigation Company (Black Star's parent company) at levels of $100 to $1,000, in order to raise the necessary capital. The headline read, "Negroes Cooperating for Black Steamship Company's Success" (Garvey 1924). During this time, the Black press, specifically the *Negro World*, appears to have used the word "cooperation" a lot. On the other hand, Floyd-Thomas notes that "despite Garvey's endorsement of racial unity and pride as well as collective economic development for African peoples, his social philosophy made quite a stir within the already volatile climate in 1920s Harlem" (2008, 137). Garvey was extremely controversial, and while he used the language of cooperation, it is not clear how fully he embraced cooperative economics.

Another interesting historical note to Garvey's failed economic attempts, particularly with the Black Star Line, and connections with other economic visions at the time, is Du Bois's attempt to resurrect the idea of a U.S.-Africa commercial shipping line. Perhaps ironically, Du Bois, basically a critic of Garvey's economic projects, had a plan to resurrect the Black Star Line in some fashion in 1923. He wrote to the secretary of state, Charles Hughes, about the failure of the U.S. Congress to confirm a Liberian loan in January 1923 (Du Bois 1923). By this time the Black Star Line was bankrupt, but according to Du Bois there was still interest in commerce between the United States and Liberia. He summarized the aftermath of the Black Star Line "fiasco":

> The difficulty with this [the bankruptcy of the Black Star Line] was that its leader, Marcus Garvey, was not a business man and turned out to be a thoroughly impractical visionary, if not a criminal, with grandiose schemes of conquest. The result was that he wasted some eight or nine hundred thousand dollars of the hard-earned pennies of Negro laborers. However, two things are clear; nearly a million dollars of Black Star Line stock of the Garvey movement is now distributed among colored

people and is absolutely without value. On the other hand, the United States owns thousands of vessels, any one or two of which might be used to initiate the plan I have spoken of. (261)

Du Bois wanted the U.S. government to provide two ships to begin a commercial trade venture between Liberia and the United States. Moreover, he asked the secretary of state if such a venture could legally be connected to the worthless Black Star stock in "an attempt to restore the confidence of the mass of American Negroes in commercial enterprise with Africa, possibly by having a private company headed by men of highest integrity, both white and colored, to take up and hold in trust, the Black Star Line certificates" (261). There is no record of a reply to that letter. However, this is more evidence of Du Bois's interest not just in Pan-African commerce but also in redeeming the concept of joint ownership.

Marcus Garvey, much like Booker T. Washington (and like Du Bois, though most of the time they thought they had very different ideas from each other), urged African Americans to find separate economic solutions to their plight and to control their own economic enterprises. Shipp contends that Garvey wanted these businesses to be managed by their members—the stockholders—and operate democratically. Advertisements in Black newspapers connected participation and investment in these enterprises with the uplift of the race, a strategy for Black liberation, and a way to make a profit by supporting Black endeavors (Briggs 2003 provides copies of some of these ads). Shipp maintains that "the cooperative or collective, as implemented by Garvey, would be a part of an expansive market area, beginning with each UNIA chapter and spreading outward to create a Pan-African trading network based on economic cooperation" (1996, 88).

The *Negro World* did cover cooperative activity in the African American community, reporting on co-op housing, buying clubs, credit unions, and the Colored Merchants Association (see chapter 6). In addition, the December 27, 1924, edition of the *Negro World* provides in-depth coverage of a new report from the Russell Sage Foundation called "Sharing Management with the Workers" (*Negro World* 1924). The subhead includes the phrase "Negroes also benefit," though it is not obvious from reading the article that any of the employees of the Dutchess Bleachery in Wappingers Falls, New York, who benefitted from the partnership plan were Black. The article does suggest that the UNIA considered this kind of information about workplace democracy important to its readers and members.

Shipp contends that Du Bois based his promotion of cooperative economic development for African Americans on Garvey's philosophy in the

1930s. However, my research and analysis of Du Bois's theory of economic cooperation (supported by Haynes 1993 and 1999; DeMarco 1974; and Rudwick 1968) find that Du Bois was already discussing economic cooperation and cooperative businesses in 1898. He wrote a book and called a conference on the subject in 1907, and read and was in contact with the major cooperative thinkers in the United States and United Kingdom by the early 1900s. He established the Negro Cooperative Guild in 1918. Du Bois, therefore, developed his cooperative economics philosophy separately from Garvey, and probably before Garvey, although it is not surprising that great minds would light on similar strategies. Indeed, one of the findings of this study is that many African American leaders and scholars supported the concept of cooperative economic development at some point (often early on) in their careers, if not throughout.

Du Bois did recognize the potential that Garvey and the UNIA had amassed. He wrote that Garvey had proved that "American Negroes can, by accumulating and ministering their own capital, organize industry, join the black centers of the south Atlantic by commercial enterprise and in this way ultimately redeem Africa as a fit and free home for black men" (1921, 977; see also Taylor 2002, 47). Also, Du Bois's letter to the secretary of state in 1923 suggests that he did not consider a venture like the Black Star Line a bad idea, just poorly executed (see also Du Bois 1921). It is also clear that he was very interested in restoring Black people's faith in joint ownership.

Marcus Garvey may have written and spoken about pooling resources, been philosophically in favor of cooperative economics, and been interested in promoting cooperative ownership in some of his projects, but the economic organizations started by the UNIA were joint-stock companies rather than cooperative businesses as defined by the Rochdale principles, and the majority of stock was owned by the UNIA. Moreover, Garvey rarely practiced financial transparency, a cooperative principle (Du Bois complained of this; see Du Bois 1921), and was known to be authoritative. Like many of the examples from Du Bois's 1898 and 1907 studies, the UNIA businesses are examples of economic cooperation among Negroes, but they were not cooperative business enterprises. The UNIA businesses had serious management problems, and none of them operated very successfully, even though they may have solved the capitalization problem by amassing so many small contributions from UNIA members. They also were sabotaged by the U.S. government and others who did not want such grand efforts to succeed. This was another example of serious physical, financial, and political challenges to collective African American economic action. Nonetheless, we see here deliberate actions by African Americans to work with others, to pool resources, to own their own businesses, to provide services to their community, and to earn a decent living—even in the face of both poverty and outside threats.

These efforts were short-lived, but they were gestures grand enough to remain in the African American collective memory—whether as an example of how the U.S. government will retaliate if you try to do too much economically for Black people, or as a lesson that collective projects end in embezzlement and financial mismanagement. While the first has much basis in fact—the Ex-Slave Pension Association was hounded by the federal government, as was the Federation of Southern Cooperatives in the 1970s—the second is a misconception that has hindered some in the Black community from becoming more involved in joint ownership and cooperative economics. For some reason, there is not as strong a collective memory about the cooperative efforts that succeeded.

It is worth noting that in addition to economic advancement—or attempts at economic advancement—Garvey's UNIA supported women's leadership. Taylor (2002, 45, 87) and others point out the ways in which women, particularly Garvey's wife, Amy Jacques Garvey, found their place in the organization and practiced "community feminism," a term that describes the Combahee River Colony and some of the other mutual-benefit societies run by women, which were successful efforts at collective economics.

Early African American Rochdale Cooperatives

In 1898, Du Bois's assessment of Black business development and cooperative businesses in general was not optimistic: "From such enterprises sprang the beneficial societies, and to-day slowly and with difficulty is arising real co-operative business enterprise detached from religious activity or insurance. On the other hand, private business enterprise has made some beginning, and in a few cases united into joint stock enterprises. It will be years, however, before this kind of business is very successful" (1898, 21–22). Du Bois counted about fifteen emerging cooperative businesses in 1898, and several cemetery associations. He remained pessimistic in 1907: "To some [cooperative business] is simply a record of failure, just as similar attempts were for so long a time among whites in France, England, and America. Just as in the case of these latter groups, however, failure was but education for growing success in certain limited directions, so among Negroes we can already see the education of failure beginning to tell" (1907, 149). Du Bois identified several challenges to cooperative business development, including the lack of capital and the nature of poor people who will not invest because they are afraid of losing their hard-earned money. He also emphasized the lack of trained managers and workers, particularly in democratic business participation. He noted that in some early attempts at cooperation, poor judgments were made. In some cases, a company did not wait until at least 25 percent of the capital stock had been raised, which often resulted in failure. This increased the perception that "promoters of cooperative enterprises were unscrupulous" (1907, 150). Despite his pessimism, Du Bois held a conference in 1907 (the twelfth Atlanta conference at Atlanta University; see chapter 4) titled "Negro Business Development and Cooperatives," promoting cooperatives and economic cooperation. The conference also launched his latest academic report on African Americans, *Economic Co-operation Among Negro Americans.*

Du Bois documented the existence of 154 African American–owned cooperatives: 14 "producer cooperatives"; 3 "transportation cooperatives"; 103 "distribution or consumer cooperatives," and 34 "real estate and credit cooperatives," in addition to hundreds of mutual-aid societies and cooperative projects through religious and benevolent institutions, beneficial and insurance societies, secret societies, schools, and financial institutions in 1907. While most of the cooperative businesses were joint-stock companies or collectively owned enterprises rather than Rochdale cooperatives, he made a case for how often it occurred, how necessary joint ownership was, and how difficult it was for African Americans. He attributed difficulties to poor management, lack of know-how, low levels of capitalization, and racial discrimination. He used the case study of Baltimore to illustrate the kinds of businesses that African Americans engaged in collectively, in some sense of the term. The "successful cooperative businesses" he studied include the Douglass Institute (a social entertainment house), the Chesapeake Marine Railway and Dry Dock Company, Samaritan Temple, the *Afro-American Ledger* newspaper, and the North Baltimore Permanent Building and Loan Association (1907, 151–78). By the early 1900s, African Americans were forming cooperative businesses based on the international principles of cooperation; these businesses are the subject of the following seven chapters.

Four early African American cooperative businesses that followed the Rochdale principles were the Mercantile Cooperative Company in Ruthville, Virginia, Citizens' Co-operative Stores in Memphis, Tennessee, the Pioneer Cooperative Society in Harlem, New York City, and the Cooperative Society of Bluefield Colored Institute of West Virginia.

The Mercantile Cooperative Company

The Mercantile Cooperative Company, the earliest urban Rochdale cooperative my research has uncovered (after the nineteenth-century unions and
farmers' alliance co-ops, and the ones mentioned by Du Bois in 1907), was
established in Ruthville, Virginia, in 1901. Charles City County, where Ruthville is located, is a relatively prosperous county for African Americans.
Until John Craig's account, however, most historians "ignored the role of the
area's free black population" and "the degree to which community cooperation during the early years of the twentieth century helped move local farmers away from economic dependence on whites" (1987, 133–34). Craig
highlights collective efforts in Ruthville and observes that Black farmers'
cooperative activity in the early twentieth century through the Mercantile
Cooperative enabled them to "achieve a level of economic independence"
that contributed to their later success in achieving voting rights and other
civil rights (134).

In the first quarter of the twentieth century, according to Craig's research,
90 percent of residents in Charles City County owned their own homes and
the land they farmed, and fewer than 6 percent of local farms had a mortgage.
These statistics stand out during a time when the number of Whites in the
county was decreasing; between 1900 and 1930, the Black population of the
county rose by 2 percent, while the White population declined by 20 percent
(139). Ruthville, a predominantly Black town, had a history of fraternal organizations. In 1901 the Odd Fellows Lodge helped to establish the Mercantile
Cooperative Company. According to Craig, this was a Black-run cooperative
store chartered by the state. Shares were sold at $5 each, and no one member
could hold more than twenty shares. Shares could be bought in installments.
Members bought a store outside Ruthville and moved it to the main cross-
roads opposite the County Training School. They raised $1,300 to buy sup-
plies in Richmond. They decided not to take credit, so that they would not
have to rely on outsiders. The cooperative coexisted on cordial terms with a
White-owned store across the street (135). By 1923, the Mercantile Cooperative had twenty-eight shareholders. The cooperative then bought trucks and
was able to hire three employees. The new United Sorghum Growers Club
met regularly above the store (136). The community also founded the Intellectual and Industrial Union, which raised money to build a new school (137–
38). Craig remarks on the "strength of community solidarity" in the town and
the way the Black community "banded together to overcome common problems." The cooperative store was an important example of this and a mainstay
of the community.

Citizens' Co-operative Stores

Citizens' Co-operative Stores of Memphis was established in direct response to a Negro Cooperative Guild meeting in August 1919 (see chapter 4).[9] From the details in a *Crisis* article, we know that the citizens of Memphis eagerly joined the project, as evidenced by the large number of participants and the resounding success of the equity drive. According to the *Crisis*, the cooperative raised more equity than expected, selling double the amount of shares initially offered. Members were able to buy shares in installments, and no one could own more than ten shares. By August 1919, five stores were in operation in Memphis, serving about seventy-five thousand people. The members of the local guilds associated with each store met monthly to study cooperatives and discuss issues. The cooperative planned to own its own buildings and a cooperative warehouse ([Du Bois] 1919).

The *Crisis* article, written by "the editor" (presumably Du Bois himself), read in part:

> The good results of co-operation among colored people do not lie alone in the return of savings. They show, also, new opportunities for the earning of a livelihood and in the chance offered our colored youth to become acquainted with business methods. . . . [They hire members of the community.] Thus, in a larger and different sense, we have another form of co-operation. Colored people are furnishing their own with work and money for services received and the recipients are handing the money back for re-distribution to the original colored sources. ([Du Bois] 1919, 50)

The Citizens' Co-operative Stores illustrate how advocacy, public education, and self-education can promote cooperative development in the Black community. This story also shows how cooperatives in low-income communities can be made affordable (shares can be bought in installments), and how cooperative businesses can improve community life by hiring local residents and allowing money to recirculate among all the participants. However, Du Bois also noted that the cooperative was later converted into a conventional stock company and went out of business (1940, 759). It was more prosperous and provided greater benefits to the community under cooperative ownership, but under pressure it ceased being a cooperative and became a conventional business.

The Pioneer Cooperative Society

According to Mr. Moore, the manager of the Pioneer Cooperative Society in Harlem, he founded the co-op because it was difficult for Blacks to buy food at affordable prices in Harlem. Moore was "interested in bringing down the high cost of living for our colored people" and was inspired by a newspaper article about cooperatives. He pulled together a group of interested people who started meeting once a week "to study and plan cooperation." The co-op started a small grocery store on September 6, 1919, with 120 members, mostly of West Indian descent. Shares cost $5 each, and every member was required to buy at least two shares—although each member had only one vote.[10] The co-op charged members the same prices as other retail stores, but at the end of the year profits were divided "in proportion to the amount of their purchases." The co-op kept records of members' purchases with stamp books. One of the ways that the Pioneer Cooperative Society recruited members and advertised the co-op was to hold a large ball. By 1920, membership had increased to two hundred, and capital accumulation stood at $4,000. Moore attributed the co-op's success in "large part due to the loyalty of [its] members" (New York Dept. of Farms and Markets 1920, 10).

The Cooperative Society of Bluefield Colored Institute

The commercial department of the Bluefield Colored Institute in Bluefield, West Virginia, formed a student cooperative store in or around 1925.[11] The store's mission was to sell needed supplies to students and others at the school, to teach cooperative economics to the students, and to be a "commercial laboratory for the application of business theory and practice" (Sims 1925, 93). A share of stock sold for less than $1. After two years in business, the cooperative had paid all its debts and owned its own equipment and inventories (Matney 1927). The store began to pay dividends of 10 percent on purchases made. The student members voted to use profits to pay for scholarships to Bluefield's secondary school and junior college. Nine scholarships had been awarded by July 1927. According to the co-op's manager, W. C. Matney, members of this cooperative were the first African Americans to attend the National Cooperative Congress.[12] They became members of the Cooperative League of the USA (CLUSA) in 1925. After several years of successful operation, however, "the state of West Virginia eventually forbade its continuance," according to Du Bois (1940, 759).

The cooperative appears to have gotten some national attention. Du Bois quotes a comment made by a member of the Harvard University Graduate School of Education to the Bluefield Cooperative Society's manager about its promise as a model: "I am convinced that you are doing a splendid piece of work with this enterprise" (1940, 759). In this cooperative, as in the Citizens' Co-operative Stores in Memphis, education and training were integral aspects of cooperative development, both initially and throughout its existence. Not only did the Bluefield cooperative educate members about cooperative ownership and business development; profits from the business were also used to send members for advanced educational degrees. Affordable membership was also a goal of this co-op—the price of shares was low. In addition, the importance and documentation of profitability and solvency were apparent. Finally, the success of the Bluefield cooperative provides insight into how African American cooperatives inserted themselves into the wider national cooperative movement by joining the national (White) association and attending national conferences.

Economic Segregation and the "Group Economy"

These examples of early African American cooperatives demonstrate how African Americans have used racial solidarity and economic cooperation in the face of discrimination and marginalization to pool their resources and create their own mutually beneficial and often democratic companies. Jacqueline Jones notes that African Americans' "ethos of mutuality" has been shaped as much by "racial prejudice as by black solidarity" (1985, 102).

In rural and urban settings, community was important, and families worked together and shared resources. Jones notes the importance of kinship networks and extended households. "Despite the undeniable economic pressures on the family, few households were thrown entirely upon their own resources" (1985, 126). In addition, "cooperative work efforts inevitably possessed a strong emotional component, for they reflected feelings of loyalty and mutual affection as well as great material need" (231).

Du Bois researched and wrote about economic cooperation among African Americans, advocating economic segregation as the path to successful "group economy" in the Black community. In a 1934 letter to NAACP executive director Walter White, Du Bois clarified what he meant by this: "I am using segregation in the broader sense of separate racial effort caused by outer social repulsions, whether those repulsions are a matter of law or custom or mere desire. You are using the word segregation simply as applying to compulsory separations" (1934c, 476). Du Bois distinguished what he meant by "group economy" from the strategies of "black capitalism" and "buying black." His notion encompassed economic activity based on solidarity among Blacks and free from discrimination. Black group economy, he wrote in his autobiography, "consists of such a co-operative arrangement of industries and services within the Negro group that the group tends to become a closed economic circle largely independent of the surrounding white world" (1940, 711). Jones observes that such a philosophy of separation and self-determination insulated Blacks from Whites "and from the disappointment that often accompanied individual self-seeking" (1985, 100), and provided the "mixed blessings of semiautonomy" (101).

Booker T. Washington also advocated economic separation as part of his promotion of Black self-help and Black business development, or Black capitalism. Washington, known for his conservatism, did promote economic independence and the dignity of work, which had a profound effect on Black entrepreneurship and Black nationalist ideology. Washington was also a founder of the National Negro Business League (see chapter 6). Marcus Garvey promoted Black capitalism and joint business ownership as strategies for economic independence, and to support the emigration of Blacks to predominantly Black Caribbean countries and the African continent—strategies that were also part of Black nationalist ideology. Garvey's political impact through the UNIA was significant as well as legendary, even though his economic philosophy was much less known and relatively unsuccessful.

Du Bois suggested that voluntary racial economic segregation, in which the "colored group" serves itself in what "approaches a complete system" (1940, 709), explains why the large number of Black businesses and professionals in the early twentieth century were little known and documented. It was a closed system that needed little if anything from the outside (White) world and operated under the radar. White society was unaware of most of these businesses and their interlocking associations, because racial segregation was increasing in the early decades of the twentieth century. Therefore, this was a hidden, almost invisible strategy, and yet in many cases it was quite successful.

Part Two

DELIBERATIVE COOPERATIVE
ECONOMIC DEVELOPMENT

When the invincible force of cooperation met the immovable mountain of prejudice, fear, ignorance, and lack of self-confidence, the mountain melted into thin air. The invincible force forged ahead and is growing by leaps and bounds, and the Red Circle Cooperative idea of two years ago is a reality today.
—ROSENBERG (1940, 118)

Almost hourly the National Office of the Young Negroes' Co-operative League is receiving the Macedonian Call from those who are convinced that the Negro's economic future is largely in his *own* hands. Today, it is a letter from Mississippi or West Virginia; tomorrow, it is one from Arizona or California. But whether it is from North, South, East or West the substance is the same—the Young Negroes' Co-operative League and its program is being looked upon as "THE WAY OUT" for the Negro.
—BAKER (N.D.)

In his 1903 book *The Souls of Black Folk*, W. E. B. Du Bois predicted that race would haunt the twentieth century; he also predicted that the pursuit of individual economic advancement would hinder African American growth and development (Du Bois 1907). At his twelfth Atlanta conference, Du Bois proposed that African Americans would do better to engage in cooperative economics. That one of the research conferences of Du Bois's famous Atlanta conferences at the dawn of the twentieth century was devoted to discussing cooperative businesses among African Americans is a testament both to Du Bois's recognition of the importance of cooperatives to the Black urban community and to the existence of significant cooperative activity in the Black community on which to report.

Part II of this book focuses on organizational promotion and development of cooperatives in African American communities through Black co-op federations and agency-driven action, particularly in the early twentieth century. This section chronicles efforts by Black organizations to promote, educate about, and create cooperative businesses. Here we take note that there have been many serious efforts at Black cooperative development, especially during the Great Depression years. Chapters in this section document and analyze the development and accomplishments of early African American cooperatives and federations such as the Negro Cooperative Guild, the Young Negroes' Cooperative League, and the Eastern Carolina Council (a federation of North Carolinian cooperatives). Chapters also include efforts by organizations such as the National Negro Business League and the International Ladies' Auxiliary to the Brotherhood of Sleeping Car Porters to promote and establish cooperatives and provide co-op education among their members. I explore the purposes and actions of these organizations, their accomplishments, and the strengths and weaknesses of the cooperative businesses that they established. Chapter 4 discusses the various kinds of education that Black cooperatives and their advocates engaged in. Chapter 5 focuses on the Young Negroes' Cooperative League and its grand visions. Chapter 6 highlights the many other cooperative activities that took place among Blacks during the 1930s, particularly those sponsored by important Black organizations. In chapter 7, I focus on Black women's cooperative activities, particularly in the 1930s but also in the 1950s and 1970s. The last chapter in this section returns us to rural cooperative efforts among Blacks.

There are many lessons learned from this history of what I call the federation strategy for strengthening the Black cooperative movement. This section explores specific programs of some of the leading Black organizations of their time, from the perspective of their position on cooperative development and their actual economic activities. All of these organizations advocated and/or practiced some form of economic cooperation, many actually establishing cooperative businesses among the members or supporting cooperative businesses in Black communities.

A Note About Cooperative Development in the 1930s

There was some cooperative economic activity among African Americans in the early 1900s, but the Great Depression saw the most active cooperative development among Blacks. The Colored Merchants Association was established in 1927 by the National Negro Business League. The Young Negroes' Co-operative League, founded in December 1930 by twenty-five to thirty African American youths in response to a call by George Schuyler, was strong in five cities by the early 1930s. The International Ladies' Auxiliary to the Brotherhood of Sleeping Car Porters also organized cooperatives during this time, and their efforts continued into the 1940s (Chateauvert 1998; Cohen 2003). In every case, study groups were formed to discuss economic problems and learn cooperative economics before starting a business. The nineteenth-century co-op attempts by the Knights of Labor and other labor unions, and by the Colored Farmers' National Alliance and Co-operative Union and the populist movement, especially in rural areas, were resurrected in significant numbers in the 1920s, '30s, and even the '40s. In urban areas, the Universal Negro Improvement Association made halfhearted attempts to promote joint-stock ownership, efforts that were taken up more seriously by different groups in the 1930s. Major co-op development and official Rochdale cooperatives among Negroes were evident by the 1930s.

The major national organizations to develop Black-owned Rochdale cooperatives were (in chronological order) the Negro Cooperative Guild, the Colored Merchants Association of the National Negro Business League, the Young Negroes' Co-operative League, the International Brotherhood of Sleeping Car Porters and its Ladies' Auxiliary, and a major regional cooperative development organization, the North Carolina Council.

By the 1950s the cooperative movement had petered out a bit, with the few remaining efforts mostly clustered around small Black colleges in the South (Brooks and Lynch 1944), or in established Black communities in major cities.

Benefits and Lessons Learned

The members of this early Black cooperative movement understood that cooperatives needed quality co-op education, alternative financing, and comprehensive support from stable institutions. Organizers and members believed in education and training, in relation to both their economic ventures and their organizational needs. They provided additional services to their communities and often stabilized them. All of these benefits, though important in any era, were particularly important during the Great Depression. Black cooperatives proliferated during that era both out of necessity and because of the values of mutual support and cooperation that so many African Americans maintained throughout their experience in the diaspora. There have also been failures—often for lack of resources (capitalization), lack of enough specific management experience and training, and poor business planning. There are also many examples of sabotage—rents increased to exorbitant rates, insurance coverage or other support services or capital withdrawn or made unaffordable, unfair competition, and other deliberate subversions, as well as physical harassment to persons and property.

Lessons learned from these early twentieth-century experiences include the following:

- These efforts were based on values as much as on need. Especially for the cooperatives started during the Great Depression, while addressing pressing needs was often the first reason to start the cooperative, almost all of the cooperatives were also started because members understood that they could make more progress by working together and helping one another—and they exhibited strong racial solidarity as they witnessed ways in which they were all weak if one was weak. African American cooperatives grew out of the mutual-aid tradition, particularly of religious and fraternal organizations of Black independent educational institutions. Values such as solidarity, concern for community, helping thy neighbor, and lifting as you climb were commonly espoused and practiced by all of the cooperatives studied here, as well as by their supporting organizations.
- Education is necessary and in some cases essential—particularly cooperative education and training in democratic organization. All of the cooperatives stressed the need to study consumers and cooperative economics, and all started with a study group of some kind.
- Success was often easier with members who had stable income and what we now call a "living wage"—enough salary to raise a family. Cooperatives whose members were mostly poor and low-income had a more difficult time raising capital, maintaining stable equity, and remaining independent of creditors. Many of the cooperatives accepted equity payments in installments, which allowed members to afford membership but left the co-op undercapitalized. Some still were able to be successful, even if dependent on debt equity; but those co-ops with members whose economic status was more stable, who had decent jobs, and who could contribute in full sooner rather than later expanded faster and often lasted longer. Often, groups of civil servants were seen as a stable pool from which to draw membership, or at least to initiate the cooperative and stabilize it.
- Strong organization both at the local level and at the national level contributed to success. Regional and national organizations that raised awareness and funds and provided state and federal advocacy were extremely helpful. National and regional organizations also provided educational materials, brought different groups of people and expertise together, and held conferences for all to attend. With the backing of the North Carolina Council, for example, a significant number of Black cooperatives and credit unions were formed in the 1930s and '40s in that state. The national Black cooperative organizations also had relationships with the White

regional and national cooperative organizations and connected the Black groups with the White groups. In addition, the national Black organizations had some relationship to one another, and often held meetings and conferences that brought different groups and leaders together, which allowed the cooperators to network with others and promote the cooperative movement.

• Strong organization among members at the local level was equally important. Cooperatives that were able to establish trust and a team mentality early on usually succeeded, and often lasted longest. While many of the co-ops depended on strong charismatic leaders (teachers, religious leaders, and leaders of mutual and fraternal societies), they depended equally on strong organizational structures. Since cooperatives operate by democratic participation, these strong organizational structures, though perhaps started in a church or other organizational atmosphere, evolved into strong team and committee structures with shared leadership, multiple leaders, and mutual responsibility among the members.

• Those cooperatives with strong and effective committee structures lasted longer, as did those whose members started with a sense of solidarity and trust in one another (or quickly built that sense of trust and community). Strong connections and loyalty among members was important, especially to keep joint ownership in place, but also in order to face the outside hostility of competitors, conservatives, and racists.

• Violence, sabotage, the hostility of competitors, and structural class and racial discrimination often made it difficult to survive and eventually defeated these cooperative efforts.

• In most cases, even when they failed, co-op members were better off when the co-op ended than they had been at the outset. In addition to providing the goods and services members needed, the cooperatives provided experiences and training that members might not get anywhere else. In addition, members were often able to establish credit, buy or develop an asset (land, machinery, etc.), and earn a financial return on their equity (interest) or on their activity (dividend or patronage refund) in the cooperative. Some of the cooperatives were also able to return each member's original equity contribution when the cooperative dissolved.

• All of the cooperatives had grand long-term plans that they did not always achieve, although many of the initial and intermediate goals were realized, some quite successfully.

These lessons suggest that sound economic strategies can bring African Americans and other marginalized communities some measure of control over their economic lives and contribute to their own and their communities' economic prosperity. In addition, even if short-lived, these cooperative experiments had far-reaching consequences for the members and their communities, which were usually better off because of these efforts. There were many obstacles to overcome. Deliberative cooperative economic development often addressed those obstacles.

4

Black Study Circles and Co-op Education on the Front Lines

We believe that the most important single factor in our progress in Gary so far has been our educational program. We realized from the beginning that if a cooperative business was going to help our people in a large way, . . . they must study its fundamental philosophy, ideals and history.

—J. L. REDDIX (QUOTED IN HOPE 1940, 40)

It is our conviction that we must be trained before trying to lead people.
—SCHUYLER (1932, 456)

Every African American–owned cooperative of the past that I have researched, and almost every contemporary cooperative I have studied, began as the result of a study group or depended on purposive training and orientation of members. The Consumers' Cooperative Trading Company is one of the best examples in the United States of the importance of education and training and the use of study circles—but is not unique. Education was and continues to be an essential element of the development and success of the cooperatives that form the Mondragon Cooperative Corporation (MCC) in Spain, for example. The very first activity related to the founding of the Mondragon cooperatives was the establishment of a community–based polytechnic high school in the early 1950s, organized by MCC founder Father José María Arizmendiarrieta. The school taught cooperative business principles along with the technical curriculum and graduated the founders of the first cooperative to form the MCC. Today, several educational institutions are members of the MCC, among them the university Mondragon Unibertsitatea. According to the Mondragon website, "Training, both academic and that linked to professional refresher courses, has always played a key role in the development of our Corporation and constitutes one of our identifying characteristics. Today, MCC has a wide-reaching educational network which includes a number of Vocational Training Centers as well as its own University" (http://www.mondragon-corporation.com/ENG/

This chapter incorporates heavy revisions of Gordon Nembhard 2008a and 2008d.

Knowledge/Training/Training-in-MONDRAGON.aspx; see also Jakobsen 2000; Meek and Woodworth 1990).

Du Bois's concepts of "intelligent cooperation" and "intelligent democratic control" in economic leaders and institutions depend heavily on public information and member education and training. In *Dusk of Dawn* he describes his efforts to educate the public through the NAACP's magazine the *Crisis*, which he edited for twenty-four years, and through meetings and conferences to discuss and train people about consumer cooperation and cooperative economics (Du Bois 1940). He also explains how important education has been to the advancement of African Americans in general, writing, "the advance of the Negro people since emancipation has been the extraordinary success in education, technique and character" (713). Du Bois believed that education and planning were essential in the development of a cooperative commonwealth.

Continuous education is one of the international principles of cooperation and an important strategy for cooperative economic development and business success.[1] The success and growth of many cooperatives appear to depend on education strategies—orientation and training about both what it means to be a good co-op member and how to operate in and manage a particular business. Future co-op business development also depends on reaching young people with knowledge about alternative economic structures and cooperative economics, as well as experiences with entrepreneurship.

In this chapter, I explore education as a cooperative resource, particularly in worker-owned cooperatives, and delineate a variety of education strategies used. We then begin the story of African American cooperation in the twentieth century with Du Bois's attempt to organize a cooperative education and development program through the Negro Cooperative Guild, in addition to his efforts to promote cooperative development in the pages of the *Crisis*.

Models of Cooperative Business Education

Human capital is traditionally viewed as a factor of labor in terms of measuring and representing labor's credentials and skills. It is usually what labor brings with it. The study of working conditions in cooperatives suggests that cooperatives also develop and generate human and social capital—it is not just what is brought to the job. "On-the-job" training in specific industry skills, business planning and accounting, strategic planning, and skills of democratic participation are developed within the cooperative business. Teamwork, meeting facilitation, leadership, and networking are also both factors of production and outcomes of the association—i.e., they become endogenous, and social capital is developed in the process of operating a cooperative. Cooperatives require trust and solidarity, and at the same time create trust and solidarity in the process of developing and maintaining the co-op. Trust and solidarity, while often necessary to make the association work, also become products or outputs of a cooperative enterprise. There is anecdotal information about this.[2] In addition, Haynes (1993 and 1994) coins the term "social energy" to capture the nontraditional collective efforts, expertise, and time put in by co-op members to make the business work, and to connect it to the profitability of the cooperative. He observes that Du Bois had a similar notion that social engagement is an economic resource in cooperative economic endeavors—both an input and an output. More research and documentation of these processes and outcomes are needed.

Cooperatives use multiple levels of educational practices: study circles, curriculum development, pretraining and orientation, committee-level in-service training (self-management and leadership development), networking and conference development and participation, and public education for customers and nonmembers (see table 4.1). Below, I describe briefly each educational strategy and provide an example of an African American cooperative that has used it.

Study Circles

Study groups were formed to discuss economic problems and learn cooperative economics. The philosophy behind study groups for cooperative business development is best articulated in a summary of the philosophy of the Antigonish cooperative movement by Miles W. Connor, who was principal of the Coppin Normal School in Baltimore, Maryland (now Coppin State University). According to Connor, Dr. Moses M. Coady, the director of the extension department of St. Francis Xavier University in Antigonish, Nova Scotia, declared that the cooperative movement was "an adult education project in which the people are made aware of their problems and through study and discussion enabled to reach a possible solution of the same." According to Connor, Coady further explained that all cooperative enterprises were "an outgrowth of months and sometimes years of study of a vital problem. . . . People, through their study clubs, become intelligent in each phase of the new enterprise and are thus able to operate with a degree of ease and understanding that practically assures success" (Connor 1939, 109). Studying how cooperative business enterprises work—how they solve economic problems in unconventional ways—is essential to their development and success,

TABLE 4.1   Educational practices used by cooperative enterprises

Type	Description
Study circles	Informal or formal; weekly group meetings with readings and discussion.
Curriculum development	Formal adult education (night school and weekend courses), community workshops and training programs, study tours (travel), reading lists, college courses.
Pretraining and orientation	Formal; week- or month-long; various degrees of intensity; industry specific as well as cooperative economics and democracy education.
In-service training (committee level, board)	Formal; ongoing; industry specific and organizational skills; may use buddy system; may rotate specific jobs and expertise; board training; self-management training.
Networking and conference development	Formal or informal; cooperation among cooperatives and with other like-minded organizations; representation at local, regional, national, and international forums; conference participation and development for networking and increased skill development and skill sharing.
Leadership development	Formal and informal; requires member responsibilities and information sharing; rotates leadership responsibilities; involves certain members in networking and/or management.
Public education (customers and community)	Formal and informal; uses flyers, brochures, newsletters, packaging, websites, etc. to educate customers and community about the co-op model and principles, as well as about the co-op services and products; offers workshops, school visits, community groups and community activities; uses community service and donations to inform public about the business and the model.

reflects Connor, an African American educator who learned this philosophy on the co-op study tour in Antigonish. He wrote his report to share this information and understanding with other African Americans. This "study-learn-implement" model was followed again and again by African Americans (and others around the world) throughout the twentieth century.[3]

As early as 1918, Black activist groups in urban areas were forming study circles to discuss economic problems and learn about cooperative economics. Remember that there was cooperative activity among African Americans in rural areas in the 1800s. The twentieth century saw co-ops develop in cities as well, and ushered in a strong cooperative education movement. As we saw in the previous chapter, for example, Citizens' Co-operative Stores in Memphis started with a study group in 1918, after its leader attended W. E. B. Du Bois's meeting of the Negro Cooperative Guild. The intent of the meeting was "to induce individuals and groups to study consumers' co-operation" and to promote that cooperation among African Americans (Du Bois 1940, 759). There is almost no documentation about how many study groups were formed after this initial meeting, but we know that at least two cooperatives (Citizens' Co-operative Stores in Memphis and the Cooperative Society of Bluefield Colored Institute in West Virginia) grew out of that meeting. And there is evidence that most cooperatives developed from study circles or initial informational meetings.

The first year of the Young Negroes' Co-operative League, 1930, was devoted to "the study of history, principles and methods of Rochdale consumers' cooperation" (Schuyler 1932, 456). The YNCL believed that leaders must be well educated and informed, and in this case the subject was economics and consumer cooperation. The YNCL provided reading lists for members, sent out newsletters, held conferences, and promoted a five-year plan that included study and discussion of cooperative economics. In addition, the YNCL planned a national tour where executive director Ella Baker would spend two days in each community, study its economic problems, introduce the concept of consumers' cooperation, provide examples of communities that had developed co-ops, and organize new YNCL councils. Part of the purpose of the tour, in addition to educating people about cooperatives, advertising the YNCL, and establishing councils, was to "act as an antidote to some of that hopelessness" that the Black community felt in the 1930s (Grant 1998, 34; Baker n.d., 1). Any city that had a YNCL council was also to establish a weekly forum "for the discussion of the economic problems of the Negro and especially the study of consumers' cooperation" (Schuyler n.d., 6). To develop effective cooperatives, Baker counseled members to "concentrate upon the intensive study and circulation of the FACTS OF CONSUMER'S CO-OPERATION. Encourage the writing of papers and holding of debates upon different phases of it. Acquaint yourselves thoroughly with the subject so that you can convince others of the value of the Y.N.C.L." (1931d, 2).

The Consumers' Cooperative Trading Company in Gary, Indiana, also provides an example of how study circles served many purposes. These purposes include initial economic analysis and business planning, better understanding of cooperative economics and the cooperative movement, networking among cooperatives, energizing and activating members to become more involved and to increase membership, industry-specific training, and research and development for expansion. In this example, as in the early history of the

Mondragon cooperatives in Spain, formalizing education also became important, i.e., the development of a course in the high school in the former example, and the establishment of a formal high school, and later a university, in the latter example.

Consumers' Cooperative Association of Kansas City formed a study group, initially of thirty people, in 1933. The group studied the history and philosophy of the cooperative movement. A local principal (H. O. Cook) and his wife went further and "personally observed and studied the operation and management of several cooperatives including ones in Pittsburgh, Columbus, Gary, Minneapolis, and Chicago" (Hope 1940, 42).

People's Consumer Cooperative, Inc. of Chicago started out with a boycott of an exploitive store in September 1936. Members of this group then investigated alternative sources of the products they needed. They also found literature about cooperatives. They met Jacob L. Reddix of Gary, who suggested a study club (Hope 1940, 44). The study group started in October 1936, and the group started a buying club a few months after that, and eventually established a store.

Study circles continue to be used today as an early step in the process of establishing a cooperative business. The Federation of Southern Cooperatives/Land Assistance Fund engaged in study groups at its beginning in the 1960s (McKnight 1992; Zippert 2005) and continues to provide its members with workshops on cooperative economics and training programs in cooperative business development and sustainable agriculture (see Gordon Nembhard 2002b and chapter 9 in this volume). In a 2007 interview by the author, Linda Leaks, a co-founder of the Ella Jo Baker Intentional Community Cooperative in Washington, D.C., said that she has found study circles very effective in every stage of the development and maintenance of cooperative housing in the 1990s and early 2000s. Moreover, because of the importance of establishing trust among members and an understanding of the mission of the cooperative, Leaks has focused more of her recent attention on the development of intentional cooperative communities—where members join the cooperative not only for the housing opportunity but also because of its philosophy, mission, and activist intentions. Continuous education and the building of trust are essential.

Another example of the growing use of study circles is their increased importance as a mechanism in the field of microlending. Loans are often awarded to members of a "lending circle" who study microentrepreneurship together, support one another, and make sure that each individual member pays back the loan (often, one loan must be repaid before another is given).[4]

Study circles are also becoming more widely used in the deliberative democracy movement and to strengthen civic participation.

Co-op Courses and Curricula Among African Americans

The early involvement of school principals and teachers is also important in the establishment of cooperatives, as well as in the provision of reading lists, cooperative economics, and curricula for members. Examples of school principals involved in cooperative education include Mr. and Mrs. H. O. Cook and the Consumers' Cooperative Association of Kansas City, J. L. Reddix and the Consumers' Cooperative Trading Company (Gary, Indiana), and various principals at the Bricks Rural Life School, Tyrrell County Training School, and Bluefield Colored Institute. The Bricks Rural Life School in Bricks, North Carolina, run by the American Missionary Association, developed a program of adult education in 1934 for African American cooperative development. Families took up residence on the school's farm to learn new farming techniques and cooperative economics. Cooperative economics courses and training workshops were provided for the community. Also in North Carolina, another charismatic principal began organizing cooperatives in the late 1930s. The principal of the Tyrrell County Training School, and members of his staff, conducted study groups on cooperative economics. This principal was familiar with the cooperatives at Bricks and had learned about cooperatives in a class on rural education at Columbia University, according to Pitts (1950).[5] They then established the Light of Tyrrell Cooperative. More cooperative activity took place in North Carolina around that time, as the Bricks and Tyrrell County co-ops joined together to organize the Eastern Carolina Council, a federation of North Carolinian cooperatives (see chapter 8).

In the 1930s, Ella Baker won a scholarship to the Cooperative Institute of CLUSA held at the Brookwood Labor College in 1931—she was the first African American to win the award (Grant 1998, 33; Cohen 2003, 50). She studied consumer problems and community building at Columbia University, the New School for Social Research (now New School University), and New York University, and served as director of the Consumer Education Division of the Works Progress Administration (Cohen 2003, 50; see also Grant 1998; Ransby 2003). Ella Baker also was chair of education and publicity for Harlem's Own Cooperative from the late 1930s until 1941 (for more on Harlem's Own, see chapter 6). This example demonstrates the various ways in which people could learn about cooperatives in the 1930s in New York City.

The *Journal of Negro Education* began publishing information about cooperatives, cooperative economics, and consumers' cooperation in 1935 (Washington 1939a). The January 1939 issue included a list of sixteen articles and books on cooperatives in the United States and Europe and among Negroes. The April 1939 issue included a list of eight public lectures at the University of Michigan's extension services on contemporary problems and the cooperative movement. Washington writes, "For those readers who have not kept track of the movement we wish at this time, not so much to give them a detailed account of what is going on, as to induce them to read and study concerning the issues, principles, and activities of this project for human betterment. Hence we present quotations, excerpts, references, newspaper clippings and personal experiences—all with the hope of awakening new interest in the subject, or feeding that which already exists" (1939a, 104–5).

The April 1939 issue of the *JNE* also included a short article by Anne Williamson promoting co-op education and advocating a regional "unified system of Negro Colleges" to develop an extensive curriculum on the cooperative movement and cooperative business development for Negroes, focusing particularly on self-help and local cooperative economic development. The Negro colleges would:

- Offer courses on the philosophy, nature, and growth of the cooperative movement
- Conduct extension courses in the organization, administration, and techniques of cooperative enterprises
- Act as a clearinghouse for problems in co-op development
- Become an experimental center for "launching Cooperative projects of individual and group nature"
- Collect data on cooperative enterprises
- Disseminate Cooperative Literature (Williamson 1939, 242)

Williamson saw the goal of this cooperative curriculum in Negro colleges as stimulating "the economic rehabilitation of the suppressed, oppressed and depressed people of the Rural South, through a program of education seeking not only better material conditions, but an awakening of the people to their innate power to solve their own problems" (242). The *JNE* reported on the study tour in 1938 of the Antigonish cooperative movement in Nova Scotia that nineteen Blacks went on with thirty-five Whites (Washington 1939a, 108). As early as 1938, in the "Bulletin of Instruction on Decisions and Orders of the First Convention of Ladies Auxiliary and International Executive Board," the Ladies' Auxiliary to the Brotherhood of Sleeping Car Porters dictated that "as soon as convenient," local auxiliaries should subscribe to "Consumers Union" and "Consumers Guide" publications. They were also directed to "information about the history and conduct of consumers' cooperatives" and "advised to study credit unions" (Wilson and Randolph 1938, 1–2). A workers' education bureau was established, and local auxiliaries were urged to develop local libraries. In 1940 the Workers Education Bureau of the Ladies' Auxiliary circulated a reading list of publications on current events, child welfare and child labor, women workers, and consumer information, including cooperative economics (Workers Education Bureau 1940, 2). Works cited included CLUSA president James Warbasse's "What Is Consumer' [sic] Cooperation," Beatrice Potter Webb's "The Discovery of the Consumer," and J. L. Reddix's article about the Gary cooperative, "The Negro Finds a Way to Economic Equality" (Reddix 1935).

One year later, the Ladies' Auxiliary continued to emphasize consumer education, cooperatives, and credit unions, along with issues about child labor and women's labor and how to support organized labor (Wilson 1941b). By this time, Halena Wilson, the president of the Ladies' Auxiliary, had written a series of bulletins about consumerism and cooperatives for the members (Wilson n.d.). One communication to the members provided a brief history of the consumer movement and the Rochdale Society of Equitable Pioneers in England and explained consumer cooperation, the benefits from consumer cooperatives, and how to conduct a consumer business (Wilson 1941a). Wilson wrote to the Ladies' Auxiliary chapter presidents and suggested that they arrange a program about consumer education, the high cost of living, and cooperatives for their members—that the times dictated this need (1941c). She outlined a set of topics to cover and directed them to CLUSA for more information. She later told the chapter presidents that she thought it was important to start members on the condensed pamphlets she had written and gradually build their knowledge of and interest in consumer cooperation "a little at a time," i.e., through sustained study: "In this graduate[d] manner an interesting Consumer Program can be established" (1941d).

In the February 1942 issue of the *Black Worker*, Wilson wrote a column called "Consumers Cooperative Movement," in which she explained clearly the importance of study groups in the cooperative movement:

> Since the Cooperative Movement is a group movement, the members are joint owners of the various enterprises. Therefore it is essential that the members become thoroughly acquainted with the principles and policies which govern their business. This is the reason for the study clubs and the discussion groups which extend over a period of many

months. During that period of study the members learn of the many advantages common to the Cooperative Movement. They learn how to get quality and value for the money being spent. They learn how to put an end to ruthless exploitation, how to lower prices and how to shorten the distance between the middle man and the ultimate consumer who happens to be themselves. They learn that the future well being of themselves and their offspring, that the success of the enterprise depends upon the consolidated efforts of the entire group. (1942a, 2)

At the January 7, 1943, meeting of the Chicago Ladies' Auxiliary, it was announced that the co-op study club had established two branches, "so members being nearest these districts may easily attend these meetings." All members were asked to join the co-op study club to help "make this movement a bigger and better one" (Williamson 1943, 2).

In addition, A. Philip Randolph was accustomed to talking to crowds and attending meetings about cooperative development among Negroes at least between 1943 and 1947. Correspondence between Randolph and Wilson documents several occasions when Randolph offered to speak about cooperatives at meetings or agreed to speak at or attend a cooperative meeting. In December 1945 he wrote to Wilson, "I hope you may be able to plan a meeting that will have wide educational value among Negroes on the importance of the cooperative movement." Before launching a cooperative store, a speech by Randolph was often part of the publicity. He is credited with stating at the Brotherhood's Consumers Cooperative Buying Club rally in 1944, for example, that cooperatives are "the best mechanism yet devised to bring about economic democracy" (Cohen 2003, 49). Randolph also wrote columns about cooperatives in the *Messenger*, the *Black Worker*, and other African American newspapers and magazines (1918 and 1944, for example).

In its more than forty-seven-year history, the Federation of Southern Cooperatives/Land Assistance Fund (FSC/LAF) has engaged in and contributed to cooperative education through series of workshops, trainings, and technical assistance offerings, often creating its own materials (see Gordon Nembhard 2002b, for example; also Zippert 2005). It is clear that many cooperatives used established curricula on cooperative economics and consumers' cooperation, and created their own materials as needed—and urged their members to read these materials. Education and group learning were encouraged and enabled. In addition, the founders and early staff of the FSC studied the Antigonish movement (see Prejean 1992; McKnight 1992), like their counterparts who attended the 1938 tour. Southern Consumers Cooperative (Lafayette, Louisiana) actually sent three staffers to an eight-week summer institute at the International School of Cooperatives and Credit Unions at St. Francis Xavier University, Antigonish, Nova Scotia—one each in the summers of 1962, 1963, and 1964—one of whom (Carol Zippert) became a founder of the FSC. Charles Prejean, the FSC's first executive director, studied cooperative management training in New England in the mid-1960s. Some members of the FSC also toured the Mondragon cooperatives in Spain in the 1970s (Zippert 2005).

Pretraining and Orientation

Many cooperatives, particularly those initiated by agencies or other organizations, begin with an extensive pretraining program and member orientation. Cooperative Economics for Women (CEW) in Jamaica Plain, Massachusetts, offered potential members an innovative, rigorous, and comprehensive six-month to one-year training program. CEW's transformative program in the late 1990s combined literacy, organizational skills, the technical know-how to run a business and a co-op, and employment experience with building trust and a sense of community among members (Gordon Nembhard 2000a).

Emma's Eco-Clean housecleaning cooperative is a project of Women's Action to Gain Economic Security (WAGES) in Redwood City, California. Five founding members, predominantly Latinas, went through a one-year business training program offered by WAGES and seventy-five hours of industrial training in ecological cleaning. Once they established their cooperative, the members formed their own internal training program. Emma's won a 1999 Silicon Valley Environmental Business Award with WAGES, and was nominated for a 2001 San Mateo County Sustainability Award (WAGES 2004). WAGES has developed and supported several other ecological cleaning cooperatives using the same model, and generally helps immigrant women jointly own their own businesses, receive the needed training, and gain control over their income (Morris 1998).

Cooperative Home Care Associates (CHCA), a home-care agency composed of women of color, blends pretraining and in-service training to develop and maintain quality of service. It developed its own not-for-profit training subsidiary to ensure comprehensive, high-quality training as well as advancement possibilities for its member-owners. Glasser and Brecher note that "since the original training was out of the hands of CHCA, it did not reflect the ethics of respect and support with which the company wished to deal with its workers" (2002, 24). As a model of how a service company can provide quality care by creating high-quality jobs, CHCA found it necessary to control job training, create its own curricula, and hire its own trainers; it then formed its own not-for-profit training subsidiary. Mondragon, similarly, has multiple education and training facilities and promotes research and development among and for its members.

Early in the process, CHCA learned to use its own workers to enhance the training and increase job opportunities and advancement. Glasser and Brecher observe that "the training program was both an opportunity to upgrade a few bright and ambitious HHAs [home health aides] and to provide trainees with instructors who were their cultural and vocational peers. This arrangement allowed trainees to communicate more honestly to the staff through the assistant instructors, and for these former HHAs to communicate their ideas to senior staff within a less threatening, more equal context" (2002, 26–27). Components of CHCA's training program include free tuition, guaranteed employment to those who pass the course, and "smooth transition from training to work" (Inserra, Conway, and Rodat 2002, 60). There is a rigorous applicant-screening process, a four- to six-week intake process that includes individual interviews and a full-day information session, a four- to five-week training course (four weeks and 160 hours in English or five weeks and 200 hours in Spanish), followed by eight hours of supervised clinical work (58–69). CHCA's training-certification program in home health care is licensed by the state of New York and surpasses federal requirements (64). CHCA's program emphasizes "process as well as content, social skills as well as technical mastery" (Glasser and Brecher 2002, 27). The training method is a learner-centered approach "designed to try to bolster individuals' confidence and self-esteem through the use of participatory techniques and emphasis on mutual respect among trainees" (Inserra, Conway, and Rodat 2002, 65). Quality of service is essential to the cooperative's success, and high-quality training and working conditions are essential to the members' provision of high-quality service. This is one of CHCA's great successes. Training also includes understanding how to participate in a democratic organization, and board training for members (worker-owners) who are elected to the board of directors of the co-op. Their high-ranking training program has also positioned them for direct replication in other places. Through all the successes, the training program continues to be challenged by increasing regulations and requirements in the field, balancing content with process, and finding and retaining appropriate instructors. In conjunction with its comprehensive training programs, CHCA also develops leadership from within, provides owner-members with opportunities to increase their skills, move up the professional ladder (from unskilled home-care provider to registered nurse or home-care instructor), and assume board and management positions. This encourages members to grow as the organization grows, and it allows the organization both to hire from within at the upper levels and to bring in new unskilled employees/potential members at the entry level.

Management by Committee, In-Service Training, and Leadership Development

The Rainbow Grocery Cooperative in San Francisco is a nonhierarchical, self-managed, interracial worker-owned cooperative that operates by a committee system. Each committee or department is semiautonomous and sends a representative to a governing committee. Members rotate among departments and learn most aspects of the business. Self-managed cooperatives in particular learn the importance of good communication, meeting facilitation, and consensus building, and make sure to train themselves in these areas in addition to the content areas related to their industry. Self-managing cooperatives such as Rainbow also engage in participatory budgeting and open-book accounting. Many such cooperatives also offer upward job mobility, horizontal promotion, and board training for their members, providing leadership development and a variety of opportunities for advancement. Members gain experience in decision making, develop leadership in context, and share their skills.[6]

Du Bois noted as early as 1907 that continuous education, especially the proper training of managers, was essential to the success of Black cooperatives (1907, 151; 1940). He also discussed the importance of selecting and developing leaders "for the discovery of ability to manage, of character, of absolute honesty, of inspirational push not toward power but toward efficiency, of expert knowledge in the technique of production and distribution and of scholarship in the past and present of economic development," leaders who would be accountable to "intelligent democratic control" (1940, 709–10). He argued, in addition, that the only way to maintain good leadership was through the deliberate and sustained education of both co-op leaders and members. "They must be taught in long and lingering conference, in careful marshaling of facts, in the willingness to come to decision slowly and the determination not to tyrannize over minorities. . . . Their real character must be so brought out and exhibited until the overwhelming mass of people who own the co-operative movement and whose votes guide and control it will be able to see just exactly the principles and persons for which they are voting" (710). Du Bois's articulation of a cooperative vision for African Americans also explains why this education is so important:

All this would be a realization of democracy in industry led by consumers' organizations and extending to planned production. Is there any
reason to believe that such democracy among American Negroes could
evolve the necessary leadership in technique and the necessary social
institutions in which would so guide and organize the masses that a
new economic foundation could be laid for a group with is today threatened with poverty and social subordination? (709)

Similarly, Ralph Paige, executive director of the FSC/LAF, suggests not
only that leadership development is essential to the success of cooperatives
but also that leadership training has been an important and successful by-
product of the support for cooperative economic development given by the
FSC/LAF. The FSC has trained members of co-ops for leadership in the
cooperative movement, but this training and leadership experience also
translates into other areas of civic society and the political arena (Paige 2001;
see also Gordon Nembhard and Blasingame 2002, Gordon Nembhard 2004b).

Networking Conferences

Many cooperatives have also formed local networks where they share product
and service information, put out a joint newsletter, and organize meetings.
Some of the networks organize educational and networking conferences and
join with other networks into regional and national organizations. At the
conferences, members share best practices, exchange information, and provide in-service training. In addition to the exchange of information and
training, attendees also engage in movement-building strategies and meet
with funders and potential funders.[7]

In addition to establishing the Negro Cooperative Guild in 1918, Du Bois
integrated discussion of cooperative economics into most of the economic
conferences and summits that he organized or spoke to, including the twelfth
Atlanta conference in 1907, the Amenia conferences in 1916 and 1933, and
even the Rosenwald economic conferences. In addition, for many years Du
Bois was in correspondence with CLUSA president James P. Warbasse, and
with many other Black and White scholars and leaders of cooperative economics. The Young Negroes' Co-operative League organized annual conferences in different locations around the country to exchange information,
support fledgling cooperatives, and educate the public.

Many of the Black cooperatives of the early twentieth century also made
sure to maintain their membership in the White cooperative national and
regional organizations and attend their conferences and annual meetings.

The Cooperative Society of Bluefield Colored Institute, for example, prided itself on joining CLUSA in 1925 and being the first African Americans to attend the National Cooperative Congress in Minneapolis in 1926 (Matney 1927). In the 1930s, the YNCL not only worked with the Colored Merchants Association but also belonged to CLUSA, attending its conferences and corresponding with its leadership (*Pittsburgh Courier* 1931).

In 1969, the National Black Economic Conference included support for cooperatives in its platform. The "Black Manifesto" (written mostly by James Forman, executive secretary of the Student Non-Violent Coordinating Committee, or SNCC), delivered at the conference, called for reparations in order to fund an "international Black appeal" that would produce capital for "the establishment of cooperative businesses in the United States and Africa," in addition to a southern land bank, a national Black labor strike and defense fund, a national welfare rights organization, Black-owned publishing houses and audio-visual networks, and research and training centers (National Black Economic Conference 1969).

THE TWELFTH ATLANTA CONFERENCE—NEGRO BUSINESS DEVELOPMENT AND COOPERATIVES

Du Bois held a conference in 1907 titled "Negro Business Development and Cooperatives," promoting cooperatives and economic cooperation. The twelfth Atlanta conference, held at Atlanta University on May 28, 1907, was a daylong program, beginning at 10:00 A.M. and ending at 10:00 P.M., and included presentations on such topics as business as a career, health and business, children's cooperation (which included songs and games presented by four kindergarten classes), and cooperative business development. Among the presentations at the final session on cooperative business were Du Bois's address "The Meaning of Co-operation" and G. Crawford's "Co-operation and Immigration" (the conference program and resolutions were published in Du Bois 1907). The conference resolution concluded that the "present tendencies among Negroes toward co-operative effort and . . . wide ownership of small capital and small accumulations among many rather than great riches among a few" should be fostered and emphasized (Du Bois 1907, 4). Conference presentations highlighted these efforts and promoted economic cooperation. The final resolution also declared that African Americans were in a crisis because "they unwittingly stand . . . at the cross roads" between the "old trodden ways of" individualistic competition (and gaining "wealth at the expense of the general well being") and "co-operation in capital and labor" (which fosters a "wide distribution of capital and a more general equality of wealth and comfort") (4). The resolution emphasized that this crisis was not the result of "idleness" or "lack of skill" but rather lack of recognition of the importance of cooperative economic development and the gains made for the race from cooperative economic endeavors.

It is significant that the topic of the twelfth conference, economic cooperation and business development, was one of the major topics Du Bois pursued and intended to revisit each decade. His extensive study of African American cooperatives and economic cooperation was the first of its kind (1898 and 1907). Currently, more than 107 years later, the 1907 monograph remains the only full-length national study of African American–owned cooperatives and collective economic activity until now.

Perhaps also significant, the first report and conference in the Atlanta series specifically studying business cooperatives among African Americans was actually one of the last to be produced before the Atlanta social study reports and conferences were terminated (in large part because of lack of financial backing). There was certainly conversation about cooperative economic action, and some examples in practice, in the years before and after that conference, but no national academic conference dedicated to Black business cooperatives and urban cooperative economic development has taken place since.[8] It is telling, therefore, that the twelfth Atlanta conference was the first and only academic conference and national study to focus on African American cooperative economics in business.

The Atlanta conferences were part of a research project that Du Bois pursued at Atlanta University with the support of its president, Horace Bumstead, from 1895 to 1908. Part of a comprehensive plan to study many aspects of the social and economic conditions of African Americans—"the complete Negro problem in the United States" (Du Bois 1940, 597)—each annual conference coincided with the release of a research report and covered one aspect of African American life. Du Bois envisioned that these annual conferences would be held in Atlanta in the succeeding decade as well—in fact, he envisioned "a hundred year program of study." Du Bois's goal was to transform Bumstead's idea of annual conferences at Atlanta University focused on city problems (to rival Tuskegee University's annual conferences on rural problems) into a national undertaking and a major research venture; in this, he anticipated the fields of urban studies and urban sociology later in the century. Du Bois explained the significance of the reports and conferences: "At the time of their publication Atlanta University was the only institution in the world carrying on a systematic study of the Negro and his development, and putting the result in a form available for the scholars of the world. In addition to the publications, we did something toward bringing together annually at Atlanta University persons and authorities interested in the problems of the South" (1940, 601–2).

Twenty-eight years later, one of Du Bois's biographers wrote, "Du Bois' Atlanta studies represent his efforts to introduce systematic induction into the field of race relations when other men were speculating about Negroes" (Rudwick 1968, 49). While noting many of the shortcomings and scholarly weaknesses of the annual research reports, Rudwick commended the effort: "Du Bois' monument was his attempt to traverse the society, observing and counting what he saw, using the schedule, questionnaire, and interview. His method of case-counting was naive and elemental, and his questions were sometimes unsophisticated. . . . But his decennial program was unique, even though none of the large universities contributed to it, as he had so much hoped" (49). Rudwick also pointed out that Du Bois's research helped to dispel many of the myths and "common sense generalizations held by many people of the period," including the misconceptions that Black men were lynched for sexual assault (in fact, this was the case in only one-third of lynchings); that Negro education was equal to White (it was inferior in every way); and that Negro education was paid for by the beneficence of Whites (Negroes paid a significant proportion of the taxes that paid for education) (49–50). Rudwick credited Du Bois's reports with improving Black morale and group pride, and with alerting Whites not only to the plight of African Americans but also to the fact that Black educational institutions were engaged in serious intellectual activity (52).

Public Education

Many cooperatives also realize the importance of public education—educating their customers, potential customers, and surrounding communities about cooperative economics and the mission of their enterprise. This may consist simply of providing informational brochures and bulletin boards about the cooperative or more extensively with forums and workshops for customers. Many cooperatives or cooperative trade associations produce newsletters, brochures, and websites to educate the public about what they do and to introduce the concept of cooperative economics. In the 1930s, the North Carolina Council for Credit Unions and Associates provided pamphlets on how to start a credit union and cooperative economics as well as workshops. These were quite effective because the number of new African American credit unions and cooperatives increased significantly during that period (see chapter 8). Prejean (1992, 17) notes that the North Carolina group had brochures and pamphlets and extensive education starting in the 1920s.

Du Bois and George S. Schuyler separately discussed cooperative efforts and principles in their newspaper columns and magazine articles, particularly in the early 1930s, and encouraged others to do so. Moreover, cooperatives were mentioned fairly regularly in newspapers and magazines by Black leaders from about 1910 to 1942. From 1910 to 1934 and again in the early 1940s, the *Crisis*, under Du Bois's leadership, published several articles and editorials on cooperative economics by both White and Black authors and sometimes highlighted a particular cooperative business (see DeMarco 1974; also Warbasse 1918; Frazier 1923; Sims 1925; Matney 1927, 1930; Rosenberg 1940a; Crump 1941). In 1918, as prelude to the establishment of the Negro Cooperative Guild, for example, Du Bois wrote a "series of editorials and explanations in the *Crisis*, advocating consumers' co-operation for Negroes" (Du Bois 1940, 759). In April 1933, one of his last editorials, "The Right to Work," proposed consumer and producer cooperation as the solution to African Americans' economic distress (Du Bois 1933b).

In 1930, Schuyler issued a call to "young Negroes" to save the race through cooperative economics (Schuyler n.d.; Calvin 1931; Ransby 2003, 82). He summarized his four-page open letter in his regular column in the *Pittsburgh Courier* (see chapter 5 for more detail). In a letter to the members of the Young Negroes' Co-operative League, Schuyler encouraged them to publicize cooperatives: "Each member must make it a point to talk up consumer' co-operation with all of his or her friends. It is necessary to prepare yourself with answers to all possible questions that might be asked. That is your ammunition—and you know you can't win a battle without ammunition" (1931, 1).

Also during the 1930s, '40s, and '50s, A. Philip Randolph's *Messenger* and *Black Worker* periodically carried articles and columns discussing cooperative ownership strategy, the consumers' cooperative movement and its relationship to the labor movement, and the development of and support for Black-owned consumer cooperatives, particularly those established by the Ladies' Auxiliary to the Brotherhood of Sleeping Car Porters (see Chateauvert 1998; see also Randolph 1918; Wilson 1942a, 1942d, 1947a, 1948a). Even Marcus Garvey's more nationalistic and economically conservative *Negro World* occasionally published an article on a Black cooperative business or housing venture in the early decades of the twentieth century (see NNBL 1929; Gothard 1931; *Negro World* 1930a, 1930c, 1931, 1932).

More recently, beginning in the 1990s, the APR Educational Fund of the A. Philip Randolph Institute, headquartered in Washington, D.C., and dedicated to Black labor and community development, has introduced worker ownership and supports the development of worker cooperatives among its members.

The strategy of using community support has helped many African American—owned cooperatives, such as the Freedom Quilting Bee in Alberta, Alabama, and the SSC Employment Agency in Baltimore. Public information and dialogue about mission and goals help to secure a client base and maintain interest in the business and its success. Part of the mission of Equal Exchange, for example (though not a predominantly African American cooperative), is to inform consumers about "honest and fair trade relationships and cooperative principles" (http://equalexchange.coop/). Because its business connects small cooperative coffee farmers in Latin America, Africa, and Asia with North American buyers, it is important that Equal Exchange customers know as much about the principles, processes, and challenges involved as possible. This increases the appeal of the product, establishes a niche market, and explains the prices.

Agency-Driven Cooperative Education Among African Americans

From these examples, we see how important cooperative economics education is for all stakeholders and at all stages of cooperative development. Throughout history, African American cooperatives, like all cooperatives, have invested time and money in self-education and training in order to strengthen their own enterprises and spread the word about this model. Three examples are the Negro Cooperative Guild, the Consumers' Cooperative Trading Company, and historically Black colleges.

The Negro Cooperative Guild

As we have seen, W. E. B. Du Bois was an early proponent of consumer cooperation and discussed its merits in his editorial columns, articles, and books. He made several attempts to interest the NAACP's board of directors in promoting cooperatives (Du Bois 1940; Rudwick 1968, 196). Du Bois asked the NAACP in 1917, for example, to support a program to teach the value of forming buyers' clubs operating on the principles of economic cooperation. According to Rudwick, at that time there seemed to be some tolerance but no particular interest on the part of the NAACP board ("the board minutes fail to note any overt antagonism either to" the editorials or to Du Bois's proposal to convene a meeting to promote cooperatives) (1968, 196).

In 1918, Du Bois held the first and only meeting of the Negro Cooperative Guild in the *Crisis* magazine offices—but apparently unofficially. Sixteen years later, Du Bois would leave the *Crisis* and the NAACP, in part because of differences of opinion over his advocacy of a racial group economy based on African American cooperative ownership ("the segregated economy theory"—see Rudwick 1968, 273; DeMarco 1974). Du Bois described his dilemma: "I could seek through my editorship of the *Crisis* slowly but certainly to change the ideology of the NAACP and of the Negro race into a racial program for economic salvation along the paths of peace and organization"— "advocating new, deliberate and purposeful segregation for economic defense in precisely the lines of business and industry" (1940, 783). To do that, however, he would need to either change the makeup of the NAACP board or leave the association. He explained the difficulty of finding directors sympathetic to this strategy, and the resistance to cooperative ownership based on racial solidarity:

> The Association seemed to me not only unwilling to move toward the left in its program but even stepped decidedly toward the right. And what astonished me most was that this economic reaction was voiced even more by the colored members of the Board of Directors than the white. One could realize why a rich white liberal should suspect fundamental economic change, but it was most difficult for me to understand that the younger and more prosperous Negro professional men, merchants, and investors were clinging to the older ideas of property, ownership and profits even more firmly than the whites. The liberal white world saw the change that was coming despite their wish. The upper class colored world did not anticipate nor understand it. (782–83)

In 1930, George Schuyler (n.d.) demonstrated a similar frustration with middle-class conservative African Americans, but he felt that salvation would be found in the younger crowd's embrace of cooperative economics.

On August 26, 1918, after publishing a series of editorials in the *Crisis* "advocating consumer's cooperation for Negroes," Du Bois went ahead and invited twelve "colored men from seven different states" to establish the Negro Cooperative Guild (Du Bois 1940, 759; see also Bunche n.d.). The meeting took place at the *Crisis* offices in New York City. The idea behind the guild was to encourage groups and individuals to study consumer cooperation, its extent and methods; to hold an annual meeting to support the establishment of cooperative stores; and to form a central committee to provide technical assistance. As Rudwick put it, "The organization wished to convince various clubs to study economic co-operation and hoped to encourage converts to open co-operative stores under its direction" (1968, 196).

After attending this meeting, a "Mr. Ruddy" returned home to Memphis, Tennessee, and organized a study group (Du Bois 1919).[9] In February 1919, the Memphis group incorporated as Citizen's Cooperative Stores to operate cooperative meat markets.

These are the known details about the formation and first (and only) meeting of the Negro Cooperative Guild in August 1918. I have found no list of names of those who attended the meeting, although from Du Bois we know that Mr. Ruddy and W. C. Matney were in attendance.[10] According to Ralph Bunche (n.d.), the meeting was a two-day conference held August 26–27, 1938, for "those interested in establishing cooperative enterprises among Negroes throughout the country." Because Bunche's description (from a one-page description of the guild among his archived papers) matches Du Bois's and Rudwick's in every respect but the year, I assume that 1938 is a typo and that he meant 1918. If there was a second meeting in 1938, I have found no other mention of it by Du Bois, Rudwick, or any other historical account.

Nor have I found any records indicating that there were any more meetings after the first, as noted above. "There is no evidence," Bunche wrote, "that the Guild ever advanced very far beyond this first conference, though Dr. Du Bois is still a staunch advocate of cooperative enterprise for Negroes" (n.d.). Du Bois admits to being distracted by a trip to Europe, his growing involvement in the Pan-African movement, "the disasters of the year 1919," and the Depression (1940, 759).

Du Bois mused in his autobiography, *Dusk of Dawn*, that the Negro Cooperative Guild and his other efforts to establish cooperatives may have been the most promising of all his endeavors—and he urged that they be revived. But he also noted that "the whole movement needed more careful preliminary spade work, with popular education both of consumers and managers; and for lack of this, it temporarily failed" (1940, 759). It is curious, however, that, writing in 1940, he did not mention the Young Negroes' Co-operative League or the efforts of George Schuyler and Ella Jo Baker to organize just such education and groundwork in the early 1930s.

As in his 1898 and 1907 writings on Black businesses, Du Bois ended his discussion of cooperatives in *Dusk of Dawn* on a pessimistic note—this time writing that he had not pursued it diligently enough and that cooperatives were a difficult model to implement without sufficient education and training. He may have had encouragement in this perspective from the Black economist and Howard University professor Abram L. Harris (even though Harris was one of the Howard professors who supported the YNCL's second national conference at Howard University in 1932). In a 1934 letter to Du Bois, Harris wrote:

I contend, however, that no program of economic welfare that is planned for the Negro is going to succeed until his so-called intelligentsia is emancipated so that it can furnish guidance. . . . Even if you would start a fool proof program of Negro economic advancement I am sure that it would soon collapse for want of determined intellectual guidance and support. . . . I do not see how very much can be done behind the back of present social changes. These changes are taking place rapidly in our industrial life and I feel that if they continue in the direction they are now going we are going to have industry permanently cartelised [sic] [i.e., under the control of a monopoly of a few large cartels]. If this takes place small industry whether individualistic or based on racial self-help is going to have hard sledding. If therefore we decided to launch a co-operative movement among the Negro as a means of economic self-help we must be prepared to see it wiped out of existence by these changes. On the other hand, [American consumers might rise up and insist on greater control]. . . . Given sufficient provocation this control might lead into the establishment of guilds through which the present ownership and management of industry will be eliminated. . . . This of course would amount to guild socialism which I am beginning to believe is the only kind we are going to see established in our life time, if at all, in this country. If present tendencies culminate into guild socialism I can see that a cooperative movement among Negroes might prove very valuable. [Whatever happens, we need independent Negro intellectuals to provide the guidance.] . . . It is my conviction, however, that nothing is going to be done with the Negro and about his special problems until we are willing to throw over board certain political and social values that govern our thinking. . . . The Negro intellectual [must] think of the race problem in terms of general economic and social changes. . . . [Otherwise,] he will effect no permanent or fundamental change in the conditions of the Negro masses. (1934, 471–72)

Harris was a leading African American economist and a leading radical economist of his time, and clearly one of the people Du Bois consulted about his ideas for cooperative economic development among Blacks. Harris's economic pessimism, as well as his strong contention that without African American intellectual support there could be no Black cooperative movement, would have been persuasive to Du Bois and fed Du Bois's own pessimism, although by 1934 Du Bois was focused more on the need to promote "economic action" than on the intellectual exchange about it. He wrote to

Harris that "the chief object of this in my mind would not be the information which they [a group of Negro scholars] can impart, but the action toward economic salvation that they can induce" (1934b, 471).[11] Although Du Bois wrote in 1940 that African American cooperative economic development was perhaps his most important project, he ended up giving it little attention, and it therefore received little publicity or serious attention from anyone else.

Manning Marable describes the period 1918–19, when Du Bois was establishing the Negro Cooperative Guild, as probably the height of Du Bois's career. He was fifty years old, the NAACP had grown significantly and had gained more grassroots supporters (many of whom had once been Booker T. Washington supporters), and monthly sales of the *Crisis* had increased to seventy thousand (Marable 1986, 97). As editor of the *Crisis*, Du Bois's national influence was at its height—seventy thousand people were reading his editorials and articles.[12] He wrote about cooperatives and about using the racial group economic strategy from the early 1900s through the 1930s, and yet by his own admission Du Bois did not put enough energy into it, and much more education was needed for the strategy to be more widely practiced. As the history of the challenges and successes of African American cooperatives unfolds in the pages of this book, perhaps we can better understand why at the height of his influence Du Bois did not seriously pursue the Negro Cooperative Guild, and why he was not able to inspire more cooperative business development among his followers.

On the other hand, Du Bois, as well as the writers of accounts for a couple of the co-op stores, credit that August 1918 meeting of the Negro Cooperative Guild with the founding of a few cooperatives. The Co-operative League of America (CLUSA) started in 1916.[13] It is clear that Du Bois and other African American leaders knew about the league by the early 1920s and had some relationship with the cooperative movement.[14] Du Bois wanted Blacks to organize separate cooperative organizations of their own, but to use CLUSA information and services.[15]

I am certain that two cooperatives are directly attributable to the August 1918 meeting. According to Du Bois (1940, 759), the meeting of the twelve members of the Negro Cooperative Guild produced six or seven cooperative efforts around the country. I found information about two of these: Citizens' Co-operative Stores in Memphis and the Cooperative Society of Bluefield Colored Institute in West Virginia. I do not know what other Black cooperatives from 1918 to 1928 were established as a result of that meeting, but presumably there were more than just these two. What we know of these two is basically positive. In addition, about a decade later, there began a period of many attempts and many successes with cooperative enterprise development among African Americans—even if not all of them can be attributed directly to Du Bois's advocacy or the Negro Cooperative Guild.

The Consumers' Cooperative Trading Company and Cooperative Education

As noted above, the Negro Cooperative Stores Association/Consumers' Cooperative Trading Company in Gary, Indiana, began with a study circle. Twenty African American families, whose annual incomes ranged from $500 to $1,000 (Hope 1940, 42), joined a study group in early 1932 to address economic problems arising from the closing of the steel mills and the ensuing economic depression in that city. The members of the study group documented and discussed economic conditions in their neighborhood, and soon focused on strategies to help alleviate the economic distress the Black community was experiencing. Their education program centered on consumer cooperation as a viable strategy. The study group held weekly educational meetings for eighteen months before opening any business. One prominent member, Jacob L. Reddix, a teacher at the local high school, attended the District Congress of the Central States Cooperative League in Cleveland, Ohio, and returned with information about consumer cooperation. He worked with the group to set up a buying club to reduce their grocery expenses and provide quality food. They raised $24 initially, which was used for publicity and the first inventory of the buying club. The study group members continued to study the history and philosophy of cooperative economics at the same time that it launched the buying club. They soon found the need to organize an official grocery store because the co-op distributor that supplied their goods could contract only with a store. In December 1932 the first store, a cooperative grocery and meat market, opened.

The study group, chaired by Reddix, continued as the education committee of the cooperative. In the fall of 1933 its members concluded that formal cooperative economics training was essential to their progress. They sponsored a class in the adult education night school of Roosevelt High School, the principal and many teachers of which belonged to the study group and buying club. The course was taught by Reddix and continued to be taught through 1935. With the largest attendance of any academic class in the evening schools at that time, two major classes were taught: the history and philosophy of cooperation, for beginners, and the organization and management of cooperatives (Hope 1940, 41). Women members of the first class organized a women's guild, and their activities inspired interest in the fledgling cooperative movement among Blacks in Gary and increased membership in the co-op (Reddix 1935). A men's council and a youth league were also established.

With increased interest in consumer cooperation, the education committee published "A Five Year Plan of Cooperative Action for Lifting the Economic Status of the Negro in Gary." The plan called for a larger, more modern grocery store and meat market, five more stores in the region, a credit union, a "motor service" station, a bakery, a dairy, and a "farm-resort." The first small store, chartered as the Negro Cooperative Stores Association in December 1932, closed after about a year of operation. It was replaced in August 1934 by a larger grocery story with a new name, the Consumers' Cooperative Trading Company. By 1935 membership had increased to four hundred. Sales in the first year amounted to $35,000, and the grocery store employed seven full-time staffers. The first dividend, of 2 percent on shares of stock owned, was paid to members in December 1935 (Hope 1940, 41). In 1936 sales reached $160,000, and the company was considered "the largest grocery business operated by Negroes in the United States" (Reddix 1974, 119). The Cooperative Trading Company also sponsored a young people's branch that operated its own ice-cream parlor and candy store. The credit union was established ahead of schedule, in November 1934, and had more than one hundred members in its first year. The cooperative became affiliated with the Central States Cooperative League and Cooperative Wholesale, Inc. of Chicago, and received advice from two White-owned cooperatives in the region. Although all of its businesses were closed by 1938, as the economy went from bad to worse, this African American cooperative society met many of its goals and influenced social and economic activity in Gary in the 1930s.[16]

Teaching Consumer Cooperation at Historically Black Colleges and Universities

During the 1940s, some Black colleges were teaching about cooperatives. Brooks and Lynch reported on coverage of the "cooperative movement" and "consumer problems" in courses in "southern Negro colleges." They surveyed seventy-five universities, colleges, and junior colleges for Negroes in the southern states in the fall of 1943. Of the fifty-seven institutions that responded, about thirty-seven indicated that study of the cooperative movement was included in their curriculum. While there was some overlap with respondents who considered discussion of consumer problems similar to teaching about cooperatives, in subsequent questions it became clear that at least twenty-five or so different institutions did teach about cooperatives, with eight indicating that they taught an entire course on the cooperative movement. Most of these courses (on both consumer education and cooperatives) had been taught since 1938 in the economics, home economics, and sociology departments of the Black universities and colleges (Black studies was not acknowledged as a discipline at this time). In addition, about twice as many of the accredited colleges as nonaccredited devoted "the equivalent of half a course or more to each of these subjects" (Brooks and Lynch 1944, 435). Faculty members were very conscious that this subject matter helped students to be more economically literate and to address problems in their communities, while developing leadership and agency. Twenty-three responded that there was a cooperative organization now functioning on their campus. The authors concluded that "the Cooperative Movement is looked upon as a way of further 'emancipation' for the Negro but with weighty qualifications which range from pessimism stemming from a realization of the basic ills of society to optimistic agreement that the Movement does offer possibilities for the up-building of the Negro" (436).

It is not clear that this tradition has continued, particularly in terms of cooperative education. A cursory recent study did not find cooperative economics taught in either economics or African studies departments in historically Black colleges and universities.[17] Nor do such courses appear significantly in the curricula of other colleges and universities, although agricultural economics departments include sections or courses on cooperative economics, and a few U.S. business schools now offer a course or partial course in cooperative economics.[18] In addition, the participation of African American students in the few courses that are available is paltry (see Gordon Nembhard 2008a). Consumer education and consumer economics, by contrast, have become a strong movement nationwide.

Of interest, in the 1944 study, sixteen respondents were able to provide examples of cooperative enterprises not connected with their college but in the immediate area. The proximity of a cooperative suggests that some of the impetus for the inclusion of the cooperative movement in the curriculum may have arisen from the existence of Black-owned cooperatives nearby and the relative prominence of the movement among African Americans during that period. Today, with attention to consumer rights and alternative community-level economic development increasing, we might expect to see more courses taught.[19]

Education as a Resource

It is impossible to trace the history of African American cooperative development without discussing the role of education and the importance of the various ways in which African Americans have disseminated information about
cooperatives and the cooperative movement in the United States and internationally. Nearly every cooperative started with a study group or some kind
of organized study. Many cooperatives shared information with one another
and with the public, using newsletters, newspaper and journal articles and
columns, and public lectures and conferences. Many cooperatives sent their
members to cooperative conferences or created their own conferences. Some
groups visited other cooperatives. It is remarkable that one-third of the participants in the 1938 study tour of cooperatives in Nova Scotia were Black
(Washington 1939a, 109). At a time when money was tight and much of the
country was deeply racially segregated, nineteen Blacks and thirty-five Whites
toured Nova Scotia together in order to learn more about cooperative education and cooperative economic development. This is a relatively obscure, lit-
tle-known fact that illustrates how important learning about cooperatives was
to a segment of the African American community.

In some ways, the history of African American cooperative development is
more about the African American promotion of cooperatives and efforts
toward cooperative economic education than about the creation and success
of cooperative businesses. While a significant number of cooperatives were
established, and while there have been many successful co-op businesses in
the Black community throughout U.S. history, as much effort and activity, if
not more, have been put into the promotion of cooperatives among African
Americans.

Sometimes there was more talk than action. This is probably because of the
difficulties of capitalizing cooperative businesses, but it was also because of
sabotage by White businesses and White supremacists who did not want these
efforts to succeed—and because of the prevailing ideology in the United States
that cooperative economics was socialist, which was then and remains today a
dirty word. Despite the difficulties they faced, African Americans did establish
cooperative businesses. The Great Depression witnessed the largest proliferation of Black-owned cooperatives in U.S. history. The next three chapters
focus on that period.

5

THE YOUNG NEGROES' CO-OPERATIVE LEAGUE

Young Negroes! It is you who must now take up the burden of leadership. You must succeed where the oldsters have failed. . . . Young Negroes! Turn your backs on the old programs and prescriptions and formulate others more in accord with the social and economic trends. Forget your petty individual interests and join in co-operative effort for the betterment of all. . . . Young Negroes! Through co-operative effort as consumers you can find your way out of the present dilemma. Collectively through democratic management of your own economic enterprises, you can supply yourselves with everything you consume, your own amusement and recreation, your own education and culture.

—SCHUYLER (N.D., 3–5)

We seek to bring women into the League on [an] equal basis with men; that where necessary Housewives' Leagues be formed and that where they are already formed the closest co-operation possible be established and maintained between them and the Y.N.C.L.

—BAKER (1931C, 1)

The Young Negroes' Co-operative League was established in December 1930. The YNCL is not usually mentioned among Black leaders, in Black history texts, or in African American scholarship in general, except in the comprehensive biographies of Ella Jo Baker (Grant 1998; Ransby 2003), who was its executive director. Its founder, George Schuyler, a journalist and satirist, was known as a Black radical in his youth and had become a Black conservative by the 1940s, but he always challenged White racism, according to Randall Kennedy (2003, 355). Schuyler was known in Black (and probably also in White) circles as a columnist for the *Pittsburgh Courier* and the author of *Black No More* (1931), and sometimes for his work with A. Philip Randolph on the *Messenger* in the 1920s. Much of his early radical activity is overlooked, and except in studies of Ella Baker and the Young Negroes' Co-operative League, there is no mention of his involvement in and founding of the YNCL.[1] The YNCL is another short-lived but important example of efforts toward cooperative economic development among African Americans. The YNCL had big

plans, accomplished much in a short time, and, I argue, affected the thinking, learning, actions, and later career of at least its executive director, Ella
Baker, if not others in the organization.

Call to Young Negroes

In the early 1930s, Schuyler declared an interest in working with a "new generation" and in running his own radical organization. In his column in the
Pittsburgh Courier (Schuyler 1930b) and in the YNCL brochure "An Appeal
to Young Negroes" (Schuyler n.d.), Schuyler admonished Black youths for
following the traditional strategies ("the old ways") for Black advancement,
which had not helped the Negro. The future, he contended, lay in the hands
of the young, and he advocated a different path for them. Young Blacks
needed to embrace and engage in cooperative economics—the only way, in
Schuyler's view, to provide economic power and security for African Americans. "The Young Negroes Co-Operative League offers an immediate way out
of our economic and social dilemma, not ten, twenty, thirty or fifty years from
now, but RIGHT NOW." He called on "those who are energetic, intelligent and
believe in the power of their own organized effort" to join the YNCL (n.d., 5).
Schuyler's column reiterated this call and the YNCL's five-year plan.

The Young Negroes' Co-operative League was a cooperative federation. It
was founded in December 1930 by twenty-five to thirty African American
youths in response to Schuyler's call (see Schuyler 1930b, 1931, and 1932;
Calvin 1931). Its goal was to form a coalition of local cooperatives and buying
clubs loosely affiliated in a network of councils (Ransby 2003). According to
its letterhead, its mission was "to gain economic power thru consumers' cooperation." The YNCL held its first national conference in Pittsburgh on
October 18, 1931. Thirty official delegates from member organizations and six
hundred participants attended (*Pittsburgh Courier* 1931, 1).[2] George Schuyler was elected president and Ella J. Baker, national director. Both Schuyler
and Baker addressed the audience. Schuyler reiterated his call and the need
and potential for economic cooperation in the Black community. Baker
closed the meeting with a discussion of the importance of cooperatives to
Black women.

The YNCL pamphlet distributed by Schuyler outlined the goals of the
organization:

- five thousand charter members, paying a $1 initiation fee, by March 15,
  1931

- a council in each community where there are five or more members, that then establishes a weekly forum to discuss economic problems of the Negro and study consumers' cooperation
- a cooperative enterprise where each council exists, by March 15, 1932
- a cooperative wholesale establishment in each state by March 15, 1933
- a cooperative bank in each community where there is a council by March 15, 1934
- factories to produce such necessities as clothing, food, and shelter by March 15, 1935 (Schuyler n.d., 6; Calvin 1931, 1)

The pamphlet summarized the cooperative principles and statistics on cooperative organizations and distributive societies around the world (Schuyler n.d., 7, 15). It also provided the bylaws of the organization, a bibliography on the cooperative movement, and a page on how to begin. It provided "a partial list" of YNCL organizers in Nashville, Tennessee; Santa Barbara and Los Angeles, California; Mobile, Alabama; Wilmington, Delaware; Buffalo and Albany, New York; Belvernon and Homestead, Pennsylvania; Covington and Ellerson, Virginia; Cincinnati and Middletown, Ohio; Washington, D.C.; Worchester, Massachusetts; Louisville, Kentucky; Topeka, Kansas; and Dallas, Texas (13–14). Officers were from New York City; Columbus, Cleveland, and Pitsburg, Ohio; New Orleans, Louisiana; Lansdowne and Monessen, Pennsylvania; Detroit, Michigan; Columbia, South Carolina; and Phoenix, Arizona. The pamphlet also included a membership form with a request for $1 as an "entrance fee"—and the group was still accepting charter members.

The YNCL contended that education was essential to good business practice and to the maintenance of cooperation. The first year was devoted to "the study of history, principles and methods of Rochdale consumers' cooperation. . . . It is our conviction that we must be trained before trying to lead people" (Schuyler 1932, 456). At its first conference, YNCL delegates resolved to "follow a well planned educational program," to develop a media strategy, and to aggressively recruit new members (Baker 1931c).

In addition to its educational mission, the YNCL sought to keep control of the organization in the hands of young people, and "to bring women into the League on [an] equal basis with men." At the first conference, delegates also agreed to adopt a defense program to protect "the Negro masses" (Baker 1931c). With Baker's leadership, women's issues were kept at the forefront, and the organization was committed to grassroots participatory democracy (Ransby 2003). Members also pledged to involve children and create children's guilds and boys' and girls' clubs. The group also resolved to remain separate from the Cooperative League of the USA (CLUSA) but to be associated with it, and to support the National Negro Business League's Colored Merchants Association stores until their own were established (Baker 1931c). However, by 1933, according to Ransby (89), the CMA and the NNBL were criticizing the YNCL, and Schuyler criticized back—thus ending any official relationship between the groups.

Connection to Other Black Organizations

Without a list of the twelve people who attended the Negro Cooperative Guild's founding meeting in August 1918, it is difficult to know whether there were any direct connections between the guild and the YNCL. While none of the documents suggests that the YNCL was in any way related or indebted to the Negro Cooperative Guild or to Du Bois's writings and urgings, it is difficult to believe that there was not some cross-fertilization, since throughout this period most of the Black political and economic leaders moved in and out of the Black business movement, the socialist and communist movements, the organized labor movement, and the cooperative movement. There is evidence of some early direct relationships between the Colored Merchants Association and the YNCL, and some of the grocery stores mentioned or supported by the YNCL were members of the CMA.[3] We also know that George Schuyler had earlier worked with A. Philip Randolph on the *Messenger*, a radical Black socialist newspaper in Harlem that sometimes promoted cooperative economics. In 1930, Randolph was deep into his ten-year commitment to organize the Brotherhood of Sleeping Car Porters, an independent labor union. Although there is no evidence that Randolph joined the Young Negroes' Co-operative League, he did promote cooperative economics and consumer cooperation, starting in 1918, within the Black labor movement, including the Brotherhood of Sleeping Car Porters. Ella Jo Baker, the YNCL's first executive director, was a close friend of Schuyler's in the late 1920s and into the 1930s. Schuyler, Baker, and Randolph had interactions with Du Bois in Harlem (where they all lived), but apparently not through the YNCL. A letter to Baker from acting YNCL field secretary Noah C. A. Walter Jr. of the United Consumers' Co-operative Association in Philadelphia, however, mentions that Du Bois "had always expressed interest in our work, true?" (Walter 1933). Walter recommended using this contact as a way to gain access to the NAACP membership, and suggested that the YNCL needed access to the National Urban League membership as well. In fact, Walter reported that he had joined the NAACP for this purpose and had contacted as many Black organizations as possible, in order to promote the YNCL nationally. The New

York office of the YNCL used the facilities of the New York Urban League to hold meetings, and a decade later Ella Baker became the NAACP's field director. However, in the YNCL papers from the 1930s, there is little evidence of direct contact between the different organizations.

There is some evidence that many of the Black leaders of the era attended labor and political meetings together, even when they did not agree on ideology or strategy (see Marable 1986). In addition, we know that Du Bois was a judge for the awarding of the CMA logo in 1930 (even though he was not supposed to be a supporter of Black capitalism and was at odds with Booker T. Washington, the founder of the National Negro Business League). In spite of all of this contact and potential contact among Black leaders and Black organizations in the early twentieth century, there is no evidence connecting any of these leaders or organizations more closely, and no other renowned Black leaders are listed as members of the YNCL. On the other hand, in founding the YNCL, Schuyler deliberately targeted Black people between the ages of sixteen and thirty-six—not the old guard and not the regulars. The lack of close connections, therefore, may be mostly generational. Du Bois, for example, though still active, was over age sixty, and A. Philip Randolph was in his forties.

Consolidation in 1932

By 1932 the YNCL had formed councils in New York, Philadelphia, Monessen, Pittsburgh, Columbus, Cleveland, Cincinnati, Phoenix, New Orleans, Columbia, Portsmouth (Virginia), and Washington, D.C., with a total membership of four hundred (Schuyler 1932). The YNCL's second national conference took place in Washington, D.C., on April 3, 1932. According to the program, the major issue discussed was the payment of dues—and the difficulty of getting members to pay regularly. The Great Depression had caused high unemployment and plunging income, especially for African Americans, which helps to explain why it was difficult for the organization to raise money, even member dues. YNCL members discussed the pros and cons of allowing members to pay dues in installments. Another discussion was about ideology and how to change people from the "private profit ideal" to cooperation. The conference ended with a mass meeting open to the public. Schuyler gave a talk titled "Why a Cooperative Movement Among Negroes?"; Thomas Dabney, "Taking Consumers' Cooperation to the Rural South"; and Ella J. Baker, "Consumers' Cooperation and the 'Race-Loyalty' Appeal." Visiting speakers included J. A. Jackson of the U.S. Department of Commerce, historian Carter

G. Woodson, and professors Benjamin G. Brawley and Abram L. Harris of Howard University (YNCL 1932). The second conference was not as well attended as the first but was still considered a success (Baker ca. 1932a). A third conference was considered for New York City or Cleveland, but there is no evidence that it took place.

YNCL officers intended that the local councils would support cooperative businesses—this was part of the organization's mission. But the organization had financial difficulties early on and did not meet most of its goals; however, it did grow steadily in the first few years (Ransby 2003) and was responsible for launching many buying clubs and cooperatives (Grant 1998, 35). Baker suggested a plan to raise money from members that would require only a small amount of money from each person—"to establish a more permanent economic program" for the cooperative movement among Negroes (Baker ca. 1932b). Her "penny-a-day plan" was a short-term national self-help scheme to raise money from among the members and affiliate organizations using "consumer power," a strategy similar to the one behind the "double-duty dollar" and "don't-buy-where-you-can't-work" campaigns. Baker deliberately suggested that the campaign run for only three months out of every year, from January through March, to encompass the celebration of the Emancipation Proclamation, Lincoln's birthday, and Negro History Week. Baker's idea was that during this period members would pledge a penny a day, which would add up to $1 from each person. The focus would be on twenty major cities with large Black populations. In addition, organizations sympathetic to the cooperative movement, such as the Federal Council of the Churches of Christ in America, the NAACP, the National Urban League, Black fraternal organizations, the Brotherhood of Sleeping Car Porters, and so on, would charge a penny admission to any of their activities during that time and donate some or all of the money to the YNCL. Baker hoped to raise about $5,000 from five to ten thousand people. In addition to fund-raising, the appeal would also be an awareness-raising effort to advertise consumer cooperation and educate the general public about cooperatives.

For the first two years, Baker and Schuyler maintained communication with members of the YNCL through newsletters, updates, conference reports, press releases, and monographs about cooperative economics. Members were kept informed about the latest accomplishments and endeavors of the league, news and statistics about the cooperative movement in the United States and Europe, and opportunities for collaboration with other Black organizations around the country. In addition, both officers continued to write to members about how to strengthen the organization. Probably in 1931, Baker released a long report titled "On Promoting Consumers' Clubs" through the YNCL's press service. In this report she suggested that with unemployment so high, "Consumers' Cooperation can take the lead" in organizing churches, lodges, and clubs to form a buying club. If the average family spent $3 on food per week, they could spend $1 through the buying club; with two hundred families, that would be enough to buy in bulk at discounted prices, and everyone's money would go much further. Baker outlined how to promote consumers' clubs:

- Organize members of the local YNCL council by their talents and delegate tasks accordingly.
- Contact leaders of all organized groups in the community; start with a letter that is respectful of their time, and follow up with a face-to-face meeting.
- Leave literature at that first meeting and make a follow-up appointment with anyone difficult to convince (also find out who else that difficult person interacts with and approach them through their friends).
- Ask to convene a meeting with their group, specifically on the topic of organizing a buying club.
- Prepare for the meeting by outlining a short address that includes a brief history of consumer cooperation; anticipate questions and concerns.
- Allow for discussion after the presentation, but "take care that the meeting does not exhaust itself in discussion alone. Focus attention upon the necessity for immediate action"; and suggest or get someone to suggest the formation of a committee.
- At that meeting or a follow-up meeting, have members leave a cash deposit for the first weekly order and explain that this business cannot be conducted with credit.
- From the first, stress the virtues of a central buying committee for all the clubs, organizing this as fast as clubs are formed. Set in action an education committee in each group, and assign some member of the YNCL council to act as counselor to every club that is formed. (Baker ca. 1931b, 2)

Baker also reminded people that with experience they could modify and strengthen these tasks, and she laid out very practical things to advance the movement, encouraging people to pass this strategy on. She also reiterated the strengths of starting with a buying club among existing organizations: "It avoids the skepticism which most people have developed towards stock-selling ventures, it touches upon the very pressing problem of unemployment, and it shows the consumer how he might spend the money that he MUST spend anyway, to his own best advantage" (2). This kind of careful, detailed information and open exchange characterizes most of the correspondence from Baker to YNCL members.

Ella Baker and Women's and Youth Leadership

The YNCL endeavored to put young people in control and to treat women as equal to men. Ella Jo Baker was a pioneer of grassroots, community-based social activism and democratic leadership development, as well as youth development and women's equality. In a speech she made in 1969 ("The Black Woman in the Civil Rights Struggle"), she said, "I don't think you could go through the Freedom Movement without finding that the backbone of the support of the Movement were women" (Grant 1998, 230). She argued similarly about the role of women in the cooperative movement, and worked closely with housewives' leagues and other women's groups. She ended that speech by arguing that "one of the guiding principles has to be that we cannot lead a struggle that involves masses of people without getting the people to understand what their potentials are, what their strengths are" (231). In the 1960s, as a co-founder and advisor to the Student Non-Violent Coordinating Committee (SNCC), Baker encouraged the young people to struggle against "tendencies toward elitism and male domination" (Ransby 2003, 297). Baker believed that radical democratic practice at both the personal and organization levels was essential to social transformation. Her biographer, Barbara Ransby, notes that "the strategy of racial uplift in the early and mid-twentieth century was rooted in the notion that the educated elite would skillfully guide the race toward progress, on the one hand lobbying and litigating for reforms and on the other grooming and socializing the 'lower-class' elements to prepare themselves for integration. Restrictive norms of masculinity and femininity were part and parcel of the mainstream, middle-class approach to social change and to leadership roles" (297). Ransby points out that Baker developed and promoted an alternative strategy: "Black leadership had to be emphasized and poor people's voices amplified because in absolutely every other facet of social life the opposite pressures and privileges were in force" (369).

Baker's early years at the YNCL contributed greatly to her later efforts and successes in promoting this strategy. In a handwritten note in her papers at the Schomburg Center in New York, for example, she wrote, "Forgetting ordinary Negro and centering it around a few elite.—Consumers coop guarantees against that through education of masses." She used this model of grassroots organizing and popular education to recruit members of the

YNCL, and to empower women and young people to fight for their rights—and especially to fashion their own economic alternatives. Ransby notes that the YNCL was "crucial in shaping Baker's own political thinking" (91). "The process of setting up co-ops," she writes, "establishing common priorities for those involved, solidifying democratic methods of decision making, and building communications networks encouraged people at the grassroots to engage in social change and transformation, changing themselves, each other and the world around them simultaneously" (90). According to Ransby, the "YNCL experiment foreshadowed" Baker's philosophy and strategy in forming and advising SNCC thirty years later. Both organizations were independent of the moderate mainstream Black organizations of their times and focused on grassroots leadership, education, democratic decision making, and a "step-by-step, transformative process of working toward long term goals" (90–91).

Cohen, too, contends that "cooperativism provided a fertile training ground for civil rights activist Baker" (2003, 50). I find that Baker developed many of her ideas about grassroots participation and leadership development not just through her work with the WPA's adult education program and the NAACP's field office, but also through her involvement in the cooperative movement. As executive director of the YNCL, she studied democratic governance and democratic economic participation, promoted youth leadership and Black women's leadership, and observed those ideals in practice in YNCL branches throughout the country. Her trips to YNCL affiliates, her efforts with starting and maintaining cooperative businesses, and her work with activists around the country gave her organizing experience. Her work with the YNCL also introduced her to people with whom she would work later in the civil rights movement (Grant 1998, 34).

It is difficult to understand Baker's pioneering of African American grassroots and women-led social change without recognizing the importance of her early training in the Black cooperative movement. Both the tenets of cooperative economics and the experience she gained as a leader in that movement contributed to her philosophy and practices, as well as her own capacity as a social and political thinker and civil rights leader. It is interesting (and frustrating) that while Ransby, one of Baker's primary biographers, recognizes this, she does not remind the reader of this in the conclusion of her study—she only discusses it in the chapter about the YNCL. In addition, while Baker is increasingly becoming recognized for her influence on our notion of grassroots democratic leadership, she still is rarely recognized as an early leader in consumers' cooperation—the White cooperative movement does not claim her, and only some elements of the Black movement recognize her contribution. This is another example of how the African American cooperative movement has had a strong but hidden influence on the theory and practice, as well as the personal development, of many African Americans and their organizations. Even many who know some of the history are underwhelmed by its significance for some reason.

Legacy

There are few examples of African American cooperative federations in the United States. The Young Negroes' Co-operative League was one of the first. It was a highly ambitious effort and succeeded in many endeavors, even though its grand vision was not realized in its short existence. Ransby observes that the league was a "short-lived experiment in collective Black self-determination"; "like many economic cooperatives; it was unable to survive the concrete pressures of a dominant social and economic system antithetical to its aims or to sustain a mass base of committed supporters" (89). Financing was the most critical unresolved problem. By September 1932 the organization had had to give up its office, stop paying the executive director, and start holding its meetings at the New York Urban League offices.[4] Baker, however, continued to act as the YNCL's unpaid executive director and continued correspondence, activities, and leadership of the organization from her home.

According to the *Negro World*, in December 1931 the Harlem Council of the YNCL announced its decision to establish a community house (*Negro World* 1931). The community house was to have a dance hall, meeting space, banquet rooms, and a dining hall, and would house the national office. Rooms on the upper floors would be rented to members. According to the article, the YNCL had already begun to sell $10 shares to capitalize the project (payable in installments of $2 per week), and had appointed a committee to select the building by January 1, 1932. The article describes the YNCL meeting as having taken place at the office of the New York Urban League. Since we know that by September 1932 the national YNCL could no longer afford its offices, it appears that this project to establish a community house was not successful.

Though short-lived, the YNCL appears to have created a ripple effect, as cooperatives continued to develop from models related to, promoted by, or started through the YNCL, or by the same people who were part of or influenced by the YNCL. Recurrent themes that emerge are the importance of internal education, public education, and publicity; attendance at and affiliation with national conferences and associations; and the problem of resources and financing. The YNCL understood that organizing at all levels was an important activity, and it had a strong organizational structure, with officers in every jurisdiction and field organizers where it could. The example of the YNCL also highlights the larger strategy of networking and of building federations of small local units (often buying clubs) into bigger, citywide and regional organizations (the councils) that feed into a national organization. The commitment to women's rights and empowering young people and children as potential leaders in the Black cooperative movement are relatively new themes that emerge with this organization as well. Baker continued that commitment throughout her career. Leaders and members of the YNCL clearly understood that cooperative economics was a strategy in pursuit of a larger goal—the elimination of economic exploitation and the transition to a new social order (Ransby 2003, 86–87). Baker and Schuyler in particular theorized and wrote about the need for and logic of such a movement, outlined economic strategies, and practiced what they preached in the years that they headed the YNCL.

The YNCL chapter in Buffalo, New York, was the first to launch a store. According to an article in the *Pittsburgh Courier*, this cooperative grocery and meat market was doing $3,000 worth of business a month by October 1931 (*Pittsburgh Courier* 1931, 1). Philadelphia had started a cooperative newsstand and stationery store by 1932. The Cincinnati Citizens' Cooperative Society affiliate established a buying club. Pittsburgh and Cleveland chapters established newspaper-distribution agencies. Columbia, South Carolina, considered opening a full grocery store. Washington, D.C., was exploring a shoeshine and cleaning and pressing establishment. New York City started a fresh egg club.[5]

Cooperative Efforts in Buffalo

The Citizens Cooperative Society of Buffalo, New York, was established in 1928 to "afford blacks of Buffalo an opportunity to help themselves and improve their standard of living through collective work and responsibility." Its founder, Dr. E. E. Nelson, was influenced by both Booker T. Washington and Marcus Garvey, as well as by George Schuyler, was an avid reader of the *Pittsburgh Courier* (according to Fordham [ca. 1976]), and worked as a dining car waiter until he could make his living from his private medical practice. In 1929 the Citizens Cooperative Society of Buffalo started an education and membership campaign. Membership cost $5 per share, and most members owned fewer than five shares (Fordham ca. 1976, 5–7). Its most ambitious project, the Citizens Cooperative Grocery market, was launched in the fall of 1931. That October, Nelson had been a founding delegate to the first conference of the Young Negroes' Co-operative League, according to YNCL letter-head. Thereafter, one R. S. Freeman was listed on the letterhead as the Buffalo representative and a charter member of the YNCL. In January 1932 Schuyler featured a picture of the storefront showing the name "Citizens Cooperative Society Meats and Groceries" in his article on the YNCL in the *Crisis* (Schuyler 1932, 456).

The co-op grocery had financial problems from the beginning, particularly since it was started during the Great Depression and unemployment was high in Buffalo. Members also had little experience running a business. The Citizens Cooperative Society disbanded around 1933. By 1934 Nelson and others had reorganized the society and were holding regular meetings. In 1935 they launched an education campaign, using the name the Buffalo Consumers Economic Society, which began operating using the international Rochdale principles. Convinced that community support was essential to the co-op's success, Nelson planned a four-year campaign, from 1935 to 1939, to attract community members and educate them about cooperative economics through weekly educational classes. He also organized the children into a "junior co-op" where they could learn the principles of business and cooperative economics. The society also operated a speakers bureau, sending members to talk at club meetings and to churches and other community groups. By 1940, almost a hundred new families had joined.

In March 1939 the society replaced the word "Consumers" in its name with the word "Cooperative," and the Buffalo Cooperative Economic Society became a legal corporation in June. The society opened a new grocery market the same month. It became an affiliate of the (predominantly White) Eastern Cooperative League. In the first year, sales brought in $21,000, with three full-time employees and several part-time workers. The society purchased a truck in order to make deliveries (Fordham ca. 1976, 6–10). By the end of 1943, the first dividend was paid to stockholders. By the end of 1944, sales had risen to about $120,000, with a net profit of more than $2,400.

The society also operated a credit union, which was not quite as successful, but stable. In 1944 the society purchased its own building. By the late 1940s, sales had begun to slip, and the cooperative store was not as successful. Stalwart members (about ten families) put their own personal money into keeping the store and society solvent. However, this was not enough, and deficits increased. The society finally disbanded in 1961 (Fordham ca. 1976, 10–13), closing the store and ceasing all activity after almost thirty years—making it one of the longest-running African American cooperatives in U.S. history. The archives include a handwritten note containing Mrs. Nelson's observations about why the store failed: because Black businesses did not patronize or support the co-op market. The neighborhood (in the Ellicott district) suffered disinvestment. Recessions in the 1950s reduced the purchasing power of members. The rising costs of overhead and an increasing number of supermarkets in the immediate area were the final elements to which Mrs. Nelson attributed the decline of the store and thus the cooperative society in Buffalo. On the other hand, for more than twenty-five years the society provided healthy food and accessible products, as well as a business education program, for the African American community in Buffalo.

Fordham's account does not mention the Young Negroes' Co-operative League, but it does mention E. E. Nelson's relationship with Schuyler. The YNCL documents mention the Buffalo cooperative's activities and highlight its accomplishments and progress. Again, the successes were tempered by the challenges of adequate capitalization and education and the need for serious, long-term community support. While the society successfully operated a store for decades, it also offered a number of workshops and educational programs that were as important as the goods supplied by the co-op store.

YNCL Activity in New York City

Ella Baker was chair of the local New York chapter of the YNCL. In 1933, according to a flyer and program in the Ella Baker Papers at the Schomburg Center in New York, the local chapter held an all-day conference. Baker gave an address titled "Consumers' Co-operation Plus 'the Race Loyalty' Appeal," and George Schuyler closed the meeting with his address "Why a Co-operative Movement Among Negroes" (presumably the same speeches they gave at the YNCL's second national conference). The flyer for the Harlem Economic Forum listed three free lectures on Sunday evenings in April 1933. D. A. Cooper, of the Brooklyn Cooperative Association, gave a speech titled "The Negro's Economic Independence—Is It a Hope or a Dream?" Baker's address was titled "Are Harlem Consumers Throwing Away Their Money?"

In September 1933, what was called "Harlem's first economic conference" was sponsored by the Problem's Cooperative Association, Inc. on West 129th Street in Harlem. The aims of the organization were to establish Rochdale cooperatives—first a market and then cooperative housing—as well as a free employment agency and, eventually, cooperative factories. The September 1933 program ran from 2:30 P.M. to 11:00 P.M. Baker gave the welcome address and Schuyler gave a speech titled "Our Community Through My Economic Lens—A Practical and Immediate Approach." The conference was opened by A. E. Lyons, the president of Problem's Cooperative Association, and S. V. L.

Campbell, the secretary and organizer of the association, reviewed the aims of the organization and the conference. Albon L. Holsey, president of the Colored Merchants Association National Stores, presented findings from an economic survey of Negroes in America. The only ad in the program was for the Harlem Mutual Exchange, one of several barter exchanges operated by the Emergency Exchange Association, Inc. The self-help barter exchange announced that it manufactured dresses for barter and also collected clothing, shoes, and furniture for barter. This shows a continued connection between cooperative economic strategies and self-help and mutual-aid practices in the 1940s.

Ella Baker wrote a memo to a Mr. Wilkins titled "Consumers' Cooperation Among Negroes" (Baker 1941), which described eleven active Black cooperatives around the country and ten African American credit unions (nine in New York City) that had been started in the 1930s (see chapter 6).

Short But Productive Life

The Young Negroes' Co-operative League lasted officially for only about three years, but it seems to have had a long-lasting effect on the continued development of African American–owned cooperatives during the Great Depression and immediately afterward, as well as on the development of Black leadership. YNCL chapters were established in many U.S. cities with major Black populations and Black activity. The portions of Baker's papers devoted to the YNCL are not comprehensive enough for us to trace all of its connections and accomplishments, but the archives do provide a snapshot of many of the activities, and her biographers filled in some blanks.

Baker's YNCL papers give us great insight into Baker's communications with the YNCL membership and her thinking on cooperative economics, Black co-op development, and fund-raising issues. They also give us a glimpse into her development as a leader, an organizer, and a thinker. Ella Jo Baker certainly cut her teeth with the YNCL, and she continued her involvement in cooperatives for most of the rest of her life, though much more quietly. Most impressive is how her leadership and experience with the YNCL helped to develop her unique style of community organizing and leadership development. I assume that being a member of the Young Negroes' Co-operative League had a similar effect on many other members, and thus may have been more influential than we have been able to gauge thus far.

6

*The Great Depression and "Consumers'
Cooperation Among Negroes"*

I still believe that black people in the United States could lift the burden of economic
exploitation from their backs by organizing a nationwide system of cooperative businesses through which they could produce and distribute to themselves and others,
such consumer needs as food, clothing, household goods and credit. Such a system
would include . . . credit unions, . . . consumer cooperative retail stores, . . . producer
cooperatives.
—REDDIX (1974, 119)

We are certain that many Journal [*Journal of Negro Education*] readers are interested
in the Cooperative Movement. It is likely that a number are participating in consumers' cooperative projects and credit unions. They will therefore grant the advisability
and timeliness of an article in this section of the Journal which takes note of a movement that is making steady strides across the American continent and that has taken
firm roots in several European countries.
—WASHINGTON (1939A, 104)

The African American cooperative movement in the 1930s was an especially
active time for the discussion and creation of Black cooperative businesses.
Scholars and activists alike were advocating the cooperative way and experimenting with co-op development. Interest in cooperative economics was so
strong that the NAACP's *Crisis* magazine, the UNIA's *Negro World*, and the
Pittsburgh Courier periodically covered the cooperative movement in Black
communities. In addition, the *Journal of Negro Education* included articles
on cooperatives and cooperative economics in more than six separate articles
and columns starting in 1935 and added consumer cooperation to their regular section on rural education for two issues in 1939 (Washington 1939a,
1939b). These articles and columns in the *JNE* included an extensive list of
readings about cooperative economics and consumer cooperation as well as
firsthand accounts of co-op businesses and conferences—"all with the hope
of awakening new interest in the subject, or feeding that which already exists"
(Washington 1939a). Alethea Washington began her "Consumers Coopera-

tion" column with the second epigraph to this chapter, which sums up the interest and involvement of Blacks in cooperatives during the 1930s.

In this chapter I continue to explore this unique period of time in African American co-op history, and evaluate the strategy and the accomplishments of African American cooperative development during the Great Depression, particularly in urban areas. This part of the narrative starts with the Colored Merchants Association of the National Negro Business League in 1927 and moves through the variety of cooperatives influenced by the Young Negroes' Co-operative League, the Committee on the Church and Cooperatives of the Federal Council of the Churches of Christ in America, and other Black community organizations. The story of this prolific period of African American cooperative development continues in chapter 7 with a discussion of the cooperatives developed by the Ladies' Auxiliary to the Brotherhood of Sleeping Car Porters and other co-op initiatives by African American women. As we have seen, a variety of cooperatives sprang up in the 1930s and '40s. The best documentation we have comes from an article by John Hope II, materials found in the Ella Baker Papers at the Schomburg Center for Research in Black Culture at the New York Public Library, and the two columns by Alethea H. Washington.

Overview

Examples of African American co-ops during this period include the Consumers' Cooperative Trading Company (Gary, Indiana), the Red Circle Cooperative (Richmond, Virginia), the Aberdeen Gardens Association (Hampton, Virginia), the People's Consumer Cooperative, Inc. (Chicago), and Cooperative Industries of Washington, D.C. (discussed in chapter 7). Of the brief information provided by Washington (1939a), the list of Negro consumers' cooperatives was obtained from correspondence with Mrs. Hugh O. Cook (Kansas City, Missouri) and Nannie H. Burroughs (Washington, D.C.). None of the co-ops is named, but some information, particularly about where they were located, is provided. The "successful" five-year-old co-op grocery and meat market in Gary, Indiana (presumably Consumers' Cooperative Trading Company) is first on the list. The Rosenwald Gardens Cooperative in Chicago is listed next (probably the same as the People's Consumer Cooperative, Inc., although unnamed in Washington's account). The report noted that the co-op was two years old, had 450 members and gross sales of $3,000, and was large and well equipped. There were smaller cooperatives in Toledo and

Cincinnati, Ohio. In addition, the list includes three co-ops in Pennsylvania—two in Pittsburgh and one in Philadelphia—and a beginning cooperative in Minneapolis, all unnamed. Washington's report also mentions a
cooperative farm in Tuskegee, Alabama, and a farmers' cooperative in Fayette
County, Texas, which operated the first cooperative sawmill in the state of
Texas, according to the U.S. Forest Service. This sawmill was portable and
could be moved from one locality to another, and was shared by White and
Black farmers (Washington 1939a, 108). This list also includes Nannie Burroughs's co-op (presumably Cooperative Industries of Washington, D.C.),
which operated out of her National Training School for Women and Girls and
included a group of industries in the city and a farming project in Maryland.

As we saw in the previous chapter, Baker's "Consumers' Cooperation
Among Negroes" (1941) described eleven active Black cooperatives around
the country and ten Black credit unions (nine in New York City) that had been
started in the 1930s. The New York cooperatives included Harlem's Own
Cooperative, the Harlem Consumers' Cooperative, the Modern Cooperative
Association, the 137th Street Housing Corporation in Harlem, the Active Citizen's Cooperative Association, and the Lackawanna Consumers' Cooperative in Buffalo. The cooperatives elsewhere in the country included the
Capital View Cooperative Association, the New Deal Cooperative, Inc., and
the Langston-Kingman Park Cooperative, all in Washington, D.C.; the Con-
sumers' Cooperative Trading Association, in Gary, Indiana; and the Red Cir-
cle Stores, Association, in Richmond, Virginia. The credit unions Baker listed
are the Tuscan Lodge Federal Credit Union, the Abyssinian Baptist Church
Federal Credit Union, the Hampton Alumni Federal Credit Union, the Postal
Alliance Federal Credit Union, the St. Martin's Episcopal Church Federal
Credit Union, the YMCA Federal Credit Union, the YWCA Federal Credit
Union, the Mount Olivet Baptist Church Federal Credit Union, and the UMBA
Federal Credit Union, all in New York City; and, in Cleveland, Ohio, a "Credit
Union (Housing Project Residents)" with an address and director's name but
no other title or information.

"Consumers' Cooperation Among Negroes" begins by observing that the
development of African American cooperatives has been similar to the early
history of the cooperative movement in the United States. Sporadic efforts
were made before the 1930s; there was a great deal of activity in the 1930s;
and in the 1940s—as a result of the efforts of the '30s—a variety of groups
(churches, labor unions, housewives' leagues, fraternal orders) sponsored
buying clubs, grocery stores, gasoline stations, producer cooperatives, and
credit unions. This document attributes much of the activity in the 1930s to

"the educational influence of the Young Negroes' Co-operative League" (Baker 1941, 1).

In addition, the document discusses the promotion of cooperatives by the Federal Council of the Churches of Christ in America. This is the second influence that Baker attributes to the increase in Black interest in cooperatives. The Federal Council hosted Japanese cooperative leader Toyohiko Kagawa in 1935, and then began to discuss cooperatives with religious leaders and church groups. The Federal Council's secretary of race relations, Dr. George E. Haynes, organized several conferences on cooperatives among Negro churchmen. Washington notes that the Federal Council's Committee on the Church and Cooperatives held eight special conferences on cooperatives and the church in 1938. In addition, the committee "disseminated literature, cooperated in study tours, contacted foreign missions, developed church summer conferences, encouraged Negro cooperatives, and stimulated friendly relationships between organized labor and consumer cooperatives" (Washington 1939b, 242). The Edward A. Filene Goodwill Fund of Boston supplied a grant to fund a full-time promotional secretary in Harlem to continue education about cooperatives. Dorothy Height (2003), social activist and president of the National Council of Negro Women, remembers that during her teenage years the New York youth group of the Greater New York Federation of Churches met at a cooperative restaurant. Height's note is another reference to the Federation of Churches' support for and involvement in the co-op movement. The role of the Federal Council of Churches, therefore, is significant to our story.

Washington (1939b) also mentions that the Congregational and Christian Churches' Congregational Council for Social Action held an economic plebiscite in 1938. Thirty-two thousand members from more than seven hundred churches around the country voted three to one to encourage the growth of consumers' cooperatives. We also know that two interfaith conferences on consumer cooperation were held in 1938 and included tours of local cooperatives—one in Washington, D.C., on February 14–15, and the other in Boston, February 20–22 (Washington 1939a). The Black Unitarian Church, through Reverend Ethelred Brown, also supported cooperative economic development. Floyd-Thomas notes that "Brown steadfastly advocated the promotion of cooperative rather than profit-making enterprises for the economic empowerment of Harlem." This was "integral to the overall social outlook of Harlem Unitarian Church" in the first half of the twentieth century (2008, 123). Therefore, the legacy of Black church involvement in mutual-aid societies and self-help projects continued in the twentieth century, as churches supported or promoted co-op and credit union development for African Americans.

Baker's "Consumers' Cooperation" memorandum concludes that although the "mortality rate" of Black co-ops "is still rather high," "enough projects have survived to prove that the technique of consumers' cooperation can be successfully employed by Negro groups" (Baker, 1941, 1). Baker suggests that the high mortality rate was caused in part by the low wages earned by the majority of African Americans. Even though low-wage earners were one of the groups that had readily embraced consumer cooperation, they had limited capital to invest in co-op shares. "Because of a combination of pressure for action and a lack of patience to wait and save slowly over an extended period of time, many cooperatives were launched with insufficient capital and/or insufficient business experience" (1). The success rate was improving with the increase in co-op members with more stable income, however. This continues to be an issue, particularly for low-income and low-wealth cooperatives. Cooperatives tend to be more successful when well capitalized; however, they can be as helpful and as effective for low-income as for middle-income members if the financing is worked out. Capital may need to come from nonmembers (in the form of a grant, for example, or patient capital with nonvoting rights), and multiple forms of equity may need to be employed.

The National Negro Business League and the Colored Merchants Association

The Colored Merchants Association (CMA) was founded by the National Negro Business League (NNBL), in Montgomery, Alabama, in 1927. The CMA was an association of independent grocers organized into a buying and advertising cooperative. The creation of the CMA was a way to support independent African American grocery stores with mutual support and collective marketing in a harsh market during difficult times. The early 1900s witnessed the consolidation of racial segregation in business (and the height of White supremacist terrorism against Black businesses), in addition to the advent and domination of chain stores. Local grocery stores were the most common African American small businesses, along with insurance companies. Segregationist policies and franchising of large White grocery stores seriously threatened the existence of Black grocery stores. The purpose of the CMA was "to pool money for buying products and advertising, and to educate African American merchants about modern business practices. Goals included increasing stores' profits by improving accounting methods; modernizing store interiors to provide a better shopping experience; and creating greater awareness of the buying power of African Americans" (Tolbert 2007, 2). According to the *Negro World,* the CMA was "the first serious attempt to organize the purchasing power of the Negro" (1930b).

Chapters were organized in cities with ten or more stores. Dues were $5 per month per store (*Time* 1930). The National Negro Business League reported in the *Negro World* in July 1929 that "cooperative merchandising is rapidly spreading among Negro retailers" and receiving strong support from Black newspapers (NNBL 1929, 8). The article noted the recent opening of a CMA in Tulsa, Oklahoma, in addition to the associations already in existence in Montgomery, Alabama, and Winston–Salem, North Carolina. According to Tolbert (2007), Winston–Salem played an important role in the development of the CMA, as the first major city to which the organization spread outside Alabama in 1929. Representatives of the NNBL came to Winston–Salem to organize the chapter. The Winston–Salem Teachers College (now Winston–Salem State University) provided resources and publicized the CMA. This was a model of development followed in many cities across the country. By 1930, 253 stores were part of the CMA network, including 32 stores in Tulsa, 25 in Dallas, 25 in Manhattan (Harlem), and 10 in Omaha (*Time* 1930). By 1932, the CMA had opened a warehouse of products using the CMA label to sell to their New York stores (Cohen 2003, 49).

As noted earlier, the NNBL was started by Booker T. Washington in 1900 at Tuskegee University in Alabama. The NNBL supported Washington's notion of Black self-help and the development of Black capitalism. Tolbert points out that merchants, educators, and housewives used grocery stores as a tool to teach improved business methods and show consumers new products, in addition to raising awareness about African American buying power. NNBL leaders "promoted the grocers' efforts as a national model for African American businessmen working in an increasingly competitive marketplace" (Tolbert 2007, 1). By 1930, the CMA was getting increasing attention, with a front-page news article in the *Negro World* and a *Time* magazine article later in the year. The *Negro World* reported in March 1930 that the NNBL had announced the winner of a contest for the "emblem and color scheme" for the CMA stores. This had been a national contest using prominent business leaders as judges.[1] There were tensions, however, between the cooperative network of grocery stores and the parent business league, and so the interest in separation grew over the years. *Time* magazine reported in May 1930 that "at last week's meeting the C. M. A. planned organization of its own personnel, apart from the N. N. B. L., and the appointment of six field men who will go to all stores, provide advice on budgets, auditing, displays" (*Time* 1930).

By 1936, the CMA was bankrupt, as chain stores and supermarkets increasingly replaced small grocery stores (Tolbert 2007).

A Note on CMA Credit Union Activity

In February 1932 the *Negro World* reported on the progress of People's Credit Union at 203 West 138th Street, New York. The credit union was a member of the NNBL. Its president, C. Benjamin Curley, was also a vice president of the CMA stores. At the time, the People's Credit Union was the only Black-owned financial institution in New York City with a state charter (*Negro World* 1932, 2).[2] In 1931, People's Credit Union paid dividends of 6 percent to its more than 250 members. It is noteworthy not only that the credit union paid dividends in 1931 but that the amount paid had increased since the previous year. This means that People's Credit Union was profitable in the early years of the Great Depression and continued to pay dividends during this period.

Black Cooperatives in New York City in the Late 1930s and Early 1940s

My research suggests that there were a significant number of cooperatives in New York City, and especially in Harlem, in the mid-1930s to early 1940s; several of these have been mentioned in earlier chapters. While it is not clear exactly which ones were created as a direct result of YNCL activities, information about many of them is found in the Ella Baker Papers. It also appears that many of the Black organizations in Harlem were involved in sponsoring or supporting the various cooperatives. Ella Baker had invited the NAACP and National Urban League to support the Young Negroes' Co-operative League, although there is no evidence that they did more than rent space to the YNCL, in the case of the New York Urban League, starting in 1932. The Harlem Consumers' Cooperative buying club operated in the basement of the New York Urban League in the late 1930s. The Dunbar Housewives' League sponsored Harlem's Own Cooperative. The president of the New York branch of the NAACP, James Egert Allen, was one of the guests invited to the Problem's Cooperative Association conference in 1932. All of this points to ways in which the Black progressive community and the Black middle class in Harlem were connected to the Black cooperative movement and knew about one another's activities.

Several cooperative stores and organizations in New York City appear in the Baker Papers. Ralph Gothard, the executive director of the Consumers and Craftsmen's Guild of Harlem, Inc., invited Baker to a meeting in May 1937 with "heads of several cooperative groups to discuss our common problem and describe the approach they are making towards the solution of it" (Gothard 1937). Its letterhead describes the guild as "a voluntary, self-help, cooperative, non-profit, membership fraternity." Archival letters show that Baker was the captain of Pure Food Co-operative Grocery Stores, Inc. on Lenox Ave. She also became the chair of education and publicity for Harlem's Own Cooperative (Cohen 2003, 50; Library of Congress 2012).

Harlem's Own Cooperative

Harlem's Own started out as a buying club affiliated with the YNCL. It was established under the auspices of the Dunbar Housewives' League in 1935, mostly as a distributor of milk (Grant 1998, 35). The "Consumers' Cooperation Among Negroes" document describes Harlem's Own Cooperative as a milk route that was six years old in 1941. In box 2, folder 3 of the Ella Baker Papers at the Schomburg Center, there is a note card with information about a "very important meeting" in the clubroom of the Paul Laurence Dunbar Apartments, organized by the Dunbar Housewives' League and the Citizens' League for Fair Play. Interested parties were urged to attend to "decide on the incorporating of a profit-sharing Consumers' Co-operative for the distribution of milk."

The cooperative started with a capital investment of $300 and grew into a $15,000 business, heavily supported by the Dunbar Housewives' League. Baker describes Harlem's Own as being "largely responsible for keeping the consumer movement alive in Harlem." The same folder in Ella Baker's papers also includes the first page of a letter to the board of directors of Harlem's Own Cooperative about the co-op's deficits. Baker reiterated the importance of good business practices and suggested that the method of milk delivery and bill collection be made much more efficient. Baker was chair of the co-op's education and publicity committee for a time, and remained connected with Harlem's Own until 1941, when her job with the NAACP required her to travel a great deal (Grant 1998). She notes that Harlem's Own merged with Harlem Consumers' Cooperative Council in 1941 (Baker 1941).

A NOTE ON THE PAUL LAURENCE DUNBAR APARTMENTS

The Paul Laurence Dunbar Apartments in Harlem, a cooperative in its early years (from 1928 to 1936), was "Manhattan's earliest large garden apartment complex" and "the first large [housing] cooperative built for blacks" (Landmarks Preservation Commission 1970, 1). This apartment complex is also well known because it has housed many famous African Americans, including W. E. B. Du Bois, A. Philip Randolph, Bill "Bojangles" Robinson (tap dancer and actor), Countee Cullen (poet), Matthew Henson (explorer), and Paul Robeson (activist and singer/actor) (Dodson, Moore, and Yancy 2000, 1928). Floyd-Thomas describes the Dunbar Apartments as a response to the "black bourgeoisie's cry for public housing"—a cooperative for middle-class Black Harlemites (2008, 120). Extending from 149th to 150th Streets between Seventh and Eighth Avenues, the Dunbar Apartment complex was designated a land-mark site in 1970. Financed by John D. Rockefeller (who later became its pri-vate owner)[3] and designed by architect Andrew J. Thomas, apartments initially were available only to tenant stockholders in the Paul Laurence Dunbar Apartments Corporation (the cooperative). A minimum down pay-ment of $150 was required (plus an additional $50 for a large apartment). The average monthly cost was $14.50, depending on the size of the apartment—55 percent of monthly "rent" covered interest and principal, and 45 percent covered all maintenance costs. Although the monthly cost was a bit higher than originally projected and was high for the neighborhood, the apartments all sold within seven months, between October 1927 and May 1928. A board was elected by the tenants.

The complex included six U-shaped buildings clustered around a large interior garden court with eight arched entryways. In addition to being well designed, light, and airy, the complex included a nursery and kindergarten, a club room for older children, a central playground, an athletic field, a men's club, and a women's club (the housewives' league). Considered a model housing development, the Dunbar complex was awarded first prize in archi-tectural excellence for walk-up apartments in 1927 by the New York chapter of the American Institute for Architects. The complex also originally housed vocational guidance and placement services, a legal aid bureau, stores, and a branch of the Black-owned and managed Dunbar National Bank, Harlem's first bank. "Thus a real community was created" (Landmarks Preservation Commission 1970, 1–2).

In a 1931 article in the *Negro World*, Gothard described the Dunbar Apart-ments as "Harlem's outstanding success in collective ownership and endeavor" (Gothard 1931, 1). Floyd-Thomas, however, mentions the paternalistic atti-tudes of privately funded housing reforms, and observes that the "residential management operated with a severe condescension" (2008, 120). As the Depression continued in the later 1930s, many of the tenants could not keep up with the mortgage payments (folded into the monthly costs). Rockefeller granted a one-year moratorium on mortgage payments in 1933 and then bought the complex himself in 1936. The cooperative was converted to a rental property, and tenant-owners' original equity was returned to them (Landmarks Preservation Commission 1970, 2). In 1937 Rockefeller sold the apartment complex to another private owner. The Dunbar remained an anchor in the neighborhood, and the housewives' league remained active throughout the 1930s and '40s.[4]

Harlem's Pure Food Co-operative Grocery Stores

Gothard's 1931 article discussed the development of a cooperative that may have become Harlem's Pure Food Co-operative Grocery Stores, or the Problem's Cooperative Association's store. After mentioning that the Dunbar Apartments were not the only cooperative effort in Harlem, Gothard reported that plans had been completed for a "large co-operative food and vegetable market in Harlem." The cooperative was to be owned by Blacks and mostly "sold to housewives in small units." Employees were to be stockholders (members). As noted above, in 1937 Gothard was executive director of the Consumers and Craftsmen's Guild of Harlem. It is not clear from his 1931 article which cooperative he was heralding at that time—perhaps one not mentioned in this chapter. From the date, it was probably Harlem's Pure Food Co-operative Grocery Stores, but I lack enough specific information about that co-op (or Problem's Cooperative Association) to be definitive.

Harlem Consumers' Cooperative Council

In the early 1940s, Baker was affiliated with the Harlem Consumers' Cooperative Council (HCCC), which also distributed milk.[5] It was a buying club that operated out of the basement of the New York Urban League. In 1941, the cooperative conducted a membership drive to establish a cooperative store in the community. Baker (1941), calling it Harlem Consumers' Cooperative, notes that it was established by "low-salaried workers" who were paying for their shares mostly in installments of twenty-five cents per week. Weekly turnover was about $130. Growth was "healthy," and the co-op conducted "consistent educational activities." According to Baker, the co-op was founded around 1939 and was in its second year when it merged with Harlem's Own Cooperative. According to the HCCC's letterhead, the same George E. Haynes from the Federal Council of the Churches of Christ in America was the HCCC's secretary, so this must have been a cooperative started or supported by the Federal Council of the Churches.

The minutes from three board meetings of the HCCC, also located in box 2, folder 3 of the Ella Baker Papers, discuss milk distribution, net losses, and the costs of "breakage and pilferage." The milk distribution had been operating at a loss for more than three months, and labor costs were considered too high. The HCCC board decided to reduce labor costs. Board members also discussed whether to move toward milk in cartons but acknowledged that bottled milk was still popular. The officers took seriously their charge to keep the organization running and to cut costs as best they could. This is another characteristic of many of the small, inadequately resourced cooperatives— their officers use all kinds of measures to try to stay in business, particularly resorting to volunteer labor.

Modern Cooperative Association, Harlem

The Modern Co-op (as it was called) in Harlem boasted that it was the first "Negro cooperative grocery store operated according to the Rochdale principles in the northeastern area" (Crump 1941, 319). Given the other information I have, it does not seem likely that Modern was the first African American Rochdale cooperative in the Northeast, let alone in Harlem, though it is possible. According to Baker, Modern Cooperative Association started in September 1940 as a buying club whose members were civil service employees. She remarked that Modern Co-op had members with "more stable income," with one-third of its 110 members holding three $10 shares, and that the goal for the entire membership was ownership of three shares per member. It realized a substantial profit, which allowed the buying club to open a co-op grocery store. Baker contended that "the store bids fair to become an outstanding example of cooperative effort in the community" (1941, 2).

According to Crump's description of the Modern Co-op, twenty "mostly middle class" African Americans came together to increase the quality and decrease the cost of their groceries. They researched the business and learned how to become a distributor of the co-op label through Eastern Cooperative Wholesale. They started with a buying club. Each member put in $5. They operated out of a member's basement. Crump emphasizes that the president of the board of directors was a "housewife"—in fact, Crump identifies her as Mrs. Thurgood Marshall, almost certainly the first wife (Vivien Burey) of the man who went on to become chief counsel for the NAACP, head the winning legal team in *Brown v. Board of Education* (overturning the "separate but equal" doctrine as applied to public schools), and in 1967 become a U.S. Supreme Court justice (330). That Mrs. Marshall was the president of the board suggests that women were assuming leadership roles.

In April 1941, the Modern Co-op began to raise capital for a retail store. The minimum investment per family was set at $15, with about a hundred members. The store opened on May 31, 1941. By summer, average weekly revenues were about $300, and the enterprise was capitalized at $50,000. Members received a patronage rebate rather than a dividend (though it was suspended in the first years until profits were regularized). Between 30 and 40 percent of the co-op's customers were nonmembers, which means that the store supplied the community, not just its membership base.

Education was important to the members of the Modern Co-op, and it maintained "weekly study classes and functioning committees" (Baker 1941, 2). This is another example of the importance of education, particularly self-education about cooperative economics in the development and maintenance of a cooperative. How to make cooperatives a more widely used strategy was also a goal of the co-op. The Modern Co-op is also an example of building from small to large, starting with a buying club and then becoming a cooperative grocery store. Other African American cooperatives (and cooperatives in general) follow a similar model of growth. One fact repeated in the reports is that many of the members were Black civil servants with an almost middle-class income and steady work. This helped the co-op to stay in business.

The Harlem River Consumers Cooperative

The Harlem River Consumers Cooperative opened in June 1968 in Harlem, at Seventh Avenue and West 147th Street by the Esplanade Gardens cooperative. The first $10,000 for the co-op was sold in shares of $5 each by teenagers going door to door in Harlem (Asbury 1967). *Time* magazine praised the effort as an example of people willing to help themselves (*Time* 1968). A popular venture, income from sales of stock was $161,000 when the store opened and grew to $209,000 after the first two months it was open (Johnson 1968), and sales in the first year reached $1.7 million (Lissner 1969). According to founder Cora Walker, Harlem River Cooperative was founded in order to combat "high prices and inferior products" in other stores in the neighborhood and to provide ethnic foods and more food choices. The co-op received a lot of press coverage (I found six articles, mostly from the *New York Times*), mostly about its success, but a couple about its labor dispute.

By 1971 the co-op boasted four thousand members (who had bought $5 and $10 shares) and announced plans to set up co-ops in twenty-six low-income areas around the city with a $20,000 contract from the New York Community Training Institute (*New York Times* 1971). The parent company of all the new stores would be called Headstart Food Cooperative. Members were celebratory also because they had just put a scandal and labor problems behind them. In mid-1969 there was a labor strike and suppliers refused to deliver food. In addition, there was a quarrel among some of the shareholders. The dispute was with the employee's union (Local 338 of the Retail, Whole-sale, and Chain Store Food Employees Union) about store management belonging to the union and how to handle layoffs when sales were slow (Liss-ner 1969). The co-op argued that the manager and assistant managers of the store should do the buying since the co-op was not a chain store and was exempt from union rules. The union argued that the department managers who were union members should do the buying. Cooperative stores do not always have unions, and those cooperatives that do were often started by the union or union members, so that labor disputes are rare. This one was pro-longed, and it almost destroyed the cooperative. The board tried to fire Walker, the co-op's founder, coordinator, and counsel, because she accused some of the board members of "betraying our cooperative community proj-ect" by supporting the union contract (Kihss 1969). She argued not only that control over buying should remain in the hands of the consumer-owners, not the union, but also that the union had too much control over who could be hired. Walker argued that if the co-op was going to help the community, it should be able to hire members of the community and train them, but this was not part of the proposed union contract. The two White board members from a supermarket chain resigned so as not to be in the middle of the dis-pute. Several months later, these issues were settled, the labor dispute was resolved, and the board and Walker were reconciled (*New York Times* 1971).

The last evidence of Ella Baker's involvement in cooperatives in Harlem comes in 1975 with this same Harlem River Consumers Cooperative. There is a copy in box 2, folder 6 of her papers at the Schomburg Center, dated Sep-tember 28, 1975, of the minutes of the "committee meeting of concerned stockholders held after the annual meeting of Harlem River Co-op." Baker is listed as a stockholder, along with twenty-three others who attended the committee meeting. It appears that the co-op was involved in a new lawsuit that went to trial. Concerned stockholders were worried that the trial had created negative public opinion about the co-op. They discussed strategies at this meeting to educate the public about the co-op and its connections to the community, and to garner more support, both ideological and financial. Strategies included picketing chain stores, mounting a telephone campaign, and contacting foundations about supporting the co-op. A letter from Walker to Baker dated November 20, 1976, two months after that meeting, provided a "pro forma" of what the cash flow could be at Harlem Co-op Supermarket if the "rebirth" effort was successful. The meeting minutes refer to raffle sales and to a monthly pledge campaign to revive the store. The "pro forma" esti-mates suggest that the store had brought in about $650,000 in revenue over thirteen weeks, with a potential net income of $51,000 after costs and paying debts. The store, though in trouble, was no small enterprise, but it suffered harsh competition from traditional chain stores in the area. I have not been able to find out what that dispute was about, but it appears that the store continued to operate, although with lower revenues, at least through 1975.

More on Black Housing Cooperatives in Harlem

Baker (1941) noted that the 137th Street Housing Corporation, like the original Dunbar Apartments, was cooperatively owned. It had twenty member-families who "rented" rooms for $8 per room per month. For several years in the 1930s, the housing cooperative gave members a rebate of a month's free rent. In addition, the Garrison House, at 149th Street and Convent Avenue, became a cooperative in 1929 (Perez 2011). Also in the 1930s, the United Harlem Tenants and Consumer Organization formed a cooperative at 211 West 111th Street after failing to get multiple violations in their apartment house addressed (Floyd-Thomas 2008, 121).

Summing up Harlem Cooperatives

This discussion of African American–owned cooperatives in New York City, particularly in Harlem, shows that there was significant cooperative activity among African Americans in New York from the late 1920s through the 1940s and beyond (and as early as 1915 or 1919 in the case of the Harlem Pioneer Cooperative Society—see Floyd-Thomas 2008, 112; New York Dept. of Farms and Markets 1920). While many of them struggled to survive, all served a purpose, pooled members' resources, provided needed goods to their members at reasonable prices, and often had an impact in their communities. Some lasted for decades in one form or another, while others were more short-lived but laid the groundwork for other community-based and cooperative activity. While not always specifically connected to the Young Negroes' Co-operative League, all had some connection to the Black cooperative movement.

Cooperatives Outside New York

Baker (1941) mentions two cooperatives—the Consumers' Cooperative Trading Company in Gary, Indiana, and the Red Circle Cooperative Association in Richmond, Virginia—that were related to each other. The Aberdeen Gardens

Association of Hampton, Virginia, had a relationship to the Red Circle Cooperative. This suggests that, in addition to the cooperative economic development in distinct African American communities during the 1930s and '40s, there was also some communication between founders and members of the various co-ops, and some effort to learn from one another's successes and failures.

Consumers' Cooperative Trading Company

In the fall of 1932, Gary, Indiana, was ravaged by the Depression. Its steel mills closed, and only one bank remained, though it also closed eventually. As noted in chapter 4, Jacob Reddix held a meeting in Roosevelt High School, which led to the formation of Gary's Consumers' Cooperative Trading Company.[6] Starting with a buying club, the Trading Company went on to operate a main grocery store, a branch store, a filling station, and a credit union. By 1934, the Trading Company had more than four hundred members and employed seven full-time workers in the grocery store. The credit union was organized in November 1934. By February 1936, it had more than a hundred members and several hundred dollars on deposit. The first dividend, of 2 percent on shares of stock owned, was paid to members in December 1935 (Hope 1940, 41). In 1936, sales for the organization stood at $160,000, and the company was considered "the largest grocery business operated by Negroes in the United States" (Reddix 1974, 119). The Cooperative Trading Company had a women's guild that developed out of the early study group organized by the founders, and supported a young people's branch that operated its own ice-cream parlor and candy store.

In addition to his remarks about the important role of women in invigorating the co-op, Reddix is quoted as saying that the "most important single factor" in the co-op's progress "has been our education program" (Hope 1940, 40). As discussed in chapter 4, the co-op held weekly educational meetings for eighteen months before opening any of the businesses. In 1933 it instituted a cooperative economic course in Roosevelt High School's evening school, which by 1936 was the largest academic class in the school (41). In 1934 the education committee published a five-year plan titled "Uplifting the Social and Economic Status of the Negro in Gary."

Again, many of the same themes, missions, and goals are mirrored in this example. Every organization found education to be one of the most important elements in the endeavor. The Gary cooperative actually integrated cooperative education into the high school's night school curriculum. This cooperative society was responding to a need in the community, particularly an economic need. The Gary cooperative also went further than most by establishing a gas station and a credit union——both to provide financial services and to help members save money—and institutionalizing its education program. Like the others, this cooperative also saw the equal inclusion of youth as important, and had strong women's leadership.

The Red Circle Cooperative Association

The Red Circle Cooperative was also mentioned in Baker's 1941 memo. Rosenberg (1940a, 1940b) provides more details about the cooperative and its origins. A Mr. E. R. Storres had the idea to form a consumers' cooperative in 1927, but the idea did not take until the executive secretary of the Richmond Urban League spoke in 1937 about the cooperative movement and used the Consumers' Cooperative Trading Company in Gary as an example (Rosenberg 1940a, 282). After a call for potential co-op members, thirty-five men, out of one hundred contacted, responded and met on June 17, 1937. The group discussed the cooperative movement and then agreed to start the Red Circle Cooperative Association, Inc. The membership fee was $1 per member (Rosenberg 1940b). The cooperative launched a campaign for more members and stock subscriptions, as well as an education drive with monthly meetings. By the end of 1937, Red Circle had 125 members and had collected $1,200 (Rosenberg 1940a, 283). Executives went to Washington, D.C., Baltimore, and Greenbelt, Maryland, "inspecting cooperative stores and getting ideas and plans of organization and operation" (Rosenberg 1940b, 118). They reported back to the board. The decision was made for the cooperative to open a grocery store that would sell meat. The store opened its doors on October 11, 1938, in the "heart of the old Jackson Ward, directly across the street from a unit of the largest chain store in the United States," which had refused to hire Negro clerks (Rosenberg 1940a, 283). Sales that first day were $350. One result of the grocery store's success was that three months after it opened, the chain store across the street hired its first Black employee and started a price war. Red Circle was able to obtain goods from a wholesaler whose prices were low enough that the co-op could compete with the chain store. The chain store actually ended up reducing its staff by two, keeping only the manager. Red Circle had four regular employees.

By 1940, the Red Circle Cooperative had four hundred members and weekly business of $700, and employed a manager, two clerks, and a delivery boy (Rosenberg 1940b). In 1939, one hundred thousand customers were served, and a 1 percent dividend was paid on purchases. The total capital invested was $2,000, and the store earned a profit of $600, or net earnings of

30 percent (Rosenberg 1940a, 283). A committee looked into organizing a credit union, service station, and second grocery store. Despite low expectations, the cooperative association was a huge success, proving that a Black-managed store could succeed. As Rosenberg observed, "when the invincible force of cooperation met the immovable mountain of prejudice, fear, ignorance, and lack of self-confidence, the mountain melted into thin air. The invincible force forged ahead and is growing by leaps and bounds, and the Red Circle Cooperative idea of two years ago is a reality today" (1940b, 118). Rosenberg attributed its success to the hard work of members, shareholders, and workers, as well as to the store's efficient service and management. He also noted that "the organization was built from the bottom up and not from the top down," another reason for its success (1940a, 283). In addition, members "did their homework" in terms of studying co-op models, even traveling to several places around the country to see other co-ops. They never stopped studying and organizing to increase efficiency. Certainly, it was a tremendous feat to stare down a local chain grocer and prevail. Rosenberg went so far as to predict that its success might "revolutionize the South" (1940a, 283).

The Aberdeen Gardens Association

Rosenberg documented a second African American–owned cooperative store in Virginia. The Aberdeen Gardens Association was a consumers' cooperative organized in a government housing project, Aberdeen Gardens, in Hampton, Virginia. As the housing complex was being built, a small group of potential residents started meeting weekly to organize a co-op store. The federal government provided a $2,000 loan. Stock sold to members for $5 a share, payable in $1 installments over the course of a year (Rosenberg 1940a, 283).

The co-op store opened on November 17, 1938, with only fifty families living in the housing complex. The co-op operated at loss for the first six months because of low volume of sales. Once more residents moved into Aberdeen Gardens, the store started to make a profit. The co-op had two regular employees. In 1939, sales amounted to $16,988.29 and earned the co-op a net profit of $761.37. A 5 percent patronage dividend was approved and distributed. Rosenberg estimates that Aberdeen Gardens residents spent about 75 percent of their food budget at the cooperative. Although there were some complaints about "government interference or red tape," the co-op made good use of the government loan, according to Rosenberg (1940a, 283). The co-op planned to open a permanent store building and to increase its business in the community.

Unlike the Red Circle Cooperative, the Aberdeen Gardens co-op did not pay rent. Red Circle raised capital from its members, whereas Aberdeen's capital came mostly from a government grant; only $55 came from members. Both co-ops operated with cash transactions and sold goods to nonmembers as well as members. Both stores also cooperated with each other. Rosenberg concludes that Red Circle had a "sounder foundation" because members had a greater stake in their cooperative. Red Circle also started with an education campaign, and members met monthly to study cooperation; Aberdeen Gardens had not started an education campaign when Rosenberg wrote his report in September 1940. Rosenberg emphasized that continuous education and a sense of ownership were important to success, although both cooperatives were doing well. He also considered both co-ops examples of economic freedom, and argued that "the way out of our economic chaos is cooperatives" (1940a, 283).

The Consumers' Cooperative Association of Kansas City

Two other cooperatives had connections with the Consumers' Cooperative Trading Company in Gary, Indiana: the Consumers' Cooperative Association in Kansas City, Missouri, and the People's Consumer Cooperative in Chicago. The first started, as most Black cooperatives did, with a study group. Hugh Cook, the principal of Lincoln High School, his wife, and about twenty-eight others studied the cooperative movement together, and the Cooks traveled to Pittsburgh, Columbus, Gary, Minneapolis, and Chicago to study cooperatives there. In 1934, the group opened its first cooperative, a service station that was "supplied by a cooperative wholesale gas and oil company in the adjoining state" of Kansas. The service station had 162 members and sold between one hundred and five hundred gallons of gas per week, with total assets of about $2,000. The co-op had a paid manager and a nine-member board of directors. The station closed in 1938. According to a letter from Mr. Cook to John Hope II, the closure had to do with the "location, membership, lack of education, and an insidious effort by the merchant association and the School Board to prevent teachers from joining the organization" (Hope 1940, 42). When the number of members more than tripled, there was no corresponding increase in education about cooperative ownership. But, as happened in the case of other Black co-ops, hostility from the surrounding White community was severe. "This organization," according to Hope, "seems distinctive in that the opposition resorted to political pressure upon municipal employees to destroy the organization as well as to economic retaliatory measures much as were used later in Chicago" (43). But this kind of response was not as rare as Hope seemed to think. On the bright side, the co-op's board told Hope that they continued to reopen, perhaps also with a grocery store, and did not intend to give up (42–43).

People's Consumer Cooperative, Inc., of Chicago

While Hope ended his description of the Consumers' Cooperative Association in Kansas City on a pessimistic note, the People's Consumer Cooperative of Chicago began with several elements in its favor. Members of the cooperative were all tenants of the Rosenwald Apartments in Chicago and thus had easy access to the co-op store. They were a "closely knit group" of stable professionals and civil servants (mostly postal employees) who used teamwork effectively. In addition, J. L. Reddix, one of the founders of the Gary cooperative, advised the Chicago group early on to start a study group (Hope 1940, 43–44). A small group did just that in October 1936.

The group then organized a buying club, starting quite small with just one product, bacon. Membership shares were sold at $3 each. For $3 per month each, two of the women agreed to work for half a day. At this early stage, the group also established several "very active committees" on buying, auditing and bookkeeping, membership, education, and store location, and made "unusually rapid and sound progress." With the high cost of food becoming a challenge and the local food store chain charging "exorbitant prices for an inferior quality of merchandise," the group was motivated to be proactive. It began a boycott of the chain store and learned about cooperatives. After forming the study group and then the buying club, the group opened a cooperative retail grocery store in July 1937 (Hope 1940, 43–45).

The cooperative faced a major obstacle at the outset, because no White real estate owners in the neighborhood would rent to it, even though there were seven vacant stores in the immediate neighborhood. The co-op prevailed and did open the store. Two months later, in September 1937, it also opened a credit union, which by February 1939 had 191 members, with outstanding loans of $1,050. During the month of February, members added $1,172.88 of new capital. Members were not allowed to invest more than $250 in the credit union (presumably as a precaution, so that no one member had so much money invested as to expect special treatment or influence on co-op decisions). By the end of February, sixteen members had already reached the maximum amount of savings. In March 1938, the co-op store added a meat market, doubling the size of the store and increasing sales from $1,749 to $4,267. At the end of 1938, the cooperative store voted to distribute a dividend of 1 percent of the value of sales per member. The remainder of the store's surplus was divided between an education fund and an expansion and protection fund. This cooperative also maintained a policy to pay interest of 4 percent on fully paid share capital. This suggests that members could pay for their shares in installments, so that the cost would not be prohibitive. By 1940, its total membership was more than 450, with 139 paid in full (Hope 1940, 45).

Hope noted that one of the elements of a strong cooperative is the willingness to donate time, or what he called "volunteer gratuitous labor service by the members." The active committee structure was also a "pillar of strength." He quotes one of the co-op's leaders, Charles A. Beckett, on the functioning of the committees and the importance of shared leadership: "What little success we might claim has been due in a very large degree to the strong committee activity in our buying club stage. There was no need for a leader. We were strong believers in the principle of division of labor. Mutual confidence and respect for our group techniques had been the life of our society. I don't think any person interested in cooperatives can possibly overemphasize this point" (Hope 1940, 44).

Hope also praised "the prudence exercised and the economic soundness of the distribution of income" practiced by the cooperative (1940, 45). Just like a commercial bank or business, the cooperative set aside funds for emergencies and for education, and did not "confuse interest and profits" (46). Fiscal soundness in combination with enthusiastic participation, democratic practice, effective shared leadership, and ongoing education are important elements for success—and are not always found in combination in any business, let alone in many of the African American cooperatives studied here. The People's Consumer Cooperative of Chicago was a model of success on every score.

The Cooperative Business Council of New Haven

Hope discusses one final urban cooperative established during the Depression to help ease the cost of healthy food. New Haven's Cooperative Business Council was established in February 1937 by postal clerks. They too began by studying cooperative economics and began to teach others about "mutual self-help." After a phase of intense study, they launched a promotion campaign with the support of some local ministers. The study group met for a year, and in December 1937 opened a co-op grocery store staffed by the volunteer labor of members. In the summer of 1938, monthly sales amounted to between $200 and $300, with a membership of about fifty people. Hope's article mentions that the cooperative was also organizing a federal credit union, according to an article in the *New Haven Register*, which suggests that this cooperative effort did receive some local publicity (1940, 48).

An Era of Growth—Summary of African American Cooperatives During the Great Depression

Most of the co-ops from this period started with study groups, and from small amounts of money pooled from members—with working-class members paying their share in installments. African American cooperative development was supported and promoted by Black educational institutions and educators, churches, community organizations, and housewives. Most Black co-ops were grocery stores, gas stations, or credit unions. Some were housing co-ops. All provided quality affordable food or services. Most employed one or two people from the community. Many were able to offer dividends or patronage refunds as they became profitable. Many struggled to raise capital and to compete with White-owned establishments. By the 1950s, the cooperative movement had petered out a bit, with the few remaining efforts mostly clustered around small Black colleges in the South (Brooks and Lynch 1944), or in established Black communities in major cities.

During this period, African American women were often integral to the Black co-op movement, as they had been integral to the Black mutual-aid and self-help movement. The Young Negroes' Co-operative League, the Consumers' Cooperative Trading Company, and other co-ops had women's guilds, women leaders, or in other ways highlighted women's roles. One significant force representing Black women's efforts in the cooperative movement was the Ladies' Auxiliary to the International Brotherhood of Sleeping Car Porters and its president, Halena Wilson. The auxiliary promoted cooperative education and the development of several cooperatives, particularly in the 1940s. The following chapter focuses on the auxiliary's philosophy and activities around cooperative economics, and highlights Black women's roles in the cooperative movement. Nannie Helen Burroughs, through her National Training School for Women and Girls in Washington, D.C., was also a force in favor of cooperatives and one of the founders of Cooperative Industries of Washington, D.C.

The Great Depression probably saw the rise of more African American–owned cooperatives than any other period in U.S. history. The Black co-op movement developed from the same philosophy and spirit that inspired most cooperative movements, particularly those among the poor and working classes. It focused on the needs of people who were left out of the market, who experienced market failure, and who were discriminated against in the market, and enabled them to join together and create their own markets and enterprises. Many Blacks (like many Whites during the Great Depression) were destitute, jobless, and without access to affordable, quality food, gas, housing, and financial services. Cooperative enterprises helped them gain access to these goods, to help one another, and to provide for their families. Cooperation appealed to their collective spirit and sometimes created a sense of optimism. Alethea Washington's description of the cooperative movement conveys the philosophy and spirit of African American cooperation, particularly during the 1930s. "The cooperative movement offers a means whereby we can work together to solve economic problems," she wrote in 1939. "The cooperative movement is based on the deep and abiding religious principles of honesty, justice, equality, brotherhood, and love. The cooperative movement is inter-faith, inter-class, and inter-race. Therefore it gives us that common meeting ground which produces the best setting for working together" (1939a, 105).

7

CONTINUING THE LEGACY

Nannie Helen Burroughs, Halena Wilson, and the Role of Black Women

You start with those who make up the majority of those living in poor communities—women—and respond to their self-defined problems. The major problem for poor women is control of income, that is, gaining access to income in ways that give women ultimate freedom in how it gets used.
—JOHNSON (1997, 3)

Addressing the status of women in cooperatives does not result in just identifying a set of "women's issues," but rather, ways of thinking about a range of issues vital to cooperatives and their placement in the economy and the community. In other words, thinking about equity for women in democratic and management structures is one of a number of "ways in" to thinking about the relevance and effectiveness of cooperatives in general. It is also a way to begin considering barriers that affect all under-represented groups.
—HAMMOND KETILSON (1998, 33)

"Women are members and men are full-time directors" (Japanese Consumers' Co-operative Union 1999, 192). This belief has been the norm in the cooperative movement throughout the world. Many observers have noted that women belong to, use, and participate in cooperative enterprises for their own and their families' benefit, but tend not to be in control. The United Nations, the International Labour Organisation, and the International Co-operative Alliance, among others, all address this issue in research and in conferences on women's roles in cooperatives in industrialized countries as well as underdeveloped countries (see, for example, ICA 1993; ILO–ICA 1995; ICA Women's Committee 1983; Centre for the Study of Co-operatives 1998). Topics addressed have ranged from the relationship between women's roles in the economy and society in general and in cooperatives, women's occupational status and economic insecurity and cooperative economic development, as well as women's access to capital (or lack thereof), women's management capacity, and women's leadership in cooperatives.

My research on African American–owned cooperatives finds that Black women have been an integral part of the Black cooperative movement—

playing roles similar to those they have played in the Black church, mutual-aid societies, and the civil rights movement. They have often been the ones organizing and managing in the background, doing much of the scut work, without the glory or formal recognition bestowed by a title or a paid or board position. At the same time, African American women in some cases were not just members but also the founders, managers, and directors of cooperative enterprises and cooperative activity in the United States. Early mutual-aid associations and collective activity in African American communities were arranged and strengthened by women's work (Jones 1985). Women like Maggie Lena Walker, Ella Jo Baker, and Fannie Lou Hamer founded, organized, and directed important economic projects and businesses along with men—sometimes playing a prominent role as president or executive director, and often doing whatever needed to be done to make the project or business work. Halena Wilson, the president of the International Ladies' Auxiliary to the Brotherhood of Sleeping Car Porters and education director of the Consumers' Cooperative Buying Club in Chicago, heavily promoted the study and practice of consumer cooperation in all the auxiliaries and in the Black trade union movement (as well as the broader U.S. trade union movement) from the 1930s to the 1950s. Others, like Nannie Helen Burroughs, Estelle Witherspoon, Rebecca Johnson, Linda Leaks, and Ajowa Nzinga Ifateyo, developed enterprises owned and managed by Black women for women's betterment (see table 7.1). In this chapter, I investigate Black women's cooperative accomplishments in more detail, focusing on the projects of the Ladies' Auxiliary to the BSCP, Cooperative Industries of Washington, D.C., Freedom Quilting Bee, and Freedom Farm.

Many Black women have participated in cooperatives and co-op development as members and supporters. We have already seen examples of their activity, such as the Independent Order of Saint Luke and the Saint Luke Penny Savings Bank (see chapter 1), and the Women's Guild of what was to become the Consumers' Cooperative Trading Company in Gary, Indiana (chapters 4 and 6). The Women's Guild was responsible for reinvigorating the co-op movement in Gary, and helped to increase membership in the Consumers' Cooperative Trading Company. The Women's Guild was formed by many of the women who attended the first evening class on cooperative economics and management taught at Roosevelt High School in 1933 by Jacob Reddix (Hope 1940). Several of the cooperatives of the 1930s and '40s had women's guilds or women's empowerment as part of their mission. The Young Negroes' Co-operative League is another important example, with its focus on youth leadership and women's equality, and Ella Jo Baker's pivotal role. Some were organized by women, and some, in addition, were owned

TABLE 7.1   Black women leaders in the U.S. cooperative movement

Date	Black women's cooperative involvement
1700s–1800s	Women leaders and organizers in mutual-aid and beneficial societies
1900–1930s	Maggie Lena Walker and the Independent Order of Saint Luke; Saint Luke Penny Savings Bank; Consolidated Bank and Trust Company, Richmond, Virginia
1930s	Ella Jo Baker and the Young Negroes' Co-operative League; Nannie Helen Burroughs and Cooperative Industries of Washington, D.C.
1940s	Halena Wilson and the International Ladies' Auxiliary to the Brotherhood of Sleeping Car Porters
1960s–1970s	Estelle Witherspoon and Freedom Quilting Bee; Fannie Lou Hamer and Freedom Farm
1980s–2000s	Peggy Armstrong and Cooperative Home Care Associates; women organizers in Workers' Owned Sewing Company and Dawson's Textile Workers in North Carolina; Avis Ransom and SSC Employment Agency, Baltimore; Shirley Sherrard (New Communities), Shirley Blakely, Alice Paris, Carol P. Zippert, and Melbah Smith with the Federation of Southern Cooperatives; emerging women leaders in new women's worker cooperatives through WAGES, Oakland, Calif.; Rebecca Johnson and Cooperative Economics for Women, Boston; Linda Leaks, Ajowa Nzinga Ifateyo, and Ella Jo Baker Intentional Community cooperative, Washington, D.C.; Ujamaa Collective, Pittsburgh

solely by women. Cooperative Industries of Washington, D.C., was one such enterprise.

Cooperative Industries of Washington, D.C.

An important endeavor during the Great Depression was an industrial co-op, Cooperative Industries of Washington, D.C., which was based on a women's cottage industry and self-help project that began with public money targeted to help put women to work in Lincoln Heights, Washington, D.C. In the summer of 1934, a joint committee representing the citizens' associations of northeast Washington organized the Northeast Self-Help Cooperative to "prevent pauperism," provide "industrial education and the opportunity to work," and "train the unemployed and handicapped in self-supporting occupations" (Northeast Self-Help Cooperative 1934, 1936). On July 16, 1934, Nannie Helen Burroughs was elected president, and H. D. Woodson, first vice president. Scholar-activist and local resident Chancellor Williams wrote immediately to Burroughs in July 1934 of his interest in the self-help movement and in working with the cooperative. He noted that the creation of the cooperative "is a timely and most important attack upon the most pressing social problem of our time," adding, "I offered a comprehensive plan to the churches of Deanwood [D.C.] to unite in an effort to do something ourselves, for ourselves, instead of waiting and depending forever and eternally upon the leadership of the white man" (Williams 1934, 1). Williams would become president of the cooperative's board of directors (the position Burroughs first held) by the end of 1934.[1]

The North East Self-Help Cooperative used the resources and physical space of the National Training School for Women and Girls (see Washington 1939a; Burroughs 1934c), of which Burroughs was founder and president.[2] The cooperative used four classrooms for the sewing unit, a room for the clinic, the kitchen for canning, as well as the dining room and chapel. From the beginning, the group targeted federal funds from the Federal Emergency Relief Administration's Division of Self-Help Cooperatives, and spent two years submitting letters of intent and proposals and meeting and corresponding with staff from the FERA (Northeast Self-Help Cooperative 1934; Burroughs 1934c; Burroughs and the Board of Directors n.d.). In its first six months, the cooperative was successful. The sewing unit was the largest in the District of Columbia, with fifty women members, and the cooperative boasted that it had done more canning than any other Black cooperative in the city (Burroughs 1934c).

In 1936, the North East Self-Help Cooperative finally received a FERA grant of $19,633, changed its name to Cooperative Industries of Washington, D.C., and was chartered as a self-help cooperative in Lincoln Heights. Hope (1940) records that Cooperative Industries was founded by Nannie Helen Burroughs and Sadie Morse Bethel. Although Alice Dunbar Nelson did not specifically mention this cooperative, she highlighted Burroughs's work in one of her columns in the *Messenger* in 1927. According to Nelson, Burroughs "conceived the idea of a Domestic Servants Organization (DSO), with rules, regulations and projects similar to the unions among men laborers or skilled workmen." A building was bought and operated for the girls in the heart of northwest Washington. The DSO operated a social center with classes, lodging rooms, recreation rooms, dining rooms, "and all the rest of it." Nelson commented that the girls needed more safe opportunities for factory work and other work outside domestic service (Nelson 1927). The DSO tried to provide this, as did other Burroughs projects. Nelson noted that Burroughs did not have the time or money to make the DSO national and was already running her own school, the National Training School for Women and Girls, started in 1909. The school curriculum uniquely combined vocational training and liberal arts education, including Bible study—and one required course in Black history. Burroughs aimed to educate all young women regardless of their position in life, and to offer women "professional training that might help them earn a higher salary and afford better living conditions" (Library of Congress 2003).

Presumably, the Northeast Self-Help Cooperative and Cooperative Industries grew out of the kind of need that Nelson described as a concern of Burroughs's almost ten years earlier, and reflected the philosophy that drove Burroughs's National Training School, which provided support for the cooperative. Washington, after talking with Burroughs, described the co-op as a cooperative project "embracing the people of the community in a group of industries and in a farming project located in Maryland" (Washington 1939a, 108). In a letter soliciting members for Cooperative Industries, Burroughs and the board of directors outlined an ambitious list of projects: a roadside market, cannery, laundry, shoe repair shop, barrel chair handicrafts production, training in beauty culture, a thrift service, and a farm (Marshall Farm near Forestville, Maryland). Potential members were invited to a cooperative study class and an introductory session about the cooperative at the training school (Burroughs and the Board of Directors n.d.). Membership dues were $5 per year. According to Hope, the cooperative consisted of unemployed workers and homemakers who were unskilled and had incomes between $500 and $1,000 per year. The co-op began as a producer cooperative for "the relief of the unemployed by allowing them to produce useful goods and gain their own livelihood by bartering their products for those of other producers" (Hope 1940, 47). Hope does not mention that this cooperative was wholly or predominantly owned by women, but I have assumed this because of the fifty women named in the sewing unit and other cooperatives projects, and because of the population with which Burroughs is known to have worked, the mission of the co-op, and the fact that the two founders were women.

From Nannie Helen Burroughs's papers at the Library of Congress, we learn that the co-op got advice from Tuskegee Institute, had a thriving chicken farm, sold its chairs and brooms as far away as Virginia and Baltimore, bought products for its retail store from Eastern Cooperative Wholesale in New York, and was represented on the Committee of Sponsors for the District of Columbia Cooperative League. Unlike most of the other cooperatives of the 1930s and '40s, Cooperative Industries was what would now be called a hybrid cooperative because it evolved into a consumers' cooperative, along with an agricultural marketing cooperative, in addition to the producer's cooperative. This way, more of the clients' needs would be met. The store carried groceries, fresh fruit and vegetables, meat, poultry, eggs, and butter.

Hope explains that this effort was different from the English co-op model, which starts with consumers' cooperatives that build demand. The demand built by a consumers' co-op provides an infrastructure that was believed to be necessary to sustain a producer's cooperative. Hope remarks that most of the Negro cooperatives followed the English model (establishing a consumers' cooperative first), but that it was "both interesting and gratifying to see" how Cooperative Industries had "taken advantage of the temporary help of the government [grant] to create a permanent cooperative society which has so charted its course as to be able to continue its independent existence by filling permanent and lasting needs of its members after government aid was withdrawn and other relief methods were substituted for the self-help cooperatives" (1940, 47). Cooperative Industries started as a producer cooperative—organizing and operating "industrial manufacturing plants [that] will aid in the educational, social and industrial welfare of the unfortunate and sell the products of such plants"—and expanded into consumer cooperative activities as well (Northeast Self-Help Cooperative 1936). It is apparent in the cooperative's constitution and by-laws that the term "consumer members" was added later. Hope also notes that while the producer cooperative started with four hundred members in 1936, it was down to eighty-seven by 1938. However, rather than a sign of failure, the smaller number of members was the result of a change of model or focus that actually strengthened the co-op. The members were more committed and more productive. Total sales were $11,380 in December 1937 with the larger program ($28.45 per capita), and $10,280.83 in December 1938 with fewer members ($118.17 per capita). Since fewer members were much more productive, the co-op continued to be successful, even though the loss of members was substantial. Burroughs explained that the main reason for establishing the cooperative was to promote "production for use" and that it was based on "a firm belief that cooperatives furnish one of the best ways for the Negro to develop initiative and self-help." The cooperative also had a unique way of handling dividends, since half of its sales were to nonmembers. The surplus that was not distributed to members was saved and divided into two funds, one reserved for contingencies and the other for education (Hope 1940, 46).

Hope's 1940 article gives us some insight into the co-op's purpose and goals, and also into Burroughs's thinking. Combining this information with knowledge of Burroughs's philosophy and accomplishments, and with documents and letters from Burroughs and the organization itself, helps us to see Cooperative Industries of D.C. as an extension of Burroughs's commitment to women's education and training and women's economic rights and well-being. It is also interesting that the two accounts of this co-op outside

Burroughs's papers are both based on interviews with Burroughs. This indicates that Burroughs talked about this co-op and was forthcoming with information—even eager for people to learn about this co-op.[3] The preamble of the co-op's constitution uses terms such as "providing means of mutual helpfulness, to promote the general welfare, to obtain the necessities of life, to advance our moral and material welfare as citizens, and to secure in a fuller degree the fruits of our labor, and a more equal distribution of wealth and opportunity for employment" (Northeast Self-Help Cooperative 1936). The membership recruitment document refers to "enlarging the cooperative movement in the District" and building "a permanent, city-wide cooperative organization" (Burroughs and the Board of Directors n.d.). Clearly, this was a grand plan that achieved some successes and was viewed favorably in Washington, D.C., and nationally.

The International Ladies' Auxiliary to the Brotherhood of Sleeping Car Porters

Black involvement with the trade union movement in the 1930s, '40s, and '50s also included support for and establishment of consumer cooperatives. Du Bois was still advocating racial cooperative development, Baker and Schuyler were creating and promoting cooperatives across the nation, and Burroughs and others were developing co-ops in their local communities. In addition, A. Philip Randolph, in the pages of the *Black Worker* and through the organization he helped to found, the International Brotherhood of Sleeping Car Porters (BSCP), was promoting consumers' cooperation. Halena Wilson, president of the BSCP's Ladies' Auxiliary, was the BSCP's strongest, most vocal proponent of cooperatives.[4]

The activities of the Ladies' Auxiliary to the International Brotherhood of Sleeping Car Porters concerning consumer education and cooperative business education and development can be pieced together from the archives of the BSCP and the Chicago chapter of the Ladies' Auxiliary (of which Wilson was also president), and from Melinda Chateauvert's 1998 study of the women of the BSCP.[5] Analysis of the activities and strategies of the Chicago auxiliary and the International Ladies' Auxiliary (operated out of the Chicago office), particularly as they interfaced with the larger labor movement, both Black and White, shows how the co-op strategy was developed among Black activists between 1935 and 1952, and sheds light on African American women's roles in advancing and implementing that strategy.

Chateauvert explains how the women of the Ladies' Auxiliary, predominantly "union wives," used their position as African American homemakers and heads of the household budget to "expand the power of the trade union movement" (1998, 138) and promote the value of organized labor at every opportunity. "Indeed, it was in the commodity market that the Auxiliary addressed the needs of both wage-earning and unwaged women. By operating consumer cooperatives and providing advice on 'better buymanship' and other consumer issues, the Auxiliary politicized the spending habits of all union women and raised members' living standards" (139). Part of the philosophy was that this kind of cooperative buying kept money in the hands of workers and kept hard-earned money circulating in the labor movement instead of leaking out in purchases from non-labor-supporting producers and sellers.

Halena Wilson was elected the first president of the Chicago Ladies' Auxiliary in October 1930 and served until 1953. She also served as the first president of the International Ladies' Auxiliary from September 1938 until 1965, and had substantial influence on the organization over the course of more than twenty-five years. According to a short, anonymous biography written in 1956 ("The Life Work of Mrs. Halena Wilson," now housed in the BSCP Collection at the Chicago History Museum), Wilson became interested in the cooperative movement after she become president of the Chicago chapter of the Ladies' Auxiliary. She was "instrumental in organizing a Consumer Cooperative Buying Club" in Chicago and was one of the few Black women (if not the only one) elected to serve on the national Consumer Cooperative Council. She also led the Chicago branch of the auxiliary in becoming a charter member of the Cooperative Union Eye Care Center (with the Coalition of Trade Unions and Consumer Cooperation in Chicago) in the 1950s. The anonymously written biography notes that "the Chicago Auxiliary is the only affiliated organization [of the eye center] composed exclusively of women." Like many Black women leaders and movers in the co-op movement who began their civic engagement doing charity and community work and honed their leadership skills in churches and benevolent societies, Wilson had been active in the social and civic movement and fraternal organizations (such as Worthy Matron of the Order of the Eastern Star) before joining the Ladies' Auxiliary.

The Ladies' Auxiliary was interested in economic justice from the beginning. Included in the "Declaration of the Object, Principles, and Aims of the Ladies Auxiliary" was the goal of providing "a common meeting ground for women who endorse the principles of democracy and who wish to see them applied to the basic field of industry" (Wilson 1942b). In addition, the "Bulletin of Instruction on Decisions and Orders" of the auxiliary, beginning in 1938, included subscribing to journals and newsletters about consumer economics and cooperatives, as well as studying credit unions and consumer cooperation (Wilson and Randolph 1938; see also chapter 4). Wilson spearheaded the auxiliary's interest in consumer education and cooperatives, working closely with Randolph. Auxiliary chapters started study groups on consumers' cooperatives in Chicago, Denver, St. Louis, Minneapolis–St. Paul, Detroit, Indianapolis, Washington, D.C., New Orleans, Omaha, Oklahoma City, Los Angeles, Seattle, Montgomery, Pittsburgh, Montreal, Buffalo, and Jersey City (Chateauvert 1998, 143). White notes that the "Denver, Chicago, and District of Columbia Auxiliaries established buying clubs, and the Chicago and Portland Auxiliaries established their own consumer cooperatives" (1999, 165). The first BSCP credit union was established by the Montreal chapter and was part of the Ladies' Auxiliary project to create credit unions to help members adjust to economic crisis through savings plans and budgeting.

The Brotherhood Consumer Cooperative store was one of the projects of the Brotherhood Consumer Cooperative buying clubs started by women from the Chicago chapter of the Ladies' Auxiliary, and it was the most ambitious of the auxiliary's cooperative projects. Its initial leadership was made up entirely of women; as the co-op grew, more men became involved (Thornton 1948). In 1941, a group of seven women from the Ladies' Auxiliary and one man started a study group to talk about establishing a cooperative in Chicago. In 1943 they opened a store that sold groceries on Saturday afternoons (Chateauvert 1998). They then moved the co-op store to the BSCP headquarters, where it was open on weekdays and Saturdays. The members served as the salespersons and clerks for the first two years. In a report to the International Ladies' Auxiliary, Wilson reminded the members that "the Chicago Auxiliary in so far as it is known is the first group of Negro women connected with labor to initiate a consumer cooperative enterprise" (Wilson 1947b).[6]

The store did well through the beginning of 1947, having a balance of nearly $3,800 on its books in March. Later in 1947, however, investment was down, and many members thought they would have to close the store; it was not in a residential area close to where most people lived, and federal price controls were being eliminated. With encouragement from A. Philip Randolph and one Ernest Smith, the co-op held on, and by 1948 it had been reenergized. Randolph addressed the co-op in 1948, which increased membership, including one new member who donated $500. The original board of the co-op consisted of four women and one man. By 1948 there were four women and five men on the board, though executive leadership remained in the hands of the women: Agnes Thornton as president, Minnie A. Lee as secretary-treasurer, and Halena Wilson as educational chair (Thornton 1948).

Around the same time, the co-op undertook a membership drive (Wilson, Lee, and Thornton 1947). Membership increased to 250, and BSCP men began to put their time and resources into the co-op. The co-op and its buying club began to look for a location for a store. The buying club was operating out of the Chicago BSCP headquarters. The co-op incorporated in the District of Columbia (which had co-op law) in 1948 and, according to Thornton, planned to issue share certificates to all members (1948, 2). In October 1948 Wilson sent a special notice about the pledge drive, the goal of which was to increase the $4,000 they had in reserves by $1,500 to $2,000, and to urge members to buy more shares (Wilson 1948b).

One year later, the store was experiencing difficulties again. A special bulletin issued in July 1949 discussed the possibility of establishing a credit union "with a view towards diverting the club's present activities in that direction" (Wilson 1949b). For two or three months, forty to fifty members had been attending meetings about establishing a credit union, and Wilson encouraged more members to attend the meetings and learn about the benefits of a credit union. In a letter to Randolph defending this move, Wilson explained that most of the members were in favor of converting to a credit union. She considered this a good way to maintain the co-op's financial stability and keep some aspect of cooperative ownership, even if the store could not sustain itself. She told Randolph that the membership had grown beyond the Ladies' Auxiliary and the Chicago chapter of the BSCP, and that the co-op members thus thought that they were relatively autonomous. According to Wilson's letter, the Chicago BSCP chapter did not approve of the conversion to a credit union. Pfeffer notes that Milton P. Webster, the BSCP's first international vice president, was actively opposed to the credit union idea and "resented all activities that took attention away from the BSCP" (1995, 570). Since the co-op was sponsored by the Chicago Ladies' Auxiliary, Wilson told Randolph, she planned to withdraw the auxiliary from sponsorship and disassociate herself from the co-op. It could then go ahead and make its own decisions. She also informed Randolph that in addition to resigning her positions in the co-op, she would also resign from all positions she held "in other co-op organizations," so that she would not be "placed in a position of talking for the Auxiliary when I am really not free to do so" (Wilson 1949a).

Wilson's letter to Randolph suggests that the Ladies' Auxiliary, and in particular the Chicago co-op, were not as autonomous as Wilson believed or wished. Other entities tried to control her projects. Interestingly, the letter also says that Agnes Thornton, the co-op's president, and others on the co-op board had vetoed her suggestion that they close the store and return everyone's share. Members were divided about whether to continue the co-op in its present form, convert to a credit union, or dissolve the business altogether. Wilson was clearly torn between following the dictates of the BSCP and working with her fellow cooperators to find a solution. It appears that she chose to remove herself from this awkward position rather than fight the BSCP or her colleagues in the co-op. "As for my part," she told Randolph, "I am satisfied with the efforts that were made to develop a co-op program. It just happens that the opposition has been too strong and too powerful to surmount. I am content to bow out gracefully and forget the whole thing, since I am not the first person who has tried and failed" (Wilson 1949a). This must have been quite a blow, in that Wilson had spent the previous ten years working on what she called "the Co-op Program." In addition, although she seemed to think that Thornton was still optimistic about the co-op's prospects, and despite some members' desire to continue it, the conclusion of her letter is quite pessimistic. In a letter to the members signed by Wilson, Thornton, and Lee on February 3, 1950, the dissolution of the Brotherhood Consumer Cooperative store was announced and members' equity was returned by check, with a note of explanation (Wilson, Thornton, and Lee 1950).

In his reply to Wilson's letter, Randolph was full of encouragement, and acknowledged her accomplishments. "I hope that you are not discouraged about the outcome of your splendid efforts in behalf of the development of a cooperative and credit union for the Auxiliary. These unions are economic agencies that require a tremendous amount of time and work to set up and maintain. You can feel that your efforts have been fruitful because you have planted the seed of cooperation among the women. This seed is bound to grow and eventually flower" (Randolph 1949). Others were also optimistic about the efforts and accomplishments of the co-op, and about Wilson's consumer cooperation program. Thornton described the establishment of the cooperatives as "in keeping with the Auxiliary program of organization, legislation, and cooperation." She contended that "it is significant that this [the Brotherhood Consumer Cooperative store in Chicago] is the first and only effort of this kind sponsored by a woman's auxiliary within the labor movement, a movement of which we are proud of and feel sure that all Auxiliaries will wish to follow" (1948, 1).

The Brotherhood co-op was not the only cooperative project of which Wilson and the Ladies' Auxiliary were a part. In 1947, several members of the Ladies' Auxiliary attended a "Co-op Labor Conference" in Chicago sponsored by the Council for Cooperative Development. In a letter to Randolph in

July 1947, C. J. McLanahan, the education director of National Cooperatives, Inc. (a BSCP partner), mentioned that he had met several women from the Ladies' Auxiliary at the Co-op and Labor Institute at the University of Wisconsin, where he discussed "their interest in the development of a cooperative program" (McLanahan 1947, 2). He also mentioned that Letitia Murray had done good work in education among the auxiliaries. Randolph replied, "Our Ladies Auxiliary is making headway in the development of an educational program in consumer cooperation. It is my hope that the Auxiliary will keep in contact with the cooperative movement which you represent, so that it will benefit from the broad stream of knowledge and inspiration that your movement affords" (1947). It is clear that the Ladies' Auxiliary had Randolph's full support in pursuing a "cooperative program."

One year later, in July 1948, McLanahan wrote to Halena Wilson about the project to "develop a type of cooperative well-fitted to fit the needs of organised [sic] labor today." He reported that National Cooperatives, Inc. was well on the way to developing a demonstration project but needed more funding. In addition to asking the Ladies' Auxiliary for funds (whether through membership fees or donations), McLanahan discussed the importance of the auxiliary's input in helping to shape "the course of a total cooperative program for the labor communities," developing "a strong cooperative that will meet the needs of union members" (McLanahan 1948). This also suggests that the larger cooperative movement understood the importance of enlisting support, input, and counsel from African American women in the labor movement. We can infer from this that the BSCP's Ladies' Auxiliary was regarded highly by both the labor movement and the cooperative movement.

In the BSCP files at the Library of Congress, there is a proposed agenda for a similar co-op labor conference in Chicago called by the Council for Cooperative Development, dated December 9 but not specifying the year (Council for Cooperative Development n.d.). This conference presumably took place before the one mentioned in McLanahan's July 1947 letter to Randolph, because it gives Chicago rather than Madison as the location. It is possible that the proposed agenda was a planning document for the Wisconsin conference and that this conference ended up taking place in Madison, but it is more likely these were two separate conferences. Perhaps the undated agenda referred to McLanahan's July 1948 letter to Wilson. It included a discussion of community cooperatives and their activities, cooperatives as "labor's community base," ownership of productive facilities ("How soon?"), and challenges to cooperative development. Wilson added a note in her own hand at the bottom of the proposed agenda for the co-op labor conference in Chicago, presumably addressed to Randolph. Her note says that she thought that

the reader would be "interested in this new development between labor and
the co-op movement" and explains that she was the only women who
attended the meeting. She was placed on the by-laws committee, charged
with drawing up the articles of consolidation between labor and the cooperative movement, but suggested that her International Ladies' Auxiliary could
not afford the $1,000 membership fee. Wilson's note also mentions other
(White?) labor union representatives in attendance. Again, these documents
suggest that, at least in co-op circles in the Midwest, and among those seeking relationships with labor, the Black women of the Ladies' Auxiliary were
involved and that their leadership was important.

Finally, in 1952, Wilson was instrumental in the establishment of the
Cooperative Union Eye Care Center, of which the Chicago chapter of the
Ladies' Auxiliary was a charter member (Wilson 1953). The "Special Letter"
in which Wilson delineated the auxiliary's relationship to the eye-care co-op,
as well as the mention of Wilson's role in the founding of that co-op in her
biographical sketch of 1956, confirms that after the demise of the Brotherhood Consumer Cooperative store, Wilson did not actually withdraw from all
of her cooperative projects or relinquish her dreams for cooperative development between African Americans and organized labor.

This more than twenty-year history of cooperative education and development promoted and sponsored by the BSCP and its Ladies' Auxiliary constitutes another important chapter in the African American co-op movement
in the United States and Canada. It is also a story of connections between the
Black labor movement and the Black cooperative movement, the Black and
White labor movements, and the Black women's labor movement and the
White labor and cooperative movements. While A. Philip Randolph is quite
well known, Halena Wilson is virtually unknown—nor have Randolph and
Wilson been remembered for their support for consumer cooperation. Nevertheless, together they had tremendous influence on the U.S. cooperative
movement, and Wilson in particular was instrumental in keeping the idea of
consumer cooperation alive and in practice in the Black community for more
than twenty years.

Women of Color and Craft and Worker Cooperatives

In the late twentieth and early twenty-first centuries, women of color, particularly immigrant women, in the United States have used cooperative economic development strategies to create good jobs in industries known for
low-paying contingent work, and to own their own companies. Below are

several examples of craft or worker cooperatives owned by Black women and other women of color.

The Freedom Quilting Bee

The Freedom Quilting Bee was established in 1967 in Alberta, Alabama, to help sharecropping families earn independent income. Some of the women in Alberta and Gee's Bend, Alabama, came together to produce and sell quilts. In a few years they had made enough money to buy land and build a sewing factory. They also provided day care and after-school services for members' children and others. The cooperative was a founding member of the Federation of Southern Cooperatives (see chapter 9) and is an example of women's leadership and control over their own work conditions and of community solidarity, in terms of the ways in which this cooperative supported and helped its community.

This handicraft cooperative was founded by women in sharecropping families who needed to increase and stabilize their meager incomes. The women began selling quilts to supplement their families' farm incomes. The seed money for the cooperative came from an initial sale of one hundred quilts, sold for them in New York by an Episcopalian minister named Francis Walters who wanted to support the effort. Co-founder Estelle Witherspoon was FQB's first president. Witherspoon officially retired at the age of seventy-five, and Lucy Pettway became CEO (FSC/LAF 1992).[7]

In 1968, the cooperative bought twenty-three acres of land on which to build the sewing plant and increase Black land ownership. It sold eight lots to families who had been evicted from their homes and land and needed to start over (Freedom Quilting Bee n.d.). Economic independence and control over land were particularly important to members of the cooperative because many families lost the land that they had been sharecropping because of their civil rights activities. Some were evicted from their farms for registering to vote, and others were evicted on their return from hearing Dr. Martin Luther King speak in a nearby town in the mid-1960s (FSC/LAF 1992). Having the cooperative own land gave members independence and an alternative source of land to farm. The twenty-three acres were thus important not only to the co-op's own survival and growth but also to that of their families and the larger community.

The quilters also began using other entrepreneurial strategies to increase the economic activity under their control. In the early years, FQB was a member of the Artisans Cooperative. Artisans helped FQB members diversify their products to include placemats, aprons, potholders, and napkins, and to sell their products in five stores in the Northeast (Freedom Quilting Bee n.d.). By the mid-1990s, the co-op members had diversified their products to include conference bags as well. One of their largest contracts was with the United Methodist Women's Conference, which ordered thirteen thousand silk-screened canvas bags in 1994. This contract alone allowed for the full-time employment of seven to twelve women that year (FSC/LAF 1992). FQB quilts have been displayed at the Smithsonian Institution and sold in such stores as Sears and Bloomingdale's. The Bear's Paw in Fayetteville, Georgia, sold FQB quilts and opened a store in Syracuse, New York, specifically to sell FQB products (Freedom Quilting Bee n.d.). A couple of the members' quilts became well known as part of the Smithsonian's Gee's Bend Quilt Exhibit, which toured the United States in the early 2000s.

By 1992 the Freedom Quilting Bee cooperative owned the sewing factory and the twenty-three acres of land, and owned or leased a day-care center. It also operated an after-school tutoring program and a summer reading program. At its height (around 1992), the cooperative had 150 members and was the largest employer in the town (Freedom Quilting Bee n.d.). At a time when the political climate had severely reduced economic options for African Americans in the South, women were able through this cooperative to augment their families' income, create alternative sustainable economic activity, save and own their farms or use some of the co-op's land for farming, and provide services to their community. They also took care of their own child care and the after-school needs of their children and provided services that the entire community could use. The increased income and control over their own business allowed them to identify needs, such as land ownership and day care, and accomplish their goals. As a women-owned cooperative, the Freedom Quilting Bee also addressed the needs of its families and their community—all under women's leadership. After a hiatus of several years, the FQB reopened in 2007, but it has had difficulty maintaining enough members to be profitable, according to an interview with Alice Paris, FSC staff member and technical assistant to the FQB, by the author.

The Workers' Owned Sewing Company

The Workers' Owned Sewing Company (WOSCO) was founded by five seamstresses and a farmer in August 1979 in Windsor, North Carolina. The company consists primarily of women machine operators who head households. The women sewing machine operators wanted to provide themselves and other industrial seamstresses with steady jobs. The farmer, Tim Bazemore, "was determined to prove that poor Americans, especially African-Americans, could run a profitable business" (Adams and Shirey 1993, 2). Previously, White seamstresses had secured the best jobs in sewing factories. A Black-owned sewing factory, Bertie Industries, had been attempted in the 1970s under President Nixon's Black capitalism program, using Small Business Administration loans and minority set-aside contracts. The company declared bankruptcy in August 1979. Bazemore met with many of the unemployed seamstresses to discuss their options and how to start a new company. They had learned about the Mondragon Cooperative Corporation at a community education center nearby, and followed a similar model to own and operate their own for-profit sewing factory.

The seamstresses worked with the ICA Group in Boston to learn how to write financing and marketing plans and by-laws and to learn pricing and self-governance. The five women founders were Carolyn Beecham, Celia Cherry, Lila Dudley, Helen White, and Louise White. Because many potential recruiters and employees did not understand their company's structure, and because the Employment Security Administration charged that they were a "communist business," they had to devise their own informal recruiting network through churches and civic groups (Adams and Shirey 1993, 5). The seamstresses began working as subcontractors but were often short of business. They secured start-up funds from the Catholic Church's Campaign for Human Development and from the Presbyterian Church, as well as private funds from Bazemore. In August 1983 they began submitting their own bids for direct contracts. Sales almost doubled in the first year (9).

Starting in 1982, the cooperative was able to provide its owner-workers with uninterrupted full-time work. Its rate of employee turnover was also uncharacteristically low, compared with average turnover rates for the industry. WOSCO instituted an innovative compensation policy based on the cooperative's profitability. The wage ratio was three to one; no worker was paid more than three times the amount earned by the least-skilled worker. Members earned more if they "made production" daily for a full week and the company was profitable. They earned an additional cash bonus if their work met or exceeded goals of productivity with quality, regular attendance, and extra effort. If this level of productivity continued every week, workers were also given an annual bonus (Adams and Shirey 1993, 15–18).

In 1986, WOSCO joined the Amalgamated Clothing and Textile Workers Union, primarily for purposes of health insurance (Adams and Shirey 1993, 19). WOSCO began paying union dues for members who were ineligible for Medicare or Medicaid. By 1992, three of the founders were still directors, and two of them had become supervisors. WOSCO's bookkeeper had started working for the company in 1980 in the least-skilled position (bagging and tagging finished garments) and moved gradually up to the bookkeeping position (5). The average number of employees in 1992 was forty-three, forty of whom were owners. At one time, the cooperative employed as many as eighty-five women (10).

Until it closed in 2000, WOSCO provided stable employment, above-average wages, and workplace democracy for its members (employee-owners). As a cooperative, the worker-owners had input into company policy on hours, wages, bonuses, and conditions on the shop floor—this in an industry characterized by low pay, low job security, high turnover, and rigidly hierarchical, often paternalistic management. The WOSCO women proved that sewing work can be profitable and can provide a safe work environment with opportunities for advancement. They also proved that women, including African American women in the American South, can own and run a for-profit business successfully.

Cooperative Home Care Associates

Cooperative Home Care Associates (CHCA), in the South Bronx borough of New York City, employs more than sixteen hundred Latina and African American women as home-care paraprofessionals in three affiliated worker-owned companies. With more than seven hundred (and counting) of these employees being worker-owners of the cooperative, it is the largest worker cooperative in the United States.[8] Since 1987, CHCA's worker-owners have earned annual dividends of between 25 and 50 percent on their initial investment. The co-op maximizes wages and benefits for members, providing paid vacations and health insurance (unprecedented in this sector) in an environment of trust and collaboration. The cooperative's workers are also unionized. CHCA offers training and career-advancement programs for its members. Average employee turnover is well below the industry average (Shipp 2000).

CHCA was started in 1985 by a "social service agency to create decent jobs and provide needed services in an impoverished community" (Glasser and Brecher 2002, vii).[9] It employs and provides ownership to African American and Latina women, three-quarters of whom had previously been dependent on public assistance. CHCA does careful screening of potential employees, offers training and career-advancement programs, and promotes management training among the worker-owners. The worker cooperative has spun off a training and development institute, the Paraprofessional Healthcare Institute, that provides the kind of training the co-op wants all its employees to have and benefits the industry citywide. Early on, it helped develop similar cooperatives across the United States. CHCA creates opportunities for advancement within the co-op and its associated enterprises. Aides can become licensed practical nurses, assistant instructors, job counselors, supervisors, or midlevel managers. A new initiative will allow many workers to be promoted as "specialized aides." In 2000, the cooperative established a third entity to deliver specialized services to the disabled. This initiative won special Medicaid funds to be allocated for home health aides for the disabled in New York and created a nonprofit organization, Independence Care System, to facilitate such aid and manage the caseloads of disabled clients. This added five hundred employees, many of whom will soon become eligible for ownership (Schneider 2009).

Cooperative Home Care Associates provides several asset-building opportunities for its member-owners. It pays annual dividends in profitable years averaging 25 percent of the initial equity investment, or $250. The cooperative leads the industry in above-average wages, benefits, career advancement, leadership training, advocacy, and low turnover (Gordon Nembhard 2004b, 2008b; Shipp 2000; Glasser and Brecher 2002; Inserra, Conway, and Rodat 2002). CHCA's worker-owners also receive a $10,000 life insurance benefit, and most owners contribute to a 401(k) plan (to which the co-op also contributes an average of $100 per employee in profitable years). As of October 2008, the value of its 401(k) plan exceeded $2.5 million, and 234 worker-owners had accumulated more than $4,000 in their accounts. CHCA also aids its employee-owners in establishing checking and savings accounts. Seventy percent of CHCA's employees use direct deposit into savings or checking accounts; before joining the company, 73 percent had not had a checking account and 79 percent did not have a savings account. The cooperative also provides small interest-free loans and allows cashing out vacation days to help members with cash-flow problems. In addition, CHCA helps about 30 percent of its worker-owners receive the Earned Income Tax Credit and Child Tax Credit and promotes free income tax preparation services (CHCA 2008). These benefits are almost unheard of in the home-care industry and rare for any low-skilled job. However, because of the company's social mission and because it is owned by its workers, these benefits are a priority for worker-owners, and the company made them possible.

CHCA promotes women's leadership in several ways. Peggy Powell (cofounder and director of education when she was interviewed by Weiss and Clamp in 1992) observes that because the Black and Latina workforce gained control of the board of directors and, through the assembly of worker-owners, influenced decisions about pay and benefits, "the women feel that they have real input and control in this company. That clearly is going to develop their ability to speak and assert [themselves]" (Weiss and Clamp 1992, 226).

Many of the original members have moved up the ranks into midlevel management positions. Economic stability, economic mobility, and leadership development for low-income women of color are some of the major accomplishments of the cooperative.

Cooperative Home Care Associates is a company that achieves economic empowerment for low-income women of color, most of whom previously relied on public assistance, in a sector known for its inadequacies. CHCA sets the standard for wages, benefits, training, and workplace democracy in its industry. It creates a significant number of meaningful jobs in the community and generates income and wealth for members. The cooperative is active in sector development in New York City and has seen the incorporation of training, leadership development, and advocacy as essential. In addition, CHCA is at the forefront of modeling involvement in policy advocacy, and in modeling strategic and effective partnerships between a worker-owned company and its union.

Cooperative Economics for Women

Cooperative Economics for Women (CEW), in Jamaica Plain, Massachusetts (a neighborhood of Boston), organized low-income women in the 1990s to create cooperative approaches to generating income while organizing for community development. The clientele were mostly women of color, immigrant and refugee women, and women survivors of domestic violence. CEW successfully helped women develop several women's cooperative businesses in sewing, housecleaning, catering, and child care. CEW used a model that gave voice, skills, and full-time employment with benefits to the poorest women. CEW began in 1994 as an effort to provide access to income through cooperatives to women who received some public assistance. It provided tutoring in English as a second language, legal services, and welfare advocacy services. Participants gained employment experience and a cooperative perspective through a rigorous and comprehensive innovative training program. Clients learned to identify their formal and informal skills and learned business skills, financial literacy, and how to work in teams to create democratic management. CEW was funded through grants from foundations and individuals, and accepted no government funding.

CEW strove to make "creative ideas work in times of cutthroat capitalism" through a transformative training program that combined literacy, organizational skills, and the technical know-how to run a business and build trust and sense of community. Rebecca Johnson, the organization's director, explained, "you start with those who make up the majority of those living in poor communities—women—and respond to their self-defined problems." Johnson finds that the cooperative process helps women gain "access to income in ways that give women ultimate freedom in how it gets used" (1997, 3). In the years it operated, CEW tended to work only with groups of women because it found that with the addition of men in the training program, the dynamics changed, and the training could not focus as clearly on building leadership qualities, empowerment, and trust among women.[10] According to a 1997 CEW brochure, the "CEW model offers a viable, powerful model for the poorest women to attain—over time—confidence, voice, skills, a community network and full-time employment with a livable wage and benefits."

Dawson Workers-Owned Cooperative

When the owners of Almark Mills, a fabric-cutting and sewing plant in Dawson, Georgia, abandoned the mill in late 1997 after thirty-one years in business, two hundred employees (down from a high of nine hundred in the 1980s) were left jobless. The property went into foreclosure and the bank locked and chained the building. Within two months, however, a plan to reopen the factory as a worker cooperative was hatched and executed. Marcus Lemacks, the president and general manager of Almark Mills, worked with the mayor of Dawson and former employees of the mill. He heard about "a small but successful textile operation in North Carolina that had restructured itself as a co-op several years before" (probably Workers' Owned Sewing Company in Windsor) (Merlo 1998b, 2; Sewell 1998). With help from a local business developer, the co-op was formed on October 6, 1997. Dianne Williams, a former employee who was elected chair of the board of the new cooperative, explained, "We had a meeting and all the employees decided this co-op was something that could work" (Merlo 1998b).

In December 1997, seventy members, all former employees of Almark Mills, started work at the old plant, now as worker-owners in a new cooperative. The majority (76 percent) of the mill's workforce was female; a third of them were single mothers; and most were Black (Merlo 1998b). Almark Mills had been the largest employer of women in Terrell County, and there were no other textile jobs within fifty miles. Reopening the plant, especially so quickly, was a significant accomplishment (see Sewell 1998).

The worker-owners used their union fund (which held decades' worth of union dues, now available because the union had been dissolved with the closing of Almark Mills) as their equity investment in the new cooperative. Because Terrell County had been identified as one of the eleven counties that suffered job losses from the North American Free Trade Agreement (NAFTA), the cooperative was able to get a sizable federal loan package of $1.4 million from the U.S. Department of Agriculture. The Clinton administration's Community Adjustment and Investment Program authorized the USDA to make loans to businesses in up to fifty rural communities adversely affected by NAFTA, through the business and industry loan-guarantee program operated by the Rural Business Cooperative Service of the USDA. This enabled the workers to pay off the bank debts, expand, and hire one hundred more employee-owners, for a total of 169. The cooperative's sales in 1998 reached almost $5 million. Ownership shares could be paid in installments of weekly payroll deductions of $7.16 over four years (Merlo 1998b).

The mayor of Dawson, Robert Albritten, stated, "Persons in this community doubted that women and minorities could make this work where it hadn't succeeded before, but we've made believers out of them" (Merlo 1998, 1). Board chair Williams remarked that the cooperative had changed the workers' lives, made them more optimistic and hopeful, and had changed the way business was done in the factory—jobs were now more secure and communication was more open and transparent. The USDA cooperative services coordinator, Gregg White, noted, "Saving jobs for the people of Dawson is a key issue. If we're going to reform welfare, cooperative development is one of the key instruments we need to use. This cooperative is giving people investment and ownership where they have their destiny in their own hands" (Merlo 1998b, 1, 5).

The Ella Jo Baker Intentional Community Cooperative

The Ella Jo Baker Intentional Community Cooperative is a fifteen-unit limited-equity housing cooperative and urban intentional community in the Columbia Heights neighborhood of Washington, D.C. It was founded by five African American women, including Linda Leaks and Ajowa Nzinga Ifateyo, who wanted to create a women-led intentional community and housing co-op where social and political activists, especially Black women, could live with like-minded people in affordable and safe housing.[11] Members started organizing in 1999 in response to gentrification and in an attempt to save affordable housing in Columbia Heights (Ifateyo 2010). Their goal was to become a model for other groups engaged in similar projects to save affordable housing in a city that was quickly losing it. Part of the strategy was to initiate legislation to allow limited-equity co-ops to pay less in taxes. The group was able to partner with a nonprofit developer and bought six row houses for one dollar. The cooperative received a mortgage to develop the fifteen units, and its members moved into the apartments in 2003. After some challenges, they finally closed on the sale of the renovated units in 2010.

The Ujamaa Collective

The Ujamaa Collective is a cooperative of African American craftswomen founded in 2007 to establish a year-round open-air artists' marketplace in Pittsburgh, Pennsylvania. "The market is designed to provide booths and tables to entrepreneurs in the early stages of their development, so that they can showcase their handmade wares, foods and goods. It is also designed to bring shoppers and visitors to the Centre Avenue business corridor" in the historic African American Hill District (Rayworth 2010). The market opened on select weekends in July 2010. The members had been "nomadic venders" (Raftis 2010) who wanted a regular place at which to sell their wares and showcase Black women's artistic talents and entrepreneurship. They began by sponsoring two successful holiday bazaars—one on the day after Thanksgiving in 2009 and the other during the Kwanzaa holiday in December 2009.

The fifteen members of the collective produce sustainable, homemade, and organic products such as jewelry, hair products, natural soaps, gift baskets, hand-painted tote bags, photographs, games, music and entertainment, and vegan, vegetarian, and West Indian food (Ifateyo 2010). The collective's mission is to "use non-traditional approaches to overcoming the long-standing economic and racial disparities in Pittsburgh's small business economy" (Rayworth 2010). Founder Celeta Hickman wanted to show that women can make their own money and help develop their communities at the same time. She wanted to connect with the Hill District's history of women's entrepreneurship and women's collaboration. Another goal was to increase Black women's wealth. The collective uses socially conscious entrepreneurship that connects African American and womanist traditions to develop women's and family-supporting, community-based businesses. The collective promotes cooperative business innovation and green entrepreneurship, teaching entrepreneurship courses and cooperative economics. The name comes from the fourth Kwanzaa principle, Ujamaa, and is the Swahili word for cooperative economics.[12] The Ujamaa Collective is supported by several local organizations, such as Sankofa Community Empowerment and the Pittsburgh Central Keystone Innovation Zone (Ifateyo 2010), and received a grant of $180,000 from McAuley Ministries (Raftis 2010).

Significance of Black Women's Involvement
in the Cooperative Movement

Women face many economic challenges: gendered occupational segregation, even after major gains in the 1980s; the highest poverty levels (women and children); a gender income gap still wide in many areas; and a huge gender wealth gap. Most women-owned businesses are small and are in the service or retail sectors; revenues are disproportionately low. Explorations of the ways in which economic development influences women's development, particularly labor force participation and income generation, tend not to analyze the ways in which cooperative economic development influences women's status, income, or wealth, and vice versa. While the focus has been on traditional capitalist development (and, for a while, state-sponsored communist development) and women's labor force participation, women have made progress through a variety of strategies and across an expanded list of indicators. Women's participation in cooperative enterprises, for example, is touted for giving women more control over economic resources; developing their leadership, managerial, and business skills; and increasing self-esteem, education, income, and wealth (see, for example, Weiss and Clamp 1992; Conover, Molina, and Morris 1993; Nippierd 1999). Because of their democratic structure and values, economic cooperatives allow women equal access to productive assets and an equal voice in governance. At the same time, women's participation in cooperatives brings diversity and innovation to cooperative enterprises and enhances the cooperative movement in general. Conn (2001), for example, notes that "co-ops present a potential solution for individual women as well as a broader strategy to improve the community economy," and are an "irresistible opportunity for women" to control their workplace and modify it to meet their family needs.

Women were important to the Black co-op movement, as they were to the mutual-aid movement and civil rights movement. Many of the Black women involved in the cooperative movement actually began as leaders in a mutual-aid society. These women used the cooperative movement to increase gains for their families and communities—to keep control over income in the hands of their communities, stabilize income, increase wealth, and control their workplaces. They saw their efforts as part of the larger Black liberation and economic justice movements.

African American women have in some ways played unique roles in the development of cooperatives in the United States. African American women in the International Ladies' Auxiliary to the Brotherhood of Sleeping Car Porters, for example, engaged in consumer and cooperative economic education, founded cooperatives, and worked with the Black and White labor movements to promote cooperatives and consumer education. That Black women had so much influence was unusual—but not unlikely. The growing use of worker cooperatives in recent years as an employment and asset-building strategy among women of color in the United States provides examples of the ways in which women of color are taking business development into their own hands, and it reflects a modern approach to using cooperatives as an economic development strategy for economically marginalized, exploited, and underserved populations.

BLACK RURAL COOPERATIVE ACTIVITY IN THE
EARLY TO MID-TWENTIETH CENTURY

In 1969 Hamer laid the groundwork for an elaborate project to make poor folks economically self-sufficient. That project became the Freedom Farm Corporation.
Through her work with the farm, Hamer broadened the meaning of civil rights activism to include addressing the economic needs of Black poor folks. . . . She was
obsessed with ending human suffering around her, and this included suffering caused
by decades of racism and poverty.
—LEE (2000, 147)

Co-ops are the best people development institutions you can have. . . . I have always
been interested in rural development in the South. It's not well understood outside of
the South that there's a connection between economic independence and political
independence—that people didn't have economic independence if when they voted
they lost their jobs or got kicked off the plantation. The whole reason for forming
cooperatives is to give people economic independence so that they could have independence in political and other matters.
—RAY MARSHALL (QUOTED IN FSC/LAF 1992, 25)

Black rural cooperative development in the early twentieth century continued the efforts of the nineteenth century. According to Curl (1980), during
the Depression many small farmers, particularly Farmers' Union members,
turned to radical action. Frazier (1923) reports on cooperative marketing
among Black farmers, particularly peanut growers in Texas. The activities of
the National Federation of Colored Farmers, Inc. are chronicled in this chapter. In addition, cooperative activity took place in North Carolina in the 1930s
and '40s, anchored by the Bricks Rural Life School and Tyrrell County Training School. These schools promoted cooperative economics education and
co-op development, and together organized the Eastern Carolina Council, a
federation of North Carolinian cooperatives. More recently, the Federation of
Southern Cooperatives, the only existing organization of African American
cooperatives, was founded in 1967 (see chapter 9). I end this chapter with a
discussion of the philosophy and efforts of Fannie Lou Hamer, the founder of
Freedom Farm Corporation, and Freedom Farm's accomplishments.

Highlights of Rural Cooperative Activity in the
Early Twentieth Century

African American rural cooperative development in the early twentieth century continued to be a struggle, yet had some successes. In 1923, E. Franklin Frazier expressed a relatively common sentiment among African Americans exposed to cooperatives: that cooperatives were a step toward economic emancipation—especially in small rural communities where Blacks had no choice but to use the White landlord's commissary (1923, 228). Frazier suggested that marketing cooperatives could be successful, especially if resources were combined and business conducted in cash. He also suggested that credit unions (cooperative banks) were a better alternative than the farm loan banks that discriminated against Black farmers.[1] The National Negro Business League similarly noted in a weekly news summary in a July 1929 issue of the *Negro World* that Black farmers would not share in the $500 million revolving fund recently approved by Congress. The NNBL attributed this exclusion of Black farmers to the lack of Black cooperative agricultural organizations (according to "a Negro statistician at the Census Bureau") and to the fact that so few Blacks owned their own farms and were thus unable to take advantage of the 1916 Federal Farm Loan Act (NNBL 1929). The NNBL was apparently not aware of the rich Black cooperative agricultural movements of the nineteenth century (see chapter 3).

Frazier concluded that "if the colored people, especially the farmers, are to avail themselves of the economic and social advantages of cooperation, in spite of the large percentage of illiteracy," then they needed to read the literature on the principles of cooperative enterprises, their leaders needed to organize consumers and farmers, and the sharecropping system had to be ended (1923, 229). Frazier concluded by remarking that a recent farmers' conference at Tuskegee Institute missed the opportunity to disseminate information about economic cooperation and discuss the challenges of cooperative marketing in which, he pointed out, some farmers were already engaged. By the late 1930s Tuskegee University would have its own cooperative (Washington 1939a, 107), perhaps in part as a response to Frazier's admonishment.

The National Federation of Colored Farmers, Inc.

Several prominent Black men—among them James P. Davis, Gilchrist Stewart, Cornelius R. Richardson, and Leon R. Harris—formed the National Federation of Colored Farmers (NFCF) in 1922.[2] By 1929, the NFCF was large enough to need full-time leadership, and in 1930 the officers incorporated it in Chicago. The NFCF's purpose was to attract Blacks and stabilize Black farm ownership and better farm living, using "cooperative buying, production and marketing" (Hope 1940, 48). The NFCF helped members purchase farms or secure better legal sharecropping contracts, and then assisted them in making a good, stable living from their farms. At the NFCF's height, its membership spanned twelve states.

The first local unit of the organization began in Howard, Mississippi, in 1929. A group of about thirty tenants and sharecroppers pooled their money to purchase goods wholesale in Memphis, Tennessee. Because wholesale prices were so much lower than what White landowners charged, more tenants and sharecroppers joined the organization, and it grew rapidly. The White planters and merchants attempted to run the purchasing cooperative out of the county. The NFCF, however, registered with the state as a legal organization, and its rights were upheld by the state's attorney general. The planters then stopped issuing tenants and sharecroppers the "limited money" or small cash advances they traditionally lent until the harvest. This reduced the amount of money that members could put into the cooperative, but it did not stop their momentum. One White planter, the exception to the rule, acknowledged that the Black tenants could get better prices through the purchasing cooperative and wanted to join them, asking only that they let him sell his commissary inventory first. So even the competition saw joint purchasing as a good idea, and White farmers often used cooperative purchasing and marketing themselves.

An October 1930 article in the *Negro World* reported that a White county agent from Lexington, Mississippi, accused the NFCF of swindling "thousands of Mississippi Negro farmers" out of $6 (a $5 membership fee and $1 publicity fee) on the promise of reduced food prices and better market prices for cotton. An NFCF spokesperson (identified as "Mr. Davis," perhaps one of the organizers, James P. Davis) denied the charges and countered that White merchants and moneylenders had encouraged the county agent to make the false accusation in an attempt to undermine the NFCF. The article noted that Black farmers had been forced to start their own cooperative after being refused membership in White farmers' cooperatives; and it quoted Davis's calculation that the NFCF would save its members twenty-five to forty cents on the dollar for every truckload of goods the Black farmers bought together (*Negro World* 1930a). In addition, NFCF members had access to credit on better terms because of their livestock securities. This saved them from 20 to 25 percent in interest. The article noted that the savings from collective buying and lower interest took money out of the pockets of the local Whites who had had a monopoly on these services—so naturally the Whites were angry. Historian J. H. Harmon Jr.'s research in 1929 confirms that White businessmen thwarted Black business development in a variety of ways and profited from discriminating against African Americans (1929, 131).

The *Negro World*'s favorable coverage of the NFCF demonstrates that not only did word of such endeavors and their challenges get out, at least in the African American media, but also that at least some of the Black media were quite sympathetic to cooperative efforts among Blacks. In 1923 the *Negro World* reported on an agreement between Black and White farmers in Aiken County, Georgia, to "co-operate and pool their interests for the general good of the local farmers" in the farmers' exchange (Associated Negro Press 1923).

The members of the Howard, Mississippi, chapter of the NFCF continued to purchase cooperatively for another three or four years, even expanding the number and kinds of items bought wholesale. They then expanded into cooperative hog and cow production and marketing, selling livestock on the Memphis market. They bought a truck and in their fifth year earned more than $3,000 from livestock sales alone—extra money above their regular activities. They were always able to find markets for their goods, which they sold in Chicago, New York, and Baltimore, although they preferred local markets when they could conduct business without racial discrimination.

Over the ten years of the cooperative's existence, most of the members, who had started out as tenants and sharecroppers, were able to buy their own farms, and thus became less dependent on government relief or loans. Similarly, Black farmers in Fayette County, Texas, operated a cooperative sawmill in the late 1930s that reduced the price of lumber and shingles and was used by both Black and White farmers. According to Alethea Washington, "The Forest Service believes that such cooperatives will increase the value of farm woodlands and greatly facilitate the use of home-grown forest products" (1939a, 108). These accomplishments are even more remarkable given that they occurred in the Jim Crow South during the Great Depression.

A NOTE ABOUT THE SOUTHERN TENANT FARMERS' UNION

In 1934, Blacks and Whites in the Arkansas cotton belt, which was dominated by huge plantations, formed the Southern Tenant Farmers' Union (STFU) in semisecrecy. This union championed cooperatives, organized buying clubs, and ran a large cooperative farm. As White growers began switching over to wage labor and evicted tenants from the land in large numbers, the STFU responded with a strike, which the growers in turn answered with a reign of terror assisted by the National Guard (Curl 1980, 43).

The North Carolina Council and Eastern Carolina Council

There was also extensive cooperative activity among African Americans in rural areas of North Carolina, notably through the Bricks Rural Life School and Tyrrell County Training School in the 1930s and '40s. These schools promoted co-op development and joined together to organize the Eastern Carolina Council, a federation of North Carolinian cooperatives. As interest in cooperatives increased among African Americans in North Carolina, members of the Bricks and Tyrrell co-ops were asked to speak to Black audiences throughout the state. In 1939, groups were called together to organize an African American federation for the development of cooperatives, and the Eastern Carolina Council was born. The organization was helped by the more established credit union division of North Carolina's Department of Agriculture and the extension service of the state's vocational program. Because of wartime restrictions during World War II, the group became inactive after 1942, but in 1945 Tyrrell County School held a workshop on cooperative living, sponsored by the Fellowship of Southern Churchmen. Organizations that participated in the workshop were the credit union division of North Carolina's Department of Agriculture, North Carolina's Department of Public Instruction, the University of North Carolina, North Carolina State College, and two "Negro colleges," as well as representatives of religious and community groups. Sixty-four people participated in the workshop over a ten-day period (Pitts 1950, 31–32).

One outcome of this workshop was a five-year plan and budget, and the creation of an advisory and administrative agency to support the development of credit unions and cooperatives—hence the North Carolina Council for Credit Unions and Associates (shortened to the North Carolina Council). The council's mission was to design a cooperative economic educational curriculum. Rosenberg described it as "an organization of credit unions and cooperatives operated by Negroes to promote new credit unions and other co-operatives throughout North Carolina and to aid existing credit unions and co-operatives" (1950, 182). Another outcome of the workshop was the creation of a primer for schools and credit union treasurers on credit union accounting (Pitts 1950, 32).

As a result of this activity to promote credit unions and other cooperatives among African Americans in North Carolina, the number of Black credit unions and other cooperatives in the state increased dramatically. According to Pitts, in 1936 there were 3 Black credit unions in North Carolina; by 1948 there were 98, along with 48 additional cooperative enterprises: 9 consumer stores, 32 machinery co-ops, 4 curb markets, 2 health associations, and 1 housing project (1950, 35).

Bricks Rural Life School

In 1934, the Bricks Rural Life School in Bricks, North Carolina, run by the American Missionary Association, developed a program of adult education for African American cooperative development. Two years later, the school organized a credit union. Members pooled their resources and borrowed from the credit union to jointly buy a tractor. In 1938, the school opened a cooperative store, and in 1939 it developed a health program. The members of these ventures raised half the cost of a full-time nurse and persuaded the state's Health Department to fund the other half. Small purchasing and service groups were established in the surrounding communities. By the late 1940s, more than three-quarters of the families in Bricks had at least one member connected with one of the co-ops (Pitts 1950, 24–26).

Tyrrell County Training School

As mentioned in chapter 4, the principal of the Tyrrell County Training School, and members of his staff, conducted study groups on cooperative economics and then developed several cooperatives. By 1939, twenty-five neighbors had established a credit union. In the first year, membership increased to 187. The credit union started a savings account program for students. Members of the Tyrrell group started a store in 1940, and in 1941 established a cooperative health insurance program that guaranteed members up to $100 for hospitalization for a membership fee of $1, monthly assessments of ten cents, and a twenty-five-cent co-payment for each hospital visit. A plan to raise money to hire a doctor was never realized. The credit union helped several families save their farms from foreclosure and enabled others to purchase a farm. It financed group purchases of farm equipment. Buying clubs and machinery-purchasing cooperatives were established through 1945 (Pitts 1950, 27–30).

Black Credit Unions in North Carolina

Writing in 1950, Rosenberg suggested that North Carolina had had the greatest credit union activity among Blacks, particularly between 1944 and 1946. Between 1944 and 1946, the number increased from thirty-two to seventy-two, mostly in rural areas of the state, capturing the market in installment loans to Blacks (1950, 188–89). Rosenberg attributes this growth both to economic necessity and to African Americans' growing interest in and enthusiasm for economic cooperation: "Public spirited and co-operative minded people were enlisted to support the credit-union program" (189). Black credit unions were successful, according to Rosenberg, "if organized by interested and capable people" (189). Also, Pitts's 1950 study documented ninety-eight credit unions in North Carolina in 1948. Pitts attributed most of the growth to the North Carolina Council. The largest Black credit union in the state was the Excelsior Credit Union of Gastonia. The Victory Credit Union of Winston-Salem and the Chowan Credit Union of Edenton were the only ones to employ paid staff.

Pig Banking and the Freedom Farm Corporation

Fannie Lou Hamer, a co-founder of the Mississippi Freedom Democratic Party well known for her work in voting rights direct action, argued that political victories were only the first step toward sustainability and social justice. Economic independence through cooperative forms of ownership, she believed, was necessary to reach the "ultimate goal of total freedom." "The concept of total individual ownership of huge acreages of land by individuals is at the base of our struggle for survival," she told an audience in her home town of Ruleville, Mississippi. "Cooperative ownership of land opens the door to many opportunities for group development of economic enterprises which develop the total community rather than create monopolies that monopolize the resources of a community" (Hamer 1971b, 5). Echoing Chancellor Williams's (1961) notions of economic sustainability, cooperation, and community, and W. E. B. Du Bois's notion of Black economic progress (1907),[3] Hamer spoke about focusing on what was best for the survival of the total community, as opposed to an individualistic notion of economic development, freedom, or progress. Woods characterizes Hamer as "a key figure in rejuvenating the historic African American land, labor, and cultural reform agenda" (1998, 12). Hamer co-founded the Mississippi Freedom Democratic Party (MFDP) in 1964, was one of the leaders of the right-to-vote campaign, and served as a member of the Student Non-Violent Coordinating Committee in Mississippi. While much of her activism in the 1960s addressed voting rights and civil rights in general, the MFDP from the beginning attempted to address poverty, not just civil rights. The MFDP was founded on a platform of free land (grants of the land that White plantation families were being subsidized not to plant), "government advice, and long term, low-interest loans for farm cooperatives," as well as "a guaranteed annual income, fair representation for the black and the poor on all state agencies receiving federal funds, expanded day care, free and complete medical care for every person from birth to death, expanded federal food programs, and free higher education" (Mills 2007, 230). Woods observes that "most of this agenda came directly out of the blues development tradition and its emphasis upon participatory democracy and global social justice" (1998, 218).

> The new institutions, communities and leaders that emerged out of the Delta freedom movement were not the creation of the . . . [traditional civil rights organizations]. They were not the creation of innovative public officials in Washington, DC, or important social theorists in New York. They emerged from the daily lives and the collective history of the people of the Delta. . . . For example, long after Delta conflicts had faded from the national headlines, Fannie Lou Hamer was still driven by her mission to give flesh and bone to her historic dreams of an ideal community. In 1970, she formed the Freedom Farm Cooperative for the purpose of helping displaced farm workers become self-reliant. (217)

By the 1970s, Hamer was focusing almost exclusively on food security and land ownership. She was a proponent of the self-help ideology that had resurfaced among Black nationalists in the mid- to late twentieth century and that built on the blues development tradition of the Mississippi Delta and the cooperative efforts of Black farmers since the 1800s. She advocated self-initiative and local control instead of reliance on government: "Instead of federal government intervention, many activists of the black nationalist persuasion espoused self-determination and community control" (Lee 2000, 123). Hunger was an increasingly pressing issue, and Hamer used her northern contacts and fund-raising to address hunger in her community (Mills 2007, 255). She also continued to pursue a dual strategy of keeping issues in the national public eye through speeches, hearings, conferences, and national television and documentaries, while also providing food directly to her community and providing her neighbors with the means to sustain themselves. In 1968, Hamer told the potential funder Measure for Measure, of Madison, Wisconsin, that since the state of Mississippi wanted Black people out and the federal government considered them "surplus," "blacks' only hope lay in acquiring land for cooperative farming and housing" (254–56). According to Lee, the purpose of Hamer's Freedom Farm project was to address economic need, human suffering, and racial discrimination by creating economic self-sufficiency for poor Blacks through co-op ownership (2000, 147).

In the 1960s, Dorothy Height, the president of the National Council of Negro Women, worked with Hamer through the Sunflower County, Mississippi, branch of the council. Height discussed with Hamer the difficulty of making political or economic progress in Mississippi. Even when registered to vote, if Blacks took time off from working in the fields in order to vote, they were fired; and Black candidates for political office still were not winning. This was an issue of great importance to Hamer. In her autobiography, Height quotes Hamer as saying, "food is used as a political weapon." "But if you have a pig in your backyard, if you have some vegetables in your garden, you can feed yourself and your family, and nobody can push you around. . . . even if we have no jobs, we can eat and we can look after our families" (Height 2003, 188).

Height suggested that they set up a "pig bank" in Mississippi, modeled after the Heifer Project's international programs (2003, 188). Biographies of Hamer (Lee 2000; Mills 2007) and Freedom Farm documents maintain that Hamer had the idea and approached Height.[4] According to a document in the Fannie Lou Hamer Papers called "Brief Historical Background of Freedom Farm Corporation," Hamer is said to have remarked, "These families cannot live on vegetables alone. There must be meat on their tables also." In any case, in 1967 the National Council of Negro Women purchased fifty-five pigs and donated them to start the pig bank in Ruleville, Mississippi. According to Height, they consulted with a farmer from Iowa and the Prentiss Institute. "Participating families were trained to care for pigs, to establish cooperatives, and to work together to improve the community's nutrition and health" (2003, 188). Participants were assigned a pregnant sow and signed a "pig agreement" stating that they would not sell the pigs but would donate two piglets from each litter to the bank, so that more pigs could be shared and help more families feed themselves. In 1975, when Hamer took Height to visit the pig bank, two thousand pigs had been raised from the initial fifty-five (237), feeding hundreds of families.

The pig bank was part of the NCNW's program of women's self-help—"helping people meet their own needs, on their own terms," and helping "themselves by helping others" (Height 2003, 199). While the project fit the mission of the NCNW, it was also consistent with the Mississippi Freedom Democratic Party's platform, and with Hamer's long-term scheme for Black rural survival (see Hamer 1970, 1971a; Freedom Farm Corporation n.d.; Lee 2000; Mills 2007). In addition, the pig farm was part of Hamer's grand plan to establish a large agricultural cooperative, Freedom Farm, which would buy up land owned by Whites, put it in the hands of African Americans, and use cooperative agriculture to keep the farm sustainable. White writes that the NCNW helped establish the Freedom Farm Corporation in 1968 (actually 1969, according to Freedom Farm documents) under Hamer's guidance, purchasing the first forty acres for the farm. The pig bank was part of this larger effort. White notes that the NCNW "initiated the first program in the country aimed at ending hunger" using public and private money (1999, 196).

The Freedom Farm Corporation was officially constituted in June 1970 as a nonprofit agricultural and charitable corporation under state charter in Mississippi (it was apparently never chartered federally as a 501[c]3 not-for-profit). The incorporators were Fannie Lou Hamer, Myles Foster, Joseph Harris, and George Jordan (Freedom Farm Corporation 1970). The official purposes of the corporation were

1. Benevolent, for the accumulation of funds and production of food for the relief of the destitute;
2. Social, to "cultivate social intercourse among the members and assist in improving moral and social conditions";
3. Property ownership, to "receive donations and to receive manage, take, and hold real and personal property by gift, grant, devise or bequest"; and
4. Other charitable and business purposes; to obtain funds or income for charitable purposes; and "purchase, receive, manage, hold and dispose of real, personal and mixed property . . . and may operate said properties or any part thereof, or any business it may acquire in any location, in the name of the corporation."

An early fund-raising letter from Hamer (1970) describes the goals of Freedom Farm as "to capitalize on the manifest need for close study of disadvantaged communities and bring changes through development." A 1973 status report describes the farm's purpose as "to develop a black controlled institution that would have its strengths in the land and would be able to support the indigent blacks and whites of the Sunflower County area that are being displaced by increased mechanization of agricultural production" (Freedom Farm Corporation 1973b, 1). Freedom Farm institutionalized a structure and process for low-income and destitute rural people (Black and White at first, and then primarily women and Blacks) to feed themselves, own their own homes, farm cooperatively, and create small businesses together in order to support a sustainable food system, land ownership, and economic independence. This community prosperity developed through mutual aid and joint ownership at the community level, connected to nationwide advocacy and philanthropy.

In a May 1970 fund-raising letter, Hamer described the "Oink-Oink or Pig Project" as well as farming, housing, education, and business initiatives proposed by Freedom Farm. The initial forty acres in Drew, Mississippi, were planted in cotton, soybeans, and vegetables. The profits from the sale of cotton and soybeans were to be used to make the land payments, and vegetables were to be gathered and given to needy families of both races. Freedom Farm planned to develop a vegetable bank as well; all who helped with the harvest would receive vegetables. Freedom Farm's first crop benefitted an estimated 250 families. In 1970, the farm donated some surplus vegetables to needy families in Chicago (Lee 2000, 149), making rural and urban connections and extending rural cooperative solutions to address urban poverty as well.

The first housing initiative consisted of purchasing three houses and two lots in Ruleville. These properties were then resold to tenants in a rent-to-own plan whereby the tenants' rent payments would be converted, in effect, into mortgage payments. The second initiative was the purchase of twenty-seven lots and would help low-income families apply for Farmers Home Administration (FHA) loans to build houses on those lots.

Freedom Farm's educational initiatives consisted mostly of a few grants to college students. The business initiatives included an African fashion shop in Drew, some small-business loans, and plans to establish a couple of sewing cooperatives. Freedom Farm Corporation made loans of up to $2,000 for Black business development. In 1969, it also bought a building in Doddsville for a sewing co-op, and had plans to open a clothing cooperative and community center in Ruleville (Lee 2000, 150). The sewing factory operated for about a year. The NCNW also helped to finance the Fannie Lou Hamer Day Care Center for women in the Doddsville garment factory (Mills 2007, 260).

A 1971 grant proposal to the Black Economic Research Council (Freedom Farm Corporation 1971) added more accomplishments to the list. In February 1971 Freedom Farm made a down payment of $84,000 on 640 acres of land (see also Lee 2000, 148). Most of the acres would be for cash crops: 300 acres in cotton and 209 in soybeans, with the remainder in fresh vegetables to be distributed to "needy families." On the housing front, Freedom Farm partnered with Delta Housing Development Corporation, "a self-help housing organization," to build sixty-four houses in Sunflower County with funding from the FHA. Construction was to begin on July 1, 1972. In addition, options were paid on eighty-nine lots for low-income families who would then apply on their own for FHA loans; all but two families were already approved for the loans. According to Mills (2007, 264), Freedom Farm's original investment in housing resulted in more than $800,000 in FHA mortgage loans for Ruleville. Freedom Farm also expanded its social services to help people purchase food stamps, food, and clothing, and to provide disaster relief after a tornado. It engaged six Neighborhood Youth Corps workers to conduct a survey to help determine the level and type of needs in the county. Freedom Farm was successful in raising funds to purchase (or received donations of) $62,480 for the purchase of three tractors, a backhoe and loader, a special combine, five cotton trailers, a plow, and some row markers, although the farm lacked adequate sheds or storage space for most of the equipment (Freedom Farm Corporation 1971; see also Lee 2000, 148).

In a 1975 funding proposal, according to Lee, Freedom Farm Corporation announced that it would target women, especially women heads of household and women farm laborers. "Hamer's targeting of women may have been a function of her involvement in gender-based politics," Lee writes, but it probably also reflected the needs of her community; changing demographics meant that there were more female-headed households in Sunflower County than ever before (2000, 152).

Often referred to as the Freedom Farm Co-op (by Hamer herself and in some grant proposals), probably because several of its projects were intended to be cooperative businesses and because it was run as a cooperative, Freedom Farm was never chartered as a cooperative of any kind but was a private not-for-profit organization. According to Lee, there was a $1 monthly membership fee, although an early document says that membership dues were $3 for a share in providing low-income families an opportunity to produce food for themselves on land owned by the corporation and to build their own homes on land "owned by their friends and brothers" with access to good farmland ("Sunflower County Freedom Farm Co-op" n.d.). Mills reports that only thirty families could afford the $1 monthly dues, but another fifteen hundred families belonged to or used the farm in some way (2007, 260). The farm's policy was that anyone who needed fresh vegetables could help harvest the crop. However, "people often helped themselves to food but did no work to keep up the farm" (260). This became a serious problem.

In 1974, with the death of business manager Joseph Harris, most of Freedom Farm's programs and activities ceased to function. Hamer was hospitalized in early 1974 and the farm lost 640 acres to creditors (Mills 2007, 269). In December 1976 Mrs. Hamer attempted to resurrect the corporation, and a new board was formed. Hamer died on March 14, 1977. The new board persevered and hoped to begin operations again on September 1, 1977, but this attempt was unsuccessful. In March 1977 the manager of the North Bolivar County Farm Co-op, Ronald Thornton, gave the Freedom Farm board an accounting of the equipment. He had repaired and maintained the equipment for a couple of years in exchange for using it at the North Bolivar Co-op and farming some of Freedom Farm's abandoned lands through an agreement with Hamer's husband. In April 1977, Freedom Farm Corporation sold the City of Ruleville six lots within the city limits for $10, on the condition that the land would be used to benefit the community, that part of two of the lots would be reserved for the burial of Fannie Lou Hamer, that the Freedom Farm Corporation would be permitted to construct a permanent memorial structure at the burial site, and that the city would maintain the site (Freedom Farm Corporation 1977).[5]

There are many reasons why Freedom Farm lasted fewer than ten years and had only a few good years during that time. Several sources shed light on what happened (Mills 2007; Lee 2000; documents from the Fannie Lou Hamer Collection at the Mississippi Department of Archives and History in Jackson; and Hamer's papers at the Amistad Research Center of Tulane University). The project needed a substantial amount of capital up front to buy land and sustain the effort through several years of drought and poor crop yields. This meant that although significant amounts of money were raised for its various projects, Freedom Farm always carried substantial debt. Hamer used grants and loans to keep the farm going, but this required her to travel a lot and maintain a national presence—all while in poor health, raising a family, and trying to get Freedom Farm's projects up and running. Hamer was thus not deeply involved in Freedom Farm's day-to-day activities, nor was she a farm manager. She was the public face of Freedom Farm.

By all accounts, Freedom Farm was more of a service organization than a profitable enterprise, partly because of its ambitious goals and partly because it was trying to sustain a farming operation during a stretch of particularly poor weather—what Helena Wilkening described as "some of the worst weather in Mississippi history" (1973, 1). Most farms relied on government subsidies, especially during periods of alternating heavy rain and drought, but Hamer refused to accept farm subsidies, though she helped members get food stamps and federal housing assistance and loans. Hamer believed wholeheartedly in self-help and was probably trying to avoid the risk of any outside control in the form of state or federal oversight (Lee 2000, 162). She reflected in November 1971, "Perhaps the major problem of Freedom Farm Corporation is simply that it is not [generating] its own capital" (158). Members who took the vegetables, benefitted from the social services, and so on, but did not give back in any way, not even with volunteer work, were also a drain on the farm.

The farm, and the organization more generally, also lacked good management. Hamer was not an administrator (Mills 2007, 272). Freedom Farm Corporation lent money to people who could not pay it back. Some of the staff did not take the job seriously and sometimes were not paid on time. Funds for the various projects were not kept separate. There was an effort to reorganize in 1972–73 (Lee 2000, 159–61), to separate social service projects from farm operations and "achieve more professional management" (Mills 2007, 265). The result of this reorganization was that the social service projects that did not generate enough income were discontinued. The farm's original, very dedicated manager died in 1974, and Hamer's ailing husband, Pap Hamer, had to manage Freedom Farm in addition to holding two other jobs. Hamer, too, was in poor health. While the farm did receive some aid and advice from the neighboring North Bolivar Cooperative, a very successful cooperative and a member of the Federation of Southern Cooperatives, this was not enough to sustain it.[6] Ronald Thornton, North Bolivar's manager, suggested that the plantation mentality and sharecropping experiences of Black farmers robbed them of good economic decision-making skills (Mills 2007, 271). In addition, there were rivalries among Black groups in Mississippi, and the Delta Foundation in particular was not supportive of Freedom Farm. According to another North Bolivar manager, L. C. Dorsey, the Farmers Home Administration and the Federal Land Bank were not supportive of cooperatives (268).

Freedom Farm took on another huge challenge in attempting to reengage low-income farmers at a time when mechanized farming was replacing traditional farming methods and many Black farmers were losing interest in farming, according to Dorsey. In addition, local farmers apparently were skeptical about being involved in a cooperative and never fully embraced the project. Dorsey emphasized that not only did many poor Black farmers no longer want to farm, but that if they were going to farm, they wanted to own their own land, not share a huge farm with others. Thornton and Dorsey managed a successful farm cooperative nearby, but they were frank about the challenges involved. Dorsey went so far as to say that cooperatives were a "foreign concept" to Blacks. "Co-ops had never been part of this society," Mills quotes her as saying, "in the sense that black folks or poor whites could participate" (Mills 2007, 271–72).

While part of this analysis is faulty—as this book documents, African Americans in the rural South do have a strong tradition of self-help and cooperative ownership—in the case of Freedom Farm, the economic cooperative concept seems to have been imported rather than homegrown. It was not begun by existing landowners who were bringing resources to an enterprise; the land had to be bought. Displaced farmers and low-income laborers, many of them destitute and weary of farming, were invited to participate but apparently were not truly engaged in the cooperative spirit of the project

or educated about what was involved in belonging to a co-op. Many had multiple challenges to overcome before they could fully engage. At the same
time, there were successful cooperative models in the region. Lee notes that
among the other southern cooperatives were the Haywood County Civic and
Welfare League in Tennessee, the Poor People's Land Corporation in Alabama, and, of course, the North Bolivar County Farm Cooperative, next door
to Sunflower County (2007, 161–62). Moreover, the Federation of Southern
Cooperatives counted more than a hundred cooperatives in its membership
by the early 1970s, and the Southern Cooperative Development Fund was
providing co-op education and start-up funds (see chapter 9). Freedom
Farm's difficulties and ultimate demise were the result of a complex set of
factors that include all the issues mentioned above, but probably were in
great part a result of lack of coordination of resources and not enough education and training about joint ownership.

Of all the Freedom Farm initiatives, the pig bank seems to have done the
best, perhaps because it was the best capitalized, was relatively self-contained,
was not capital- or labor-intensive, was run by women, and did not depend
much on the weather. Mills delineates many of Freedom Farm's accomplishments by 1973: its members hired a manager, a secretary-bookkeeper, 4 full-
time laborers, and 35 part-time workers; helped 13 seasonal workers catch up
with their mortgages; enabled more than 80 families to receive clothing;
assisted 25 families in applying for food stamps; and helped 57 families apply
for welfare and Social Security (2007, 267). Given all that it tried to achieve and
all that it did accomplish, Freedom Farm should not be considered a failure. As
Mills puts it, "The question is not so much why Freedom Farm failed but how it
managed to operate as long as it did" (272). In November 1971, Hamer declared
the farm a humanitarian success at feeding people, giving people a chance to
heal, and giving voice to "the silent ones." She admitted that while "the only
thing Freedom Farm is generating is food—and lots of it," it was "feeding people who previously starved in one of the richest agricultural [areas] in the
world. It is building pride, concern and all the other superlatives professionals
use to describe hard-working folk" (Lee 2000, 158). White notes that, "although
the only part of the program to survive was the Head Start Center, the initiative
brought hope, and meat to the families in Sunflower County" (1999, 196).

Maintaining the Cooperative Legacy in the Rural South

This chapter has highlighted the ways in which the rural agricultural cooperative movement continued among African Americans well into the twentieth

century. While there were many challenges—including drought, poverty, racial segregation, and lack of access to capital—there were also successes. People were fed, some Black farms stayed in business and sustained families, some land remained in African American hands, some affordable housing was created, credit unions provided needed credit, health care was supported collectively, and many cooperatives were formed and sustained. In addition, there was often good publicity about attempts to create and maintain Black cooperatives, and in the case of Fannie Lou Hamer's national campaign to fund Freedom Farm, many northern foundations and progressive groups aided the Black co-op movement. Out of this legacy some impressive organizations were built, in particular the Federation of Southern Cooperatives, which started before Freedom Farm but after the other examples discussed in this chapter and which remains in existence today, almost half a century later.

Part Three

TWENTIETH-CENTURY PRACTICES,
TWENTY-FIRST-CENTURY SOLUTIONS

The origins of a new form of regional development in the Delta are to be found within the region itself among the scattered, misplaced, and often forgotten movements, projects, and agendas of its African American communities and of other marginalized groups. Generation after generation, ethnic and class alliances arose in the region with the aim of expanding social and economic democracy, only to be ignored, dismissed, and defeated. These defeats were followed by arrogant attempts to purge such heroic movements from both historical texts and popular memory. Yet even in defeat these movements transformed the policies of the plantation bloc and informed daily life, community-building activities, and subsequent movements. Within the unreconstructed oral and written records of these arrested movements resides the knowledge upon which to construct new relationships and new regional structures of equality.
—WOODS (1998, 4)

The pooling of resources in one form or another has helped solve the problems of other groups almost since the beginning of time and it is only logical to conclude that the same principle can be made to help solve the problems of our own racial group.
—WILSON (1942A, 2)

I propose as the next step which the American Negro can give to the world a new and unique gift. We have tried song and laughter and with rare good humor a bit condescending the world has received it; we have given the world work, hard, backbreaking labor and the world has let black John Henry die breaking his heart to beat the machine.

It is now our business to give the world an example of intelligent cooperation so that when the new industrial commonwealth comes we can go into it as an experienced people and not again be left on the outside as mere beggars. . . . If leading the way as intelligent cooperating consumers, we rid ourselves of the ideas of a price system and become pioneer servants of the common good, we can enter the new city as men and not mules.
—DU BOIS (1933C, 162–63)

In the transitions from enslavement to wage labor, from industrialization to the postindustrial information age, African American and other subaltern populations held little control over the economic processes of change, or the assets required for success.[1] As a result, many subaltern communities are underdeveloped, marginalized, and underserved. Persuad and Lusane note that "benefits have gone disproportionately to those who strategically manage and control capital" (2000, 27), even in what is called the "new economy." Economic inequality and discrimination at all levels of society are well documented (see, e.g., Darity and Mason 1998). At the same time, subaltern populations have been instrumental in contributing to the successes of each era—performing much of the hard labor, providing productive services, and inventing new technologies. Twenty-first-century solutions to reducing poverty and increasing subaltern groups' control of capital require creativity, flexibility, and diversity—the solutions cannot afford to be exclusive or exploitive. Throughout history, members of subaltern populations have wanted to control resources, income, and assets. Rather than continue to be "beggars" and recipients of inappropriate and outmoded models of industrial and economic development imposed by others, subaltern populations can and sometimes do use alternative economic models to fashion their own economy. Part III of this book explores the ways in which African Americans have used their own community-based democratic enterprises to create economic opportunities and stabilize their communities.

The African American cooperative movement had started to revive by the 1960s. Co-ops, sometimes quietly, became intricately connected to the efforts of civil rights organizations and the Black power movement in the urban North, West, and South, and in Black struggles for economic independence in rural areas. The later twentieth-century urban projects used cooperatives as part of a larger strategy of Black empowerment, and while they were often deliberate about creating cooperatives, co-op development was a minor aspect of a larger strategy. Chapter 9 provides a brief history of the Federation of Southern Cooperatives/Land Assistance Fund, a cooperative support and development organization focused on African American and low-income rural cooperative economic development and land ownership. The FSC/LAF is the only existing African American regional or national cooperative organization in the United States. This chapter also looks at some relatively recent efforts of the FSC/LAF to develop and sustain cooperative economic activity in the South and to support Black farmers. The final chapter, chapter 10, makes connections between the different cooperatives and development models throughout African American history, identifies common elements and themes, and attempts to evaluate their impact, particularly on youth.

This chapter pulls together the many ways in which cooperatives have used solidarity and group cohesion to benefit African American communities.

The cooperative enterprises discussed in this book have many things in common. Their members came from marginalized communities and were not being served well, or at all, by prevailing market forces or government agencies. They needed to generate income and build assets, and they needed more control over their own economic lives and their community's economic activities. They came together (often with the help of a leader or community organization), studied their circumstances, studied the alternatives, and pooled their talents and capital. They launched businesses that would address their needs and keep them in control. Many followed a charismatic leader. Many started through a church or school. Others were initiated by an agency or organization that recognized a need and pulled together a group of people who could work together.

They were all stable enterprises anchored in their communities, with no desire or incentive to leave. They usually provided permanent jobs with livable wages and benefits for their workers/owners, often setting a high standard for the industry in their region. Many provided comprehensive services, or at least services that went beyond those specific to their industry. Because they were member-owned, they provided asset-building opportunities and increased both individual and community wealth. The benefits of these businesses spilled over into the broader community, often providing training and education for members and consumers in the community, buying from other local businesses, fostering business spinoffs, increasing civic participation, and advocating for industry or community change.

This study of African American economic history suggests that being masters of their own economic destiny and positioning themselves at the cutting edge of new economic formations has been helpful to African Americans. African American history has generally been a story of underdevelopment, discrimination, and lack of control, with pockets of economic independence continually challenged. I have endeavored to demonstrate the feasibility of fashioning financial redevelopment, both urban and rural, around proactive, egalitarian strategies for democratic ownership and control of productive assets in African American communities. These two final chapters demonstrate how community-controlled democratic enterprises can provide economic stimulus, create wealth, and reduce exploitation and inequalities for African Americans.

9

THE FEDERATION OF SOUTHERN COOPERATIVES

The Legacy Lives On

Since 1967, we at the Federation of Southern Cooperatives/Land Assistance Fund (Federation/LAF) have remained true to our founding purposes of helping people to help themselves through cooperatives. . . . We have developed family farmers, especially those of color, [and helped them to] remain and develop their landholdings as a key to rural community development. . . . We have accepted the challenge of working with the poorest, most neglected and isolated people in the rural Southeast to help them make a difference in their lives and livelihoods.

—PAIGE (2012, 1)

Since the civil rights movement, cooperatives have played an important part in helping black farmers to sustain or develop as independent operators. As a public issue, the objectives have been civil rights and fighting poverty, and not independent farming. . . . But to black farmers and community leaders, building and sustaining operating independence is a concomitant objective and cooperatives have a major role in achieving that end.

—REYNOLDS (2002, 2)

The Federation of Southern Cooperatives was founded in 1967 to promote cooperative economic development as a strategy (and philosophy), to support and sustain Black farmer ownership and control over land, to support the economic viability of family and independent farm businesses—especially small, sustainable, and organic farms—and to advance the stewardship of Black-owned land and other natural resources in rural low-income communities in the southern United States. After merging with the Emergency Land Fund in 1985, the organization became the Federation of Southern Cooperatives/Land Assistance Fund (FSC/LAF), and the stewardship of land became as important a goal as cooperative development. It has recently added creating "local food economies and systems that can sustain the communities in which our members live" as another objective (FSC/LAF 2013, 4). The FSC/LAF today is a network of rural cooperatives, credit unions, and state associations of cooperatives and cooperative development centers in the southern United States.

This chapter contains material originally published in Gordon Nembhard 2004b.

The FSC/LAF provides technical and legal assistance, financial support, education, and advocacy for its members and low-income populations in the South. In addition, the organization promotes and supports state and federal policy changes and legislation favorable to small farmers and low-income rural populations, as well as supporting cooperative development. The FSC/LAF is the heart and soul of the current African American cooperative movement.

In its first twenty-five years of existence, the FSC/LAF has helped to create or support more than two hundred cooperatives and credit unions, most of them in the seven states where it has offices. The list of member organizations includes, in Alabama: the Freedom Quilting Bee, the Panola Land Buyers Association and PLBA Housing Development Corporation, SOGOCO Goat Producers Cooperatives, the Federation of Greene County Employees Federal Credit Union, and Women in Land Ownership; in Mississippi: the North Bolivar County Farm Cooperative, Beat 4 Farms Cooperative A.A.L., the Indian Springs Farmers Association, Inc., the Shreveport Federal Credit Union, the New Community Cooperative, and the Milestone Cooperative Association (previously the Middle Mississippi Farmers Cooperative); in South Carolina: the Carver Homes Worker's Cooperative, the South Carolina Sea Island Farmers Cooperative, the Orangeburg Young Farmers Cooperative, and the People's Cooperative; in Georgia: the Southern Alternatives Cooperative and the Southwest Georgia Farmers Cooperatives; in Louisiana: the Southern Consumers' Cooperative, the Grand Marie Sweet Potato Cooperative, the South Plaquemines United Fisheries Cooperative, and the Point Coupee Farmers Cooperative; and in Florida: the New North Florida Cooperative.[1] The federation runs a Rural Training and Research Center that showcases sustainable forestry, provides co-op education, and helps to develop Black youth-run co-ops. The FSC/LAF also engages in cooperative development in Africa and the Caribbean. The organization has a wide reach throughout the South, is connected to the larger U.S. cooperative movement, and has successfully advocated for important measures in U.S. farm bills to support Black farmers, Black land ownership, and co-op development.

This chapter provides an analysis of the history and accomplishments of the FSC/LAF. The early story of the FSC is also the history of the Southwest Alabama Farmers' Cooperative Association and the Southern Cooperative Development Fund.

The Southwest Alabama Farmers' Cooperative Association

During the 1960s, some civil rights organizers sought to establish more formal cooperative enterprises as a way to support African American rural commercial efforts to address the many challenges of rural commerce, and to help reduce Black migration from rural areas by enabling Black farmers and their families to earn a sustainable living (Reynolds 2002, 11; de Jong 2005, 399).[2] Cooperatives were proposed as a mechanism to enable Black farmers to reduce costs, convert from cotton to vegetable crops, increase technical capacity, and improve their collective leverage by pooling resources, marketing their products together, and transporting products to distant markets. Cooperatives would thus help to decrease interaction with White merchants and product brokers (Reynolds 2002, 10; de Jong 2005, 399). In a 2005 interview by the author, John Zippert, a co-founder of the FSC and the current director of program operations at the FSC/LAF's Rural Training and Research Center in Epes, Alabama, explained that the way cooperatives share benefits "based upon participation was a good way to work with people because it contained elements of equity, democracy, and sharing—and blended in with the movement philosophy." Charles Prejean, the co-founder and first executive director of the FSC, noted in a 1992 interview that from 1954 through the 1960s, he worked with Father Al McKnight to promote adult literacy and educate people about cooperative economics, starting credit unions, and supporting cooperative development.[3] McKnight and Prejean operated through the Southern Consumers' Cooperative in Louisiana. Community economic development and cooperative business development efforts were also pursued in Mississippi, North Carolina, South Carolina, Georgia, Tennessee, and Kentucky, according to Prejean (1992, 16; see also FSC/LAF 1992; Woods 1998; and Zippert 2005).[4] The Southwest Alabama Farmers' Cooperative Association (SWAFCA) and the FSC emerged out of these efforts.

SWAFCA was formed in 1967 by a group of African American farmers whose families had farmed the same land for more than two centuries. Its goal was to keep Black farmers and former sharecroppers in the region and on their land (de Jong 2005, 399). SWAFCA developed out of Black farmers' interest in diversifying and was followed by a campaign that included voter registration and other activities. The organizers of SWAFCA brought together eighteen hundred Black farmers through outreach, voter registration drives, and other mutual-assistance activities (Reynolds 2002, 12).

The federal Office of Economic Opportunity (OEO) provided SWAFCA with a grant of $399,967 as part of its new mandate in 1967 to fund rural programs that would counter the trend of migration out of the South. In 1968 the OEO granted the group another $595,751, and the Economic Development Administration gave them a planning grant of $87,000 to study the viability of expansion (de Jong 2005, 399–400). The project was to serve eight hundred families in ten Black Belt counties. SWAFCA became an example of "what could be achieved through local initiative combined with federal assistance" (400). In the first year, it saved its members an average of $2 per ton on fertilizer and enabled members to sell their crops for a total of $52,000. SWAFCA worked with the Farmers Home Administration to help members qualify for mortgages and loans—a strategy pursued by Freedom Farm in the 1970s, as we saw in the previous chapter. While SWAFCA achieved significant marketing successes, despite White opposition, challenges arose with respect to its management, cooperative education program, and access to markets (Reynolds 2002, 12). Overall, however, the cooperative increased members' economic security by working with them to reduce their operating costs, diversify their crops, and raise their incomes.

In 1968, the OEO awarded grants to four more southern cooperatives, and the USDA reported lending more than $13 million to eleven hundred low-income cooperatives in twenty-two states, among them the North Bolivar County Farm Cooperative (NBCFC). USDA officials pledged to intensify their efforts to help poor people establish cooperatives. According to de Jong, "Federal interest and the examples set by projects like SWAFCA and the NBCFC encouraged a proliferation of rural cooperatives in the South in the late 1960s" (2005, 402). Where cooperative development was connected to Black political power, poverty was reduced, Black local populations increased, and out-migration decreased. Activists realized that political gains, not just economic resources, had to be secured: "black activists rejected migration as a solution to social problems and instead sought improved public services and economic development for their communities" (de Jong 2005, 404; see also FSC/LAF 1992; Hamer 1971b; Woods 1998, 2007). Cooperatives proved to be an important economic support for that strategy. While there was opposition—both local Whites and southern Whites in Congress tended to oppose these programs (see Woods 1998)— opponents could sometimes be persuaded by the self-help nature of cooperative development and the lessening of the financial burden on southern state coffers.

SWAFCA, like other emerging cooperatives across the South, had to address the usual challenges: lack of both adequate capital and organizational and technical expertise. In response to these challenges, organizers saw the need to create a regional entity that could "serve as a means of connecting and supporting all the diverse co-op efforts struggling to get under way in the South" (Bethell 1982, 6). In February 1967, twenty-two cooperatives, including SWAFCA, came together and established the Federation of South Cooperatives (Reynolds 2002, 11).

The Early Years of the FSC

The FSC was part of the effort on the part of African Americans to formalize their cooperative efforts and obtain needed financial and technical assistance (Reynolds 2002). Zippert (2012) credits support with helping to establish the FSC from a coalition of civil rights organizations—including the Congress of Racial Equality, the Student Non-Violent Coordinating Committee, and the Southern Christian Leadership Conference—whose purpose was to develop a regional economic development capacity in the South (see also de Jong 2010, 80). Prejean reflects that the FSC was "founded in [the] climate of raised expectations, determination, and hopefulness" created by the successes of the civil rights movement, adding, "clothed in the garment of first class citizenship rights, economic betterment seemed more achievable than ever" (1999, 12, 13).

Part of that activism and sense of possibility included finding resources to support the economic empowerment side of the movement. Several regional organizations in the South developed in the mid-1960s to engage not only in cooperative development but also in policy advocacy, in part to direct federal resources (in particular, the Southern Regional Council and the National Sharecroppers Fund) to this kind of development in the South (Prejean 1992). Prejean mentions that the Southern Regional Council and the National Sharecroppers Fund helped to convene meetings of all the entities in the region involved in cooperative economic development, and from those meetings the FSC developed (1992, 23). According to the FSC/LAF's 1992 annual report (the twenty-fifth-anniversary edition), one specific meeting convened by the Southern Regional Council in the spring of 1966 at the Mt. Beulah Center in Mississippi led a small group of leaders and representatives from several southern cooperatives and support groups to draft a proposal to the Ford Foundation for the establishment of what they called the Southern Cooperative Development Program. The Cooperative League of the USA (CLUSA) and the International Self-Help Housing Association also supported this effort. At the same time, groups from other southern states joined the meetings, and interest grew in forming a larger regional organization—a federation—that could do more (FSC/LAF 1992, 8). The groups identified common needs and agreed that they could best be met by an effective regional federation. These needs included management skills, capital for development and expansion, and operational funds, board of directors' training, member training, and management training, and technical assistance (Prejean 1992, 24). According to Bethell, the idea for the FSC arose from questions about how to address the challenges of finding capital, and the "absence of organizational and technical expertise" for cooperative development in the South (1982, 6). De Jong includes interest on the part of federal officials in the "War on Poverty" to stop the Black out-migration and to reduce southern Black poverty as also contributing to the climate and context for the development of the FSC (early grants came from this source).

The Federation of Southern Cooperatives was chartered on August 4, 1967, under the Cooperative Associations Act of the District of Columbia. The FSC was founded by twenty-two cooperatives who had met in February of that year at the Interdenominational Theological Center in Atlanta, Georgia, agreed to form a federation, and elected a steering committee to develop the articles of incorporation and by-laws for the new organization (FSC/LAF 1992, 8). The FSC was founded to put together a new umbrella organization intended to serve as a means of connecting and supporting all of the diverse co-op efforts in the South at that time (Bethell 1982, 6), and to promote cooperative development among low-income and Black farmers and rural communities.

The founding cooperatives and credit unions in seven southern states were primarily agricultural marketing and supply co-ops, although they included some fishing, consumer, handicraft production, housing, and other co-ops. The FSC was organized with representation through state associations. Member organizations (the cooperatives and other community organizations) belonged to state associations and voted for representatives to the board of directors. The organization grew rapidly. By October 1968 membership had increased to forty-five cooperatives, with about 10,000 individual members. By August 1970, the FSC had 100 member cooperatives and 25,000 individual members (Busby 1970, 1). The staff increased from 5 to 62 during the same period. Reynolds notes that from its original 22 members, the Federation leaped to 130 cooperative members by the mid-1970s (2002, 12). The FSC spans fourteen states, but most of its members are from Alabama and Mississippi, with the largest FSC cooperative being the Southwest Alabama Farmers' Cooperative Association.

Early assistance came to the FSC from CLUSA, which used part of an OEO grant to hire the FSC's first executive director, Charles Prejean. The FSC established its headquarters in Atlanta. At the same time that the FSC was forming, the Ford Foundation funded the Southern Cooperative Development Program for three years, and the steering committee named Father Albert McKnight its director in Louisiana. In addition, among the 1968 OEO grants mentioned above was a grant of $592,870 to the Federation of Southern

Cooperatives "to provide research and technical support services to its thirty-eight member organizations" (de Jong 2005, 402).

The FSC also had plans to start a rural training center, and began to search for appropriate land to purchase. The Panola Land Buyers Association, with the help of the FSC and some of its support organizations, purchased a 1,164-acre tract of land near Epes, Alabama, in 1970.[5] This was a difficult transaction because local White elites, led by the mayor of Livingston, sought to oppose their efforts (Bethell 1982, 8; Zippert 2005). "Panola members [eventually] built homes on part of it, while FSC established a training center and demonstration farm on the remaining part" (Reynolds 2002, 12). The PLBA eventually established a housing cooperative, the Wendy Hills Co-op Community, in 1980 with forty units of housing (FSC/LAF 1992, 66). The PLBA then constructed two more subsidized multifamily housing units, the Griffin-Mandela Apartments in Greensboro, Alabama, and the Sanders and Black Apartments in Eutaw, Alabama.

The FSC's Rural Training and Research Center in Epes trains young people in cooperative business development and sustainable farming and forestry, and supports a demonstration farm where the federation "raised pigs and vegetables, built greenhouses, and repaired farm equipment in its own welding shop" (Bethell 1982, 9). In addition, the training center maintains a small conference center with an eighty-bed dormitory. The center received new funding starting in 1972, with a grant from the Office of Minority Business Enterprise. This allowed the FSC to open thirteen offices in seven southern states and provide technical assistance and loan packages for rural business ventures and cooperative development (FSC/LAF 1992, 66). The training center facilitated much of this early technical assistance. John Zippert became the director of the training center and director of programs for the FSC/LAF, a position he continues to hold today.[6]

A Note About the Southern Cooperative Development Fund

In 1970, the staffs of the FSC and the Southern Cooperative Development Program were joined under the FSC. But Father McKnight soon separated permanently from the FSC. In 1969, the FSC worked with the Ford Foundation on the feasibility of establishing a developmental loan/equity fund. According to the FSC/LAF, the feasibility study recommended the development of a separate corporation, to be called the Southern Cooperative Development Fund (SCDF), that would be a subsidiary of sorts of the FSC, with a partially overlapping board of directors. The initial funding went to the FSC, which established the SCDF and created its board of directors (including some board members selected by outside investors, as the study suggested). Since the Southern Cooperative Development *Program* was coming to an end, the FSC board designated Father McKnight as the director of the SCDF. Loans from the SCDF were originally restricted to member cooperatives of the FSC (FSC/LAF 1992, 26).

By 1971, the political climate in the federal government was changing. The Nixon administration was less than enthusiastic about the antipoverty programs put in place by the Johnson administration. According to the FSC/LAF, the OEO started requiring external evaluations of the cooperative development programs it had funded as a way to reduce or defund them. The FSC board joined other OEO-funded cooperative development programs to oppose the evaluation. When it came time to renew OEO funding in 1972, an organization could not receive new funds without the external evaluation. The FSC refused the evaluation but submitted a proposal anyway. The OEO negotiated instead with Father McKnight separately, and funded the SCDF but not the FSC (FSC/LAF 1992, 27; see also Prejean 1992; Zippert 2005). The funders pushed for the separation. This split the SCDF board of directors, but the SCDF did vote to accept the money. At the same time, the Ford Foundation changed the focus of the FSC's new grant away from broad regional cooperative development and movement building to supporting a few economically viable cooperatives. Ford also suggested a restructuring of the FSC's board to include non-co-op representatives. The FSC's board did not accept these conditions. The Ford Foundation then negotiated with Father McKnight and the SCDF board to establish a new not-for-profit, the Southern Development Foundation, along with the SCDF. The Southern Development Foundation was set up to promote the same kind of southern cooperative development in which the FSC was already engaged.

There is a more complicated story here than I have space or inclination to cover. I will not attempt to provide any more details or analyze why this happened.[7] The organizations severed ties in 1972. The Southern Development Foundation was short-lived, but the SCDF remains in existence. The FSC/LAF eventually started its own revolving loan fund. Things appeared to have been reconciled by the time the FSC celebrated its twenty-fifth anniversary in 1992. The annual report for that year includes a short reflection by Father McKnight, who praised the FSC: "Unlike so many organizations that have gone out of existence, the fact that the Federation/LAF is still here shows its staying power. One of the things that I've always admired of the personel [sic] at the Federation is their commitment to the struggle."

I will comment that the forced separation of the SCDF from the FSC, and the creation of the rival Southern Development Foundation, caused a serious split in the Black cooperative movement in the South. The FSC/LAF's 1992 report concludes, "Many of us in the cooperative movement feel that the funding sources, for their own reasons and interests, conspired to drive a wedge into the growing unity and development of the cooperative movement in the South. It is clear in retrospect that some ways should have been found to overcome these conflicts and outwit those who sought to diminish or possibly to destroy the power and influence of a united cooperative movement" (27).

FSC Accomplishments

The 1960s and early 1970s were a time of significant cooperative development among southern Blacks (and northern Blacks as well; see the time line at the end of the book). They built upon the previous history of cooperative development from the late 1800s and the 1930s and '40s. The infusion of public money was important because many Black farmers were quite poor, and small family farms were being displaced by large corporate agriculture. The consolidation of education and other technical assistance to African American cooperatives was also important, and it allowed for the proliferation of cooperatives. While significant public and private grants helped develop and support agricultural cooperatives in African American communities in the South, these grants came with strings attached and undermined the unity among Black cooperators. In this complicated and frustrating climate, African Americans joined together to form the Federation of Southern Cooperatives, which remains to this day a strong and viable support organization.

In 1985, the FSC and the Emergency Land Fund association merged so as to better protect Black landowners. Ralph Paige became executive director of the new FSC/LAF, and he continues to serve in this capacity.[8]

The FSC/LAF has held together a membership of what has sometimes been more than a hundred cooperatives, credit unions, and community-based economic development organizations involving twenty-five thousand mostly Black rural and low-income families, including some ten thousand family farmers who own half a million acres of land. The FSC/LAF's budget grew from $547,473 in 1970, to $3,196,746 in 2001, to $3.5 million in 2010–11, with $3.5 million in total assets; its annual budget in the 2000s was roughly $3 million (FSC/LAF 2012). Over its forty-seven-year history, the FSC/LAF and its state associations of cooperatives have developed and assisted hundreds of cooperatives, credit unions, and community-based economic-development projects in fourteen states. Currently, there are approximately seventy-five active members of the FSC/LAF. In each of its fiscal years 2011–12 and 2012–13, the organization helped start five new cooperatives and held more than ninety workshops, conferences, and board trainings (FSC/LAF 2012, 2013).

For most of its history, the FSC/LAF's programs have pursued the following six goals:

- to develop cooperatives and credit unions as a means for people to enhance the quality of their lives and improve their communities;
- to save, protect and expand the land holdings of black family farmers and landowners in the South;
- to develop a unique and effective Rural Training and Research Center to provide information, skills and awareness, in a cultural context to help our members and constituents to build strong rural communities;
- to promote and develop safe, sanitary and affordable housing opportunities for our members in rural communities;
- to develop and advocate and support public policies to benefit our membership of black and other family farmers; and low-income people living in rural communities;
- to support and sustain the work of the Federation for the long term by developing a succession plan, capital campaign and fully funding the "Forty Acres and A Mule Endowment Fund." (FSC/LAF 2007, 18)

The FSC/LAF also devotes some of its time to state and federal policy advocacy to support Black farmers, Black land retention, and cooperative development. It contributes to the development of agriculture policies and advocates for measures to be included in state and federal farm bills and other legislation, and provides legal advice to members and the community about land retention and their rights in land disputes and unfair treatment by government agencies. In this capacity, the FSC/LAF is a networking organization and coalition builder, working with rural coalitions, small farmers, organic farmers' organizations, the sustainable agriculture movement, and the U.S. cooperative movement. The FSC/LAF also provides members with estate planning to help reduce their property disputes. Following the Hurricane Katrina disaster in the Gulf Coast in 2005, the FSC/LAF developed an emergency relief capacity and replicated the "Farmers as First Responders

TM" program to provide hurricane survivors directly with fresh produce as soon after a disaster as possible.

I have worked with the FSC/LAF to help articulate and measure the federation's and its affiliate cooperatives' and development centers' impacts on their local communities. The FSC/LAF has provided numerous services and leadership experiences; saved family estates; reduced farmers' costs; increased revenues and enhanced stability for members (through producer, marketing, consumer, and credit cooperatives); and taught techniques and skills to hundreds of people. We tried to calculate the worth of all these services, but it was impossible because there were so many indirect and informal services and benefits attached to every service. In addition, other services and benefits were leveraged from the direct services, and many intangible benefits thus spilled over. A rough estimate of the monetary impact of the first forty years of the FSC/LAF, beyond its direct calculable services, is more than $500 million. Over its first forty years, the FSC/LAF leveraged resources worth five times the amount of direct funding raised (more than $50 million). The FSC/LAF has facilitated savings of more than $34.7 million by 16,155 people in member credit unions, and has made more than 79,000 loans to low-income people, totaling more than $239 million. The FSC/LAF has facilitated $80 million in sales through cooperative marketing, created $26 million worth of housing units (constructed and rehabilitated), and saved more than $200 million worth of land (FSC/LAF 2007, 11). The FSC/LAF also assisted five thousand Black farmers in saving more than 175,000 acres of land, and helped more than seven hundred families find affordable housing (FSC/LAF 2002, 7–8). It has employed and trained more than five hundred people, including VISTA volunteers, interns, and trainees. Its workshops and education programs have provided skills, knowledge, awareness, and sensitivity to working creatively on behalf of poor people, in addition to providing introductory cooperative business development courses and board training. Many former employees of the FSC/LAF have gone on to work in positions of significance in the region, among them members of Congress, state legislators, county commissioners, school board members, program directors, bank managers, attorneys, social workers, college faculty, and foundation staff (Paige 2001).

The FSC/LAF's land-retention activities have allowed members not only to keep control over inherited property but to make a living from farming, engage in sustainable agriculture, branch into alternative crops, increase their farm income, and decrease their off-farm income. As noted above, the organization also provides training and legal services, all of which contribute to income generation, wealth creation, and quality of life in rural southern communities.

Through the FSC/LAF, individuals and communities create opportunities for themselves and find a safe haven and productive work that facilitate their economic well-being and stability and help them improve their lives and remain active in civil rights and the political arena. Cooperative ownership provides meaningful, steady, profitable work, access to financial services, human capital development, and a panoply of increased opportunities. In addition, the FSC/LAF provides young people with skills, educational opportunities, and economic activities that contribute to their becoming productive adults, good citizens, and partners with adults in cooperative enterprises. The federation also publicizes its achievements in leadership development and highlights the significant roles of women in the organization (Paige 2001).

Asset Building Through the FSC/LAF

Cooperative agricultural production and marketing help individuals maintain land ownership and make a living from farming. Cooperatively owned processing plants help farmers earn more money from their produce, retain earnings, and invest in more equipment, supplies, and land. African American land retention and sustainable co-op agriculture are major objectives of the FSC/LAF. In its first thirty-five years, the federation helped save $87.5 million worth of land (175,000 acres at an average of $500 per acre) and construct or rehabilitate $26 million worth of affordable housing units (see table 9.1).

There is more concrete financial data about the community development credit unions (CDCUs) affiliated with the FSC/LAF. They all share the same mission—to provide financial services and loans to mostly rural low-income African Americans and other people of color. These credit unions provide financial services, savings opportunities, and loans to their members, thus

TABLE 9.1   FSC/LAF land retention, 1995–2002

	Acres	Value
Total land saved	4,054	$3,356,720
Total land purchased	1,633	$1,408,550
Five-year comparison	1995	2000
Number of farms	125	192
Alternative crops	54%	87% (2001)
Average gross income	$40,665	$55,413
Off-farm income	64%	52%

Source: FSC/LAF 2002.

helping low-income southern Black communities build assets. While keeping these credit unions in business has continued to be a challenge, especially when the large employers that are sometimes a credit union's base leave the area, some of the FSC/LAF-sponsored CDCUs have increased their assets and number of members (see table 9.2).

The number of CDCUs affiliated with the FSC/LAF has fallen to six, down from a high of eighteen in 2000. Table 9.2 shows, however, that the CDCUs have been increasing in number of members and assets, particularly before the economic downturn in 2008. Total assets were growing until that year: to approximately $39.6 million, or about $2,449 per member for eleven credit unions. In 2009, the total assets of the FSC/LAF CDCUs dropped significantly, but they recovered in 2010, only to drop again in 2011 and 2012 (partly because the number of CDCUs also dropped, although the reduction in assets continued even after the number of CDCUs stabilized). By 2012, the total assets of these credit unions had decreased to $21.8 million, and the average assets per member in the six CDCUs stood at $2,759, down from a high of $3,328 in 2010. At the beginning of the decade, the decline in the number of credit unions had only a small effect on the credit unions' membership numbers, total assets, and value of shares as a whole. Each year since 2010, however, CDCU assets have been declining, as have the number of members and value of shares. The earlier trend of increasing financial assets wavered and now is in decline. Loans have increased: in 2008, eleven CDCU's made 79,286 loans, the total value of which was $239.5 million. In 2012, the total number of loans made by the six remaining CDCUs, was 57,662—still a significant number and an increase from 2011. The total value of those loans—$194.3 million—was high, but outstanding loans had suffered a huge decline by 2012. Shares (holdings or savings in share accounts) for the members of these credit unions have fluctuated, reaching a high of $34.7 million in 2008, recovering a bit in 2010, and falling since then. The value of shares was down to $17.3 million in 2012. The value of shares per member, however, increased from $2,152 in 2008 to $2,715 in 2011, but then decreased in 2012. This is important because even the amount of $2,189 per member represents significant average savings for low-income people, especially during a period of serious recession and high unemployment, when many people were losing assets, had no assets at all, and/or were in debt. It is also a significant amount given that African Americans' median net worth in 2009 was less than $6,000 (Kochhar, Fry, and Taylor 2011). That members of these credit unions can average almost $2,000 in savings accounts is impressive and hopeful. In addition, the credit unions provide personal loans, car loans, and home mortgages to some of their depositors, thus facilitating asset building in this population. The FSC/

TABLE 9.2 FSC/LAF credit unions: Members, assets, savings, loans, 2000–2012

Year and # of CDCUs	Number of members	Assets (in millions of dollars)	Average assets per member	Member shares saved in millions of dollars	Average value of shares per member	Outstanding loans (in millions of dollars)	Total number of loans	Total value of loans (in millions of dollars)
2000 (17)	12,140	$23.3	$1,923	$19.4	$1,594	$17.23	63,710	$72.3
2001 (16)	13,743	$27.2	$1,980	$22.2	$1,614	$16.3	50,154	$97.5
2002 (16)	15,046	$30.1	$2,000	$24.2	$1,605	$18.5	53,207	$113.3
2003 (14)	14,971	$32.3	$2,157	$25.9	$1,728	$21.1	56,415	$144.3
2004 (14)	19,785	$37.6	$1,980	$29.8	$1,614	$20.4	60,392	$157
2005 (14)	27,225	$36.6	$1,344	$30.5	$1,122	$32.6	69,059	$205.5
2006 (14)	27,649	$38.1	$1,378	$26.9	$972	$25.3	75,516	$211.4
2007 (11)	16,648	$38	$2,284	$33	$1,983	$27.2	–	–
2008 (11)	16,155	$39.6	$2,449	$34.7	$2,152	$25.2	79,286	$239.5
2009 (8)	11,219	$33	$2,941	$28.9	$2,576	$24.1	–	–
2010a (8)	11,478	$38.2	$3,328	$29.1	$2,538	$26.2	76,837	$262.6
2010b (6)	8,637	$27.2	$3,149	$23.4	$2,709	$19.5	–	–
2011 (6)	8,542	$26.1	$3,056	$23.2	$2,715	$19.4	56,214	$190.2
2012 (6)	7,902	$21.8	$2,759	$17.3	$2,189	$4.1	57,662	$194.3

Sources: FSC/LAF annual reports, 2000–2012; assets per member and shares per member calculated by author.
Note: Data are not available for the cells that contain no figures. There are two rows for 2010 so that results for 2010a, based on eight credit unions, can be compared with 2009. By 2011, only six credit unions affiliated with the FSC/LAF remained. I provide data for these six in 2010b so that they can be compared with 2011 and 2012 statistics.

LAF notes that these "locally owned and operated financial institutions help people to pool their savings and assets to work toward self-directed community development from the 'bottom-up' " (2012, 16).

A Note on the Decrease in the Number of Credit Unions Associated with the FSC/LAF

As of 2011, the number of credit unions associated with the FSC/LAF stood at an all-time low of six. There was also a significant decrease in FSC/LAF credit union members in 2007, which reflects the smaller number of credit unions. The reason for this drop is that over the previous decade, some of the smaller credit unions were forced to merge with larger credit unions, not all of which were in the FSC/LAF. This happened around the country to small rural and urban credit unions alike, but this trend hit the CDCUs of the FSC/LAF particularly hard. During this period, the federal regulator, the National Credit Union Administration (NCUA) liquidated or consolidated more than half of the FSC/LAF's CDCUs because of their small size. This explains the dramatic decrease in the number of CDCUs left in the FSC/LAF network, and why no new CDCUs have been chartered in the South in the past ten years. The FSC/LAF explains that "the cautious regulatory policies of NCUA defeat a major organizing strategy of the Federation, which is helping low-income people and distressed communities in the rural Black Belt South to organize and develop their own financial institutions" (2012, 16). The NCUA's lack of understanding of the importance of these grassroots financial institutions to the Black community limits the ability of the FSC/LAF to provide support and asset-building opportunities to its members.

The Federation Weathers Federal Investigation

For its entire existence, the FSC/LAF has operated in the racially challenging context of the rural South. Attempts to undermine its effectiveness are not unusual. The federation has been vulnerable because it supports not just the economic development of Black farmers in the South but also cooperative development and African American land ownership. In addition, the FSC was active in organizing farmers to press for civil rights and for "more favorable, equal access to public policies" (Reynolds 2002, 12). Such multiple roles, while necessary, have provoked deep hostilities in the racially segregated politics of the South (see Woods 1998; Reynolds 2002). The most difficult challenges have arisen when local hostilities and federal policies combined to undermine the federation and its programs. As we have seen, the FSC initially received significant support from federal authorities, including grants from the OEO, USDA, and the Department of Labor. Yet, with the transition in federal leadership during the Nixon era, national agencies began to harass and oppose African American economic experiments. For example, the USDA, which funds cooperative extension services at land-grant universities and supports outreach to farmers across the country, blocked initiatives for training about cooperatives for Black farmers in the late 1960s and 1970s (Reynolds 2002, 13). The collusion of federal and local authorities against Black cooperatives even led to a federal investigation of the FSC in the late 1970s.[9]

According to Bethell, local Whites strategized about how to undermine the FSC, which they considered a threat. In May 1979, a number of Whites, including representatives of Alabama's U.S. senators, congressional representative Richard Shelby, and others, came together to discuss the FSC. Eventually, Shelby requested an investigation by the GAO (at that time the General Accounting Office, now the Government Accountability Office, the investigative arm of Congress) into the FSC on charges of abuse of federal funds (Bethell 1982, 14). The GAO concluded in September of 1979 that an investigation was unwarranted.

In early December 1979, however, the FBI began an investigation of the FSC, requesting broad information about the organization, including membership lists, curricula used in training sessions, and funding proposals. On December 31, 1979, the FBI issued a subpoena to executive director Charles Prejean. Uncertain of the reasons for the investigation or the charges, the FSC responded that it would be willing to provide information into specific allegations of individual wrongdoing, but would not agree to turn over the information on a general request. A second subpoena was then provided, which detailed more specific items. The FSC complied and shipped twenty-two file drawers of information to the FBI office in Birmingham. The FBI then began to visit FSC members and citizens broadly affiliated with FSC activities. These visits were not simple inquiries or fact-finding missions; instead, agents asked questions such as, "Did you know that the Federation was ripping off the government?" and "Who did you have to sleep with while you were [at the FSC dormitories]?" (Bethell 1982, 14–15). Moreover, grand jury proceedings investigating the charges against the FSC occurred regularly.

The grand jury investigation had a significant impact on the FSC. Unlike the usual political attacks by political enemies, it had a legitimacy that frightened community supporters and members alike. Prejean estimated a fundraising loss of close to $1 million, above and beyond the costs of staff time and legal defense. The loss of federal funds at this time was particularly damaging because the Carter administration had appointed officials who were sympathetic to the federation's goals (Bethell 1982, 16, 2). The FSC at this point brought together a few foundations and organizations working on civil rights to publicize the FBI's harassment and to attempt to get the Department of Justice to respond.

On May 20, 1981, the U.S. attorney for the northern district of Alabama announced that it would not prosecute the FSC. Moreover, neither the U.S. attorney's office nor its superiors would provide information on the reason for the eighteen-month grand jury investigation or the reason for its termination (Bethell 1982, 2). Even with the effective termination of the grand jury inquiry and the lack of indictment, this case initiated the withdrawal of federal support from the FSC. This incident had a lasting impact on the FSC and its members, who have since been suspicious of certain kinds of support. Even more important, the incident increased the organization's vulnerability and marginality. It is also another example of the kinds of harassment and sabotage that Black cooperative organizations have suffered throughout their history.

Brief Highlights of Some FSC/LAF Member Cooperatives

The North Bolivar County Farm Cooperative

In 1973, Helena Wilkening described the North Bolivar County Farm Cooperative (NBCFC) to potential funders as a cooperative incorporated in December 1969 "for the purposes of economic development, education support and welfare assistance," and noted that the cooperative supported "a community center in Rosedale, the Afro-American Book Store and Library in Mound Bayou [its headquarters], several sewing and clothing cooperatives in Rosedale and Shelby, and a low-income housing development covering 20 acres in Rosedale" (Wilkening 1973, 3). In 1973, the farm had 424 acres of land planted mostly in soybeans, with some in cotton and a few vegetables. According to Lefkowitz, the NBCFC was started by the North Bolivar County Health Council and the Tufts-Delta Health Center in Mound Bayou, Mississippi, as "a more permanent response to the problem" of malnutrition that would treat health issues rather than just their symptoms. It was "born not only of hunger but also from the realization that growing crops was one thing the North Bolivar County residents could do well" (Lefkowitz 2007, 38–39). Similarly, de Jong describes the NBCFC as an outgrowth of the Tufts-Delta Health Center, started in April 1968 with initial funding from the Office of

Economic Opportunity and "an anonymous northern donor."[10] De Jong also reports that the NBCFC bought forty acres of land and rented another eighty acres from local Black farmers, and put 250 members to work for $4 in cash plus $6 in food credit per day. In addition, members could buy food from the co-op at minimal cost. In its first season, the cooperative produced more than one million pounds of food, enough to "end hunger in the area served by the co-op" (de Jong 2005, 401). The NBCFC was a founding member of the FSC, and its managers were advisors to Fannie Lou Hamer and Freedom Farm in the early 1970s. It continues to be a successful farm cooperative today.

South Plaquemines United Fisheries Cooperative

The South Plaquemines United Fisheries Cooperative in Louisiana took shape after Hurricane Katrina hit the Gulf Coast in August 2005, when members attended cooperative education workshops that were part of the FSC/ LAF hurricane-relief efforts (Livingston 2007b, 20). For generations, the fishers of Plaquemines Parish had access only to private commercial docks to buy essential services and to sell their catch. Most families lived below the poverty line.

When Hurricane Katrina hit, 80 percent of the parish's commercial fleet was destroyed and almost every dock was washed away, along with the equipment and businesses of those who lived by the water. The "multicultural fishing community," surmounting "overwhelming obstacles," came together to form a cooperative in the aftermath. This diverse community included African Americans and Native Americans whose families have lived in the area for generations, as well as Vietnamese and other Southeast Asian newcomers looking for work and entrepreneurial opportunities. With the help of the FSC/LAF and the USDA's rural development specialists, the group's steering committee developed a feasibility study and business plan. Committee members also surveyed potential members and found that the fishers (men and women) in the area were very interested in forming a cooperative and in working together to "create a more robust community" (Livingston 2007, 20–21). This would allow them to own their own boats and their own company. In all, fifty families joined the new marketing cooperative, trading in shrimp, crab, and oysters. The South Plaquemines United Fisheries Cooperative has earned grants for boat repairs and co-op facilities, in addition to a large Community Development Block Grant from the state of Louisiana to develop a docking facility. The new dock gave co-op members better access and ability to fish. Collective marketing has also helped them earn a good price for their catch and allowed them to connect with lucrative markets.[11]

Carver Homes Worker's Cooperative

The Carver Homes Worker's Cooperative started with a convenience store in the Carver Homes public housing community that operated from 1976 to 1988 in Atlanta, Georgia. The housing project's manager, Louise Watley, had been interested in starting such a store in the 1960s, but things did not come together until 1976. The co-op started with a grant from the U.S. Department of Housing and Urban Development. From there, money was raised to start a sewing cooperative to employ women-owners from Carver Homes. Grants from local churches as well as the FSC made this possible. Funding from a Community Development Block Grant enabled the co-op to renovate a school building for the sewing factory, which also houses a community center with a wellness center and food and clothing banks (FSC/LAF 1992, 47).

Concluding Observations

As noted above, the FSC/LAF is the largest and most influential African American cooperative development organization in the United States. It is the only system of networked co-op development centers controlled by African Americans in the country. That it has persisted for forty-seven years, in both good and bad financial times, and has supported major cooperative endeavors throughout the South, even when the U.S. government and funders tried to undermine its effectiveness, attests to the fortitude of the member organizations and individuals, and to the persistence of its leadership. This chapter is a brief case study of a complex organization with a long history. Much more needs to be documented and analyzed.[12]

The FSC understood from its inception in 1967 the necessity of Black control over land and African American economic self-sufficiency. The southern states were then, and remain today, some of the poorest in the country. In the 1960s and '70s, African American poverty was severe. The plantation bloc and remnants of Confederate rule made it difficult to make reforms or institute meaningful antipoverty strategies for Blacks. African American sharecroppers were evicted from their farms, and laborers lost their jobs because they exercised their right to register to vote or even to listen to a civil rights speech. Agricultural and marketing cooperatives, credit unions, and legal services provided or supported by the FSC/LAF decreased the economic insecurity and exploitation imposed by the White plantation bloc, and helped to sustain Black communities on their own terms. The FSC/LAF has also helped to slow the loss of Black-owned land in the South.

Although economic cooperation has a long history in African American communities, the FSC/LAF's efforts are particularly noteworthy. Few organizations in the South can claim to have done as much in advancing the interests of African American farmers, protecting land ownership, and building cooperative enterprises, thus supporting rural development. As Paige put it in 1992, "being out there in the trenches has been a constant battle, but we are providing an alternative to the existing system. We're empowering people to take control over their own lives, which often forces change on the entire community . . . changes that demand community institutions to be more just" (FSC/LAF 1992, 11). It is not just the organizational and economic accomplishments that are noteworthy, but also the development of the members. The leadership and skill development of the people associated with the FSC/LAF has been one of the organization's major successes. The history and growth of the federation not only demonstrates the African American pursuit of economic cooperation; it also provides insight into the nuances of development strategy in the challenging context of the rural South. Issues of structure, strategy, and leadership within the organization must be seen in the context of the racial and political dynamics of the deep South.

In many ways, the story of the Federation of Southern Cooperatives/Land Assistance Fund tells in microcosm the broader history of African American cooperatives. The reasons why it was started, its goals and aims, its challenges and threats, its focus on grassroots empowerment, economic independence, leadership development, and women's development—all are elements of the entire experience of the Black cooperative movement.

10

ECONOMIC SOLIDARITY IN THE AFRICAN AMERICAN COOPERATIVE MOVEMENT

Connections, Cohesiveness, and Leadership Development

The economic basis of African life was originally cooperative. . . . Cooperation was one of nature's more important schemes for survival.
—WILLIAMS (1993, 151)

It is the opinion of the writer, based on several years of study of co-operation and having sat in two of the National Co-operative Congresses, that co-operation offers great promise of being the solution for the economic riddle confronting the Negro, just as it has been a way out for other oppressed groups for over three-quarters of a century.
—MATNEY (1930, 49)

The past three years show us why it is time to consider a different approach to owner-ship: cooperatives. If more assets and businesses were owned and controlled by the people who use them, our economy could be more stable.
—LEIGH (2011, 1)

Almost all African American leaders and major thinkers, from the most con-servative to the most radical, have at some point promoted cooperative eco-nomic development as a strategy for African American well-being and liberation. We have seen examples of how cooperative economic development provides economic stability, camaraderie, resource and profit sharing, educa-tion and training, high-quality goods and services, and community develop-ment. W. E. B. Du Bois expressed the sentiments of many when he said that by using cooperative economic development, Blacks could change the paradigm, create African American leadership of a new industrial structure, and enter the "new city" as men and women, not chattel (1933a, 162–63). These senti-ments point to the need for African Americans to create their own eco-nomic reality, to think outside the box economically, and to use cooperative

This chapter incorporates, in heavily revised form, parts of Gordon Nembhard and Haynes 2002; Gordon Nembhard 2004b, 2006b, and 2008d; and Haynes and Gordon Nembhard 1999.

economics as a way to develop industrial leaders among the race. In many ways, the documentation provided in this book is a history of just that.

This chapter focuses on the ways in which the African American cooperative movement has been built around an ideology of economic solidarity. The first section explores the notion of solidarity as it relates to cooperative economics, and especially to camaraderie, networking and clustering, collective financing, and worker sovereignty among subaltern groups, as shown in the first nine chapters of this book. In addition, this chapter reviews examples of youth involvement in cooperatives, past and present, particularly as youth development and engagement in cooperative business ownership point us toward the future. A brief section discussing the importance of leadership development in cooperatives, and ways in which leadership spills over into civic engagement more broadly, follows. The chapter ends with some reflections on the significance of African American cooperative development, particularly for Black communities.

Solidarity

From Gherardi and Masiero we learn that cooperation is a deliberate and necessary expansion of in-group solidarity and cohesion: "Solidarity regulates cooperation on the basis of shared customs, values and norms. Or else it works through a process whereby actors identify themselves with a social group and create a collective identity. . . . [We define] solidarity as a relational pattern, a form of collective behavior and a networking activity based on trust" (1990, 554). Shipp recognizes solidarity as important to the success of the Mondragon Cooperative Corporation, for example, where solidarity "was achieved through cultural cohesiveness." "The importance of culture as a binding agent," Shipp contends, "explains how disadvantaged groups come together to achieve a common purpose—e.g., to fight against oppression" (quoted in Feldman and Gordon Nembhard 2001, 28).[1]

The cooperative movement among African Americans has also been strongly influenced by feelings of racial and community solidarity. African Americans have come together to solve their economic problems using their racial and economic identity, religious affiliations, and commonality of need. The ex-slave pension movement used a sense of solidarity and the experience of common exploitation to come together and form a mutual-aid society and launch a political advocacy movement for reparations. The members of the APR Masonry Arts Corporation came together to address marginalization in their union and economic discrimination (see below). Black farmers needed collectively to combat land loss, discrimination in credit markets, and limited access to and fairness in product markets.

Many new urban cooperatives include in their mission improving the quality of life and community empowerment. Jobs are anchored in the community and local products are supported. Good, healthy, local food and green energy are provided. Many cooperatives also tend to use local suppliers and to share resources with other cooperatives and with community organizations and residents. The pooling of resources is empowering because it reduces dependence on outsiders—on businesses hostile or indifferent to the group or the cooperative structure—and increases self-reliance and locally controlled income generation. Many cooperatives take their commitment to the community seriously, and put aside funds for community development and community charities, in addition to depending on community support. Large corporations, franchises, and branch offices, by contrast, tend to send dollars out of a community without circulating much within the community first, and rarely have a local focus that would bring either tangible or intangible benefits to the local community (see Fairbairn et al. 1991).

Cooperatives allow members to help one another—to reduce the cost of living and buy one another's products, for example. Perhaps the most successful economic outcome is that cooperatives provide African Americans with affordable, high-quality products, especially healthy food, and often environmentally friendly products and practices. They promote local products, inspire the community with a vision of alternatives, and provide goods and services that neither the government nor the private sector provides, at least not adequately or affordably. This is particularly true in the areas of healthy food, organic food, alternative and green energy, child care, health care, home health care, utilities, and banking. Local agriculture and buying clubs, for example, help lessen food insecurity and are viewed as community-building activities (*Journal of Cooperative Development* 1998a).The Federation of Southern Cooperatives/Land Assistance Fund also addresses food insecurity and local control over healthy food systems.

African American cooperatives formed in the 1930s and '40s provided affordable food, gasoline, and banking services. We saw this in the Consumers' Cooperative Trading Company of Gary, Indiana; the Red Circle Cooperative of Richmond, Virginia; Harlem's Own Cooperative and the Modern Co-op in New York City; and the Walker Credit Union in Montreal (started by the Brotherhood of Sleeping Car Porters). More recently, the Chester Community Grocery Co-op in Chester, Pennsylvania, was established in 2006, after Chester went without a supermarket for sixteen years, thanks to the city's deindustrialization (Livingston 2007a, 22); the Mandela Foods Cooperative in

Oakland, California, similarly arose in response to a lack of supermarkets and fresh vegetables in the community. A chapter of the Nation of Islam started a food cooperative—the OST/MacGregor Food Cooperative—in Houston, Texas, on June 30, 2012, in an attempt to provide healthy, high-quality food choices to a neighborhood suffering from a lack of fruit, vegetables, and other healthy affordable food. Student minister Robert Muhammad worked with Muhammad Mosque no. 45 to research and design this co-op (Muhammad 2012).

The cooperative movement among Black trade unionists, led by the Knights of Labor and the Colored Farmers' National Alliance and Co-operative Union in the late nineteenth century, for example, and the Ladies' Auxiliary to the Brotherhood of Sleeping Car Porters in the mid-twentieth, also kept dollars in the hands of workers and helped them control what they made and what they consumed, strengthening Black workers' positions and their families' rights and well-being.

Worker Sovereignty

Worker sovereignty is also a form of economic solidarity. Worker sovereignty refers to privileging labor over capital, or balancing returns to labor and returns to capital. Many of the cooperatives studied in this book, especially the worker cooperatives, strove to create good, even great, jobs, with good working conditions and benefits, decent pay, flexibility, dignity, and profit sharing. Returns to capital are important, but solvency, employee benefits, and high-quality products are more important. While the focus of cooperatives in all communities is often on consumers, concern for workers and increasing the quality of both the work and the product have also been issues, especially for Black cooperators, and have become increasingly important.

The cooperatives started by or affiliated with labor unions exemplify this. Chapter 1 of this book looked at efforts by the Knights of Labor and other early Black trade unions. Chapter 4 explored the efforts at cooperative education and development by the International Brotherhood of Sleeping Car Porters. In the late twentieth century, Cooperative Home Care Associates unionized in order to focus on engaging members in improving workplace conditions and to offer affordable health insurance for the worker-owners. The APR Masonry Arts Corporation was a unionized, worker-owned African American masonry construction company organized in the late 1990s. Unionized African American bricklayers in Los Angeles were underemployed and felt discriminated against. The union was not successful in addressing their needs. Both the union and management agreed that helping the African

American bricklayers form their own company, particularly as a cooperative, would be the best solution. After seven years of organizing and fund-raising, with help from the A. Philip Randolph Educational Fund, a not-for-profit in Washington, D.C., and from Ownership Associates in Boston, the cooperative was launched in August 1998 (Hill and Mackin 2002). It worked mostly on jobs in the Black community and made sure that all members had work. Cash-flow difficulties contributed to the business's shutting down in 2005.[2]

The Lusty Ladies Theater, a peep show worker cooperative in San Francisco, was bought by the theater's workers, bouncers, and janitors after winning union representation, when the owner decided to sell rather than own a union ship. The worker co-op rotates management positions between the member-owners, gives all dancers access to the more lucrative windows, hires women of all races and body types, and provides women of color with the same conditions and opportunities as every other dancer.[3] This is unprecedented in that industry.

In one case that I found in my research, there was tension between the cooperative and the union. For Harlem River Cooperative, a consumer co-op whose workers were members of a traditional union, the union did not understand the co-op model, and the co-op manager could not figure out how to combine the consumer co-op's need for member and community control over some decisions with the union's need to maintain control over certain workplace processes. They eventually came to an agreement, but not without first endangering the success of the co-op and polarizing the board and community around the issues. In general, however, the connection between labor unions and cooperative development is historic and continues relatively successfully in each era.

Solidarity in Late Twentieth-Century Black Cooperatives

Solidarity and cultural/racial loyalty have been important motivators for cooperative development among African Americans, especially in the twentieth century, as we saw in the Universal Negro Improvement Association's economic projects and those of the Ladies' Auxiliary to the Brotherhood of Sleeping Car Porters. According to Curl, the Poor People's Corporation, organized in 1965 by a former SNCC field worker in Jackson, Mississippi, provides another example. Within four years the PPC was running thirteen producer cooperatives and a marketing co-op, producing sewing, leather and wood crafts, and candles, and had more than eight hundred members, mostly former sharecroppers. The 1964–65 Black voter registration drives and the Selma-to-Montgomery "March for Freedom" contributed to the formation of the Southwest Alabama Farmers' Cooperative Association, discussed in chapter 9. Within a few years, this co-op included eighteen hundred families, making it the largest agricultural co-op in the South. Originally, eight of the families were White. But harassment by racist politicians and businessmen followed, and banks and suppliers refused to deal with the co-op until the Whites withdrew (Curl 1980, 45).

John Lewis, former head of SNCC and a U.S. congressman from Georgia for the past twenty-seven years, describes the work he did with the Southern Regional Council's Community Organizing Project, which began in the late 1960s and reflects the sense of solidarity behind Black cooperative development. Lewis became director of the Community Organizing Project in October 1967. He explains that the project's main focus was to establish "cooperatives, credit unions and community development groups" throughout the deep South. Lewis describes participating in intensive grassroots organizing to help people obtain food, shelter, and jobs. In these places, "the civil rights movement was old news," with press coverage moving north to cover the Black Panthers, riots, campus unrest, and Vietnam War protests, according to Lewis. People could vote, but they did not have enough to eat. "My job was about helping these people join together," Lewis writes, "helping them help one another to fill those needs. It was about showing people how to pool what money they had to form a bank of their own, a credit union. Or how to band together to buy groceries, or feed, or seed, in bulk amounts at low prices—how to form cooperatives" (Lewis 1998, 398–99). Lewis discusses helping farmers' wives organize quilting cooperatives and using the money to buy a refrigerator, stove, or washing machine. He mentions working with Charles Prejean, the director of the Southern Regional Council and the first executive director of the Federation of Southern Cooperatives. For Lewis, community organizing for cooperative development was important training in direct organizing and finding collective solutions. Similarly, Fannie Lou Hamer found in the 1970s that working for voting rights was not enough; Whites used economic retaliation, and people needed to control their own food, housing, land, and work. She turned to cooperative economic development.

Curl summarizes activities by the Black Panthers in the late 1960s and early 1970s. The "inter-communalist" Black Panther Party, begun in 1966 in Oakland, organized a host of "survival programs pending political revolution." These included distribution of free shoes (from their own factory), clothing, food, health care, plumbing repair, pest control, and transportation for the aged. Communal houses provided shelter for BPP workers. The Panthers also promoted cooperative housing for the community and established cooperative bakeries and free breakfast programs for children (see also Joseph 2012). According to Jamal Joseph, one of the New York Panther 21, in addition to self-defense, the Panthers' major objective was economic development and self-help in Black urban communities. Their free breakfast programs included collecting neighborhood food and financial donations, and educating children about their African heritage and civil rights. Their community organizing and economic programs included selling newspapers and joint ownership and collective businesses to provide employment and needed products. In addition, the Black Panthers in Oakland successfully used long boycotts to pressure community businesses to invest in the community through the Panthers' social projects (Curl 1980, 45, 49).

According to Ellison (1980), the most important organization promoting Black cooperatives was the Congress of African Peoples (CAP), led by the poet and playwright Amiri Baraka, a leader of the Black arts movement. The CAP later became the Revolutionary Communist League and then the U.S. League for Revolutionary Struggle, focusing on the struggle for liberation of the Black working class (Frazier 2006, 155). Ellison notes that CAP inspired community-action agencies to organize consumer cooperatives and low-income credit unions, especially in Brooklyn in the 1970s, as well as in Cleveland, Pittsburgh, Detroit, Youngstown, Chicago, Houston, Milwaukee, San Francisco, and Los Angeles. In addition, the Black Media, Inc. Cooperative (BMI Cooperative) of Black newspapers provides advertising and other services for the more than one hundred papers that are members. BMI Cooperative also produces a monthly supplement, the *National Black Monitor.* Ellison also discusses community investment cooperatives established in several Black cities in the 1970s.

The Apex Taxi Cab Cooperative in Milwaukee, Wisconsin, began in January 1973 and closed in late 1974. Although it had a short history, it showed that cab ownership was viable for African Americans.[4] (Washington, D.C., also had an African American–owned cooperative cab company for several years.) The company bought thirty new cabs at the outset. One of the company's competitive advantages was that, unlike the White cab companies, its drivers were willing to take passengers to any part of the city. Here is where solidarity with the community gave Apex a market advantage. After eighteen months of relatively successful operation, however, the taxi cooperative could not afford the high insurance premiums and went out of business soon after dropping the exorbitant group insurance, even though some of the taxi drivers paid their own insurance premiums. In this case, a viable concept was thwarted by a hostile insurance provider.

The SSC Employment Agency in Baltimore was a worker-owned cooperative temp agency in the hospitality industry.[5] Baltimore BUILD (Baltimoreans

United in Leadership Development), a community-organizing and advocacy organization, wanted to support businesses that would hire "hard-to-employ" local residents, develop their skills and career mobility, and provide good jobs with ownership possibilities. BUILD established SSC in 1997, at the height of the growth in the hospitality industry around the revitalized Baltimore Harbor. Providing temporary workers in a fast-growing industry positioned SSC to succeed. BUILD hired a local Black-owned management company to run the business until the workers were trained to take over. After working for 160 hours, workers were eligible to apply to become members, at an investment of $100 each. As more and more workers became eligible to be owners, the agency became self-managing and truly worker-owned. As the company grew, it provided annual dividends to each owner in addition to job security within the cooperative, decent wages, and opportunities for advancement.

External Solidarity

Solidarity can extend past one's own group or community. Melman (2002) uses the term "social cement" to describe what co-op members in Spain's Mondragon Cooperative feel: both an internal sense of cultural and ethnic solidarity and loyalty to the group, and an external solidarity with other groups and movements in the world (see also MacLeod 1997). External solidarity is related to the principles of intercooperation and concern for community. The sense of cohesion, trust, and teamwork extends outward to others engaged in similar cooperative projects around the world. African Americans have supported cooperative efforts in other countries, particularly in Africa; the FSC/LAF supports cooperative development programs in several African countries and the Caribbean.

The extension of solidarity beyond the immediate group is also exemplified in national support for local efforts. Fannie Lou Hamer depended on national support for Freedom Farm. Hamer worked with Measure for Measure out of Madison, Wisconsin, and accepted speaking engagements all over the country to raise money for Freedom Farm and its projects (Mills 2007; Lee 2000). In 1969, high school students from northern cities conducted a series of walks against hunger, raising $120,000 that Freedom Farm spent on farm equipment and the down payment on 620 acres of farmland. The singer and activist Harry Belafonte made several contributions to Freedom Farm. He also wrote a fund-raising letter in May 1969 in which he described Freedom Farm as an "example of initiative, racial cooperation and political militancy worthy of the support of all decent Americans" (Mills 2007, 258, 260).

Such contributions definitely extended the sense of solidarity to a broad community of support.

The FSC/LAF and its member cooperatives joined local credit unions and other cooperatives in responding after Hurricane Katrina devastated the Gulf Coast in August 2005. These groups and their members helped with disaster relief and in revitalizing farmers' markets, cooperative businesses, farms, and local economies in general with physical, financial, and spiritual support. Similar aid was provided by the FSC/LAF in 2011, after fierce tornados swept through western Alabama. Small worker cooperatives are helping to revitalize immigrant communities in Brooklyn (Bransburg 2011), communities of color in Oakland (Abell 2011; Mandela Foods Cooperative 2010), and Black women's prospects in the Hill District of Pittsburgh (Raftis 2010).

These projects and many others are not reinventing the wheel of cooperative development among low-income and subaltern populations—they are continuing the legacy. Working together, sharing resources, developing workshops, creating jobs, providing goods and services, developing leaders, building economic solidarity to match their social cohesion—Black cooperators are showing the courage and fortitude of their ancestors, their past leaders, and their neighbors. This book has shown that there has been a continuous thread of cooperative activity and development in Black communities over the past two centuries. The few attempts at national federations, such as the Young Negroes' Co-operative League, were only somewhat successful, but they were nonetheless serious and significant. Inadequate support and outside threats have been an ongoing challenge, but the overall accomplishment has been the planting and nurturing of the seeds of cooperation, the maturation of fledgling efforts, and the flowering of viable cooperative businesses.

Networking and Regional Economic Development

Making connections with other cooperatives; sharing information, education, and training; buying in bulk; advertising and marketing together—these are all ways in which cooperatives network and form necessary alliances. While all of these elements are important, networking is one of the most important, because often a local cooperative cannot meet all of its own needs, as we saw in the case of Freedom Farm. Networking, especially with other cooperatives, tends to be one of the most efficient ways to address these needs. Cooperatives that have strong networks tend to be more successful than those that do not.

The Young Negroes' Co-operative League, the Eastern Carolina Council, and the FSC/LAF are national or regional cooperative organizations discussed in detail in previous chapters. The FSC/LAF is the best present-day example of this networking strategy, but it by no means incorporates all the elements of cooperative networking. The YNCL attempted to create a networked system in the early 1930s that would connect cooperative councils in major cities to a national infrastructure to develop and supply cooperatives throughout Black communities during the Great Depression. The YNCL's goal was to supply all needs within the cooperative movement, especially the African American cooperative movement, and thus to create the products and employment African Americans needed and keep the wealth flowing within the African American community.

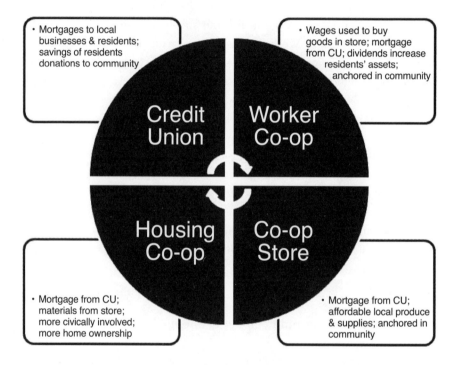

Figure 10.1 provides the skeleton of a model of a networked local cooperative system that reduces dependence on outside resources, links cooperatively owned businesses, and keeps exchanges recirculating among cooperatively owned enterprises. While such a model is still rare, in that most cooperatives are relatively isolated, the networked model graphically portrays potential linkages and shows how cooperative principles work together and how a cooperative commonwealth could work.

Another approach to networking, or building a cooperative commonwealth, refers to creating a system of interlocking cooperatives that supply one another and help to keep local money recirculating among grassroots and local businesses (see Fairbairn et al. 1991). The Mondragon Cooperative Corporation (MCC) is usually showcased as an example of interlocking cooperative systems within the greater Basque communities throughout northern Spain, because it started from a community high school and a worker-owned factory in 1956 and became a cooperative holding company that includes hundreds of worker cooperatives and a credit union that became the seventh-largest financial institution in Spain. The MCC boasts its own social security system, a university, and a nationwide consumer retail store, and it galvanized worker cooperative development in the region (see http://www.mondragon-corporation.com/language/en-US/ENG.aspx; Melman 2002; Gordon Nembhard and Haynes 2002). The MCC became a regional organization that then extended internationally. It is one of the most successful cooperative systems in the world. The recirculation of money within the network, the use of services, know-how, and surplus from one sector in aiding another sector, and the linkage of all the cooperatives through financial services, a social security system, and research and development all contribute to Mondragon's successes.

One development strategy for marginal, disadvantaged, underserved, and oppressed groups is to use economic cooperation and group solidarity to create businesses that will provide meaningful work and income, greater control for workers, and the possibility of wealth creation. The cooperative history documented in this book confirms that cooperatives are an important community economic development tool in Black communities because of their economic and social benefits. They recirculate local resources; support education and training; create jobs and meaningful work; address market failure and marginality; are economically and environmentally sustainable; facilitate joint ownership; build wealth; require democratic participation; develop leadership capacity; and promote civic participation. They are a mechanism to provide most of the elements that we look for in economic development: efficient resource allocation, profit or surplus, human capital development, social capital leveraging, and individual and community prosperity. Table 10.1 provides a summary of some of the ways in which cooperative ownership addresses challenges in rural and urban development. The examples in this book have illustrated how a housing cooperative, for example, provides affordable, dignified housing, or how a credit union provides affordable financial services, especially in areas abandoned by traditional banks or preyed upon by subprime and payday lenders.

TABLE 10.1   Urban and rural challenges and cooperative solutions

	Urban and rural challenges	Cooperative solutions
Capital	Export of capital and industry to foreign soil and to other areas of the United States Inadequate wages Few employment benefits Out-migration and loss of youth	Cooperative solutions Worker-owned and managed businesses Community-owned businesses Geographic stability One member, one vote: no tyranny of capital Nontraditional assets developed, alternative resources leveraged Individual and community entrepreneurship nurtured
Credit	Credit crunch, redlining Lack of banking services Predatory lending and alternative finance businesses (check cashing, title loans, payday loans, pawnshops) Impaired credit Lack of asset-building opportunities	Community development credit unions (CDCUs) Alternative and creative community financing Public/private partnerships and leveraging Pooling capital and other resources (lending circles, solidarity groups) Use of nontraditional resources and alternative assets (social energy, "sweat equity," etc.)
Industry and employment	Underdevelopment Remnants of old industrial practices Unoccupied sites and businesses Weak resource sectors Unemployment, underemployment	Democratic governance and ownership foster use of effective, innovative, flexible strategies and organizational forms that support competitive enterprises Individual and community entrepreneurship given formal structures and support Social entrepreneurship and investing Income-generating and wealth-producing enterprises developed Marketing or producer cooperatives Worker cooperatives
Education and training	Poor quality of education Lack of skills, inadequate or inappropriate labor force training and participation Skills mismatch High rates of adult illiteracy	Educational mission; continual education is a priority Learning by doing is rewarded Commitment to training workers, managers, and new members Self-management Vertical and horizontal mobility "Social energy," nontraditional skills recognized
Housing and property values	Skyrocketing property values Lack of affordable housing Inadequate housing—poor quality, poor location	Affordable housing through cooperative housing and land trusts Community land trusts Increased quality of economic activity increases land use; ownership structure can keep properties affordable Community-based revitalization of commercial areas
Elder services	Increasing poor elderly population	Cooperative housing and cooperative home health-care services, for example, are low-cost, high-quality alternatives particularly suited to serve the elderly
Food sufficiency	Lack of access to affordable and quality food Poor dietary practices	Cooperative grocery stores Food buying clubs Community gardens in housing communities and schools
Child care	Poor child-care services	Worker co-op (quality employment creates quality services) Parent-run (consumer) co-op Nonprofit day-care operation

Source: Revised version of table 1 in Gordon Nembhard 2006a.

Policy and Legislative Advocacy

Networking and regional collaboration also includes collaboration in policy advocacy. Cooperatives and their support organizations, such as Cooperative Home Care Associates in New York City, ChildSpace in Philadelphia, and the FSC/LAF in the South, are advocates in both the training and policy arenas. They bring together coalitions, for example, to influence policy to improve working conditions, pay, and benefits in their industries. CHCA helped to form the New York City Home Care Work Group to promote restructuring of the industry, created the nonprofit Paraprofessional Healthcare Institute to provide training in this area and to replicate the CHCA model, and then, in cooperation with other health-care and consumer organizations, started the nonprofit Independence Care System, Inc. to serve people with disabilities who receive Medicaid (Glasser and Brecher 2002; see also http://www.chcany.org). CHCA has strong connections with its union (SEIU 1099), and together they promote internal policies to support employees and strengthen employee-management relations. ChildSpace also collaborates with unions, child-care advocates, other practitioners, and the public sector to advocate for public policies to support increased quality of life for child-care workers (Clamp 2002).[6]

As we saw in chapter 9, the FSC/LAF has initiated and supported legislation that helps small farmers at the state and national levels, and engages in class-action suits, helping farmers file petitions and make legal claims (see the FSC/LAF annual reports for 2009 and 2010, available from the FSC/LAF; Paige 2001). These examples of policy advocacy demonstrate the ways in which cooperatives are able to influence regulations and practices in their industries that not only help their businesses and aid their workers but also aid their clients and others in their industry.

Financial Support and Capitalization

Financial support, financial services, reinvestment, and general capitalization are crucial to the success of cooperatives. Networked cooperative enterprises often address the need for these goods by pooling resources in an institutionalized way and through joint ownership and profit sharing. Here, credit union examples are the most relevant. The Mondragon Cooperative Corporation's credit union, Caja Laboral, has played a crucial role in the development and maintenance of the Mondragon system (see Thomas 2000; Mathews 2002). Credit unions have provided access to credit and safe places to save money, and have used members' savings to help other members own a car or home, start a business (or cooperative), etc. (see Gordon Nembhard 2010). Many of the early Black co-op societies established credit unions to pool deposits, provide affordable financial services, and improve members' access to credit and mortgages. There are about two hundred community development credit unions (CDCUs) in the United States whose purpose is to provide financial services to low-income communities. Some of the CDCUs are predominantly Black, and about six of them (down from sixteen at the beginning of this century) are affiliated with the FSC/LAF, as we saw in the previous chapter. In the United States, most credit unions can engage in only a small percentage of commercial and business services (even to other cooperatives) but can provide full services for individual members of cooperatives. CDCUs are permitted in engage in more small business services, often for other cooperatives. Credit unions, particularly CDCUs, are important community-based institutions that provide fair, low-cost credit and financial services to those who lack access to banks, as well as to low-wealth communities. Credit unions have community-lending boards and use alternative lending criteria. They rely less, for example, on credit reports and more on employment status and the ability of members to pay rent and utility bills. In using such alternative methods to decide to provide loans to low-income families, CDCUs help low-income families build credit. Some of the credit unions also offer innovative services and instruments designed to be flexible in helping their members, or specifically designed to help them start saving or increase their savings. Members can open and maintain accounts with low balances, and they often earn higher interest rates than they would with conventional banks (Gordon Nembhard 2010).

In 1969 the "Black Manifesto" of the National Black Economic Development Conference in Detroit offered another strategy for capitalizing Black cooperatives. The manifesto demanded reparations of $500,000 for African Americans, in part to establish a southern land bank and cooperative businesses in the United States and Africa (National Black Economic Conference 1969). The National Black Economic Development Conferences in 1969 and 1972 stressed economic empowerment and cooperative economics, demanding reparations for investment in those strategies. Similarly, Callie House and the Ex-Slave Mutual Relief, Bounty and Pension Association demanded slave pensions (reparations), and started using dues from members to finance their mutual-aid society and community activities (Berry 2005). Another example is the FSC/LAF's participation in the suit against the U.S. Department of Agriculture for financial compensation for unfair loan conditions and unfair denial of loans to African American farmers (see chapter 9).

African Americans have experienced cooperatives as viable businesses with good returns to their owners and the community. Over the past century,

Black-owned cooperatives have provided dividends to their members, in addition to economic control over land, land and homeownership, quality products, and jobs. In 1871, for example, the collectively owned Chesapeake Marine Railway and Dry Dock Company paid members a stock dividend totaling $14,000 (on eight thousand outstanding shares). In the 1920s, the Cooperative Society of Bluefield Colored Institute in North Carolina paid dividends of 10 percent on purchases made to its student-owners. In 1932, People's Credit Union in New York City paid dividends to members (for 1931) at 6 percent, for a total of $350. "More than 250 members received from 5 cents to $30, according to the number of shares held, and the length of time they had held the shares" for more than thirty days (*Negro World* 1932, 2).

In 1935, Consumers' Cooperative Trading Company in Gary, Indiana, began to pay dividends of 2 percent on shares of stock owned. In the 1990s, Cooperative Home Care Associates started paying their worker-owners dividends worth 25 percent of the initial investment in profitable years (Schneider 2009). The FSC/LAF's member credit unions have helped members save more than $2,500 per member on average. These are not trivial accomplishments.

Financing, therefore, is about both pooling resources and creating mechanisms for pooling resources, but it is also about identifying the sources of financial discrimination and demanding reparations or compensation. Using solidarity, racial pride, and a sense of belonging—both to connect people, organizations, and enterprises and to satisfy these kinds of needs—has been crucial to the development of African American cooperatives. At the same time, even as many cooperatives have faced problems with raising capital and gaining credit for expansion, or to address temporary cash flow imbalances, some have been assets for their members through dividend payments.

Youth Development

There is increasing evidence that young people who engage in entrepreneurial projects, especially cooperative businesses, gain benefits such as more confidence, increased general and technical skills, more motivation to learn, and the incentive (and sometimes the funding) to go on to college.[7] Participation in cooperative business endeavors teaches students business, math, research, and communication skills, resourcefulness and problem solving, teamwork, and the facilitation skills needed to participate in democratic enterprises. At the same time, it fosters concern for community and facilitates community-building strategies among youth (Gordon Nembhard and Pang 2003; Pang, Gordon Nembhard, and Holowach 2006). Curriculum development sensitive to the needs of democratic businesses can combine teaching critical thinking, problem solving, and team building, along with the necessary technical and business skills (see Skilton-Sylvester 2003). Schools can facilitate experiences that develop good learning habits and creative, flexible thinking by teaching cooperative economics and providing cooperative entrepreneurship experiences. Through school-based cooperative economic experiences, young people can also become active participants in democratic enterprises and civil society.

Schools and education programs have also been important cooperative developers in the African American community, sometimes through churches, but often in public and private high schools. Examples include the Bluefield Colored Institute, Bricks Rural Life School, Tyrrell County Training School, and the Consumers' Cooperative Trading Company in the 1930s, and some of the southern Black colleges and junior colleges in the 1940s (see chapter 4). The YNCL focused on engaging and training African American youths in cooperative economics in the 1930s. More recently, school gardens have led some students to participate in farmers markets' and develop their own co-ops.

School-Based and Other Youth Cooperatives

In the modern period, school-based cooperative businesses range from in-class role playing and model city experiments such as "Sweet Cakes Town" (Skilton-Sylvester 1994), to schoolwide credit unions and school stores, to school-based farmers markets and buying clubs, to other businesses and projects that operate on school grounds during the school day, after school, and during the summer. In addition, some youth-development programs outside schools use students from a particular school or class, or provide services, workshops, or training to school-age children, sometimes in a school setting. Cooperative entrepreneurship is being fostered in some schools as part of the school gardening experience.

Food from the 'Hood

In the fall of 1992, students from Crenshaw High School in South Central Los Angeles revitalized the school garden to help rebuild their community after the 1992 rebellion in Watts, a neighborhood that erupted in frustration after the police who beat Rodney King were acquitted. The students donated the food they had grown to the homeless. After turning a profit selling produce at a farmers' market, they decided to develop a business plan for product development. Food from the 'Hood began selling salad dressing made from the produce they grew in the school garden. This enterprise was managed by the students and run like a cooperative business. At least 50 percent of the profits were dedicated to college scholarships. Over a ten-year period, more than $180,000 was awarded in college scholarships to seventy-seven student managers (Dorson 2003).[8]

The Urban Nutrition Initiative

Similarly, the University of Pennsylvania partnered with the West Philadelphia Partnership and Philadelphia public schools to promote school-based community health with the Urban Nutrition Initiative (UNI). This interdisciplinary program uses college students studying horticulture and nutrition to teach high school students, who then teach middle school students, who then teach elementary school students, about health, nutrition, and business development. This is a learning-by-doing experience for all involved at every level. It is a "dynamic educational process based on experiential learning and community problem-solving" integrated with public service (UNI 2002, 3). The program combines a community health curriculum, school-based urban gardens, and entrepreneurial and business development. Students (mostly African American) combine learning about nutrition, teaching it to others, growing healthy food, and creating businesses to sell and market the food. The businesses they create are cooperative purchasing clubs, food co-ops, and farmers' markets. The young participants develop entrepreneurship and many related skills (math, science, marketing, communication), engaging in school and community service through a "democratic collaborative process" (8, 3). In 2003, for example, as part of the summer jobs program of the Center for Community Partnerships, six students from University City High School's eco-tech learning community, using funds from the school district, worked with UNI to develop plans for a food cooperative in the neighborhood (Rossi 2003). The purpose was to supplement the Saturday farmers' market that the UNI had already established. Students and the community wanted to provide affordable healthy food for the neighborhood on a daily basis, as well as jobs for the students using an empowering ownership structure.

Sankofa Youth Agricultural Project and the FSC/LAF

The youth-development arm of the Federation of Southern Cooperatives/ Land Assistance Fund teaches African American youths about economic paradigms, cooperatives, and business development. One strategy is to help young people make connections between democratic economic concepts and their own cultural and family values (Gordon Nembhard 2002b). For example, FSC/LAF educators remind students of the principles celebrated during the Kwanzaa festivals (in particular Ujamaa, or cooperative economics; see Karenga 1989). Another strategy is to point out everyday paradigms or systems, discuss them, and show how they can be changed (see Gordon Nembhard 2002b; Gordon Nembhard and Pang 2003). Only after these preliminaries do the programs address democratic economic structures and the question of how young people can begin to create their own businesses and cooperative enterprises. The FSC/LAF provides both cooperative development workshops and summer programs for youth.

One of the federation's youth projects is the Sankofa Youth Agricultural Project, started in March 2004, which helps young people enter the field of agriculture and introduces them to cooperatives "as instruments that are capable of advancing the agenda of rural economic and social development" (Sankofa Youth Agricultural Project 2011). Young people learn farming techniques, raise chickens, sell produce and homemade T-shirts, and develop business skills. The project also established a youth worker cooperative, the Ella Baker Youth Cooperative.

Chain Reaction

Another project combines youth entrepreneurship and sustainable transportation. Chain Reaction was a project of the EcoDesign Corps of Shaw Eco-Village in Washington, D.C., founded in 1997. Shaw EcoVillage's mission is to develop youth leaders and build sustainable communities. Youths in the EcoDesign Corps participate by creating educational workshops and creating and implementing their own community-development and urban-planning projects (Shaw EcoVillage 2005). High school students work with college-age leaders and professional mentors.

After conducting an experiment about effective modes of transportation in Washington, D.C., the youth corps created Chain Reaction to educate young people about bicycle transportation and teach them how to repair, recycle, and resell bicycles in the Shaw neighborhood. The EcoDesign Corps used as a model a New York City youth bike-repair program. Between 2001, when the full-service bicycle shop opened, and 2005, about 120 youths became active members and mechanics, cooperatively managing the business. Six young mechanics (each in the program for at least two years) graduated to careers in the bicycle industry. More than two hundred bicycles were donated to the program, and more than 180 were recycled for new owners. More than fifty young people were trained in basic bike repairs and safe riding techniques. Chain Reaction provided bicycle-repair workshops in schools around Washington, D.C., in-school bike-safety clubs, and vocational training camps, in addition to community bike festivals and the full-service store. All revenues were reinvested to support the work of the young mechanics, educational workshops, and for inventory. Chain Reaction won the Washington Area Bicyclists Association Award in 2003 (Varney 2003; Shaw EcoVillage 2005).

Toxic Soil Busters Cooperative

Toxic Soil Busters Cooperative is a lead-abatement business created and managed by youths in Worcester, Massachusetts.[9] Started in 2006 by two youths as part of an extracurricular project sponsored by the not-for-profit Worcester Roots, young people learn about environmental hazards and environmental racism, and how to be proactive about environmental sustainability. They help to detoxify their communities and advocate for environmental policies. They use theater to advertise their services, communicate their message, and educate their audiences about lead poisoning and other toxic waste in their homes and backyards. The students first research the issue, receive training in soil cleansing, and hone their communication skills. They provide soil testing, consultation and detoxification services, lead-safe landscaping services, outreach services, video production, and training. While not explicitly school-based, Toxic Soil Busters is part of a youth-development program that combines study, policy advocacy, and economic action with self-education, public education, and entrepreneurship.

The Impact of Cooperative Engagement Among Black Youths

These examples illustrate the potential for cooperative development through youth development. They represent a range of activities available to schools and after-school programs to involve students in their own economic development as well as their community's well-being. The use of cooperative economic principles enables these students to develop social capital and benefit materially as well as academically and personally. Preliminary analyses of these programs show that students increase academic confidence; gain academic, communication, and business skills; sustain viable businesses; and educate other students and residents about their businesses and their goals and mission (Gordon Nembhard 2008a, 2008d). These enterprises also serve as training grounds for more formal cooperative business development when these young people become adults.

The relative lack of cooperative education in high school curricula may be a significant oversight, particularly for inner-city youths of color, who are likely to live in an economically underserved or underdeveloped community and to experience a lack of capital, a lack of access to capital, and racial discrimination in labor and capital markets and workplaces. At the same time, they may have strong bonds with their peers and an interest in helping their communities (Gordon Nembhard and Pang 2003). Often, what is dismissed as undesirable activity—such as involvement in a gang or an illegal trade—has the potential to become the basis for building strong peer bonds and entrepreneurship. Cooperative business development is a viable strategy for helping students creatively produce a good or service on their own terms. Educating inner-city youths not only in economic decision making but also about cooperatives can help them to use peer bonds in legitimate businesses. These businesses allow them to work together, share ideas, learn skills, earn money, and minimize financial risks. Cooperatives facilitate entrepreneurial activity as the engine of economic growth and originality. There are tremendous barriers to starting businesses in inner cities, such as raising the necessary startup money, finding space and affording a good location, training employees and managers, and securing clients. A strong, creative economics curriculum that includes the study of cooperatives and business development can help students expand their economic potential by exposing them to a variety of economic business options, increasing their skill sets, and reducing barriers to entry. School-based cooperative businesses also face fewer barriers than other startups, since the school usually provides the space and business advisors, and sometimes also funding and clientele.

I have written about using collective entrepreneurship and cooperative development to help motivate high school students to continue in school and become activists (Gordon Nembhard 2005, 2008d). Some examples exist of high school curricula that include teaching students how to run their own businesses, how to operate cooperative businesses, and how to be more involved in community development, school gardens, and other forms of urban renewal and community revitalization. Students in these programs learn to operate legitimate, viable businesses. These programs find that students are more engaged, graduate from high school, and in many cases even go on to college (see Gordon Nembhard 2005; Gordon Nembhard and Pang 2003; Pang, Gordon Nembhard, and Holowach 2006). These are promising curricular innovations that need more study and replication. More such programs would increase the number of high school graduates taking college economics and business courses, who are already thinking out of the box and eager to study alternative economics and community building. It could also increase the number of young people willing and able to establish or join cooperative enterprises.

Giving young people opportunities to build their communities, be involved in leadership development, and study and practice economic democracy in action involves them early in economic activity and may motivate them to be academic achievers. It increases their problem-solving and critical-thinking skills and develops their leadership skills. It also increases their involvement with adults and in developing their local community, as well as their connections to the Black cooperative movement and the broader cooperative and worker–cooperative movements.

Leadership Development and Social Capital

Cooperatives have always been aware of developing human capital (knowledge and training) along with trust among the members (social capital), but more recently they have also begun to articulate broader skills in social capital and leadership development in particular. The benefits to youths of involvement in worker and consumer cooperatives are just one example. My engagement in participatory action research and in observing co-op member meetings, conferences, and workshops suggests a growing recognition of and interest in the development of a variety of kinds of social capital within cooperatives. Shipp (2000) also finds social capital development in Black cooperative ownership. Indeed, the structure of democratic governance and the necessity of building trust and trustworthiness in order to operate a cooperative efficiently demand both skill and social capital development. This develops members' leadership skills within the co-op and equips them to go on and become leaders in other contexts. Cooperative members often point to members who "grew into" a position or became a leader within the organization or even out in the community (PTA leader, credit union board chair, community activist, etc.) (see Paige 2001 and Weiss and Clamp 1992 for examples).

Leadership development is often assumed but not well articulated as a benefit of cooperative ownership and participation. Cooperative members rarely articulate leadership development as an outcome or impact of democratic ownership. They do, however, sometimes discuss feeling more comfortable actively participating in their child's PTA at school, engaging more with their child's teacher, starting a community-based organization or being a board member (first of the cooperative and then in other organizations in the community), running for office—and in other ways being more active and assuming leadership outside the cooperative where the leadership was encouraged and groomed. Several of the staff members of the FSC/LAF, for example, maintain that leadership development has been one of the organization's major accomplishments, in addition to providing a means of making a living for many if not all of their members.

Weiss and Clamp found in their interviews with women worker-owners that cooperatives "afford women a number of important benefits, including empowerment, leadership training, learning opportunities not available in traditional work settings, and increased self-esteem" (1992, 225). Some of the members of the Watermark Association of Artisans in North Carolina (a co-op made up largely of women), for example, became generally active in their communities, completed college degrees, and served on the local PTA after becoming members of the cooperative (McKecuen 1992, 25). Cooperative Home Care Associates has been grooming worker-owners to become members of the board of directors and middle managers of the company. The SSC Employment Agency's worker-owners took over their company after incubation.

Civic Participation

Gordon Nembhard and Blasingame (2002, 2006) have explored the ways in which the skills and capacities developed in cooperative activities spill over into other areas of life and contribute to civic engagement and political participation.

Democratic participation and decision making, as well as skill and leadership development, often spill over into other arenas, as co-op members become more active in civic organizations and politics. Greenberg's study of the (predominantly White) Plywood Cooperatives, for example, examines the relationship between workplace democracy and political participation:

> With the exception of voting, about which no differences are found, worker-shareholders were significantly more active in all phases of political life than workers in conventional firms. Furthermore, the gap between workers in cooperatives and conventional firms increased over time, suggesting the existence of a political learning process. Finally, the data suggests that the experience of participation by worker-shareholders in enterprise decision making serves as the principal educative tool for political participation and increases involvement with various voluntary and community organizations. (1986, 131)

Gordon Nembhard and Blasingame have found that the political learning and governance experience in democratic workplaces help to develop transferable skills and capacities for increased political participation. "Co-op members and employee owners become used to the transparency and accountability in their own organizations (open book policies, one member one vote, shared management, etc.). They come to expect transparency and accountability and help re-create this in civil society and political arenas" (2002, 24). Networking and working together become normal behavior in similar situations, and the skills that facilitate this are developed in most co-op members. Cooperatives similarly develop and empower young people. Members of housing cooperatives are also more civically active (Kleine 2001).

Erdal 1999 found that social health and civic participation are positively related to measures of democratic ownership in Italy. Erdal compared three towns with similar demographics that differed in levels of cooperative ownership. The town with the highest cooperative (and worker) ownership had the highest levels of well-being and civic participation. Many of the African American cooperative strategies discussed in this volume were based on a notion of interlocking support systems that would help members avoid indifferent and hostile outside forces.

Back to the Future

History has shown that cooperatives are an important strategy for economic collaboration, racial economic independence, and community well-being. They develop leadership capacity and promote civic participation. Combining Du Bois's concept that through economic racial segregation African Americans could create, and position themselves at the cutting edge of, new economic relationships and formations, with the notion of a solidarity economy among subaltern populations creates a powerful tool for analyzing the accomplishments of African American cooperatives and their potential for future growth.[10]

We learn from the Mondragon experiment in Spain that a sense of solidarity combined with democracy and community involvement can spur economic development—sometimes even more successfully than other strategies can (see Abascal-Hildebrand 2002; Gherardi and Masiero 1990). As the Mondragon movement showed, success depends in large part on the ability of communities to identify existing individual and community assets and pool and organize them as a resource for production in cooperative enterprises (Gordon Nembhard and Haynes 2002, 2003). The Mondragon movement used a variety of strategies and activities to identify and activate these assets: participatory and applied research, popular education, networking, and various other innovations that cultivate knowledge of self and community, as well as skills in governance and enterprise development. The Mondragon model is an exciting example of how to combine humane interactions, solidarity and concern for community, cooperative organization, democratic governance, participatory management, and competitive business practices into a network of interlocking and mutually supportive economic and social enterprises that continually develop and change.

Are co-op members more involved in their communities? Do they join more organizations, assume leadership positions, run for office? Do fellow members or outsiders notice greater involvement by co-op members? I have argued in this chapter that the answer to all of these questions is yes, and the research supports this, but we do not yet have all of the answers. More research is still needed, because what we know is mostly anecdotal and from case studies. What we do know is that throughout African American history, leaders in many arenas were first involved in cooperatives in one way or another. While it has been difficult to connect the dots of individual African Americans moving from one cooperative activity to another, I have found that many of the people involved in one area of social change had also been involved with the cooperative movement or the promotion of cooperative principles—early Black trade unionists and clergy, W. E. B. Du Bois, Marcus Garvey, A. Philip Randolph, Halena Wilson, Nannie Helen Burroughs, John Hope II, E. Franklin Frazier, Ella Jo Baker, John Lewis, and Fannie Lou Hamer, to name some of the most significant. In terms of grassroots leadership, many more were active in their local communities, even if they did not gain national prominence. Once one studies the Black cooperative movement, it is impossible to ignore these connections.

We have learned from this history that cooperatives combine social and economic development. They use a sense of solidarity and concern for community to promote economic alternatives that create economic growth and sustainability. At the same time, their solidarity and collective action increase productivity and help to stabilize their economic circumstances. Moreover, cooperative economics is often viewed as a tool or strategy of a larger movement toward the elimination of economic exploitation and the transition to a new social order.

The history of cooperative ownership among African Americans presented in this book demonstrates how cooperatives have enabled low-income residents, women, and others to generate income and at the same time be family and community friendly and civically responsible. They have enabled low-income residents, women, immigrants, and other underserved people to provide affordable, high-quality goods and services, generate jobs, stabilize their communities, and accumulate some assets. As it continues to unfold, the history of African American cooperative ownership demonstrates that Black Americans have been successful in creating and maintaining collective and cooperatively owned enterprises that often provided not only economic stability but also developed many types of human and social capital, as well as economic independence. They have provided an alternative economic model based on recognizing and developing internal individual and community capacities. They have created mechanisms that distribute, recycle, and multiply local expertise and capital within a community, creating a solidarity economy. The potential is great, and the future of African American cooperatives is wide open—not just to continue on the margins but to flourish more fully. The seeds have been planted.

Time Line of African American Cooperative History, 1780–2012: Selected Events

1780   Establishment of the African Mutual Aid Society in Rhode Island by the African Methodist Church.

1787   The Free African Society is founded in Philadelphia by Richard Allen and Absalom Jones, the second African American mutual-aid society to open in the United States.

1790s   Women's mutual-aid societies proliferate.

1825   The Nashoba Commune is founded by Frances Wright for Blacks in Tennessee. It is an established community that divides hours between academic work and manual labor and prepares African American members for freedom and colonization outside the United States.

1830   The Negro convention movement in Philadelphia is an important stimulus to the growth of beneficial societies across the nation.

1831   The Wilberforce Colony in Ontario, Canada, is a Black self-sustaining commune, owning livestock, land, and a school.

1837   The Dawn Settlement in Dresden, Ontario, Canada, is founded by Josiah Henson, who escaped from enslavement in the United States.

1842   The Northampton Association of Education and Industry, founded in Northampton, Massachusetts, is an intentional, racially integrated community based around a communally owned silk mill.

1863   The Combahee River Colony, a collective in the South Carolina Sea Islands, is established by several hundred African American women during the Civil War (it remained relatively self-sufficient and semiautonomous).

1865   The Chesapeake Marine Railway and Dry Dock Company is established by the African American community of Baltimore as a "cooperative" joint-stock shipyard and caulking company, to provide work for skilled Blacks. It closes in 1883 after eighteen years, for a variety of reasons, including financial and management challenges.

1867   The Independent Order of Saint Luke, an African American women's sickness and death mutual-benefit association, is established in Maryland. Maggie Lena Walker becomes grand secretary in 1899, when the headquarters is reestablished in Richmond, Virginia.

Mid-1870s   The Colored Farmers Association is established in Texas.

1880   The Colored Grange of Tennessee is established.

1881   The Grand United Order of the True Reformers is established in Richmond, Virginia. Its branches grow throughout the South and East. This Black mutual-aid society owns real estate and a premium insurance company, and conducts banking services.

1882   The Negro Farmers' Alliance (or the Negro Alliance of Arkansas) is organized in Prairie County, Arkansas. Other African American farmers' alliances follow in other states, such as Texas.

1886   Colored Agricultural Wheels organize in the South, focusing on economic cooperation in addition to political and economic rights. They spread particularly in Alabama, Tennessee, and Arkansas.

Cooperative Workers of America is established in South Carolina, as is the Colored Alliance in Texas.

The Knights of Labor, a racially integrated union, expands significantly in the South and includes goals for the development of a "cooperative commonwealth." In September an all–African American chapter of the Knights of Labor convenes.

Leonora Barry is elected head of the new department of women's work at the Knights of Labor convention (Barry is the first professional woman labor organizer in U.S. history). Between 1886 and 1888 the Knights establish two hundred industrial co-ops, including an African American–owned cotton gin in Alabama and African American co-op villages in Birmingham.

Haymarket strike of 1886. Knights of Labor co-ops begin to decline economically as railroads refuse to haul their products, manufacturers refuse to sell them machinery, and wholesalers refuse them raw materials. Banks will not lend them money. The White National Farmers Alliance opposes and physically attacks the African American alliances.

The Colored Farmers' National Alliance and Co-operative Union (1886–91) forms in Houston County, Texas, to join the various local and statewide alliances, assist African Americans with marketing and mortgage payments, and protect African American farmers from the Ku Klux Klan and exploitive practices. It holds its first national meeting in 1888, and has more than a million members at its peak. It establishes exchanges (co-op stores) in African American communities in Norfolk, Charleston, Mobile, New Orleans, and Houston.

1894   The Workers' Mutual Aid Association is organized in Virginia.

1895   Lexington Savings Bank is incorporated in Baltimore with $10,000 raised by Black leaders.

The International Co-operative Alliance is founded in Europe and codifies the Rochdale principles, a set of ideals for operating cooperatives.

1896   The National Ex-Slave Mutual Relief, Bounty and Pension Association (a part-mutual-aid association) is founded in Tennessee, advocating for reparations for ex-slaves.

1897   The Coleman Manufacturing Company of Concord, North Carolina, is incorporated with $50,000 of stock. The objective of this company is to build a cotton mill for African Americans.

1898   W. E. B. Du Bois publishes *Some Efforts of American Negroes for Their Own Social Betterment*, which includes discussion of Black cooperatives and collective ownership.

1901   Odd Fellows Lodge establishes the Mercantile Cooperative Company in Ruthville, Virginia, and also builds a school and buys trucks. After twenty years, the co-op store closes, around 1921.

1903   The North Carolina Mutual Insurance Company, the largest state-based, locally owned insurance company, becomes the largest Negro-owned insurance company in the world. In 1912 it qualifies as a legal reserve company with loans from Fidelity Bank.

        Maggie Lena Walker founds the Saint Luke Penny Savings Bank in Richmond and becomes its president, making it the first bank founded by an African American woman to be chartered in the United States. The Order of Saint Luke also opens a department store. By 1920 the order owns six hundred homes.

1904   The first annual meeting of the North Carolina Mutual Insurance Company at the Colored State Fair in Raleigh promotes the message of racial solidarity.

1907   W. E. B. Du Bois holds his twelfth Atlanta conference on Negro business development and cooperatives, where he promotes cooperatives and economic cooperation. (The Atlanta conferences began in 1900 at Atlanta University as part of Du Bois's research project to study the social and economic condition of African Americans.)

        Du Bois publishes *Economic Co-operation Among Negro Americans*, documenting 154 African American–owned cooperative businesses.

1915   Pioneer Cooperative Society forms in Harlem, New York City.

1916   W. E. B. Du Bois organizes the Amenia economic conference of 1916 in Amenia, New York (this was followed by a second conference in 1933, also organized by Du Bois).

        The Co-operative League of America (which changed its name to the Cooperative League of the USA, or CLUSA, in 1922) is founded to promote cooperative economic development and support cooperatives in the United States.

1917   W. E. B. Du Bois requests that the NAACP support a program to teach the value of forming buyers' clubs operating on the principles of economic cooperation, but the program is not established.

1918   Du Bois founds the short-lived Negro Cooperative Guild.

        The Universal Negro Improvement Association (originally formed in Jamaica in 1914 as a mutual-benefit and reform association focused on uplifting the race) is incorporated in New York. It becomes one of the largest mass movements in African American history, promoting Black-owned grassroots joint-stock companies in shipping (Black Star Line, 1920–22) and clothing factories (Negro Factories, 1920s).

        Co-operative League of America president James Warbasse publishes "The Theory of Cooperation" in the NAACP's magazine, the *Crisis*.

        A. Philip Randolph publishes "The Co-operative Movement Among Negroes" in the *Messenger*.

1919   Citizens' Cooperative Stores, an African American cooperative meat market in Memphis, owns five co-op stores serving 75,000 people.

The Harlem Pioneer Cooperative Society opens a small grocery store in Harlem, New York City.

1922   The National Federation of Colored Farmers is formed in Chicago.

1923   The *Negro World* reports an agreement between Black and White farmers in Aiken County, Georgia, to participate together in a farmers' exchange.

1925   Students in the commercial department at the Bluefield Colored Institute in West Virginia manage a co-op supply store. Profits fund scholarships for students to pursue higher education.

The Cooperative Society of Bluefield Colored Institute joins CLUSA. In 1926 members of the Bluefield cooperative become the first African Americans to attend the national cooperative conference in Minneapolis.

1927   The Colored Merchants Association, a marketing cooperative of independent African American grocers, is founded by the National Negro Business League in Montgomery, Alabama. (Booker T. Washington started the NNBL in 1900 at Tuskegee University to support Black self-help and the development of Black businesses.) By 1930, 253 stores are members. By 1936, the CMA is bankrupt, as chain stores begin to replace small grocery stores.

The Paul Laurence Dunbar cooperative apartment complex is awarded first prize in architectural excellence for walk-up apartments by the New York chapter of the American Institute for Architects.

1928   The Citizens Cooperative Society of Buffalo, New York, is established. In 1929 it starts an education and membership campaign.

1929   The first local unit of the National Federation of Colored Farmers in Howard, Mississippi, joins with thirty tenants and sharecroppers who pool their money to purchase goods wholesale in Memphis.

Maggie Lena Walker establishes the Consolidated Bank and Trust Company in Richmond, Virginia, and becomes chair of its board.

Garrison House cooperative opens in New York City.

The North Carolina Mutual Insurance Company's president, Charles Clinton Spaulding, works with the federal government in President Hoover's "black capitalism" initiative.

1930   Ella Jo Baker and George Schuyler establish the Young Negroes' Co-operative League. Baker is its first secretary-treasurer and is chair of the New York Council.

Halena Wilson is elected the first president of the Chicago chapter of the BSCP's Ladies' Auxiliary in October and serves until 1953.

Citizens' Cooperative Society of Omaha, Nebraska, is established in November.

1931   At the YNCL's first conference in Pittsburgh, held to promote cooperatives in the African American community, Ella Jo Baker is elected its first executive director and gives a speech titled "What Consumers' Co-operation Means to Negro Women." George Schuyler is elected president.

Citizens Cooperative Grocery market is launched in Buffalo.

1931–34   Philadelphia's United Consumers' Co-operative Association calls itself "the grocery store owned by its customers."

1932   The People's Credit Union in New York City pays yearly dividends of 6 percent to more than 250 members.

          By 1932, the YNCL has formed councils in New York; Philadelphia; Monessen, Pennsylvania; Pittsburgh; Columbus; Cleveland; Cincinnati; Phoenix; New Orleans; Columbia, South Carolina; Portsmouth, Virginia; and Washington, D.C., with a total membership of four hundred.

          Harlem's Pure Food Co-operative Grocery Stores operate.

          The Consumers' Cooperative Trading Company is formed in Gary, Indiana. In 1933 it establishes a cooperative economics course in the night school at Roosevelt High School.

          The youth branch of the Consumers' Cooperative Trading Company operates an ice-cream parlor and candy store in Gary.

1933   The Consumers' Cooperative Association of Kansas City, Missouri, forms a study group to study the history and philosophy of the cooperative movement.

          The Problem's Cooperative Association sponsors "Harlem's First Economic Conference" in September. Baker delivers the welcome, and Schuyler, the keynote address.

1934   The Consumers' Cooperative Trading Company opens a credit union that has more than one hundred members by 1936.

          The Bricks Rural Life School, run by the African Missionary Association, develops a program of adult education for African American cooperative development.

          The Southern Tenant Farmers' Union is founded in the Arkansas cotton belt.

1935   The 137th Street Housing Corporation in New York City has twenty member families.

          Harlem's Own Cooperative is founded by the Dunbar Housewives' League. Ella Jo Baker serves as chairperson of education and publicity.

1936   The People's Consumer Cooperative, Inc. of Chicago is established in September by the residents of the Rosenwald Apartments with the boycott of an exploitive store. Soon thereafter, the organization starts a study group and begins a buying club, followed by the opening of a store. In September 1937 the cooperative starts a credit union, which has 191 members by 1939.

          Cooperative Industries of Washington, D.C., is chartered as a self-help cooperative in Lincoln Heights with a grant from the federal government. It is co-founded by Nannie Helen Burroughs, president of the National Training School for Women and Girls.

          The Cooperative Business Council of New Haven is established in February in New Haven, Connecticut. It starts a study group on cooperative economics in December.

          The Red Circle Cooperative Association is founded in Richmond, Virginia. By the end of the year, the organization has 125 members, and in 1938 it opens its first grocery store.

Harlem Consumers' Cooperative Council distributes milk and operates a buying club out of the basement of the New York Urban League.

Ella Jo Baker speaks on consumer cooperation at the twenty-seventh annual conference of the NAACP.

The Consumers' Cooperative Trading Company in Gary opens a second, larger grocery store, with total sales of $160,000 (considered "the largest grocery store owned by African Americans"). It also operates a co-op gas station.

Bricks Rural Life School (North Carolina) organizes a credit union. In 1938 it opens a cooperative store, followed by a health program in 1939.

1937   The Housewives' Cooperative League in Pittsburgh studies consumer empowerment and cooperative efforts around the country, and promotes supporting Black businesses and facilitating cooperative buying.

1938   The Aberdeen Gardens cooperative store opens in Hampton, Virginia, for fifty families living in the apartment complex.

The International Ladies' Auxiliary to the Brotherhood of Sleeping Car Porters is established in September when representatives of twenty-eight Women's Economic Councils of the BSCP convene in Chicago. Halena Wilson is elected the first president and serves until 1965.

The Ladies' Auxiliary promotes the study of consumer economics and cooperatives.

1939   The Tyrrell County Training School (North Carolina), after forming study groups on cooperative economics, starts a credit union. In 1940 it adds a co-op store, and in 1941, a cooperative health insurance program.

The Eastern Carolina Council is created after the Bricks Rural Life School and the Tyrrell County Training School join other interested groups to organize an African American federation for the development of cooperatives in North Carolina.

The Buffalo Cooperative Economic Society becomes a legal cooperative and opens a new grocery market. The society becomes an affiliate of the predominantly White Eastern Cooperative League.

Langston-Kingman Park Cooperative in Washington, D.C., operates with residents of the Langston Terrace housing project.

1940   The Workers' Education Bureau of the BSCP Ladies' Auxiliary circulates a reading list of publications on current events, child welfare and child labor, women workers, and "consumer information" (including cooperatives).

1941   Ella Jo Baker compiles "Consumers' Cooperation Among Negroes," which documents several African American cooperatives around the country and observes that the development of Black cooperatives has been similar to that of the broader cooperative movement in the United States.

African American members of the Modern Co-op in Harlem launch a collectively owned grocery store.

Harlem's Own Cooperative merges with Harlem Consumers' Cooperative Council.

The Ida B. Wells Cooperative operates on the South Side of Chicago, as do Thrift Cooperative and Morgan Park Cooperative. Other African American cooperatives in Chicago include Open Eye Consumer's Cooperative (affiliated with Pilgrim Baptist Church) and Citizen's Non-Partisan Cooperative of Olivet Baptist Church.

A group of seven women from the BSCP's Ladies' Auxiliary in Chicago and one man start a study group to talk about establishing a cooperative. In 1942 they start a buying club.

BSCP Ladies' Auxiliary chapters start study groups in Denver, St. Louis, Minneapolis–St. Paul, Detroit, Indianapolis, Washington, D.C., New Orleans, Omaha, Oklahoma City, Los Angeles, Seattle, Montgomery, Pittsburgh, Montreal, Buffalo, and Jersey City. Denver also establishes a buying club.

1943   The Chicago BSCP cooperative buying club joins Central States Cooperative Wholesale and opens a retail co-op grocery store on Saturdays. Later that year it moves the store to the BSCP headquarters and operates regularly on weekdays and Saturdays.

The BSCP Ladies' Auxiliary chapter in Washington, D.C., hosts a speaker from the Cooperative League of the USA, and several members attend a six-day summer course on cooperatives at Howard University.

Authors Brooks and Lynch (1944) survey Black universities, colleges, and junior colleges in southern states and find that thirty-seven of fifty-seven respondents include the cooperative movement in their curriculum. Many of the campuses have cooperatives associated with them or in a neighboring town.

1944   African American credit unions in North Carolina begin to expand in number throughout the state, increasing from thirty-two to seventy-two in mostly rural areas.

1945   The Credjafawn Social Club (1928–80), in St. Paul, Minnesota, opens Neighborhood Co-operative Store No. 3, the first Black neighborhood cooperative store in St. Paul. The club also establishes one or two credit unions, hires local Blacks, supports a junior club for youths, and awards scholarships for college.

The North Carolina Council for Credit Unions and Associates is established and designs a cooperative economic educational curriculum and a primer for schools and credit union treasurers on credit union accounting. Over the next twelve years, ninety-five new credit unions and forty-five new cooperatives are formed in North Carolina.

1945–47   The Montreal chapter of the International Brotherhood of Sleeping Car Porters establishes the first credit union affiliated with the organization, the Walker Credit Union.

1947   Several members of the Chicago chapter of the BSCP Ladies' Auxiliary attend a co-op labor conference in Chicago, sponsored by the Council for Cooperative Development.

1948   The BSCP Cooperative Buying Club, established with help from the Chicago chapter of the Ladies' Auxiliary, is incorporated, and grows to 250 shareholding members. It is probably the only cooperative of the era founded and controlled by African American women.

1950   The BSCP Cooperative Buying Club is dissolved and checks are disbursed to members.

Morningside Heights Consumers Cooperative opens in New York City and operates for more than ten years (50 percent of its members are African American or Puerto Rican).

1956   The Mondragon Cooperative Corporation, which started as a community-based polytechnic high school, is founded in the Basque community of northern Spain by Father José María Arizmendiarrieta. It becomes a model for networked cooperative economic development centered around worker cooperatives in an ethnic minority community.

1964   Southern Consumers' Cooperative is founded in Louisiana.

1966   The Black Panther Party, founded in Oakland, California, organizes "survival programs pending political revolution" that include free breakfast and education programs for children and the provision of free shoes (from the Panthers' own factory), clothing, food, health care, plumbing repair, pest control, and transportation for the aged; the Panthers also sponsor cooperative housing and cooperative bakeries.

1967   The Freedom Quilting Bee is established in Alberta, Alabama, with Estelle Witherspoon as co-founder, to help sharecropping families earn independent income. By 1992 the co-op owns twenty-three acres of land and has 150 members.

The Southwest Alabama Farmers' Cooperative Association (SWAFCA) is formed by a group of African American farmers whose families have farmed the land for more than two centuries.

In August, the Federation of Southern Cooperatives (FSC) is established by twenty-two cooperatives, among them the Southern Consumers' Cooperative, the SWAFCA, and the Freedom Quilting Bee.

The Southern Cooperative Development Program is funded as a co-project with the FSC.

Fannie Lou Hamer and the National Council of Negro Women start a pig bank by purchasing fifty-five pigs. Participating families are trained to care for pigs, establish cooperatives, and work together to improve their communities' nutrition and health.

Harlem River Consumers Cooperative in Harlem, New York City, raises $152,000 from twenty-five hundred African American members (at $5 a share) to open a cooperative supermarket in Esplanade Gardens Cooperative. The supermarket offers affordable prices and ethnic foods and plans to create fifty jobs.

1968   The federal Office of Economic Opportunity grants $592,870 to the FSC for research and technical support services to its thirty-eight member organizations.

Co-op grocery stores and buying clubs are established after riots in Detroit (e.g., Community Consumer Co-op, Inc.) and Los Angeles (e.g., Unity Market).

1969   The North Bolivar County Farm Cooperative (originally an outgrowth of Tufts-Delta Health Center, founded in April 1968) is incorporated in Bolivar County, Mississippi, and becomes a member of the FSC.

The National Black Economic Conference calls on the U.S. government and churches for reparations, to be used in part to fund African American cooperative ownership.

The Southern Cooperative Development Fund receives its first funding as a project of the FSC.

Fannie Lou Hamer launches the Freedom Farm Cooperative in Sunflower County, Mississippi (incorporated in June 1970). The Freedom Farm Co-op buys a building in Doddsville, Mississippi, for use as a sewing co-op, and plans to open a clothing cooperative in Ruleville.

1970s   The Congress of African Peoples inspires community-action agencies to organize consumer cooperatives and low-income credit unions, especially in Brooklyn, Cleveland, Pittsburgh, Detroit, Youngstown, Chicago, Houston, Milwaukee, San Francisco, and Los Angeles.

Black Media, Inc. Cooperative (BMI Cooperative), a consortium of Black newspapers in the United States, provides advertising and other services for the more than one hundred newspapers that are members.

1970   The Paul Laurence Dunbar apartments, originally a housing cooperative built for Blacks in Harlem, New York, is designated a landmark site.

The Southern Cooperative Development Program and the FSC staff merge.

1972   The Southern Cooperative Development Fund separates from the FSC and forms its own Southern Development Foundation.

1973   Apex Taxi Cab Cooperative is established in Milwaukee but closes eighteen months later because of high insurance premiums.

1979   The Workers' Owned Sewing Company (1979–2000) is founded by five seamstresses and a farmer in Windsor, North Carolina.

1980   The U.S. government launches an eighteen-month investigation of the FSC on charges of misuse of federal funds, reducing the organization's ability to raise money and cover its expenses. In 1981, the U.S. attorney for the northern district of Alabama announces that it will not prosecute the FSC, finding no evidence of wrongdoing.

The Panola Land Buyers Association establishes a housing cooperative, Wendy Hills Co-op Community, with forty units of housing near Gainesville, Alabama.

1985   The FSC merges with the Land Emergency Fund to become the Federation of Southern Cooperatives/Land Assistance Fund, the only networked regional organization of African American cooperatives and development centers in the United States; it is still in operation today.

Cooperative Home Care Associates, a worker-owned home-care cooperative based in the South Bronx, is founded. The majority of members are Latina and African American. CHCA becomes the largest worker cooperative in the United States and is still in operation today.

1986   The Workers' Owned Sewing Company of Windsor, North Carolina, joins the Amalgamated Clothing and Textile Workers Union.

1987   Co-op City, a housing complex in the Bronx, New York City, becomes majority non-White.

1990   Oceanhill Brownsville Tenants Association forms the Central Building Fedayeen Construction Company, a worker cooperative with fifteen worker-owners.

1992   Food from the 'Hood, a student-led co-op at Crenshaw High School in Los Angeles, starts a school garden, gives produce to the poor, sells at a farmers' market, and begins a multiyear project to sell salad dressing made from produce grown in its garden. By 2003, seventy-seven members have graduated and gone on to college using money earned from working in the co-op.

          Oceanhill Brownsville Tenants Association forms the worker cooperative Oceanhill Brownsville Security Company. About 20 percent of the forty-two worker-owners are former prison inmates or substance abusers.

1994   Cooperative Economics for Women is founded in Jamaica Plain (Boston), Massachusetts, and offers a thorough training program focusing on literacy, organizational skills, cooperative economics, and business management for women of color, immigrant and refugee women, and survivors of domestic violence.

1995   Women's Action to Gain Economic Security (WAGES) is founded in Redwood City, California, to provide business and industrial training to immigrant women for the purpose of developing cooperatives. By 1999, WAGES began to specialize in training Latinas to create environmentally friendly housecleaning co-ops; it is still in operation today.

          Cooperative Janitorial Services, a worker cooperative, opens in Cincinnati, Ohio, and remains in operation today.

1997   Dawson Workers-Owned Cooperative is founded in Dawson, Georgia. The majority of the workers are female, a third of them single mothers.

          Baltimoreans United in Leadership Development (BUILD) establishes the SSC Employment Agency, a Baltimore-based worker-owned temporary employment agency, as a job-creation strategy for the hard to employ.

1998   In response to discrimination and underemployment, African American workers in Los Angeles start the APR Masonry Arts Corporation with help from its union and the A. Philip Randolph Educational Fund and its union.

          Enterprising Staffing Solutions, an experiment in worker-owned temporary employment services in Washington, D.C., opens in the Shaw neighborhood.

1999   Emma's Eco-Clean, a housecleaning cooperative in Redwood City, California, begins as a project of Women's Action to Gain Economic Security.

          The Ella Jo Baker Intentional Community Cooperative is established in Washington, D.C., to save affordable housing in response to gentrification. Members move into six row houses in Columbia Heights in 2003. It remains in operation today.

2001   Chain Reaction, a project of the EcoDesign Corps of Shaw EcoVillage in Washington, D.C., opens its youth-managed full-service bicycle shop cooperative.

2004   The FSC begins the Sankofa Youth Agricultural Project, an agricultural cooperative.

2006   Toxic Soil Busters, a youth-managed lead-removal and landscaping cooperative supported by the not-for-profit Worcester Roots, is founded in Worcester, Massachusetts.

Chester Community Grocery Co-op is established in Chester, Pennsylvania, after sixteen years with no supermarket, the result of the city's deindustrialization.

"Uplifting and Strengthening Our Community: Through Alternative Economic Development and Action," a conference on cooperative economic strategies for Harlem, is sponsored by the CEJJES Institute (Pomona, New York), the Institute for Urban and Minority Education (Columbia Teachers College), and the African American Studies Department of the University of Maryland, College Park, and takes place at the Abyssinian Development Corporation in Harlem on April 28.

2007   The Ujamaa Collective, a cooperative of African American craftswomen and businesswomen, is established with the launch of a year-round open-air artists' marketplace in Pittsburgh.

Green Worker Cooperative, a cooperative development organization in the South Bronx, is established to incubate worker-owned and environmentally friendly co-ops in response to high unemployment and "decades of environmental racism." Green Worker also establishes a Co-op Academy to provide training in cooperative business development to community members.

Bike Church Repair Shop, a youth-managed cooperative in Philadelphia, is sponsored by the youth agency Neighborhood Bike Works.

The Freedom Quilting Bee reopens after an extended hiatus.

2009   Mandela Foods Cooperative, a worker- and community-owned co-op, opens in West Oakland, California, as part of a strategy to address food insufficiency in the neighborhood.

2012   Nation of Islam members in Houston, Texas, launch the OST/MacGregor Food Cooperative in the third ward of the city.

Notes

Introduction

1. Technically, the ICA indirectly represents more than a billion people around the world through the memberships of the national trade associations in the ICA that represent cooperative enterprises in member countries. There are probably more cooperators in co-ops not officially recognized in this way. The United States has the largest absolute number of people indirectly represented by the ICA, with 305.6 million people in thirty thousand cooperatives, employing two million people. China, India, and Japan are the countries with the next-largest numbers of people in cooperatives represented by the ICA. In Canada, a country with a much smaller population, 25 percent of the people belong to a cooperative, giving Canada one of the highest proportions of cooperative members in the world (ICA 2012a).

2. For more information on cooperatives, see Gordon Nembhard 2008c; see also the ICA website, http://www.ica.coop, and http://ica.coop/en/what-co-op/co-operative-identity-values-principles. The website of the National Cooperative Business Association, the U.S. co-op trade association, is located at http://www.ncba.coop/. For more specifically about worker co-ops and their benefits, see Gordon Nembhard 2004b, 2002a; Haynes and Gordon Nembhard 1999; and http://www.usworker.coop.

3. The seven cooperative principles are voluntary and open membership; democratic member control; member economic participation; autonomy and independence; education, training, and information; cooperation among cooperatives; and concern for community. See ICA 2012b.

4. Emelianoff summarizes an Italian study of cooperatives done by M. Marini in 1906 (1995, 20–22). Fairbairn similarly highlights the "multidimensionality" and closeness between the co-op and its members; members "are customers as well as owners" (2003, 5).

5. There is increasing recognition of cooperatives (including credit unions) in the media as a viable economic development tool. Many writers and reporters acknowledge the importance of cooperative economics for economic revitalization and the role of cooperatives in the aftermath of a disaster, particularly after the devastation of the Gulf Coast from the flooding caused by Hurricane Katrina in 2005, after the Japan earthquake in 2011, and since the Great Recession that began in 2008 (see, for example, Nader 2005; Livingston 2007b; Hart and Touesnard 2008; Hocker 2009; Marte 2009; Leigh 2011; Hightower 2012; and Takanarita and Tsuchiya 2012). See also Gordon Nembhard 2006b on cooperatives and economic recovery in New Orleans.

6. Throughout his career, Du Bois had an extensive and complicated analysis of the importance and benefits of cooperatives for African Americans (see Du Bois 1907, 1933b, 1940). Du Bois's analysis of cooperative economics as an economic strategy for African Americans is scattered throughout this volume (see esp. chaps. 1, 2, and 4).

7. Haynes and I devised a theory from Du Bois's writings on cooperatives (Du Bois 1907, 1925, 1933b, 1933c, 1940), Demarco's 1974 and 1983 explorations into Du Bois's social and economic thought, and Hogan's 1984 analysis of African Americans' relationship to labor (the need for Black people to control their own labor). We theorized that cooperative economics addresses the total condition of depressed communities and should be an important strategy for effective African American community economic development. Haynes and Gordon Nembhard 1999 sketched an alternative framework for analyzing inner-city development, and concluded that conditions in inner cities and persistent poverty suggest the need for alternative paradigms in economic development. We proposed cooperative enterprise development as a viable economic strategy for inner-city redevelopment; and in Gordon Nembhard and Haynes 2002 and 2003, we suggested that the Mondragon Cooperative Corporation is an example of how another ethnic minority group applies this theory. Fairbairn et al. 1991 and Birchall 2003 explore similar theories about cooperatives, poverty reduction, and community economic development, and provide policy analyses of the contributions of cooperative enterprises to economic development.

8. The Mondragon Cooperative Corporation is a complex of about 258 industrial, financial, distributional, research, and educational cooperatives and enterprises in the Basque region of northern Spain, with ninety-three production plants and nine corporate offices located outside Spain. The corporation, which started with one small worker-owned ceramic heating factory in 1956, is rooted in grassroots networks of Basque-owned worker cooperatives. The Basque are an ethnic (language and cultural) minority in Spain. The Mondragon complex uses a system of interlocking cooperatives to handle all levels of business development, including education and training, development, financial services, and social security. It has provided a mechanism for some members of the Basque community to form and control their own businesses, schools, and financial institutions, according to shared values and shared work. The Mondragon system of cooperatives is discussed again in chapters 4 and 10 in this volume. See also Gordon Nembhard and Haynes 2002 and 2003; Mondragon Cooperative Corporation 2011; and the Mondragon website at http://www.mondragon-corporation.com/ENG.aspx.

9. The earliest known mutual insurance company in the United States was the Philadelphia Contributionship, a mutual fire insurance company established in 1752. Benjamin Franklin's Union Fire Company in Philadelphia met with other firefighting companies in 1751 to form the insurance company. The members agreed that it would be a mutual company, with every member owning an equal number of shares.

Chapter 1

1. The Co-operative League of America changed its name to the Cooperative League of the USA (CLUSA) in 1922, and then to the National Cooperative Business Association (NCBA) starting in the 1980s. See http://www.ncba.coop, "History."

2. New Harmony followed the socialist philosophy of Robert Owen, a nineteenth-century Welsh social reformer. According to Donnachie 2006, Owen's utopian solution to social distress was to design "villages of unity and mutual cooperation" for working people that satisfied human needs without exploitation. Several Owenite communities sprang up in the nineteenth century, particularly in Britain and the United States, among them New Harmony and Orbiston.

3. DeFilippis refers to Nordoff's seminal work here: Charles Nordhoff, *American Utopias* (Stockbridge, Mass.: Berkshire House, 2003).

4. In fact, according to Berry, "The concept of burial assistance was so traditional that men in the Tuskegee Syphilis Study participated in part because they were offered burial assistance" (2005, 263n21).

5. In addition, at the end of the nineteenth century, many formerly enslaved persons who had been emancipated at age thirty or so were now sixty and older, and suffered from

"a variety of ills." "The rapidly aging members overwhelmed local benevolent societies" (Berry 2005, 64)—this is why the ex-slave association in Tennessee needed to keep pushing for pensions but also needed to provide aid. Aid was needed more than ever, but so were strategies for providing income for destitute families.

Chapter 2

1. As noted in the introduction, a Rochdale cooperative is a formal cooperative business that follows the European "Rochdale Principles of Cooperation," established by the Rochdale Pioneers in England in 1844. A Rochdale cooperative is a cooperatively owned enterprise governed democratically according to the Rochdale principles codified by the International Co-operative Alliance (ICA) in 1895 (ICA 2012b). I follow Hope 1940, which uses the term "Rochdale cooperative" to describe more formal cooperative business enterprises, rather than an informal economic cooperation or collective effort. In the United States today, an official cooperative business follows ICA principles, is incorporated under a specific state law (which varies by state), and usually qualifies for certain tax credits or allowances under U.S. tax law.

2. Clare Horner, "Producer Co-operatives in the United States" (PhD diss., University of Pittsburgh, 1978), 228–42, quoted in Curl 2009, 4.

3. Susan B. Anthony was also an active KOL member (Curl 2009, 101).

4. Reverend Love said, "There is no reason why the Negro should not control the Negro trade and handle the money the Negro has to spend." Quoted in Ali 2003, 77n5.

5. The Florida Farmers Union was dominated by 1,720 African American members from fourteen all-Black local clubs, compared to 1,166 White members in twenty-one all-White clubs (Ali 2003, 71).

6. The Knights of Labor also collapsed by the end of the 1880s, and the National Farmers Alliance exchanges suffered a similar fate a decade or so later, as corporate rule consolidated (Curl 2009).

Chapter 3

1. See the introduction, note 3, for the seven Rochdale cooperative principles, which are the guidelines that cooperatives use to put into practice the internationally recognized cooperative values of self-help, self-responsibility, democracy, equality, equity, and solidarity (see ICA 2012a and 2012b).

2. Woodson notes that "insurance companies have been more prosperous than any other large enterprises among Negroes" (1929, 202).

3. See also http://www.mdarchives.state.md.us/msa/stagser/s1259/121/6050/html/cmrddc.html.

4. The failure of the Freedman's Savings Bank is associated with several problems, including too many speculative ventures, spending on a new building in Washington, D.C., and the Panic of 1873. While most of its trustees were White, it was considered a Black-owned bank and its failure was attributed to misguided conventional wisdom that African Americans cannot run a business properly. Frederick Douglass had just been appointed president before the bank went under. There was a plan to reimburse the majority of depositors' savings, but much of that money was not disbursed. This left many Blacks with a distrust of banks in general and of Black-owned businesses specifically (see Hine, Hine, and Harrold 2010; Gilbert 1972).

5. As noted above, the Mondragon Cooperative Corporation is a holding company in the Basque region of northern Spain; see note 8 to the introduction as well as discussions at the beginning of chapter 4 and briefly in chapter 10 in this volume. For more about

Mondragon, see Gordon Nembhard and Haynes 2002. See also http://www.mondragon -corporation.com/language/en-US/ENG.aspx; MacLeod 1997; Melman 2002; Morrison 1991; Whyte and Whyte 1991; and Thomas 2000.

6. Garvey quoted in the *Negro World*, May 1, 1920 (Martin 1976, 151).

7. According to Martin, as early as 1918 the UNIA's Negro Factories Corporation managed laundries, restaurants, a doll factory, tailoring and millinery establishments, and a printing press (13).

8. In 1922, Garvey was indicted for mail fraud—namely, fraudulent use of the U.S. mail to sell Black Star Line stock. In 1925, he was convicted of the charge, though most observers agree that he was more guilty of mismanagement and incompetence than of deliberate fraud (Hine, Hine, and Harrold 2010, 455). Note here the similarity in tactics, as the earlier Ex–Slave Mutual Relief, Bounty and Pension Association was also accused of mail fraud.

9. The account in the *Crisis* does not use the name Negro Cooperative Guild, identifying a Mr. Ruddy only as attending "a meeting called by Du Bois." However, in his autobiography, Du Bois (1940, 759) mentions that several co-op stores were established after that meeting.

10. Members were allowed to own up to five hundred shares, but as of the 1920 report, no one owned more than twenty. The first two shares earned 4 percent interest; additional shares earned 5 percent (New York Dept. of Farms and Markets 1920, 10).

11. While I have no definite proof, Du Bois (in his 1940 autobiography) and Matney's writings suggest that Matney attended the meeting of the Negro Cooperative Guild in 1918. Because Du Bois identifies this as a project that came out of the Negro Cooperative Guild, the Cooperative Society of Bluefield Colored Institute may have started before 1925. However, Sims 1925 provides the best information we have about the cooperative without providing the exact date of its establishment.

12. They attended this national congress in Minneapolis in 1926, so this was probably CLUSA's national conference.

Chapter 4

1. The cooperative principles are recognized the world over as part of the cooperative statement of identity adopted in 1995 by the International Co-operative Alliance. The fifth principle highlights the importance of education and training on all levels.

2. I have begun to document cooperative activities that build trust and solidarity by studying member orientation manuals and programs developed by worker-owned cooperatives to orient and train their members, and methods that worker cooperatives use to self-manage. Effective meeting facilitation and consensus-building strategies, the different faces of leadership, board training in general, and training that targets democratic participation are essential to effective democratic governance of a cooperative, specifically worker co-ops. I analyze the ways in which worker co-ops provide specialized training to increase their members' skills and facilitate career ladder mobility within the cooperative. I also analyze community education and marketing strategies that work to engage the communities around worker co-ops in supporting such businesses as consumers, partners, and advocates. There are studies about the use of trust in cooperatives and the importance of social capital and "solidarity" (see Ellerman 1990; Engelskirchen 1997; Bergström 1999; Bickle and Wilkins 2000; Shipp 2000; Abascal-Hildebrand 2002; and chapter 5 in this volume). Also, Linda Leaks, in a 2007 interview by the author, suggested that education and a sense of trust are essential in making cooperative housing work, particularly limited-equity cooperative housing that requires that member-residents understand the mission and purpose (to keep the housing affordable).

3. From several presentations at the "Towards a Global History of the Consumer Cooperative Movement" conference sponsored by ABF-huset, the Labour Movement Archives

and Library in Stockholm, Sweden, May 2–4, 2012, it is apparent that many cooperative movements in Africa and Asia have used the Antigonish model and made study tours to Coady's cooperative program at Xavier University. The Puerto Rican cooperative movement, for example, owes much to the Antigonish movement and to Father Joseph A. McDonald, who moved from Antigonish to Puerto Rico to help develop cooperatives there (see http://www.oralhistorycentre.ca/fonds/laidlaw-alex).

4. For more about microenterprise development and microlending, particularly as they relate to cooperatives, see Gordon Nembhard 2011; ILO-ICA 2005; ILO 2005; Dumas 2001; Feldman 2002.

5. This was probably the co-op study tour of Nova Scotia referred to in Washington 1939a, one of two tours in 1937 and 1938 to study the Antigonish cooperative movement of Nova Scotia. The 1938 tour was led by Mabel Carney of Teachers College, Columbia University. Thirty-five Whites and nineteen Blacks participated in the study tour. That number of African Americans participating with Whites in studying cooperatives in Canada is significant. I have not been able to find the names of those who attended that tour.

6. Most of this information comes from workshops led by members of the Rainbow Grocery Cooperative between 2000 and 2006 (at the CooperationWorks cooperative training program in December 2000, the Eastern Conference for Workplace Democracy conferences in 2002, 2003, and 2005, and the first national conference of the U.S. Federation of Worker Cooperatives in 2006), as well as from the Rainbow Grocery Cooperative "Owner's Manual."

7. U.S. cooperative development centers, organized as CooperationWorks!, also have joined together to form a joint training program for cooperative developers (see http://www.cooperationworks.coop).

8. In the early twenty-first century, I have organized some panel discussions about Black cooperative businesses at meetings of the National Urban League, the National Economic Association (in connection with the American Economic Association's annual meetings), and with community groups in Harlem, New Orleans, and Baltimore. However, there still has not been a major university conference dedicated to this subject since 1907.

9. Presumably, Ruddy's action was the result of his having attended the August 1918 meeting establishing the Negro Cooperative Guild, but it is not clear why Du Bois, who wrote the article titled "Ruddy's Citizen's Cooperative Stores" in the December 1919 issue of the *Crisis*, does not mention this specifically or name the organization. Perhaps, because he was not sure of the NAACP's support, he did not want to mention the meeting or the guild, or perhaps at that first meeting there had been no consensus on calling the new group the Negro Cooperative Guild, or on holding additional meetings.

10. In addition, while A. Philip Randolph does not mention attending the August 1918 meeting, he wrote an article in the *Messenger* called "The Co-operative Movement Among Negroes" in the same year. And in the October 2, 1919, issue of the *Messenger*, in an article titled "The Failure of the Negro Church," he wrote that "the churches of the Black community should become bases of cooperative economic activity for the black working-class" (quoted in Floyd-Thomas 2008, 109). Is this just a coincidence? Did Randolph write the 1918 piece on cooperatives, and did he urge Black churches to become involved in cooperative development in 1919, because he attended the meeting that established the Negro Co-operative Guild and was doing his part to promote cooperatives? Or did he write these things because he heard about the meeting and was not invited, and wanted to show that he had an opinion on the subject? Or did he write the article in 1918 because many Black leaders at that time were thinking about using the co-op model, given the establishment of the Co-operative League of America in 1916, a reminder that Blacks should be involved in the cooperative movement as well? Or was it a combination of several of these possibilities? In my view, the chronology of events and interconnections between progressive African American leaders suggest that Randolph may have attended the August 1918 meeting. Both Jervis Anderson's 1986 biography of Randolph and the biographical information

provided by the A. Philip Randolph Institute (http://www.apri.org/ht/d/sp/i/225/pid/225) are essentially silent about Randolph's view of cooperative economics and do not mention any connection he might have had to the cooperative movement, so are not helpful here.

11. In 1934, Du Bois was focused not so much on his early notion of a "talented tenth" who could lead the movement as on promoting purposive cooperative economic development in Black communities. Harris sounds more like the one pushing for a talented tenth, or a cadre of intellectuals to lead the way.

12. While this is an impressive readership, Marcus Garvey's Universal Negro Improvement Association began publishing the *Negro World* in English, Spanish, and French in August 1918, after only a little more than a year in the United States. The *Negro World* had a weekly circulation of two hundred thousand worldwide (Dodson, Moore, and Yancy 2000, 159). Occasionally, the *Negro World* reported on cooperative activities and cooperative housing in the African American community (*Negro World* 1930a, 1930b, 1930c, 1931, 1932). Cyril Briggs founded the monthly magazine the *Crusader* in August 1918 as well. In 1917, other Black progressive and socialist magazines came into print, among them Hubert H. Harrison's *Voice* and A. Philip Randolph's *Messenger,* joining the Black-owned newspapers scattered around the country. So, while cooperatives were being discussed among Blacks during this time, Du Bois had serious competition for readers—the *Crisis* was not the only publication Blacks were reading. In addition, the United States had joined the Allied forces in World War I in April 1917. Blacks debated whether or not to support the war effort. A strong antilynching movement had also developed during this period, and antilynching activists petitioned President Woodrow Wilson to make lynching a federal crime. The cooperative movement and discussion of cooperative development among African Americans may have seemed less relevant than all the other events and issues on people's minds. All of this may help put into perspective the limitations of Du Bois's influence in the African American community at that time, particularly on the subject of cooperative economics. Even Du Bois himself was distracted.

13. Founded in 1916, the Co-operative League of America became known as the Cooperative League of the USA (CLUSA) in 1922. In 1985 the name was changed to the National Cooperative Business Association, the name by which it is known today. The first national organization for cooperatives in the United States, it is "dedicated to developing, advancing and protecting cooperatives" (see http://www.ncba.coop/, "About NCBA").

14. As noted above, Du Bois corresponded with the league's president, James Warbasse, and Warbasse wrote an article called "The Theory of Cooperation" in the *Crisis* in 1918. Matney 1927 boasts that the Bluefield co-op joined CLUSA and attended the national conference in 1926. In 1932, CLUSA's executive secretary, Oscar Cooley, sent greetings to the second national conference of the Young Negroes' Co-operative League (Cooley 1932b).

15. The Brotherhood of Sleeping Car Porters actually required that members read CLUSA literature. In 1925, Du Bois wrote to Warbasse asking for advice and funding suggestions for starting cooperatives in Harlem. Warbasse replied that CLUSA had had several visits from Blacks interested in cooperatives and offered to put Du Bois in contact with them. He also suggested several fields and industries that might be conducive to Black cooperatives, especially cooperative housing, since it already had strong roots in New York City. He even suggested that because cooperative housing reduced the cost of second mortgages, such a project would not need much philanthropic support (Warbasse 1925, 306).

16. Most of the information in this case study has been pieced together from accounts in Hope 1940 and Reddix 1935 and 1974.

17. The decline in teaching cooperative economics and the history of the cooperative movement, particularly in African American colleges, may be explained by the political repression that began with the McCarthy era in the 1950s. In response to a question about the conscious separation of economic rights from the struggle for political (civil) rights during the civil rights movement in the 1960s, Lawrence Guyott, during a 2007 interview by the author, suggested that cooperatives and economic democracy were off the table

because of the dangerous political climate. African American civil rights advocates were very sensitive to the congressional House Committee on Un-American Activities probes, threats, blacklisting, and imprisonment of anyone suspected of supporting communism in the 1950s, and to COINTELPRO investigations of Black organizations in the 1960s. In addition, as late as 1979–80, the federal government investigated the Federation of Southern Cooperatives for possible misuse of its not-for-profit status (see Bethell 1982). Most observers believe that this was an attempt to undermine its support for cooperative development in the South.

18. See, for example, Southern New Hampshire University, http://www.snhu.edu/online-degrees/graduate-degrees/community-economic-development-MS-online/curriculum.asp.

19. As this book goes to press, a couple of important developments are worth noting. The FSC/LAF is working with Tuskegee University (a historically Black college) to create a course on cooperative economics. Also, the Economics Department of the University of Massachusetts, Amherst, has approved a certificate in cooperative economics.

Chapter 5

1. Kennedy does mention Schuyler's fleeting interest in Black separatism (2003, 355), which could include (or be a code word for) his work with the YNCL—which advocated that Blacks form their own cooperative businesses separate from the White economy. Interestingly, at the time that Schuyler was so involved in founding the YNCL, his famous satirical novel Black No More was widely discussed and debated, but not his YNCL involvement. He also satirized Du Bois and Garvey in that novel, both of whom had advocated economic cooperation and cooperative ownership among Blacks a decade earlier, if only in the form of joint-stock ownership. Presumably, their support for some kind of cooperative economics was also not well popularized. Schuyler thus may not have known that his work with the YNCL followed in their footsteps—or he may not have been willing to admit it, since he should have known, given the circles in which he traveled.

2. Ransby suggests that the number of delegates was small, but the conference drew a "capacity crowd" of six hundred onlookers (2003, 82).

3. I suspect that the Citizens Cooperative Grocery market in Buffalo may have been a member of the CMA, and it seems to have been the first store opened by the YNCL. Also, some of the grocery co-ops in Harlem were members of the CMA.

4. A receipt from the New York Urban League at 202–206 West 136th Street for meeting privileges in March 1932 is in the Ella Baker Papers, box 2, folder 2, Schomburg Center (see also Ransby 2003, 85).

5. This information comes from a newsletter from the national office of the YNCL written by Ella Baker and addressed, "Dear Fellow Cooperator." The letter mentions 1932, so it was written either in late 1932 or early 1933 (Baker ca. 1932a).

Chapter 6

1. This report also noted that W. E. B. Du Bois was one of the judges of this contest, along with the editors of the Progressive Grocer and Business Week and other business leaders. Here again we see overlap between Du Bois, then editor of the Crisis and a self-proclaimed proponent of cooperatives, and other business leaders, labor leaders, and supporters of cooperatives—although there is only scattered evidence that these interests overlapped among African American leaders.

2. I listed above the several federally chartered credit unions named in "Consumers' Cooperation Among Negroes." This credit union, however, was not included there.

3. In 1925 the Urban League had approached Rockefeller for help in financing second mortgages in Harlem (Landmarks Preservation Commission 1970, 2), which sounds very similar to a project that J. P. Warbasse of CLUSA suggested to W. E. B. Du Bois in a letter dated February 1925 (Warbasse 1925, 306)—perhaps the projects have a common origin. According to the New York City Landmarks Preservation Commission, Rockefeller was more interested in constructing housing and thus bought the property on 149th–150th Streets in early 1926 and developed it into the Dunbar complex.

4. The Dunbar was not the only Black or predominantly Black housing cooperative in New York City (or the country). New York City contains more cooperative housing (and probably more Black co-op housing) than any other U.S. city. Washington, D.C., and other cities also have several Black housing co-ops, and rural areas in the South have organized housing cooperatives.

5. This information was gleaned from copies of executive board reports of the Harlem Consumers' Cooperative Council, Ella Baker Papers, box 2, folder 3, Schomburg Center.

6. While there is no mention of this being part of a larger national movement, Reddix may have been connected to Du Bois or to the YNCL. He seems to have been well connected in the U.S. cooperative movement; according to his memoirs, he was offered the first directorship of the USDA Cooperative Services Agency (Reddix 1974).

Chapter 7

1. In an August 1934 letter to Owen Woodruff, director of the Federal Emergency Relief Administration's Division of Self-Help Cooperatives (the co-op's funder), Burroughs listed the co-op's officers and trustees. Chancellor Williams is listed as vice president (Burroughs 1934b). In October 1934, Burroughs wrote to Williams and the associates of the cooperative identifying Williams as the co-op's president (Burroughs 1934a).

2. Burroughs was also a founder, corresponding secretary, and president of the National Baptist Women's Convention for more than sixty years (Library of Congress 2003). The National Baptist Convention and its Women's Convention provided the support needed to establish her school in 1909. She was also president of the National Association of Wage Earners (with Mary McLeod Bethune as vice president). In addition to being a religious leader, teacher, and school principal, Burroughs was a journalist, orator, and women's rights and workers' rights activist.

3. Hope interviewed the managers and founders of all the cooperatives he reported on, so although it was not unusual for Burroughs to talk about her co-op (or that Hope interviewed the founders and managers), it is interesting that as a woman in the movement, Burroughs talked up her co-op more than once. Alethea Washington also interviewed Burroughs about this cooperative (1939b). In addition, the Nannie Helen Burroughs Papers in the Library of Congress include hundreds of letters about Cooperative Industries between Burroughs and others in the cooperative movement. Burroughs did attend some conferences and gave some speeches on the subject. In addition, she received orders from Baltimore and other places for brooms and other products of Cooperative Industries, and had inspectors from all over the country attest to the quality of the chickens and other farm animals and produce.

4. This is obvious from the many letters to and from Wilson about cooperatives in the various BSCP archives in the Library of Congress, Chicago Historical Society, and the Bancroft Library of the University of California at Berkeley, and from Wilson's own activities and conference participation while president of the Ladies' Auxiliary (see also Chateauvert 1998).

5. Special thanks to Melinda Chateauvert for sharing her notes and files on the Ladies' Auxiliary to the BSCP.

6. Wilson may be correct, but a couple of cooperatives were initiated by Black women connected with labor in the 1800s, though these may have been producer or worker co-ops. In addition, Burroughs's Cooperative Industries co-op eventually became a consumers' cooperative and may be considered founded by Black women with connections to the labor movement. Nonetheless, the Chicago buying club was important and historic, and may have been the first initiated by Black women connected to the labor movement, as Wilson claims.

7. The FSC/LAF named their prestigious lifetime achievement award after Witherspoon in 2002—the Estelle Witherspoon Lifetime Achievement Award—and began to hold annual fund-raising dinners around the presentation of the award.

8. Technically, CHCA has a high member-owner proportion of about 70 percent. However, the figure for the total number of employees includes employees in the partner organization Independence Care System, which provides services to people with disabilities and whose employees are not yet worker-owners but will be offered ownership once the parent company is able to accommodate more owners. This was explained in an address by Stu Schneider at the Fair Work Conference in New York City in December 2009, and also on a tour of CHCA, Bronx, New York, in October 2009.

9. The information in this section is based primarily on CHCA's website, http://www.chcany.org/; Shipp 2000; Glasser and Brecher 2002; and Weiss and Clamp 1992.

10. In a workshop presented at the National Cooperative Business Association's Cooperative Development Forum in Atlanta in 1998, members of CEW discussed the difficulties of starting cooperatives with a mixed group of men and women. They have been more successful with their empowerment training in all-women groups. From the perspective of increasing women's empowerment, a preliminary review of the literature suggests that this experience might be universal.

11. This information comes from an interview by the author with co-founder Linda Leaks in Washington, D.C., November 2007, and from a presentation by co-founder Ajowa Nzinga Ifateyo in 2010.

12. Kwanzaa is the African American holiday founded by Maulana Karenga and celebrated from December 26 to January 1. Each day celebrates one of the seven Nguzo Saba (principles): Umoja, Kujichagulia, Umija, Ujamaa, Nia, Kuumba, and Imani (see Karenga 1989).

Chapter 8

1. More and more evidence has come to light of discrimination by federal agencies, especially the U.S. Department of Agriculture, against Black farmers throughout the twentieth century. *Pigford v. Glickman* (1999) is one example. In that case, Black farmers who were denied federal financial support after World War II, including during the era after passage of the Civil Rights Act of 1964, pursued a successful class-action suit against the USDA. Loans for production and operations, housing, economic opportunity, and other forms of credit were systematically denied to Black farmers by agencies such as the Farmers Home Administration, and farmers were charged higher interest rates than Whites when they did receive loans. The result has been massive foreclosures and the loss of millions of acres owned by African Americans, particularly productive farms. After years of filing grievances, organizing at the state and federal levels, and suing the USDA, African American claimants accepted a settlement from the USDA in 1999. While the USDA did not actually admit racial discrimination, the settlement acknowledged wrongdoing and required the federal government to compensate Black farmers who could provide documentation to support their claims (see Daniel 2007).

2. Most of the details of this account come from Leon Harris's interview by John Hope II (Hope 1940, 48–51). Harris was a co-founder and president of the National Federation of Colored Farmers at the time of the interview.

3. The resolution of the twelfth Atlanta conference on Negro business development and cooperative economics, held in May 1907, reflected Du Bois's conviction that "present tendencies among Negroes toward co-operative effort and . . . wide ownership of small capital and small accumulations among many rather than great riches among a few" should be fostered, and that the individualistic pursuit of wealth would not help the race (1907, 4).

4. The information in this section comes primarily from Freedom Farm Corporation, "Brief Historical Background of Freedom Farm Corporation," Fannie Lou Hamer Papers, box 11, folder 1, Amistad Research Center.

5. For more information on the Freedom Farm Corporation, see Lee 2000, chap. 8, "Poverty Politics and the Freedom Farm"; and Mills 2007, chap. 14, "Got My Hand on the Gospel Plow."

6. The two cooperatives were very different. North Bolivar was a farmers' cooperative started by experienced, landowning farmers and managed professionally. Its managers had abundant experience in running a farm; some came from three generations of farmers. They handled their assets better—kept their equipment in proper sheds, for example—and operated with an effective business plan.

Part III

1. The epigraph by Du Bois is the ending of an address he delivered in May 1933 at the Rosenwald Economic Conference in Washington, D.C., titled "Where Do We Go from Here? (A Lecture on Negroes' Economic Plight)." The Rosenwald Economic Conference represented an important opportunity for Du Bois to offer this strategy and admonish the United States for its neglect of African American talents.

Chapter 9

1. For a complete list of FSC/LAF member cooperatives, see http://www.federation .coop. Former members are listed in the organization's various annual reports. The information on the FSC/LAF in this chapter comes primarily from FSC/LAF 1992 and 2002, with updates from 2012 and 2013.

2. While many of the most prominent civil rights activists deliberately avoided the subject of economic justice and economic empowerment in order to focus strategically on political rights and not antagonize major corporate and plantation bloc interests (see Young 2005; Reynolds 2002), many of the grassroots civil rights activists, including members of SNCC, promoted cooperative economic development as a strategy for reducing poverty, empowering Black farmers, and stabilizing communities (see Prejean 1992; Reynolds 2002; FSC/LAF 1992; Lewis 1998; and Zippert 2012). In this effort, they joined African Americans who were already working together in mutual-aid societies (Prejean 1992; Jones 1985) and other collective efforts (Woods 1998).

3. Before joining the FSC, Prejean worked with the Southern Consumers' Cooperative in Louisiana. Albert J. McKnight was a Black parish priest engaged in community organizing and cooperative development in Louisiana and the founder of the Southern Consumers' Cooperative. According to de Jong, by 1962 McKnight had been involved in the establishment of more than two thousand cooperatives in southwestern Louisiana (2010, 163).

4. Early FSC/LAF staff member Wendell Paris, for example, notes the cooperative development efforts of Tuskegee Institute and the Southeast Alabama Self-Help Association, which helped establish cooperatives, credit unions, and affordable housing in the early 1960s (FSC/LAF 1992, 24). Woods 1998 makes several references to cooperative efforts among African Americans in the Mississippi Delta.

5. The Panola Land Buyers Association was formed by former sharecroppers/tenant farmers in Sumter County, Alabama, who sued their landlords (plantation owners) for "their legal share of the government price support payment on cotton" with help from the Sumter County Movement for Human Rights, a local affiliate of the Southern Christian Leadership Conference (FSC/LAF 1992, 9). While they won the suit, many tenants were evicted from the plantations they worked on, and most received no money because their landlords, in an age-old practice of deceit and discrimination, claimed that the tenants owed money from prior living expenses and advances. The former tenant farmers who formed the PLBA requested assistance from the Southern Cooperative Development Program and were able to work with one of the local White landowners whose property was being foreclosed. The deal was that the PLBA would help the White landowner redeem all three tracts, with the right to purchase two of the tracts, for a total of 901 acres (FSC/LAF 1992, 24, 25).

6. Zippert joined the effort to develop the federation in 1967 as a co-founder of the Grand Marie Sweet Potato Cooperative in Opelousas, Louisiana, a charter member of the FSC. He had been a CORE volunteer in Louisiana and became Father McKnight's assistant in the Southern Cooperative Development Program when it was first funded by the Ford Foundation (FSC/LAF 1992, 19; Zippert 2005). After the staffs merged in 1970, Zippert moved to Alabama and became the director of the FSC's Training and Research Center.

7. More details can be found in FSC/LAF 1992, other FSC/LAF annual reports, and other documents in the FSC archives located in the Amistad Research Center at Tulane University. The SCDF archives are also located at the Amistad Research Center.

8. Paige began as a volunteer organizer for the West Georgia Farmers Co-op in 1969. He then became a field organizer, a coordinator for the Georgia State Association, a director of marketing at the FSC, and eventually the FSC/LAF's executive director—FSC's third, after Charles Prejean and Jim Jones, who had a short tenure (FSC/LAF 1992, 11, 27; Paige 2001).

9. This type of investigation was not unique to the FSC. Prejean notes that the Southern Consumers' Cooperative, for example, was attacked as a subversive communist organization as it became more effective and better known in the mid-1960s (1992, 14). In 1966 it was investigated locally for alleged misuse of federal and foundation grant funds. The NAACP Legal Defense Fund provided legal support to help the SCC challenge the charges and exonerate itself. De Jong reports a less threatening but equally vexing kind of attack, a White Citizens' Council newsletter ridiculing a new Black cooperative bakery (probably a fruitcake bakery in Louisiana sponsored by the SCC) (2010, 37). De Jong's book contains abundant evidence of physical violence against cooperative businesses and their members (see also Woods 1998).

10. The FSC also established a community health center, the Black Belt Community Health Program, in Sumter County, Alabama, near the training center in Epps. It eventually merged with West Alabama Health Services (FSC/LAF 1992, 66).

11. This account of the South Plaquemine United Fisheries Cooperative comes largely from the FSC/LAF's 2009 annual report.

12. John Zippert, the director of the FSC/LAF's Training and Research Center, has expressed an intention to write a book about the organization, and such a project is certainly warranted.

Chapter 10

1. See also Shipp 2000, on cultural capital, and Abascal-Hildebrand 2002, on Mondragon's social principles, social mechanism system, and "ethos in action."

2. This information comes from an informal interview by the author of Chris Mackin of Ownership Associates, the co-author of an article on APR Masonry Arts (Hill and Mackin 2002), New York City, October 2006.

3. This information comes from discussions with African American member-owners of Lusty Ladies during a workshop I conducted about women in cooperatives in 2009, and through an informal interview with one African American dancer-worker-owner, who also provided a tour of the facilities, August 10, 2009.

4. Information about Apex comes from a plaque in the African American History Museum in Milwaukee.

5. This information is from McCulloch 2001, 69, and from my personal discussions with Avis Ransom of R&B Unlimited, Inc., providers of management assistance to SSC.

6. ChildSpace is a worker cooperative child-care provider in Philadelphia. It operates on a model developed by the ChildSpace Development Training Institute, which incubates worker cooperatives that employ low-income women to provide quality child-care services in high-quality jobs. The worker co-op contracts with a local nonprofit or government agency to provide "developmental learning programs" (Clamp 2002, 47). The ChildSpace Development Training Institute has also started day-care centers in Richmond, California, and Denver, and supports two centers in Philadelphia.

7. I have written elsewhere about cooperative development among Black youths (Gordon Nembhard 2005, 2006b, 2008a, and 2008d); in this section, I use information that was first introduced in this earlier work. Earlier versions of my articles on this subject received substantial research assistance from T. J. Lehman in 2003, thanks to support from the Democracy Collaborative at the University of Maryland and its funders. Updates were provided in 2007 by Chryl Laird, through the African American Studies Department at the University of Maryland, College Park. Moussa Walker Foster provided research and editorial assistance in the final stages of the 2008 versions. Some of this earlier work examines the ways in which entrepreneurial training and experience running cooperative businesses help students, particularly African American students, gain important knowledge and skills for participation in the economy as well as for their academic achievement and their leadership in economic transformation (see Gordon Nembhard 2005, 2008a, 2008d; see also Nagel, Shahyd, and Weisner 2005; Dorson 2003; Skilton-Sylvester 1994; Brooks and Lynch 1944).

8. For more on Food from the 'Hood, visit http://try-change.blogspot.com/2007/11/food-from-hood.html; and see the video at http://www.youtube.com/watch?v=XPvuyXo6Smo.

9. Most of this information comes from the Worcester Roots website, (http://www.WorcesterRoots.org), but also from my attendance at workshops and presentations by the young owners over the past eight years, and from informal conversations with several of these owners at worker-cooperative conferences.

10. The term "solidarity economy" has become increasingly popular since the first World Social Forum in Brazil. The U.S. Solidarity Economy Network (http://www.ussen.org) describes a solidarity economy as an alternative economic framework grounded in shared values, solidarity, and cooperation that promotes social and economic democracy, equity in all dimensions (e.g. race, class, gender), and sustainability. It is pluralist and organic in its approach, allowing for different nonhierarchical forms and strategies in different contexts, and always building from the grass roots up. The term "economic solidarity" refers to economic activities whose purpose is to support, promote, and develop a particular group using shared values, trust, and loyalty (see Gherardi and Masiero 1990).

References

All sources in the Ella Baker Papers are located at the Schomburg Center for Research in Black Culture, New York Public Library, New York (hereafter Schomburg Center); all sources listed under Ella J. Baker are in box 2, folder 2. All sources in the Fannie Lou Hamer Papers are located at the Amistad Research Center, Tulane University, New Orleans (hereafter Amistad Research Center).

Abascal-Hildebrand, Mary. 2002. "Culture, Geography, and the Anthropology of Work: Textual Understandings of *Equilibrio* and *Solidaridad* in the Mondragon (Basque) Cooperatives." Manuscript, University of San Francisco, School of Education. http://cog.kent.edu/lib/Abascal-Hildebrand.htm.

Abell, Hilary. 2011. "WAGES Model and the Value of Partnerships." *GEO: Grassroots Economic Organizing Newsletter*, no. 8 (Summer): 27–31.

Abramowitz, J. 1953. "The Negro in the Populist Movement." *Journal of Negro History* 38 (3): 257–89.

Adams, Bristow. 1920. "Direct Dealing Between Producers and Consumers." In "Cooperation Among Producers and Consumers in New York State," special issue, *Foods and Markets* 2 (March–April): 47–50.

Adams, Frank T., and Gary B. Hansen. 1992. *Putting Democracy to Work: A Practical Guide for Starting and Managing Worker-Owned Businesses*. Rev. ed. San Francisco: Berrett-Koehler.

Adams, Frank T., and Richard Shirey. 1993. *The Workers' Owned Sewing Company: Making the Eagle Fly Friday; An ICA Group Case Study*. Boston: ICA Group.

AFL-CIO Housing Investment Trust. 2000. "Homeownership and Wealth Accumulation." Paper presented at the Joint 2000 Cooperative Development Forum and the Cooperative Housing Coalition, Washington, D.C., October 24.

"Aggie." 1975–76. "Some Background on the Interview." *Scoop Newsletter*, no. 12 (December–January): 12.

Ali, Mazher, Jeannette Huezo, Brian Miller, Wanjiku Mawangi, and Mike Prokosch. 2011. *State of the Dream 2011: Austerity for Whom?* Boston: United for a Fair Economy.

Ali, Omar H. 2003. "Black Populism in the New South, 1886–1898." PhD diss., Columbia University.

———. 2005. "Independent Black Voices from the Late Nineteenth Century: Black Populists and the Struggle Against the Southern Democracy." *Souls* 7 (2): 4–18.

———. 2010. *In the Lion's Mouth: Black Populism in the New South, 1886–1900*. Jackson: University Press of Mississippi.

Allen, Mary. 1948. "How Can the Cooperative Movement Help Workers?" *Black Worker*, March, 5.

American Bankers Association. 2010. "NCUA Actions to Support Corporate Credit Unions." http://www.aba.com/aba/documents/groce/ncuaactions.pdf.

Anand, Nikhil, and Henry Holmes. 2000. *Failed Promises: Why Economic Growth and the Global Economy Cannot Achieve Social Justice and Ecological Sustainability, and What Can.* San Francisco: Sustainable Alternatives to the Global Economy.

Anderson, Jervis B. 1986. *A. Philip Randolph: A Biographical Portrait.* Berkeley: University of California Press.

Asbury, Edith Evans. 1967. "Co-op Store for Harlem; Harlem to Build a Co-op Market." *New York Times,* December 21. http://select.nytimes.com/gst/abstract.html?res=F70A15F934591B7B93C3AB1789D95F438685F9.

Associated Negro Press. 1923. "Negro and White Georgia Farmers Pool Interests." *Negro World,* October 27.

Badgett, M. V. Lee, and Rhonda M. Williams. 1994. "The Changing Contours of Discrimination: Race, Gender, and Structural Economic Change." In *Understanding American Economic Decline,* ed. Michael A. Bernstein and David E. Adler, 313–29. Cambridge: Cambridge University Press.

Baker, Bruce E. 1999. "The 'Hoover Scare' in South Carolina, 1887: An Attempt to Organize Black Farm Labor." *Labor History* 40 (August): 261–82.

Baker, Ella J. ca. 1931a. "From the National Director." Ella Baker Papers, box 2, folder 2, Schomburg Center.

——. ca. 1931b. "On Promoting Consumers' Clubs." Ella Baker Papers, box 2, folder 2, Schomburg Center.

——. 1931c. "Report of the First National Conference of the Young Negroes' Co-operative League." Ella Baker Papers, box 2, folder 2, Schomburg Center.

——. 1931d. *Straight Talk,* no. 1 (July). Ella Baker Papers, box 2, folder 2, Schomburg Center.

——. ca. 1932a. "Dear Fellow Cooperator." Ella Baker Papers, box 2, folder 2, Schomburg Center.

——. ca. 1932b. "Penny-a-Day Plan." Ella Baker Papers, box 2, folder 2, Schomburg Center.

——. 1941. "Consumers' Cooperation Among Negroes." Memorandum from Baker to Mr. Wilkins, August 12. Ella Baker Papers, box 2, folder 2, Schomburg Center.

[——.] n.d. "Dear Friend and Cooperator." Ella Baker Papers, box 2, folder 2, Schomburg Center.

Baker, Ella J., and Marvel Cooke. 1935. "The Bronx Slave Market." *Crisis,* November, 330–31, 340.

"Barb." 1975–76. "C.O. Update." *Scoop Newsletter,* no. 12 (December–January): 12.

Barkley Brown, Elsa. 1989. "Womanist Consciousness: Maggie Lena Walker and the Independent Order of St. Luke." *Signs* 14 (Spring): 610–33.

Barone, Charles A. 1991. "Contending Perspectives: Curricular Reform in Economics." *Journal of Economics Education* 22 (Winter): 15–26.

Baugh, Joyce. 1987. "Employee Ownership as a Strategy for Black Economic Empowerment." In *The Ohio Buyout Handbook,* ed. John Logue, 64–72. Athens, Ga.: Centers for Labor-Management Cooperation.

Baumol, William J., John C. Panzar, and Robert D. Willig. 1982. *Contestable Markets and the Theory of Industry Structure.* New York: Harcourt Brace Jovanovich.

Bendick, Marc, Jr., and Mary Lou Egan. 1995. "Worker Ownership and Participation Enhances Economic Development in Low-Opportunity Communities." *Journal of Community Practice* 2 (1): 61–85.

Bergström, Cecilia. 1999. "People Develop Themselves: A Socio-Economic Approach." Paper presented at International Co-operative Alliance research conference, "Values and Enterprise for Co-operative Advantage," Quebec City, August 28–29.

Berkeley, Kathleen C. 1985. "'Colored Ladies Also Contributed': Black Women's Activities from Benevolence to Social Welfare, 1866–1896." In *The Web of Southern Social Relations*, ed. Walter J. Fraser Jr., Frank Saunders Jr., and John L. Wakelyn Jr., 181–201. Athens: University of Georgia Press.

Berry, Mary Frances. 2005. *My Face Is Black Is True: Callie House and the Struggle for Ex-Slave Reparations.* New York: Knopf.

Bethell, Thomas N. 1982. *Sumter County Blues: The Ordeal of the Federation of Southern Cooperatives.* Washington, D.C.: National Committee in Support of Community Based Organizations.

Bickle, Richard, and Alan Wilkins. 2000. "Co-operative Values, Principles, and Future— A Values Basis to Building a Successful Co-operative Business." *Journal of Co-operative Studies* 33 (August): 179–205.

Birchall, Johnston. 2003. *Rediscovering the Cooperative Advantage: Poverty Reduction Through Self-Help.* Geneva, Switzerland: International Labour Office.

Birchall, Johnston, and Lou Hammond Ketilson. 2009. *Resilience of the Cooperative Business Model in Times of Crisis.* Geneva, Switzerland: International Labour Office.

Blinder, Alan S., ed. 1990. *Paying for Productivity: A Look at the Evidence.* Washington, D.C.: Brookings Institute.

Bois, Danuta. 1998. "Maggie Lena Walker (1867–1934)." http://www.distinguishedwomen .com/biographies/walker-ml.html.

Boston, Thomas D., and Catherine L. Ross. 1997. *The Inner City: Urban Poverty and Economic Development in the Next Century.* New Brunswick, N.J.: Transaction.

Bowman, Elizabeth A., and Bob Stone. 2003. "New Orleans' Alternative Economy." *GEO: Grassroots Economic Organizing Newsletter,* no. 57 (May–June): 12.

Boylan, A. M. 1984. "Women in Groups: An Analysis of Women's Benevolent Organizations in New York and Boston, 1797–1840." *Journal of American History* 71 (3): 497–523.

Bransburg, Vanessa. 2011. "The Center for Family Life: Tackling Poverty and Social Isolation in Brooklyn with Worker Cooperatives." *GEO: Grassroots Economic Organizing Newsletter,* no. 8 (Summer): 13–16.

Briggs, Emanuel Denard. 2003. "Analysis of Cooperative Economic Development Strategies Fostered in the Black Community." Senior thesis, Department of African American Studies, University of Maryland, College Park.

Britton, Eric D., and Mark C. Stewart. 2001. "Selling to Your Employees Through a Worker Cooperative—And Sheltering Your Capital Gain." dept.kent.edu/oeoc/ OEOClibrary/Coop1042Rollover.htm.

Bromell-Tinubu, Gloria. 1998. "The Cooperative Continuum of Asset Accumulation and Ownership: Why Focus on Assets?" In *1998 Cooperative Development Forum Proceedings,* ed. NCBA, 57–63. Washington, D.C.: National Cooperative Business Association.

———. 1999. "Individual and Community Asset-Building Through Cooperative Enterprises: Economic and Social Justifications." Paper presented at the National Economic Association/ASSA annual meeting, New York, January 3–5.

———. 2000. "Creating a Cooperative Culture: A Systems View of Economic and Social Cooperation." Paper presented at the Association of Cooperative Educators Institute, Saskatoon, Saskatchewan, May.

Brooks, Lee M., and Ruth G. Lynch. 1944. "Consumer Problems and the Cooperative Movement in the Curricula of Southern Negro Colleges." *Social Forces* 22 (May): 429–36.

Browne, Irene, ed. 1999. *Latinas and African American Women at Work.* New York: Russell Sage Foundation.

Browne, Robert S. 1974. "Wealth Distribution and Its Impact on Minorities." *Review of Black Political Economy* 4 (Summer): 27–37.

Bullard, Robert D., Glenn S. Johnson, and Angel O. Torres. 2000. *Sprawl City: Race, Politics, and Planning in Atlanta.* Washington, D.C.: Island Press.

Bunche, Ralph. n.d. "The Negro Cooperative Guild." Mimeograph. Ralph J. Bunche Papers, 1922–1988, box 33, folder 4, collection no. SC MG 290, Schomburg Center.

Burroughs, Nannie Helen. 1934a. Letter to Chancellor Williams and the Trustees of the Northeast Self-Help Cooperative, October 31. Nannie Helen Burroughs Papers, box 52, folder 3, Library of Congress, Washington, D.C.

———. 1934b. Letter to Owen Woodruff, August 31. Nannie Helen Burroughs Papers, box 52, folder 3, Library of Congress, Washington, D.C.

———. 1934c. Letter to Owen Woodruff, December 6. Nannie Helen Burroughs Papers, box 52, folder 3, Library of Congress, Washington, D.C.

Burroughs, Nannie Helen, and the Board of Directors. n.d. [ca. late 1936.] "Dear Fellow Citizens." Nannie Helen Burroughs Papers, box 52, folder 3, Library of Congress, Washington, D.C.

Busby, William H. 1970. "Evaluation of the Third Annual Meeting of the Federation of Southern Cooperatives, Held August 28–30, 1970." Mimeograph. Federation of Southern Cooperatives/Land Assistance Fund, East Point, Ga.

Bynum, Bill. 2010. "Community Development Financial Institutions: Their Unique Role and Challenges Serving Lower-Income, Underserved, and Minority Communities." Testimony before the U.S. House Financial Services Committee, March 9. http://financialservices.house.gov/media/file/hearings/111/bynumγtestimony.pdf.

Calvin, Floyd J. 1931. "Schuyler Launches Program to Awaken Race Consciousness." *Pittsburgh Courier*, February 7.

Cartmell, Samuel. n.d. "Consumers' Cooperation." Ella Baker Papers, box 2, folder 1, Schomburg Center.

Case, J. 2003. "The Power of Listening: How Does an Old-Line Manufacturer in a Stagnant Industry Manage to Grow 25% a Year for 10 Years?" *Inc. Magazine*, March, 77–84, 110.

Centre for the Study of Co-operatives. 1998. *Proceedings from the Women in Co-operatives Forum, November 7–8, 1997.* Saskatoon: University of Saskatchewan, Centre for the Study of Co-operatives.

Chaddad, F. R., and M. Cook. 2004. "Understanding New Cooperative Models: An Ownership-Control Rights Typology." *Review of Agricultural Economics* 26 (Autumn): 348–60.

Chang, Mariko Lin. 2006. "Women and Wealth." In *Wealth Accumulation and Communities of Color in the United States: Current Issues*, ed. Jessica Gordon Nembhard and Ngina Chiteji, 112–30. Ann Arbor: University of Michigan Press.

Chateauvert, Melinda. 1998. *Marching Together: Women of the Brotherhood of Sleeping Car Porters.* Urbana: University of Illinois Press.

CHCA (Cooperative Home Care Associates). 2008. "Helping Low-Income New York City Residents Develop Assets." Mimeograph. "Expanding Asset Building Opportunities Through Shared Ownership," Annie E. Casey Foundation Conference, Baltimore, December 2.

Chesnick, David S. 2000. "Asset Growth for Largest Co-ops Shows Resilience to Declining Revenues." *Rural Development* (January). Washington, D.C.: United States Department of Agriculture. http://www.rurdev.usda.gov/rbs/pub/jan00/asset.htm.

Chipeta, W. 1971. "On the Classification of African Indigenous Cooperatives." *African Studies Review* 14 (April): 95–100.

Churchill, Neil C. 1995. "Analysis, Overview, and Application to Pedagogy." In *Entrepreneurship: Perspectives on Theory Building*, ed. I. Bull, H. Thomas, and G. Willard, 159–70. Tarrytown, N.Y.: Pergamon Press.

Clamp, Christina. 2002. "Case 5: Childspace Development Training Institute, Philadel-
    phia." In Feldman and Gordon Nembhard, *From Community Economic Develop-
    ment*, 47–48.

Cobbs, John L. 1976. "A Job That Badly Needs Doing: A Business Editor Looks at Econom-
    ics Education." *Journal of Economics Education* 8 (Winter): 5–8.

Cohen, Lizabeth. 2003. "Depression: Rise of the Citizen Consumer." In Cohen, *A Con-
    sumers' Republic: The Politics of Mass Consumption in Postwar America*, 18–61.
    New York: Knopf.

Coleman, Daniel A. 2000. "Combining Worker and Consumer Ownership: The Experi-
    ence of Weaver Street Market." *Journal of Co-operative Studies* 33 (April): 7–14.

Collaborative for Educational Services. 2009a. "Radical Equality: 1842–1846—Abolition."
    http://radicalequality.emergingamerica.org/background/abolition/.

———. 2009b. "Radical Equality: 1842–1846—Democracy." http://radicalequality.emerging
    america.org/background/democracy/.

———. 2009c. "Radical Equality: 1842–1846—Overview." http://radicalequality.emerging
    america.org/background/overview/.

Coltrain, David, David Barton, and Michael Boland. 2001. "Differences Between New
    Generation Cooperatives and Traditional Cooperatives." Staff paper no. 01–08.
    Department of Agricultural Economics, Kansas State University.

Conn, Melanie. 2001. "Women, Co-ops, and CED." *Making Waves*, Spring, 34–36.

Connor, Miles W. 1939. "The Nova Scotia Cooperatives as Seen by Miles W. Connor." In
    Alethea H. Washington, "Section B: Rural Education—The Cooperative Move-
    ment." *Journal of Negro Education* 8 (January): 108–110.

Conover, Nancy, Frieda Molina, and Karin Morris. 1993. *Creating Jobs Through Cooper-
    ative Development*. Davis, Calif.: University of California, Davis, Center for
    Cooperatives.

Conrad, Cecilia A. 1998. "National Standards or Economic Imperialism?" *Journal of Eco-
    nomic Education* 29 (Spring): 167–69.

Conrad, Cecilia, John Whitehead, Patrick Mason, and James Stewart. 2005. *African
    Americans in the United States Economy*. Lanham, Md.: Rowman & Littlefield.

Cook, Michael L. 1995. "The Future of U.S. Agricultural Cooperatives: A Neo-Institutional
    Approach." *American Journal of Agricultural Economics* 77 (December): 1153–59.

Cooley, Oscar. 1932a. Letter to George S. Schuyler, March 31. Ella Baker Papers, box 2,
    folder 1, Schomburg Center.

———. 1932b. "Greetings to the National Conference of the Young Negroes Cooperative
    League." Ella Baker Papers, box 2, folder 1, Schomburg Center.

Corporation for Enterprise Development. 1999. *Ideas in Development: Growing Assets,
    Expanding Opportunity*. Washington, D.C.: Corporation for Enterprise Develop-
    ment.

Cotton, Jeremiah. 1992. "Towards a Theory and Strategy for Black Economic Develop-
    ment." In *Race, Politics, and Economic Development: Community Perspectives*,
    ed. James Jennings, 11–32. New York: Verso.

Council for Cooperative Development. n.d. "Co-op Labor Conference Proposed Agenda."
    December 9. A. Philip Randolph Collection, box 75, folder 7, Library of Congress,
    Washington, D.C.

Couto, Richard A., with Catherine S. Guthrie. 1999. *Making Democracy Work Better:
    Mediating Structures, Social Capital, and the Democratic Prospect*. Chapel Hill:
    University of North Carolina Press.

Cox, O. 1948. *Caste, Class, and Race: A Study in Social Dynamics*. New York: Doubleday.

Craig, John M. 1987. "Community Cooperation in Ruthville, Virginia, 1900–1930." *Phylon*
    48 (2): 132–40.

Crisis. 1934. "Dr. Du Bois Resigns." August, 245–46. Reprinted in Huggins, *W. E. B. Du
    Bois: Writings*, 1259–63.

Crump, Charlotte. 1941. "The Co-op Comes to Harlem." *Crisis*, October, 319, 330.

Curl, John. 1980. *History of Worker Cooperation in America: Worker Cooperatives or Wage Slavery; Co-ops, Unions, Collectivity, and Communalism from Early America to the Present.* Toledo, Ohio: Homeward Press. http://www.red-coral.net/WorkCoops.html.

———. 2009. *For All the People: Uncovering the Hidden History of Cooperation, Cooperative Movements, and Communalism in America.* Oakland, Calif.: PM Press.

Daly, Herman E., and John B. Cobb Jr. 1994. *For the Common Good: Redirecting the Economy to the Community, the Environment, and a Sustainable Future.* 2nd ed. Boston: Beacon Press.

Daniel, Pete. 2007. "African American Farmers and Civil Rights (*Pigford v. Glickman*)." *Journal of Southern History* 73 (February), http://www.federationsoutherncoop.com/pigford/AfricanAmericanfarmers.pdf.

Danielson, C. 2003. *Enhancing Student Achievement: A Framework for School Improvement.* Alexandria, Va.: Association for Supervision and Curriculum Development.

Darity, William A., Jr., and Jessica Gordon Nembhard. 2000. "Racial and Ethnic Economic Inequality: The International Record." *American Economic Review* 90 (May): 308–11.

Darity, William A., Jr., and Patrick L. Mason. 1998. "Evidence of Discrimination in Employment: Codes of Color, Codes of Gender." *Journal of Economic Perspectives* 12 (Spring): 63–90.

Darity, William A., Jr., and Melba Nicholson. 2005. "Racial Wealth Inequality and the Black Family." In *African American Family Life: Ecological and Cultural Diversity,* ed. Vonnie McLoyd, Nancy Hill, and Kenneth Dodge, 78–85. New York: Guilford Press.

Davies, James B., Susanna Sanstrom, Anthony Shorrock, and Edward N. Wolff. 2006. "The World Distribution of Household Wealth." http://www.wider.unu.edu.

Davis, Angela Y. 1981. *Women, Race, and Class.* New York: Random House.

Davis, F. 1972. *The Economics of Black Community Development.* Chicago: Markham.

Davis, Peter. 1999. "Contested Terrain: Co-operation as a Social Movement for Economic and Political Justice." *Journal of Co-operative Studies* 32 (September): 147–60.

DeFilippis, James. 2004. *Unmaking Goliath: Community Control in the Face of Global Capital.* New York: Routledge.

———. n.d. "Place, Politics, and Worker-Ownership in the United States." Manuscript, King's College, London.

de Jong, Greta. 2005. "Staying in Place: Black Migration, the Civil Rights Movement, and the War on Poverty in the Rural South." *Journal of African American History* 90 (Fall): 387–409.

———. 2010. *Invisible Enemy: African American Freedom Struggles After 1965.* West Sussex, UK: Wiley Blackwell.

Deller, Stephen, Ann Hoyt, Brent Hueth, and Reka Sundaram-Stukel. 2009. *Research on the Economic Impact of Cooperatives.* Madison: University of Wisconsin Center for Cooperatives.

DeMarco, Joseph P. 1974. "The Rationale and Foundation of Du Bois' Theory of Economic Cooperation." *Phylon* 35 (1): 5–15.

———. 1983. *The Social Thought of W. E. B. Du Bois.* Lanham, Md.: University Press of America.

Democracy Collaborative. 2005. *Building Wealth: The New Asset-Based Approach to Solving Social and Economic Problems.* Washington, D.C.: Aspen Institute.

Dernovsek, Darla. 2007. "CDCUs Push the Envelope." *Credit Union Magazine*, September, 46–51.

Dodson, Howard, Christopher Moore, and Roberta Yancy. 2000. *The Black New Yorkers: The Schomburg Illustrated Chronology.* New York: John Wiley & Sons.

Donnachie, Ian. 2006. "Orbiston: The First British Owenite Community, 1825–28." *Spaces of Utopia: An Electronic Journal* 2 (Summer). http://ler.letras.up.pt/uploads/ficheiros/1635.pdf.

Dorson, Cheryl. 2003. "Grounds for Learning: Hope for America's Derelict Schoolyards." http://www.asbj.com/.

Douglass, Frederick. 1882. *The Life and Times of Frederick Douglass, 1817–1882.* London: Christian Age.

——. 1895. "What I Found at the Northampton Association." *Old Community Times.* Reprinted in *A History of Florence, MA*, ed. C.A. Sheffield (Florence, Mass.: by the author, 1895), 129–32. http://archive.org/stream/historyofflorencooshef/historyofflorencooshef_djvu.txt.

Du Bois, W. E. B. 1898. *Some Efforts of American Negroes for Their Own Social Betterment.* Atlanta: Atlanta University Press.

——. 1899. "Postscript: On the Duty of Negroes." In Du Bois, *The Philadelphia Negro: A Social Study* (Philadelphia: University of Pennsylvania). Reprinted in Paschal, *W. E. B. Du Bois Reader*, 193–97.

——. 1903. *The Souls of Black Folk.* Chicago: A. C. McClurg.

——. 1907. *Economic Co-operation Among Negro Americans.* Atlanta: Atlanta University Press.

[——.] 1919. "Ruddy's Citizen's Cooperative Stores." *Crisis*, December, 48–50.

——. 1921. "Marcus Garvey, Part 2." *Crisis*, January. Reprinted in Huggins, *W. E. B. Du Bois: Writings*, 972–79.

——. 1923. Letter to the Hon. Charles Hughes, January 5. In Aptheker, *Correspondence of W. E. B. Du Bois*, 1:260–61.

——. 1925. Letter to Dr. Warbasse, February 13. In Aptheker, *Correspondence of W. E. B. Du Bois*, 1:305.

——. 1933a. "Pan-Africa and New Racial Philosophy." *Crisis*, November, 247, 262.

——. 1933b. "The Right to Work." *Crisis*, April, 93–94. Reprinted in Huggins, *W. E. B. Du Bois: Writings*, 1235–38 (citations are to this edition).

——. 1933c. "Where Do We Go from Here? (A Lecture on Negroes' Economic Plight)." Address delivered at the Rosenwald Economic Conference, Washington, D.C., May. Reprinted in Paschal, *W. E. B. Du Bois Reader*, 146–63.

——. 1934a. Letter of Resignation as Editor. *Crisis*, August.

——. 1934b. Letter to Abram L. Harris, January 3. In Aptheker, *Correspondence of W. E. B. Du Bois*, 1:470–71.

——. 1934c. Letter to Walter White, January 17. In Aptheker, *Correspondence of W. E. B. Du Bois*, 1:475–76.

——. 1935a. "A Negro Nation Within a Nation." In *Current History*, 42:265–270. New York: New York Times Company.

——. 1935b. "The Present Economic Problem of the American Negro." Reprinted in Paschal, *W. E. B. Du Bois Reader*, 163–79.

——. 1940. *Dusk of Dawn: An Essay Toward an Autobiography of a Race Concept.* New York: Harcourt, Brace. Reprinted in Huggins, *W. E. B. Du Bois: Writings*, 549–801 (citations are to this edition).

——. 1958. "The Negro and Socialism." In *Toward a Socialist America—A Symposium of Essays by Fifteen Contemporary American Socialists*, ed. Helen Alfred, 179–91. New York: Peace Publications. Reprinted in Paschal, *W. E. B. Du Bois Reader*, 179–93 (citations are to this edition).

——. 1970. *Black Reconstruction in America, 1860–1880.* New York: Atheneum.

——. 1971. *A W. E. B. Du Bois Reader.* Edited by Andrew G. Paschal. New York: Collier Books.

———. 1973. *The Correspondence of W. E. B. Du Bois.* Vol. 1, *Selections, 1877–1934.* Edited by Herbert Aptheker. Amherst: University of Massachusetts Press, 1973.

———. 1978. *On Sociology and the Black Community.* Edited by Dan S. Green and Edwin D. Driver. Chicago: University of Chicago Press.

———. 1986. *W. E. B. Du Bois: Writings.* Edited by Nathan Huggins. New York: Library of America.

Dumas, Colette. 2001. "Evaluating the Outcomes of Microenterprise Training for Low Income Women: A Case Study." *Journal of Developmental Entrepreneurship* 6 (August): 97–128.

Dymski, Gary. 1995. "Exploitation and Racial Inequality: The U.S. Case." Working Paper in Economics no. 96–06. Department of Economics, University of California, Riverside.

———. 2001. "Can Entrepreneurial Incentives Revitalize the Urban Inner Core? A Spatial Input-Output Approach." *Journal of Economic Issues* 35 (June): 415–22.

Elden, J. Maxwell. 1981. "Political Efficacy at Work: The Connection Between More Autonomous Forms of Workplace Organization and a More Participatory Politics." *American Political Science Review* 75 (1): 43–58.

Ellerman, David P. 1990. *The Democratic Worker-Owned Firm.* Boston: Unwin Hyman.

Ellison, Julian. 1980. "Cooperation and Struggle: The African American Cooperative Tradition." *Scoop Newsletter,* no. 50 (September): 2.

Emelianoff, Ivan V. 1995. *Economic Theory of Cooperation: Economic Structure of Cooperative Organizations.* Davis, Calif.: University of California, Davis, Center for Cooperatives.

Engelskirchen, Lynne E. 1997. "Meeting the Challenge of Economic Development: Productivity, Efficiency, and Participation in Employee Owned Firms in New York State." PhD diss., Columbia University.

Erdal, David. 1999. "Egalitarianism in Human Evolution." PhD diss., University of St. Andrews, Scotland.

Fairbairn, Brett. 2003. "Three Strategic Concepts for the Guidance of Co-operatives: Linkage, Transparency, and Cognition." Saskatoon: University of Saskatchewan, Centre for the Study of Co-operatives.

Fairbairn, Brett, June Bold, Murray Fulton, Lou Hammond Ketilson, and Daniel Ish. 1991. *Cooperatives and Community Development: Economics in Social Perspective.* Saskatoon: University of Saskatchewan, Centre for the Study of Co-operatives.

Fannie Mae Foundation. 2003. "Stretch Loan, ASI Federal Credit Union." Washington, D.C.: Fannie Mae Foundation. http://content.knowledgeplex.org/kp2/cache/documents/5629.pdf.

Feldman, Jonathan Michael. 2002. "From Microenterprise to Franchise Cooperative: A New Model for Ethnic Entrepreneurship." In Feldman and Gordon Nembhard, *From Community Economic Development,* 92–114.

Feldman, Jonathan Michael, and Jessica Gordon Nembhard. 2001. "Towards a New Community Development Paradigm: The Political and Economic Agenda." *Planners Network Newsletter,* no. 149 (September–December): 21–34.

———, eds. 2002. *From Community Economic Development and Ethnic Entrepreneurship to Economic Democracy: The Cooperative Alternative.* Umea, Sweden: Partnership for Multiethnic Inclusion.

Fenton, Tracey L. 2002. *The Democratic Company: Four Organizations Transforming Our Workplace and Our World.* Arlington, Va.: World Dynamics.

Fitzgerald, Dianne. 1999. "Cooperativism at Its Best: Through CEPP, Social Assistance Recipients Become Income Tax Payers." *GEO: Grassroots Economic Organizing Newsletter,* no. 38 (September–October): 10–12.

Fitzgerald, Joan, and Nancey Green Leigh. 2002. *Economic Revitalization: Cases and Strategies for City and Suburb.* Thousand Oaks, Calif.: Sage Publications.

Fletcher, William, and Eugene Newport. 1992. "Race and Economic Development: The Need for a Black Agenda." In *Race, Politics, and Economic Development: Community Perspectives*, ed. James Jennings, 117–30. New York: Verso.

Floyd-Thomas, Juan M. 2008. *The Origins of Black Humanism in America: Reverend Ethelred Brown and the Unitarian Church*. New York: Palgrave Macmillan.

Folbre, Nancy, and Julie A. Nelson. 2000. "For Love or Money—Or Both?" *Journal of Economic Perspectives* 14 (Fall): 123–40.

Fordham, Monroe. ca. 1976. "The Buffalo Cooperative Economic Society: A Short History." Buffalo Afro-American Collection and the Buffalo State College Regional History Collection, Buffalo State College Archives, SUNY, Buffalo.

Frazier, E. Franklin. 1923. "Cooperation and the Negro." *Crisis*, March, 228–29.

Frazier, Robeson Taj P. 2006. "The Congress of African People." *Souls* 8 (September): 142–59.

Freedom Farm Corporation. 1970. "Charter of Incorporation." Fannie Lou Hamer Collection, Tougaloo College Civil Rights Collection T/012, Mississippi Department of Archives and History, Jackson.

———. 1971. Letter to Robert S. Brown, BERC, August 23, with funding proposal. Fannie Lou Hamer Papers, box 11, Amistad Research Center.

———. 1973a. "Progress Report" (March). Fannie Lou Hamer Papers, box 11, Amistad Research Center.

———. 1973b. "Status Report and Request for Funds" (March). Fannie Lou Hamer Papers, box 11, Amistad Research Center.

———. 1977. "Quitclaim Deed." Freedom Farm Corporation to City of Ruleville, March 18. Fannie Lou Hamer Collection, Tougaloo College Civil Rights Collection T/012, Mississippi Department of Archives and History, Jackson.

———. n.d. "Brief Historical Background of Freedom Farm Corporation." Fannie Lou Hamer Papers, box 11, folder 1, Amistad Research Center.

Freedom Quilting Bee. n.d. "History, Activities, Plans." http://www.ruraldevelopment.org/FQBhistory.html.

Frey, Bruno. 2001. *Inspiring Economics: Human Motivation in Political Economy*. Cheltenham, UK: Edward Elgar.

Friedman, Thomas L. 1999. *The Lexus and the Olive Tree: Understanding Globalization*. New York: Farrar, Straus and Giroux.

FSC/LAF (Federation of Southern Cooperatives/Land Assistance Fund). 1992. "25th Anniversary Annual Report, 1967–1992." East Point, Ga.: FSC/LAF.

———. 2002. "Thirty-Fifth Anniversary—2002 Annual Report." East Point, Ga.: FSC/LAF.

———. 2006. "The Federation's Katrina Relief and Recovery Program." *Rural Agenda*, Fall/Winter (entire issue).

———. 2007. "Celebrating Forty Years 'Working Together for Change.'" East Point, Ga.: FSC/LAF.

———. 2012. "Cooperatives Make a Better World: 45th Anniversary Annual Report, 2011–12." East Point, Ga.: FSC/LAF.

———. 2013. "Rural Communities Matter: Fighting for Fair and Equitable Policies; Annual Report, 2012–13." East Point, Ga: FSC/LAF.

Fulton, Murray, and Julie Gibbings. 2006. "Cognitive Processes and Co-operative Business Strategy." University of Saskatchewan, Centre for the Study of Co-operatives. http://usaskstudies.coop/pdf-files/FultonGibbings.pdf.

Fusfeld, Daniel R. 1980. "Capitalist Exploitation and Black Labor: An Extended Conceptual Framework." *Review of Black Political Economy* 10 (3): 244–46.

Galloway, Ian J. 2009. "Peer-to-Peer Lending and Community Development Finance." Community Development Investment Center, Working Paper 2009–06. http://www.frbsf.org/publications/community/wpapers/2009/wp2009–06.pdf.

Gallup Organization and National Center for Research in Economic Education. 1996. *Entrepreneurship and Small Business in the United States: A Survey Report on Minority and Gender Attitudes and Opinions Among High School Youth.* Kansas City, Mo.: Center for Entrepreneurial Leadership.

Ganibe, Salome. 1998. "Women in Leadership and Decision-Making Roles in Co-opera-tives." In *Proceedings from the Women in Co-operatives Forum, November 7–8, 1997,* 54–60. Saskatoon: University of Saskatchewan, Centre for the Study of Co-operatives.

Garcia, Michelle. 2005. "For a Former Panther, Solidarity After the Storm." *Washington Post,* December 4.

Gardner, R., and A. H. Miranda. 2001. "Improving Outcomes for Urban African American Students." *Journal of Negro Education* 70 (4): 255–63.

Garrett-Scott, Shennette. 2009. "A Historiography of African American Business." *Free Library,* January 1. http://www.thefreelibrary.com/A historiography of African American business.-a0220202784.

Garvey, Marcus. 1924. "Negroes Cooperating for Black Steamship Company's Success." *Negro World,* May 24, 1.

——. 1986. *The Philosophy and Opinions of Marcus Garvey: Or Africa for the Africans,* comp. Amy Jacques Garvey. 2 vols. Dover, Mass.: Majority Press.

Gemerer, Greg. 2008. "Financial Trends in Community Development Credit Unions: A Statistical Analysis (January 1–December 31, 2007)." New York: National Federa-tion of Community Development Credit Unions.

Gherardi, Silvia, and Attilio Masiero. 1990. "Solidarity as a Networking Skill and a Trust Relation: Its Implications for Cooperative Development." *Economic and Industrial Democracy* 11 (November): 553–74.

Gilbert, Abby L. 1972. "The Comptroller of the Currency and the Freedman's Savings Bank." *Journal of Negro History* 57 (April): 125–43.

Giloth, Robert. 1998. "Jobs and Economic Development." In *Jobs and Economic Devel-opment,* ed. Robert Giloth, 1–18. Thousand Oaks, Calif.: Sage Publications.

Glasser, C. 1989. *The Quality School.* Chatsworth, Calif.: William Glasser Institute.

Glasser, Ruth, and Jeremy Brecher. 2002. *We Are the Roots: The Organizational Culture of a Home Care Cooperative.* Davis, Calif.: University of California, Davis, Center for Cooperatives.

Gordon, Edmund T. 1994. "Cultural Politics of the African American Male Cultural Form." Paper presented at the Working Conference on African American Males, the Black Community Crusade for Children, Children's Defense Fund, Haley Farm, Clinton, Tennessee, October.

——. 1997. "Cultural Politics of Black Masculinity." *Transforming Anthropology* 6 (1–2): 36–53.

Gordon, Edmund W., Beatrice L. Bridglall, and Aundra Saa Meroe. 2005. *Supplementary Education: The Hidden Curriculum of High Academic Achievement.* Lanham, Md.: Rowman & Littlefield.

Gordon Nembhard, Jessica. 1999. "Community Economic Development: Alternative Visions for the Twenty-First Century." In *Readings in Black Political Economy,* ed. John Whitehead and Cobie Kwasi Harris, 295–304. Dubuque, Iowa: Kendall/ Hunt.

——. 2000a. "Democratic Economic Participation and Humane Urban Redevelopment." *Trotter Review:* 26–31.

——. 2000b. "Post-Industrial Economic Experiences of African American Men, 1973–1993." In *Edmund W. Gordon: Producer of Knowledge, Pursuer of Understand-ing,* ed. Carol Camp Yeakey, 241–62. London: Elsevier.

——. 2002a. "Cooperatives and Wealth Accumulation: Preliminary Analysis." *American Economic Review* 2 (May): 325–29.

——. 2002b. "Education for a People-Centered Democratic Economy." *GEO: Grassroots Economic Organizing Newsletter*, nos. 53–54 (July–October): 8–9.

——. 2004a. "Cooperative Ownership and the Struggle for African American Economic Empowerment." *Humanity and Society* 28 (August): 298–321.

——. 2004b. "Non-Traditional Analyses of Cooperative Economic Impacts: Preliminary Indicators and a Case Study." *Review of International Co-operation* 97 (1): 6–21.

——. 2005. "On the Road to Democratic Economic Participation: Educating African American Youth in the Post-Industrial Global Economy." In *Black Education: A Transformative Research and Action Agenda for the New Century*, ed. Joyce King, 225–39. Fairfax, Va.: Tech Books.

——. 2006a. "Entering the New City as Men and Women, Not Mules." In *The Black Urban Community*, ed. Lewis Randolph and Gail Tate, 75–100. New York: Palgrave Macmillan.

——. 2006b. "Principles and Strategies for Reconstruction: Models of African American Community-Based Cooperative Economic Development." *Harvard Journal of African American Public Policy* 12 (Summer): 39–55.

——. 2008a. "Alternative Economics—A Missing Component in the African American Studies Curriculum: Teaching Public Policy and Democratic Community Econom- ics to Black Undergraduate Students." In "Incorporating Black Political Economy into Black Studies," ed. Jessica Gordon Nembhard and Mathew Forstater, special issue, *Journal of Black Studies* 38 (May): 758–82.

——. 2008b. "Asset Building Through Cooperative Business Ownership: Defining and Measuring Cooperative Economic Wealth." Concept paper, University of Wisconsin Center for Cooperatives. http://reic.uwcc.wisc.edu/discussion/papers/ nembhard.pdf.

——. 2008c. "Cooperatives." In *International Encyclopedia of the Social Sciences*, 2nd ed., ed. William A. Darity, 123–27. Farmington Hills, Mich.: Macmillan Reference USA.

——. 2008d. "Educating Black Youth for Economic Empowerment: Democratic Eco- nomic Participation and School Reform Practices and Policies." In *Handbook of African American Education*, ed. Linda Tillman, 481–98. Thousand Oaks, Calif.: Sage Publications.

——. 2010. "Taking the Predator Out of Lending: The Role Played by Community Devel- opment Credit Unions in Securing and Protecting Assets." Working paper, Howard University Center on Race and Wealth.

——. 2011. "Micro Enterprise and Cooperative Development in Economically Marginal- ized Communities in the U.S." In *Enterprise, Social Exclusion, and Sustainable Communities: The Role of Small Business in Addressing Social and Economic Inequalities*, ed. Alan Southern, 254–76. New York: Routledge.

Gordon Nembhard, Jessica, and Anthony Blasingame. 2002. "Economic Dimensions of Civic Engagement and Political Efficacy." Working paper, Democracy Collabora- tive–Knight Foundation Civic Engagement Project, University of Maryland, Col- lege Park.

——. 2006. "Wealth, Civic Engagement, and Democratic Practice." In *Wealth Accumu- lation in Communities of Color in the United States: Current Issues*, ed. Jessica Gordon Nembhard and Ngina Chiteji, 294–325. Ann Arbor: University of Michigan Press.

Gordon Nembhard, Jessica, and Curtis Haynes. 2002. "Using Mondragon as a Model for African American Urban Redevelopment." In Feldman and Gordon Nembhard, *From Community Economic Development*, 51–67.

——. 2003. "Networked Cooperative Economic Development: Mondragon as a Model for African American Urban Revitalization." Working paper, University of Maryland, College Park.

Gordon Nembhard, Jessica, and Valerie O. Pang. 2003. "Ethnic Youth Programs: Teaching About Caring Economic Communities and Self-Empowered Leadership." In *Critical Race Theory Perspectives on Social Studies: The Profession, Policies, and Curriculum*, ed. G. Ladson-Billings 171–97. Greenwich, Conn.: Information Age.

Gothard, Ralph O. 1931. "Race Men Plan Co-operative Food Market." *Negro World*, May 9, 1.

——. 1937. Letter to Ella Baker, May 1. Ella Baker Papers, box 2, folder 2, Schomburg Center.

Grant, Joanne. 1998. *Ella Baker: Freedom Bound.* Hoboken: John Wiley & Sons.

Gray, Thomas W. 2007. "Co-ops Focus Collective Action: Business Structure Helps Producers Address Power Disparity in the Marketplace." *Rural Cooperatives*, May–June, 33–35.

Greenberg, Edward S. 1986. *Workplace Democracy: The Political Effects of Participation.* Ithaca: Cornell University Press.

Grimes, Paul W. 1994. "Public Versus Private Secondary School and the Production of Economics Education." *Journal of Economics Education* 25 (Winter): 17–30.

Gross, Daniel. 2008. "A Risk Worth Taking: Many Ethical Subprime Lenders Still Manage to Make Plenty of Money." *Newsweek*, November 14, http://www.thedailybeast.com/newsweek/2008/11/14/a-risk-worth-taking.print.html.

Groves, Frank. 1985. "What Is Cooperation? The Philosophy of Cooperation and Its Relationship to Cooperative Structure and Operations." University of Wisconsin Center for Cooperatives, Occasional Paper no. 6. http://www.uwcc.wisc.edu/info/ocpap/groves.html.

Guarneri, Carl J. 1991. *The Utopian Alternative: Fourierism in Nineteenth-Century America.* Ithaca: Cornell University Press.

Gutierrez-Johnson, Ana. 1984. "The Mondragon Model of Cooperative Enterprise: Considerations Concerning Its Success and Transferability." *Changing Work*, no 1, 35–41.

Haddad, W., and G. Puch, eds. 1969. *Black Economic Development.* Englewood Cliffs, N.J.: Prentice Hall.

Hamer, Fannie Lou. 1970. Fund-raising letter for Freedom Farm Corporation, May 15. Fannie Lou Hamer Papers, box 11, Amistad Research Center.

——. 1971a. Funding proposal to Field Foundation for Freedom Farm Corporation, November 16, addressed to "Mr. Dunbar." Fannie Lou Hamer Papers, box 11, Amistad Research Center.

——. 1971b. "If the Name of the Game Is Survive, Survive." Speech given in Ruleville, Mississippi, September 27. Fannie Lou Hamer Collection, box 1, folder 1, Tougaloo College Civil Rights Collection T/012, Mississippi Department of Archives and History, Jackson.

Hamer, John H. 1981. "Preconditions and Limits in the Formation of Associations: The Self-Help and Cooperative Movement in Sub-Saharan Africa." *African Studies Review* 24 (March): 113–32.

Hammond Ketilson, Lou. 1998. "Who Is Driving the Bus?" In *Proceedings from the Women in Co-operatives Forum, November 7–8, 1997*, 14–34. Saskatoon: University of Saskatchewan, Centre for the Study of Co-operatives.

Handy, John W. 1993. "Community Economic Development: Some Critical Issues." *Review of Black Political Economy* 21 (Winter): 41–64.

——. 1998. "The Shadow of the Future and the Complexity of Cooperation." *Review of Black Political Economy* 26 (Summer): 57–73.

Hansen, W. Lee. 1998. "Principles-Based Standards: On the Voluntary National Content Standards in Economics." *Journal of Economic Education* 29 (Spring): 150–56.

Hanson, Warren. 1975–76. "Interview: Moe Burton." *Scoop Newsletter*, no. 12 (December–January): 13–14.

Harmon, J. H., Jr. 1929. "The Negro as a Local Business Man." *Journal of Negro History* 14 (April): 116–55.

Harris, Abram L. 1934. Letter to W. E. B. Du Bois, January 6. In Aptheker, *Correspondence of W. E. B. Du Bois*, 1:471–72.

Harris, Donald. 1978. *Capital Accumulation and Income Distribution.* Stanford: Stanford University Press.

Hart, Stuart L., and Monica Touesnard. 2008. *Back to the Future: Integrating Sustainability into Credit Union Strategy.* Madison, Wisc.: Filene Research Institute.

Haynes, Curtis, Jr. 1993. "An Essay in the Art of Economic Cooperation: Cooperative Enterprise and Economic Development in Black America." PhD diss. University of Massachusetts, Amherst.

———. 1994. "A Democratic Cooperative Enterprise System: A Response to Urban Economic Decay." *Ceteris Paribus* 4 (October): 19–30.

———. 1996. "Mondragon and the African American Community: An Interview with Curtis Haynes, Jr." *GEO: Grassroots Economic Organizing Newsletter*, no. 10 (January–February): 8–9.

———. 1999. "Du Bois and Economic Cooperation." Working paper, Buffalo State College.

Haynes, Curtis, Jr., and Jessica Gordon Nembhard. 1999. "Cooperative Economics—A Community Revitalization Strategy." *Review of Black Political Economy* 27 (Summer): 47–71.

Height, Dorothy. 2003. *Open Wide the Freedom Gates: A Memoir.* New York: Public Affairs.

Henderson, Beth. 1998. "Opportunities and Challenges." In *Proceedings from the Women in Co-operatives Forum, November 7–8, 1997*, 64–66. Saskatoon: University of Saskatchewan, Centre for the Study of Co-operatives.

Henson, Eric, Anna Lee, and Luxman Nathan. 2005. "Rural Wealth Building." Manuscript. Harvard Project on American Indian Economic Development and Lexecon, John F. Kennedy School of Government, Harvard University.

Higgs, Robert. 1977. *Competition and Coercion: Blacks in the American Economy, 1865–1914.* Chicago: University of Chicago Press, 1977.

Hightower, Jim. 2012. "Cooperatives over Corporations." Op-ed. *Truthout*, February 24, http://www.truth-out.org/.

Hill, Norman, and Christopher Mackin. 2002. "Case 1: The A. Philip Randolph Educational Fund's Craft Union Cooperatives, Washington, DC." In Feldman and Gordon Nembhard, *From Community Economic Development*, 40–42.

Hill, Roderick. 2000. "The Case of the Missing Organizations: Cooperatives and the Textbooks." *Journal of Economics Education* 31 (Summer): 281–95.

Hilliard, Asa. 1997. *SBA: The Reawakening of the African Mind.* Gainesville, Fla.: Makare.

Hine, Darlene Clark, William C. Hine, and Stanley Harrold. 2010. *The African-American Odyssey.* Upper Saddle River, N.J.: Pearson Prentice Hall.

Historic Northampton. n.d. "Northampton Association of Education and Industry." http://www.historic-northampton.org/highlights/educationindustry.html.

Hochman, Anndee. 2007. "A Cooperative Spirit Is Truly in the Air: From Bike Church to Babysitting Groups, Co-ops Are Catching on in the Region and Around the Nation." *Philadelphia Inquirer*, July 20.

Hocker, Cliff. 2009. "Get Schooled on Thriving in Hard Times." *Black Enterprise*, May 8, http://www.blackenterprise.com/wealth-for-life/2009/05/08/get-schooledon-thriving-in-hard-times/.

Hogan, Lloyd, ed. 1980. *The State of the Black Economy: Issues in Community Revitalization.* New Brunswick, N.J.: Transaction.

———. 1984. *Principles of Black Political Economy.* Boston: Routledge & Kegan Paul.

———. 1992. "The Role of Land and African-Centered Values in Black Economic Development." In *Race, Politics, and Economic Development: Community Perspectives*, ed. James Jennings, 165–74. New York: Verso.

Holmes, William F. 1973. "The Laflore County Massacre and the Demise of the Colored Farmers' Alliance." *Phylon* 34 (3): 267–74.

———. 1975. "The Demise of the Colored Farmers' Alliance." *Journal of Southern History* 41 (May): 187–200.

———. n.d. "Colored Farmers' Alliance." *Handbook of Texas Online.* http://www.tsha online.org/handbook/online/articles/aaco1.

Holmquist, June Drenning. 2004. *They Chose Minnesota: A Survey of the State's Ethnic Groups.* Reprint, St. Paul: Minnesota Historical Society.

Hope, John, II. 1940. "Rochdale Cooperation Among Negroes." *Phylon* 1 (1): 39–52.

Howard, Ted. 1999. "Ownership Matters." *Yes! A Journal of Positive Futures* 9 (Spring): 24–27.

Hoyt, Ann. 2001. "The Twenty-First Century Case for Urban Cooperative Development." *Journal of Cooperative Development* 2 (Spring): 1, 17.

HUD (U.S. Department of Housing and Urban Development). 2000. *The State of the Cities, 2000.* Washington, D.C.: U.S. Department of Housing and Urban Development.

Huet, Tim. 1997. "Can Coops Go Global? Mondragon Is Trying." *Dollars and Sense,* November–December, http://dollarsandsense.org/archives/1997/1197huet.html.

———. 2000. "Can MCC Go Global?" *Peace Review* 12 (2): 283–86.

———. 2001a. "Some Possible Elements of a Leadership Development Program." *GEO: Grassroots Economic Organizing Newsletter,* no. 55, http://www.geo.coop/ archives/leaders1202.htm.

———. 2001b. "Worker-Owned Cooperative Case Study." AA Technical Course on Cooperative Development, session 2. Cooperation Works. November 5–7, Bailey, Colo.

Humphrey, Richard M. 1891. "History of the Colored Farmers' Alliance and Co-operative Union." In *The Farmers' Alliance History and Agricultural Digest,* ed. Nelson A. Dunning, 288–92. Washington, D.C.: National Farmers' Alliance.

Hunter, Carol. 1998. "Women in Co-operatives: Some Benchmarks." In *Proceedings from the Women in Co-operatives Forum, November 7–8, 1997,* 1–9. Saskatoon: University of Saskatchewan, Centre for the Study of Co-operatives.

ICA (International Co-operative Alliance). 1993. "ICA Policy on Women in Co-op Development." http://www.uwcc.wisc.edu/icic/orgs/ica/dev/policy/women.html.

———. 2001. "Gender Issues in Co-operative Development: An ILO–ICA Perspective." May 2. http://www.ica.coop/gender/ica-ilo-manual/topic3.html.

———. 2005. "Microfinance Is Our Business—Co-operating Out of Poverty." Press release, July 2, Geneva, Switzerland. http://www.aciamericas.coop/IMG/pdf/ 2005-idc-en.pdf.

———. 2007. "Statement on the Co-operative Identity: Cooperative Identity, Principles, and Values." http://www.ica.coop/coop/principles.html.

———. 2012a. "Co-operative Facts and Figures." http://2012.coop/en/whats-co-op/ co-operative-facts-figures.

———. 2012b. "Co-operative Identity, Values, and Principles." http://2012.coop/en/what-co-op/co-operative-identity-values-principles.

ICA Women's Committee. 1983. "Women as Equal Partners in Third World Co-operative Development." http://www.uwcc.wisc.edu/icic/orgs/ica/pubs/Other-ICA -Publications1/Women-as-Equal-Partners-in-Third-World-C1.html.

Ifateyo, Ajowa Nzinga. 2010. "Current Day Black Cooperatives." Presentation at the "Mapping African American Cooperatives" session, North American Students of Cooperation Institute, Ann Arbor, Michigan, November 7.

Ijere, Martin O. 1972. "Whither Economics in a Black Studies Program?" *Journal of Black Studies* 3 (December): 149–65.

ILO (International Labour Organisation). 2002. "Recommendation 193: Recommendation Concerning the Promotion of Cooperatives." http://www.ilo.org/coop/.

ILO-ICA (International Labour Organisation–International Co-operative Alliance). 1995. "Brief Overview of Gender Issues in Cooperatives." http://www.uwcc.wisc.edu/icic/issues/gender/ilo-ica/overview.html.

———. 2005. "Cooperating Out of Poverty to Achieve the Millennium Development Goals by Empowering the Poorest of the Poor." Geneva, Switzerland, October 17. http://www.aciamericas.coop/IMG/pdf/2005-ilo-ica-poverty.pdf.

Inserra, Anne, Maureen Conway, and John Rodat. 2002. *Cooperative Home Care Associates: A Case Study of a Sectoral Employment Development Approach*. Washington, D.C.: Aspen Institute.

Insight Center for Community Economic Development. 2010. *Lifting as We Climb: Women of Color, Wealth, and America's Future*. http://www.insightcced.org/uploads/CRWG/LiftingAsWeClimb-WomenWealth-Report-InsightCenter-Spring2010.pdf.

Institute for Community Economics. 2012a. "Institute for Community Economics." http://www.nhtinc.org/ice.php.

———. 2012b. "2012 Annual Report." http://www.nhtinc.org/downloads/instituteforcommunityeconomics2012annualreport.pdf.

International Labour Office. 2005. "Microfinance Is Our Business—Co-operating Out of Poverty." Message from the ILO director-general on the eighty-third ICA International Cooperative Day, eleventh UN International Day of Cooperatives, Geneva, Switzerland, July 2. http://www.copac.coop/idc/2005/2005-idc-ilo.pdf.

Jakobsen, Gurli. 2000. "Co-operative and Training Dimensions in Entrepreneurship: A Study of the Methodology of the Saiolan Centre in Mondragon." *Review of International Co-operation* 92–93 (March): 47–54.

James, NeEddra. 2009. "A Market for West Oakland: The Mandela Foods Cooperative." Food First Institute for Food and Development Policy, September 25. http://www.foodfirst.org/en/West+Oakland+Mandela+Market.

Janis-Aparicio, Madeline, and Roxana Tynan. 2005. "Power in Numbers: Community Benefits Agreements and the Power of Coalition Building." *Shelterforce* 27 (November–December): 8–11.

Japanese Consumers' Cooperative Union. 1999. "Women's Work, Men's Work: To Live a Better Life Beyond Gender." *Journal of Co-operative Studies* 32 (December): 182–96.

Jennings, James, ed. 1992. *Race, Politics, and Economic Development: Community Perspectives*. New York: Verso.

Johnson, Rebecca. 1997. "Poor Women, Work, and Community Development: A Reflection Paper." Mimeograph. Cooperative Economics for Women, Jamaica Plain, Massachusetts.

Johnson, Rudy. 1968. "Harlem Market Thrives as Co-op." *New York Times*, August 11.

Jones, H. H. 1920. "How the Division of Foods and Markets Aids Consumers' Cooperation." In "Cooperation Among Producers and Consumers in New York State," special issue, *Foods and Markets* 2 (March–April): 51–56.

Jones, Jacqueline. 1985. *Labor of Love, Labor of Sorrow: Black Women, Work, and the Family from Slavery to the Present*. New York: Basic Books.

Joseph, Jamal. 2012. *Panther Baby: A Life of Rebellion and Reinvention*. Chapel Hill, N.C.: Algonquin Books.

Journal of Cooperative Development. 1998a. "Building Community with Affordable, High Quality Food." *Journal of Cooperative Development* 1 (Spring): 6–8.

———. 1998b. "Providing Living Wages for Childcare Workers." *Journal of Cooperative Development* 1 (Spring): 4–5.

———. 1999. "Manna CDC Is Revitalizing the Shaw Community." *Journal of Cooperative Development* 2 (Fall): 8, 13.

Karenga, Maulana. 1989. *The African American Holiday of Kwanzaa: A Celebration of Family, Community, and Culture.* Los Angeles: University of Sankore Press.

Kaswan, Jaques. 1999. "Cooperatives as a Socioeconomic Alternative to the Mainstream: Are We Ready?" *GEO: Grassroots Economic Organizing Newsletter,* no. 38 (September–October): 2–3, 12.

Katz, Alyssa. 2002. "Bed-Stuy Credit Union Gets a Long Island Label." *New York City Limits Weekly,* September 2.

Katz-Fishman, Wanda. 1992. "Women: The Neglected Majority." In *From the Ground Up: Essays on Grassroots and Workplace Democracy by C. George Benello,* ed. Len Krimerman, Frank Lindenfeld, Carol Korty, and Julian Benello, 177–83. Boston: South End Press.

Kaushik, Surendra K., and Raymond H. Lopez. 1994. "The Structure and Growth of the Credit Union Industry in the United States: Meeting Challenges of the Market." *American Journal of Economics and Sociology* 53: 219–43.

Kenkel, Phil, and Bill Fitzwater. 2004. "Impact of a Stock Write Down on Cooperative Members." Oklahoma Cooperative Extension Service, CR-989.0104. http://agecon .okstate.edu/coops/files/cr-989web.pdf.

Kennedy, Randall. 2003. "Passing and the Schuyler Family." In Kennedy, *Interracial Intimacies: Sex, Marriage, Identity, and Adoption,* 339–66. New York: Pantheon Books.

Kessler, Sidney H. 1952. "The Organization of Negroes in the Knights of Labor." *Journal of Negro History* 37 (July): 248–76.

Kihss, Peter. 1969. "Harlem Store Torn by Dispute: Meeting of Stockholders Called." *New York Times,* February 17.

Kleine, Doug. 2001. "Urban Housing Cooperatives—Benefits Beyond the Walls." *Journal of Cooperative Development* 2 (Spring):12–13, 16.

Kochhar, Rakesh, Richard Fry, and Paul Taylor. 2011. "Twenty to One: Wealth Gaps Rise to Record Highs Between Whites, Blacks, and Hispanics." July 26. Pew Research Social and Demographic Trends, Pew Research Center, Washington, D.C. http:// www.pewsocialtrends.org/files/2011/07/SDT-Wealth-Report_7-26-11_FINAL .pdf.

Kourilsky, M. L., and M. Esfandiari. 1997. "Entrepreneurship Education and Lower Socioeconomic Black Youth: An Empirical Investigation." *Urban Review* 29 (September): 205–15.

Kraenzle, Charles A. 1994. "Full-Time Employees, Sales, and Assets of Selected Farmer Cooperatives: 1981, 1986, and 1991." ACS Research Report 129. Washington, D.C.: U.S. Department of Agriculture.

Kretzmann, John P., and John L. McKnight. 1993. *Building Communities from the Inside Out: A Path Toward Finding and Mobilizing a Community's Assets.* Chicago: ACTA Publications.

Kreuberm, Sherman. 2003. "Sectoral Strategies in CED: Critical Factors in the Success of CHCA and Childspace." *Making Waves* 14 (Fall): 4–10.

Krimerman, Len, and Frank Lindenfeld, eds. 1992. *When Workers Decide: Workplace Democracy Takes Root in North America.* Philadelphia: New Society.

Krimerman, Len, Frank Lindenfeld, Carol Korty, and Julian Benello, eds. 1992. *From the Ground Up: Essays on Grassroots and Workplace Democracy by C. George Benello.* Boston: South End Press.

Kromm, Chris, and Sue Sturgis. 2008. "Hurricane Katrina and the Guiding Principles on Internal Displacement: A Global Human Rights Perspective on a National Disaster." *Southern Exposure* 35 (January), http://www.southernstudies.org/southern_ exposure/2008/01/hurricane-katrina-and-human-rights.html.

Kunjufu, Jawanza. 2002. *Black Economics: Solutions for Economic and Community Empowerment.* 2nd ed. Chicago: African American Images.

Labelle, Luc. 2000–2001. "Development of Cooperatives and Employee Ownership, Quebec Style." *Owners at Work* 12 (Winter): 14–17.

Landman, Ruth H. 1993. *Creating Community in the City: Cooperatives and Community
Gardens in Washington, D.C.* Westport, Conn.: Bergin & Garvey.

Landmarks Preservation Commission. 1970. "Dunbar Apartments." Letter LP-0708, July
14, no. 4. http://www.neighborhoodpreservationcenter.org/db/bb_files/DUNBAR
-APTS.pdf.

Lawrence, John W. 2008. "Raising Capital for Worker Cooperatives." *GEO: Grassroots
Economic Organizing Newsletter*, no. 74, http://www.geo.coop/node/60.

Lawrence, Keith. 1999. "Race and Community Building." Mimeograph. Aspen Institute
Roundtable on Comprehensive Community Initiatives, December 8.

Lee, Chana Kai. 2000. *For Freedom's Sake: The Life of Fannie Lou Hamer.* Urbana: University of Illinois Press.

Lee, Jinkook, and William A. Kelley Jr. 2001. *Who Uses Credit Unions?* 2nd ed. Madison,
Wisc.: Filene Research Institute.

Lefkowitz, Bonnie. 2007. *Community Health Centers: A Movement and the People Who
Made It Happen.* New Brunswick: Rutgers University Press.

Leigh, Wilhelmina A. 2011. "Co-ops on Main St. and Wall St." *New York Times*, August
16, http://www.nytimes.com/roomfordebate/2011/08/16/a-chance-to-reshape
-the-economy/more-businesses-could-become-cooperatives.

Leikin, Steve. 1999. "The Citizen Producer: The Rise and Fall of Working-Class Cooperatives in the United States." In *Consumers Against Capitalism: Consumer Cooperation in Europe and North America, 1840–1990*, ed. Ellen Furlough and Carl
Strikwerda, 93–114. Lanham, Md.: Rowman & Littlefield. http://www.uwcc.wisc
.edu/info/history/citizen_producer.pdf.

Lerner, Gerda. 1974. "Early Community Work of Black Club Women." *Journal of Negro
History* 59 (April): 158–67.

Levine, David, and Laura D'Andrea Tyson. 1990. "Participation, Productivity, and the
Firm's Environment." In *Paying for Productivity: A Look at the Evidence*, ed.
Alan S. Blinder, 183–243. Washington, D.C.: Brookings Institute.

Lewis, John, with Michael D'Orso. 1998. *Walking with the Wind: A Memoir of the Movement.* San Diego: Harcourt Brace.

Library of Congress. 2003. "Discovering Hidden Washington: A Journey Through the
Alley Communities of the Nation's Capital; Special Presentation—Nannie Helen
Burroughs." Library of Congress Virtual Programs and Services. http://www.loc
.gov/loc/kidslc/sp-burroughs.html.

———. 2012. "The Civil Rights History Project: Survey of Collections and Repositories;
Ella Baker Papers." Library of Congress, American Folklife Center. http://www.loc
.gov/folklife/civilrights/survey/view_collection.php?coll_id=2778.

"The Life Work of Mrs. Halena Wilson." 1956. Mimeograph. BSCP Collection, box 34,
folder 3, Chicago History Museum.

Livingston, Jane. 2007a. "Future of Local Food." *Rural Cooperatives*, July–August, 22–23.

———. 2007b. "Miracle on the Bayou: How One Louisiana Parish Is Resurfacing from
Disaster." *Rural Cooperatives*, March–April, 20–21.

Lissner, Will. 1969. "Peace Talks Collapse in Strike at Harlem Co-op Supermarket." *New
York Times*, July 31.

Logue, John, and Jacquelyn Yates. 2005. *Productivity in Cooperatives and Worker-
Owned Enterprises: Ownership and Participation Make a Difference!* Geneva,
Switzerland: International Labour Office.

Long, Richard J., and Bodil Thordarson. 1987. "A Comparison of Worker-Owned Firms
and Conventionally Owned Firms in Sweden." In *Advances in the Economic
Analysis of Participatory and Labor-Managed Firms*, vol. 2, ed. Derek C. Jones
and Jan Svejnar, 225–42. Greenwich, Conn.: JAI Press.

MacLeod, Greg. 1997. *From Mondragon to America: Experiments in Community Eco-
    nomic Development.* Sydney, Nova Scotia: University College of Cape Breton
    Press.

Mammen, Kristin, and Christina Paxson. 2000. "Women's Work and Economic Develop-
    ment." *Journal of Economic Perspectives* 14 (Fall): 141–64.

Mandela Foods Cooperative. 2010. "African American Economic Development in Oakland
    Tour." Presentation and discussion at Mandela Foods Cooperative, in conjunction
    with the U.S. Federation of Worker Cooperatives conference, Berkeley, California,
    August 8.

———. n.d. "About Mandela Foods." http://www.mandelafoods.com/.

Manson, Wendy. 1998. "Strategies for Change." In *Proceedings from the Women in
    Co-operatives Forum, November 7–8, 1997,* 35–39. Saskatoon: University of
    Saskatchewan, Centre for the Study of Co-operatives.

Marable, Manning. 1986. *W. E. B. Du Bois: Black Radical Democrat.* Boston: Twayne.

Marshall, Shashkin. 1984. "Participative Management Is an Ethical Imperative." *Organi-
    zational Dynamics* 12 (Spring): 5–22.

Marte, Jonnelle. 2009. "Safe Havens: Credit Unions Earn Some Interest." *Wall Street
    Journal,* March 15, http://online.wsj.com/article/SB123708535764231521.html
    ?mod=googlenews_wsj#printmode.

Martin, Tony. 1976. *Race First: The Ideological and Organizational Struggles of Marcus
    Garvey and the Universal Negro Improvement Association.* Dover, Mass.: Majority
    Press.

Maryland State Archives. 1998. "The Lexington Savings Bank." In "The Road from Freder-
    ick to Thurgood: Black Baltimore in Transition, 1870–1920." http://www.mdarchives
    .state.md.us/msa/stagser/s1259/121/6050/html/17453000.html.

Mason, Anne. 1946. Letter to Halena Wilson, March 21, and "Daily Field Report" from the
    Department of Information of the Office of Price Administration, February 26. A.
    Philip Randolph Collection, box 76, folder 1, Library of Congress, Washington, D.C.

Mason, Patrick L., and Mwangi wa Githinji. 2008. "Excavating for Economics in Africana
    Studies." In "Incorporating Black Political Economy into Black Studies," ed. Jes-
    sica Gordon Nembhard and Mathew Forstater, special issue, *Journal of Black
    Studies* 38 (May): 731–57.

Massey, Douglas S., and Nancy A. Denton, eds. 1993. *American Apartheid and the Mak-
    ing of the Underclass.* Cambridge: Harvard University Press.

Mathews, Race. 1999. *Jobs of Our Own: Building a Stakeholder Society, Alternatives to
    the Market and the State.* Sydney, Australia: Pluto Press.

———. 2002. "Mondragon: Past Performance and Future Potential." Paper presented at
    the Kent State University Capital Ownership Group conference, Washington, D.C.,
    October.

Matney, W. C. 1927. "Teaching Business." *Crisis,* July, 157, 177–78.

———. 1930. "Exploitation or Co-operation?" *Crisis,* February, 48–49, 67.

Mayberry, B. D. 1989. *The Role of Tuskegee University in the Origin, Growth, and Devel-
    opment of the Negro Cooperative Extension System, 1881–1990.* Tuskegee: Tuske-
    gee University Cooperative Extension Program.

McCulloch, Heather, with Lisa Robinson. 2001. *Sharing the Wealth: Resident Ownership
    Mechanisms.* Oakland, Calif.: PolicyLink.

McKecuen, Carolyn. 1992. "Watermark Artisans: A Lifetime Path of Economic and Per-
    sonal Empowerment." In *When Workers Decide: Workplace Democracy Takes
    Root in North America,* ed. Len Krimerman and Frank Lindenfeld, 21–25. Phila-
    delphia: New Society.

McLanahan, C. J. 1947. Letter to A. Philip Randolph, July 21. A. Philip Randolph Collec-
    tion, General Correspondence, 1947, box 1, Library of Congress, Washington, D.C.

——. 1948. Letter to Halena Wilson, July 26. A. Philip Randolph Collection, box 75, folder 6, Library of Congress, Washington, D.C.

Mead, Margaret, ed. 1968. *Cooperation and Competition Among Primitive Peoples*. Boston: Beacon Press.

Medoff, Peter, and Holly Sklar. 1994. *Streets of Hope: The Fall and Rise of an Urban Neighborhood*. Boston: South End Press.

Meek, Christopher B., and Warner P. Woodworth. 1990. "Technical Training and Enterprise: Mondragon's Educational System and Its Implications for Other Cooperatives." *Economic and Industrial Democracy* 11 (November): 505–28.

Megson, Jim, and Janet Van Liere. 2001. "The Role of Worker Cooperatives in Urban Economic Development." *Journal of Cooperative Development* 2 (Spring): 2, 18.

Melman, Seymour. 2002. "Mondragon: A Model for Linking Innovation, Productivity, and Economic Democracy." In Feldman and Gordon Nembhard, *From Community Economic Development*, 99–110.

Mendell, Marguerite. 2008. *The Social Economy in Quebec: Lessons and Challenges for Internationalizing Co-operation*. Saskatoon: University of Saskatchewan, Centre for the Study of Co-operatives.

Merlo, Catherine. 1998a. "A Few Good Women." *RBS Rural Cooperative Magazine*, March–April, http://www.rurdev.usda.gov/rbs/pub/mar98/contents.htm.

——. 1998b. "The Triumph of Dawson's Textile Workers." *RBS Rural Cooperative Magazine*, March–April, http://www.rurdev.usda.gov/rbs/pub/mar98/contents.htm.

Miller, Floyd J. 1972. "Black Protest and White Leadership: A Note on the Colored Farmers' Alliance." *Phylon* 33 (2): 169–74.

Mills, Kay. 2007. *This Little Light of Mine: The Life of Fannie Lou Hamer*. Lexington: University Press of Kentucky.

Mississippi Market Natural Foods Co-op. 2012. "The Credjafawn Co-op Store—A Piece of St. Paul Co-op History." *M: Mississippi Market Newsletter*, February 2, http://msmarket.coop/2012/02/the-credjafawn-co-op-store-a-piece-of-st-paul-co-op-history/.

Mohanty, Sunil K. 2006. "Comparing Credit Unions with Commercial Banks: Implications for Public Policy." *Journal of Commercial Banking and Finance* 5 (1–2): 97–113.

Mondragon Cooperative Corporation. 2009. "2009 Annual Report." http://www.mcc.es/LinkClick.aspx?fileticket=TeHx6JRmJRE%3d&tabid=331.

——. 2010. "Mondragon Corporate Profile: 2010." http://www.mondragon-corporation.com/mcc_dotnetnuke/Portals/0/documentos/eng/Corporative-Profile/Corporative-Profile.html.

——. 2011. "Mondragon Corporate Profile: 2011." http://www.mondragon-corporation.com/language/en-US/ENG/Economic-Data/Corporate-Profile.aspx.

Montgomery, David. 1999. "A Neighborhood Cleans Up; Community Laundry Sells Shares, Turns a Profit." *Washington Post*, March 8.

Morris, Karin. 1998. *The Wages Curriculum: Teacher's Guide to Starting Worker Cooperatives in Low Income Communities*. Davis: University of California, Davis, Center for Cooperatives.

Morrison, Roy. 1991. *We Build the Road as We Travel: Mondragon, a Cooperative Social System*. Philadelphia: New Society.

Moss, C. B., S. A. Ford, and W. G. Boggess. 1989. "Capital Gains, Optimal Leverage, and the Probability of Equity Loss: A Theoretical Model." *Agricultural Finance Review* 49:127–34.

Muhammad, Jesse. 2012. "An Oasis in the 'Food Desert': Houston Mosque Launches Food Cooperative to Bring Fresh Fruit and Produce to Third Ward." http://jessemuhammad.blogs.finalcall.com/2012/07/an-oasis-in-food-desert-houston-mosque.html.

Nadeau, E. G. 2001. "A Food Co-op Thrives on Diversity in Brooklyn." *Journal of Cooperative Development* 2 (Spring): 15.

Nadeau, E. G., and David J. Thompson. 1996. *Cooperation Works!* Rochester, Minn.: Lone Oak Press.

Nader, Ralph. 2005. "Cooperatives." http://www.nader.org/template.php?/archives/203 -Cooperatives.html#extended.

Nagel, Kiara, Khalil Shahyd, and Michael Weisner. 2005. "Youth Cooperative Toolkit." Paper, MIT Department of Urban Studies and Planning. http://community-wealth .org/content/youth-cooperative-toolkit.

National Black Economic Conference. 1969. "Black Manifesto." *New York Review of Books,* July 10, http://www.nybooks.com/articles/archives/1969/jul/10/black- manifesto/?pagination=false. (Incorrectly identified as the Black National Economic Conference in the *New York Review of Books* reproduction of the manifesto.)

National Center for Education Statistics. 2001. "The 1998 High School Transcript Study Tabulations: Comparative Data on Credits Earned and Demographics for 1998, 1994, 1990, 1987, and 1982 High School Graduates, Revised." NCES Working Paper 2001–498. Washington, D.C.: U.S. Government Printing Office.

National Community Land Trust Network. n.d. "What Are Community Land Trusts?" http://www.cltnetwork.org/About-CLTs/What-Are-Community-Land-Trusts.

National Cooperative Bank. 2008. "A History of Co-op Impact." Washington, D.C.: National Cooperative Bank. http://www.ncb.coop/uploadedFiles/2008Co-op100 _final.pdf.

National Cooperative Business Association. 1998. *Cooperative Approaches to a Living Wage: Reducing Costs and Enhancing Income; Proceedings of the 1998 Cooperative Development Forum, Atlanta Georgia, October 28–31.* Washington, D.C.: National Cooperative Business Association.

———. n.d. "What Is a Co-op?" Washington, D.C.: National Cooperative Business Association. http://www.ncba.coop/what-is-a-coop?

National Credit Union Administration. n.d. "A Brief History of Credit Unions." http:// www.ncua.gov/about/history/Pages/CUHistory.aspx.

National Federation of Community Development Credit Unions. 2013. "What Is a CDCU?" http://www.cdcu.coop/about-us/what-is-a-cdcu/.

Negro World. 1924. "Wage Earners and Employes Co-operate." December 27, 2.

———. 1930a. "Colored Farmers Getting Together." October 18, 1.

———. 1930b. "National Negro Business League Prizes Awarded to Business Man and Artist: Bright, Sun-Proof Red and Gold Sign Will Mark C.M.A. Stores." March 22, 1.

———. 1930c. "Rosenwald Apts. a Huge Success in Windy City." October 18, 1.

———. 1931. "Cooperative League Plans Community House." December 19, 2.

———. 1932. "People's Credit Union Pays Yearly Dividend." February 27, 2.

Neifeld, M. R. 1931. "Credit Unions in the United States." *Journal of Business of the University of Chicago* 4 (October): 320–45.

Nelson, Alice Dunbar. 1927. "The Problem of Personal Service." *Messenger,* June, 184.

Nelson, Jack L., Stuart B. Palonsky, and Kenneth Carlson. 2000. *Critical Issues in Education.* Boston: McGraw-Hill.

Nereim, Vivian. 2009. "Hill District's Ujamaa Collective Offered Black Friday Alternative." *Pittsburgh Post-Gazette,* November 28.

New York Department of Farms and Markets, Division of Foods and Markets. 1920. "Pictures of Successful Cooperative Undertakings." *Foods and Markets* 2 (May): 8–16.

New York Times. 1971. "Co-op in Harlem Plans to Help Poor to Set Up Stores." June 5.

Nippierd, Anne-Brit. 1999. "Gender Issues in Co-operatives." *Journal of Co-operative Studies* 32 (December): 175–81.

NNBL (National Negro Business League). 1929. "Weekly News Summary of Negro Economic Conditions." *Negro World*, July 18, 8.

Northeast Self-Help Cooperative. 1934. Letter from the cooperative's joint committee to Jacob Baker, July 17. (Also signed by Mrs. Adab C. Herrod, chair, and Mr. W. A. Bethel, secretary.) Nannie Helen Burroughs Papers, box 52, folder 3, Library of Congress, Washington, D.C.

————. 1936. "Constitution and By-Laws of the Northeast Self-Help Cooperative (Cooperative Industries, Inc.)." Mimeograph, February 20. Nannie Helen Burroughs Papers, box 52, folder 2, Library of Congress, Washington, D.C.

Northern California Land Trust. 2013. "What Is a Community Land Trust (CLT)?" http://www.nclt.org/index.php?option=com_content&view=article&id=1&Itemid=154.

Ofari, Earl. 1970. *The Myth of Black Capitalism.* New York: Monthly Review Press.

Off Center Video. 2001. "Democracy in the Workplace: Three Worker-Owned Businesses in Action." Video, 26 mins. Berkeley, Calif.: Off Center Video. http://www.offcentervideo.com/.

Ohio Employee Ownership Center. 2000–2001. "Company Networks Improve Performance." *Owners at Work* 12 (Winter): 1–3.

Oliver, Melvin J. 2000. "A Tribute to the Federation of Southern Cooperatives/Land Assistance Fund." *Journal of Cooperative Development* 2 (Spring): 1, 3.

Oliver, Melvin J., and Thomas Shapiro. 2006. *Black Wealth/White Wealth: A New Perspective on Racial Inequality.* 2nd ed. New York: Routledge.

Olson, Deborah Groban. 1993. "Development, Growth, and Experiences of ESOPs and Democratic Employee Buyouts in the USA." Paper presented at Foras Aiseanna Saothair conference on Strategies for Democratic Employee Ownership, Dublin, Ireland, October 21. cog.kent.edu/lib/Olson/BuyOut.htm.

Olson, Lynne. 2001. *Freedom's Daughters: The Unsung Heroines of the Civil Rights Movement from 1830–1970.* New York: Scribner.

Otaka, Kendo. 1999. "Community Development Through Economic Cooperation." Paper presented at the International Co-operative Alliance research conference, "Values and Enterprise for Co-operative Advantage," Quebec City, August 28–29.

Ownership Associates. 2003. "ESOPs and Employee Wealth." Employee-Ownership Briefing Paper, Research Highlights 2, brief 7.2, May 20. http://www.ownershipassociates.com/pdf/brief7.2.pdf.

Paige, Ralph. 2001. Interview by author, Washington, D.C., April.

————. 2012. "Message from the Executive Director." http://www.federation.coop.

Pang, Valerie Ooka, Jessica Gordon Nembhard, and Kathleen Holowach. 2006. "What Is Multicultural Education? Principles and New Directions." In *Multicultural Education: Principles and Practices,* ed. Valerie Ooka Pang, 23–43. Westport, Conn.: Praeger.

Pateman, Carole. 1970. *Participation and Democratic Theory.* Cambridge: Cambridge University Press.

Pease, William H., and Jane H. Pease. 1963. *Black Utopia: Negro Communal Experiments in America.* Madison: State Historical Society of Wisconsin.

Perez, Judith A. 2011. "Middle-Class Journeys: A Comparative Study of the Residential and Housing Outcomes of Caribbean Latino, Black, and White Native New Yorkers." PhD diss., Fordham University.

Perlo, Victor. 1976. *The Economics of Racism, U.S.A.: Roots of Black Poverty.* New York: International Publishers.

Persuad, Randolph B., and Clarence Lusane. 2000. "The New Economy, Globalisation, and the Impact on African Americans." *Race and Class* 42 (July–September): 21–34.

Pestoff, Victor. 1999. "The Future of Consumer Co-operatives in Post-Industrial Societies." *Journal of Co-operative Studies* 32 (December): 208–19.

Pfeffer, Paula F. 1995. "The Women Behind the Union: Halena Wilson, Rosina Tucker, and the Ladies' Auxiliary to the Brotherhood of Sleeping Car Porters." *Labor History* 36 (Fall): 568–71.

Pichardo, Sonia. 2010. "Graduating Green Dreams: Green Worker Cooperative Academy Is Helping Worker Co-ops Flourish in the South Bronx." *GEO: Grassroots Economic Organizing Newsletter*, no. 5, http://geo.coop/node/434.

Pitts, Nathan Alvin. 1950. *The Cooperative Movement in Negro Communities of North Carolina*. Washington, D.C.: Catholic University of America Press.

Pittsburgh Courier. 1931. "Schuyler Heads Up League." October 24.

Pollard, Leslie J. 1980. "Black Beneficial Societies and the Home for Aged and Infirm Colored Persons: A Research Note." *Phylon* 41 (3): 230–34.

Powell, Dana. 1999. "In Her Own Words: Dana Powell's Thoughts on 'Why Enterprising Staffing Services.'" *Journal of Cooperative Development* 2 (Fall): 9, 13.

Prejean, Charles. 1992. Interview by Robert Korstad and Neil Boothby. Tape recording. Duke Sanford School of Public Policy and Dewitt Wallace Center for Media and Democracy, Duke University, Chapel Hill, North Carolina. Transcript at http://dewitt.sanford.duke.edu/rutherfurd-living-history/southern-rural-poverty-collection/#prejean.

———. 1999. *Training the Community Organizer: Organizing Low Income Southern Rural Communities to Engage in Cooperative Enterprise Development.* Jackson: Mississippi Center for Cooperative Development.

Rachleff, Peter. 2012. "Labor History for the Future." *Social Policy* 42 (Fall): 34–36.

Raftis, Alaina. 2010. "Ujamaa Collective Market Will Open Saturday in Hill District." *Pittsburgh Tribune-Review*, July 28.

Randolph, A. Philip. 1918. "The Co-operative Movement Among Negroes." *Messenger*, 23–24.

———. 1944. "Cooperatives Are One of 'Four Democracies.' Urges Negro People to Use Cooperatives as Way to Achieve Better Living." *Prosveta*, January 6. A. Philip Randolph Collection, box 57–58, Library of Congress, Washington, D.C.

———. 1945a. Letter to Halena Wilson, August 29. A. Philip Randolph Collection, box 76, folder 1, Library of Congress, Washington, D.C.

———. 1945b. Letter to Halena Wilson, December 31. A. Philip Randolph Collection, box 75, folder 7, Library of Congress, Washington, D.C.

———. 1947. Letter to C. J. McLanahan, July 29. A. Philip Randolph Collection, General Correspondence, 1947, box 1, Library of Congress, Washington, D.C.

———. 1949. Letter to Halena Wilson, September 9. A. Philip Randolph Collection, box 75, folder 7, Library of Congress, Washington, D.C.

Ransby, Barbara. 2003. *Ella Baker and the Black Freedom Movement.* Chapel Hill: University of North Carolina Press.

Ransom, Roger L., and Richard Sutch. 1977. *One Kind of Freedom: The Economic Consequences of Emancipation.* New York: Cambridge University Press.

Rayworth, Melissa. 2010. "Beautiful Things to Benefit the Hill: Ujamaa Collective's New Market." *Pop City*, July 28, http://www.popcitymedia.com/forgood/ujamaamarket-place072810.aspx.

Reddix, Jacob L. 1935. "The Negro Finds a Way to Economic Equality." *Consumers Cooperation*, October, 173–76.

———. 1974. *A Voice Crying in the Wilderness: The Memoirs of Jacob L. Reddix.* Jackson: University Press of Mississippi.

Reynolds, Bruce J. 2001. "A History of African-American Farmer Cooperatives, 1938–2000." Paper delivered at the annual meeting of the NCR-194, USDA/RBS/Cooperative Services. U.S. Department of Agriculture.

———. 2002. *Black Farmers in America, 1865–2000: The Pursuit of Independent Farming and the Role of Cooperatives.* Washington, D.C.: U.S. Department of Agriculture.

Rhodes, V. James. 1987. "Cooperatives and Contestable/Sustainable Markets." In *Cooperative Theory: New Approaches*, ed. Jeffrey S. Royer. Washington, D.C.: U.S. Department of Agriculture. http://www.rurdev.usda.gov/rbs/pub/sr18/contents.htm.

Robles, Barbara. 2006. "Wealth Creation in Latino Communities: Latino Families, Community Assets, and Cultural Capital." In *Wealth Accumulation and Communities of Color in the United States: Current Issues*, ed. Jessica Gordon Nembhard and Ngina Chiteji, 241–66. Ann Arbor: University of Michigan Press.

Rohe, William M., George McCarthy, and Shannon van Zandt. 2000. "The Social Benefits and Costs of Homeownership: A Critical Assessment of the Research." Research Institute for Housing America, Working Paper no. 00–01. Washington, D.C.: Research Institute for Housing America.

Rokholt, Per Ove. 1999. "Strengths and Weaknesses of the Co-operative Form: A Matter of Perspective and Opinion." Paper presented at the International Co-operative Alliance research conference, "Values and Enterprise for Co-operative Advantage," Quebec City, August 28–29.

Rose, Kristine G. 2002. "Leadership Pathways: Women Agricultural Cooperative Directors." Master's thesis, College of St. Catherine, St. Paul, Minnesota.

Rosen, Corey. 1992. "ESOPs: Hype or Hope?" In *When Workers Decide: Workplace Democracy Takes Root in North America*, ed. Len Krimerman and Frank Lindenfeld, 184–87. Philadelphia: New Society.

Rosenberg, Samuel A. 1940a. "Negro-Managed Cooperatives in Virginia." *Crisis*, September, 282–83.

———. 1940b. "Richmond's New Negro Cooperative." *Opportunity*, April, 118.

———. 1950. "Credit Unions in North Carolina." *Journal of Business of the University of Chicago* 23 (July): 182–90.

Rosenthal, Clifford, and Min Kyung Kim. 2010. "Low-Income Communities and the Great Recession: Financial Trends in Community Development Credit Unions, 2009." National Federation of Community Development Credit Unions. http://www.cdcu .coop/files/public/Low-Income_Financial_Trends_in_CDCUs_2009_FINAL.pdf.

Rosenzweig, M. R. 2000. "Schooling, Learning, and Economic Growth." In *Back to Shared Prosperity: The Growing Inequality of Wealth and Income in America*, ed. R. Marshall, 229–37. Armonk, N.Y.: M. E. Sharpe.

Rossi, E. 2003. "Local Students Join to Create Food Co-operatives." *Daily Pennsylvanian*, October 20, http://www.thedp.com/r/32c2228f.

Royer, Jeffrey S. 1992. "Cooperative Principles and Equity Financing: A Critical Discussion." *Journal of Agricultural Cooperatives* 7:79–98.

Rudwick, Elliott M. 1968. *W. E. B. Du Bois: Propagandist of the Negro Protest*. 2nd ed. Philadelphia: University of Pennsylvania Press.

Saegert, Susan, Lymari Benitez, Efrat Eisenberg, Melissa Extein, Tsai-shiou Hsieh, and Chung Chang. 2005. "The Promise and Challenges of Co-ops in a Hot Real Estate Market." *Shelterforce* 27 (July–August): 16–18.

Sankofa Youth Agricultural Project. 2011. "Our Story." http://www.facebook.com/note .php?note_id=262855003755816.

Scharf, Adria. 2001. "Show Them the Money." *ESOP Report*, November–December. http://www.ownershipassociates.com/esopwealth.shtm.

Schenk, Mike. 2013. "Commercial Banks and Credit Unions: Facts, Fallacies, and Recent Trends: Year-End 2012." Madison, Wisc.: Credit Union National Association Economics and Statistics Department. http://www.cuna.org/Research-And-Strategy/ Credit-Union-Data-And-Statistics/.

Schneider, Stu. 2009. "Cooperative Home Care Associates." Paper presented at Fair Work conference, New York City, December.

Schrader, L. F. 1989. "Equity Capital and Restructuring of Cooperatives as Investor-Oriented Firms." *Journal of Agricultural Cooperatives* 4:41–53.

Schutz, Aaron. 2006. "Home Is a Prison in the Global Economy: The Tragic Failure of School-Based Community Engagement Strategies." *Review of Educational Research* 76 (Winter): 691–743.

Schuyler, George S. 1930a. "Dear Colleague," November (with personal note to "Miss Baker"). Ella Baker Papers, box 2, folder 2, Schomburg Center.

———. 1930b. "Views and Reviews." *Pittsburgh Courier,* November 15.

———. 1931. "To the Members of the Y.N.C.L." Ella Baker Papers, box 2, folder 2, Schomburg Center.

———. 1932. "The Young Negro Co-operative League." *Crisis,* January, 456, 472.

———. n.d. "An Appeal to Young Negroes." YNCL brochure. Ella Baker Papers, box 2, folder 2, Schomburg Center.

Sewell, Dan. 1998. "Sweat Equity Keeps Plant Humming—Workers-Turned-Mill-Owners Pinch Pennies and Keep Jobs." *Seattle Times,* May 9, http://community.seattle-times.nwsource.com/archive/?date=19980509&slug=2749636.

Sexton, Richard J. 1984. "Perspectives on the Development of the Economic Theory of Cooperatives." *Canadian Journal of Agricultural Economics* 32 (July): 423–36.

Sexton, Richard J., and Terri A. Sexton. 1987. "Cooperatives as Entrants." *RAND Journal of Economics* 18 (Winter): 581–95.

Shaffer, James D. 1987. "Thinking About Farmers: Cooperatives, Contracts, and Economic Coordination." In *Cooperative Theory: New Approaches,* ed. Jeffrey S. Royer. Washington, D.C.: U.S. Department of Agriculture. http://www.rurdev.usda.gov/rbs/pub/sr18/contents.htm.

Shavelson, Jeff. 1990. *A Third Way: A Sourcebook; Innovations in Community-Owned Enterprise.* Washington, D.C.: National Center for Economic and Security Alternatives.

Shaw EcoVillage. 2005. "Our Mission"; "Chain Reaction"; "Success Stories." http://www.shawecovillage.com/.

Shipp, Sigmund C. 1996. "The Road Not Taken: Alternative Strategies for Black Economic Development in the United States." *Journal of Economic Issues* 30 (March): 79–95.

———. 2000. "Worker-Owned Firms in Inner-City Neighborhoods: An Empirical Study." *Review of International Co-operation* 92–93 (March): 42–46.

Siegfried, John J., and Bonnie T. Meszaros. 1998. "Voluntary Economics Content Standards for America's Schools: Rationale and Development." *Journal of Economic Education* 29 (Spring): 139–49.

Simms, Margaret C. 2002. "Women-Owned Businesses in 1997: A Step in the Right Direction." Paper presented at the Allied Social Sciences Association meeting, Atlanta, Georgia, January 4.

Sims, R. P. 1925. "Co-operation at Bluefield." *Crisis,* December, 92–93.

Skilton-Sylvester, Paul. 1994. "Elementary School Curricula and Urban Transformation." *Harvard Educational Review* 64 (Fall): 309–31.

———. 2003. "Less Like a Robot: A Comparison of Change in an Inner-City School and a Fortune 500 Company." *American Educational Research Journal* 40 (Spring): 3–41.

Smith, Ruby Green. 1920. "Cooperation and Living Cost Problems." In "Cooperation Among Producers and Consumers in New York State," special issue, *Foods and Markets* 2 (March–April): 14–20.

Spear, Roger. 1999. "The Co-operative Advantage." Paper presented at the International Co-operative Alliance research conference, "Values and Enterprise for Co-operative Advantage," Quebec City, August 28–29.

———. 2000. "The Co-operative Advantage." *Annals of Public and Cooperative Economics* 71 (4): 507–23.

Spriggs, William Edward. 1979. "The Virginia Colored Farmers' Alliance: A Case Study of Race and Class Identity." *Journal of Negro History* 64 (Summer): 191–204.

Stewart, James B. 1984. "Building a Cooperative Economy: Lessons from the Black Com-
    munity Experience." *Review of Social Economy* 42 (December): 360–68.
———, ed. 1997. *African Americans and Post-Industrial Labor Markets.* New Brunswick,
    N.J.: Transaction.
———. 2004. "Globalization, Cities, and Racial Inequality at the Dawn of the Twenty-First
    Century." *Review of Black Political Economy* 31 (Winter): 11–32.
"Sunflower County Freedom Farm Co-op." n.d. Fannie Lou Hamer Papers, box 11, Amistad
    Research Center.
Swinney, Dan. 1998. *Building the Bridge to the High Road.* Chicago: Midwest Center for
    Labor Research.
Tabb, William K. 1970. *The Political Economy of the Black Ghetto.* New York: W. W. Norton.
Takanarita, Takeshi, and Takako Tsuchiya. 2012. "Japan Workers' Co-operative Union's
    Reconstruction Efforts to Cooperate with Disaster Victims." *Social Policy* 42 (Fall):
    16–26.
Tansey, Charles D. 2010. "Community Development Credit Unions: An Emerging Player
    in Low Income Communities." Brookings Institute. http://www.brookings.edu/
    articles/2001/09metropolitanpolicy_taney.aspx.
Taylor, David. 1974. "Historical Sketch of the Cedjafawn Social Club." Credjafawn Social
    Club Records, Minnesota Historical Society. http://www.mnhs.org/library/findaids/
    P732.xml.
Taylor, Ula Y. 2002. *The Veiled Garvey: The Life and Times of Amy Jacques Garvey.*
    Chapel Hill: University of North Carolina Press.
Thomas, Henk, and Chris Logan. 1982. *Mondragon.* Boston: George Allen & Unwin.
Thomas, Karen. 2000. "Lessons of Mondragon's Employee-Owned Network." *Owners at
    Work* 12 (Summer): 5–9.
Thompson, David. 1981. "Feminist Cooperative History: The Role of Women Co-operators
    in the Birth of the British Cooperative Movement." *Co-ops Today*, May, 14–16.
Thordarson, Bruce. 1999. "Co-operative Legislation and the Co-operative Identity State-
    ment." *Journal of Co-operative Studies* 32 (September): 87–93.
Thornton, Agnes. 1948. "Brief History of the Brotherhood Consumer Cooperative Store."
    Mimeograph. BSCP Collection, box 34, folder 6, Chicago History Museum.
Thornton, Ronald. 1977. "Report to the Board of Directors of Freedom Farm Coopera-
    tive," March 17. Fannie Lou Hamer Collection, Tougaloo College Civil Rights Col-
    lection T/012, Mississippi Department of Archives and History, Jackson.
Time. 1930. "Business: Negro Chain." May 12, http://www.time.com/time/magazine/
    article/0,9171,752535,00.html.
———. 1968. "Enterprise: Helping Themselves." June 7, 100.
Tolbert, Lisa. 2007. "Challenging the Chain Stores." *Tar Heel Junior Historian* 46
    (Spring), http://ncpedia.org/industry/colored-merchant-assoc.
Truth, Sojourner. 1850. *The Narrative of Sojourner Truth.* Edited by Olive Gilbert.
    Boston: by the author. http://digital.library.upenn.edu/women/truth/1850/
    1850.html.
Turner, Chuck. 1992. "Empowering Communities of Color." In *From the Ground Up:
    Essays on Grassroots and Workplace Democracy by C. George Benello,* ed. Len
    Krimerman, Frank Lindenfeld, Carol Korty, and Julian Benello, 185–92. Boston:
    South End Press.
UN (United Nations). 2011. "International Year of Cooperatives." http://social.un.org/
    coopsyear/.
UN Development Program. 1994. *Human Development Report.* New York: United
    Nations.
UNI (Urban Nutrition Initiative). 2002. "Annual Report, May 2001–May 2002." Center for
    Community Partnerships, University of Pennsylvania, Philadelphia. http://www
    .upenn.edu/ccp/uni.shtml.

University of Wisconsin Center for Cooperatives. 2012. "Business Structure Comparison." UWCC Archives, University of Wisconsin, Madison. http://www.uwcc.wisc.edu/whatisacoop/BusinessStructureComparison/.

U.S. Department of Health and Human Services, Administration for Children and Families, Office of Community Services. 1994. "Micro-Business and Self-Employment." Monograph Series 200–90. Washington, D.C.: U.S. Department of Health and Human Services.

Vance, Laura. 1998. "Asian and Canadian Perspectives on Women." In *Proceedings from the Women in Co-operatives Forum, November 7–8, 1997*, 61–63. Saskatoon: University of Saskatchewan, Centre for the Study of Co-operatives.

Vanek, Jaroslav. 1971. *The Participatory Economy: An Evolutionary Hypothesis and a Strategy for Development.* Ithaca: Cornell University Press.

Varney, Darcy. 2003. "Shaw EcoVillage: Starting a Positive Chain Reaction." *Children, Youth, and Environments* 13 (Spring). http://www.colorado.edu/journals/cye.

WAGES. 2013. "Emma's Eco-Clean." http://www.wagescooperatives.org/co-op-network/co-op-network.

Wagner, Angela. 2006. "Data Collection in the Co-operative Sector: Sources of Other Business Statistics in Canada and the United States." Saskatoon: University of Saskatchewan, Centre for the Study of Co-operatives.

Wagner, Fritz W., Timothy Joder, and Anthony Mumphrey Jr. 1995. *Urban Revitalization: Policies and Programs.* Thousand Oaks: Calif.: Sage Publications.

Walker, Jim. 1999. "Enterprising Staffing Services—A Temporary Services Firm Working for Permanent Change." *Journal of Cooperative Development* 2 (Fall): 8–9, 13.

Walstad, William B., and Ken Rebeck. 2000. "The Status of Economics in the Curriculum." *Journal of Economics Education* 31 (Winter): 95–101.

Walter, Noah C. A., Jr. 1933. Letter to "Co-Worker Baker," November 2. Ella Baker Papers, box 2, folder 6, Schomburg Center.

Warbasse, James P. 1918. "The Theory of Cooperation." *Crisis*, March, 221–24.

———. 1920. "Consumer's Cooperation in United States." In "Cooperation Among Producers and Consumers in New York State," special issue, *Foods and Markets* 2 (March–April): 20–26.

———. 1925. Letter to W. E. B. Du Bois, February 19. In Aptheker, *Correspondence of W. E. B. Du Bois*, 1:305–6.

Washington, Alethea H. 1939a. "Section B: Rural Education—The Cooperative Movement." *Journal of Negro Education* 8 (January): 104–11.

———. 1939b. "Section B: Rural Education—The Cooperative Movement (Continued)." *Journal of Negro Education* 8 (April): 238–43.

Weare, Walter B. 1993. *Black Business in the New South: A Social History of the North Carolina Mutual Life Insurance Company.* Durham: Duke University Press.

Weiss, Chris, and Christine Clamp. 1992. "Women's Cooperatives: Part of the Answer to Poverty?" In *When Workers Decide: Workplace Democracy Takes Root in North America*, ed. Len Krimerman and Frank Lindenfeld, 225–28. Philadelphia: New Society.

White, C. R. 1920. "Report of Committee on Cooperative Organizations." *Foods and Markets* 2 (February): 29–31.

White, Deborah Gray. 1999. *Too Heavy a Load: Black Women in Defense of Themselves, 1894–1994.* New York: W. W. Norton.

Whitehead, John, David Landes, and Jessica Gordon Nembhard. 2005. "Inner-City Economic Development and Revitalization: A Community-Building Approach." In *African Americans in the U.S. Economy*, ed. Cecilia A. Conrad, John Whitehead, Patrick Mason, and James Stewart, 341–56. Lanham, Md.: Rowman & Littlefield.

Whyte, William F., and Kathleen K. Whyte. 1991. *Making Mondragon.* 2nd ed. Ithaca, N.Y.: ILR Press .

Wiener, Hans, and Robert Oakeshott. 1987. *Worker-Owners: Mondragon Revisited.* London: Anglo-German Foundation for the Study of Industrial Society.

Wilkening, Helena. 1973. Fund-raising letter for Freedom Farm Corporation and other co-ops in Mississippi, August 25. Fannie Lou Hamer Papers, box 11, Amistad Research Center.

Williams, Chancellor. 1934. Letter to Miss Burroughs, July 20. Nannie Helen Burroughs Papers, box 52, folder 3, Library of Congress, Washington, D.C.

———. 1961. "The Economic Basis of African Life." In Williams, *The Rebirth of African Civilization,* 151–84. Reprint, Chicago: Third World Press, 1993 (citations are to this edition).

Williams, Rhonda M. 2000. "If You're Black, Get Back; If You're Brown, Stick Around; If You're White, Hang Tight: A Primer on Race, Gender, and Work in the Global Economy." Working paper. Washington, D.C.: Preamble Center.

———. 2005. "Getting Paid: Black Women Economists Reflect on Women and Work." In *Sister Circle: Black Women Represent Work,* ed. Sharon Harley, 84–101. New Brunswick: Rutgers University Press.

Williams, Richard C. 2007. *The Cooperative Movement: Globalization from Below.* London: Ashgate.

Williams, Russell E. 2000. "Business Ownership Patterns Among Black, Latina, and Asian Women in Massachusetts." *Trotter Review:* 5–14.

Williamson, Anne O. H. 1939. "The Cooperative Way Out: A Challenge to the Negro College." In Alethea H. Washington, "Section B: Rural Education—The Cooperative Movement (Continued)," *Journal of Negro Education* 8 (April): 240–42.

Williamson, T. L. 1943. "Chicago Ladies Auxiliary to the Brotherhood of Sleeping Car Porters." Minutes of the January 7 and 21 regular meetings, BSCP Collection, box 29, folder 1, Chicago History Museum.

Williamson, Thad, David Imbrocio, and Gar Alperovitz. 2003. *Making a Place for Community: Local Democracy in a Global Era.* New York: Routledge.

Wilson, Halena. 1941a. "Brief History of the Consumer Movement." July 16. C. L. Dellums Papers, carton 24, BANC MSS 72/132, "Ladies Auxiliary, 1940–44" folder, Bancroft Library, University of California, Berkeley.

———. 1941b. Letter to the president, April 25. C. L. Dellums Papers, carton 24, BANC MSS 72/132, "Ladies Auxiliary, 1940–44" folder, Bancroft Library, University of California, Berkeley.

———. 1941c. Letter to the president, August 22. C. L. Dellums Papers, carton 24, BANC MSS 72/132, "Ladies Auxiliary, 1940–44" folder, Bancroft Library, University of California, Berkeley.

———. 1941d. Letter to the president, September 25. BSCP Collection, box 27, folder 3, Chicago History Museum.

———. 1942a. "Consumers Cooperative Movement." *Black Worker,* February, 2.

———. 1942b. "Declaration of the Object, Principles, and Aims of the Ladies Auxiliary to the Brotherhood of Sleeping Car Porters." Mimeograph. BSCP Collection, box 28, folder 2, Chicago History Museum.

———. 1942c. Letter to Lucille Jones, January 26. BSCP Collection, box 27, folder 3, Chicago History Museum.

———. 1942d. "More About the Rochdale Co-operative Principles." *Black Worker,* May, 3.

———. 1945a. Letter to A. Philip Randolph, January 4. A. Philip Randolph Collection, box 76, folder 1, Library of Congress, Washington, D.C.

———. 1945b. Letter to A. Philip Randolph, July 6. A. Philip Randolph Collection, box 76, folder 1, Library of Congress, Washington, D.C.

———, ed. 1947a. "Cooperation: The Middle Way of Sweden." *Black Worker,* December, 6.

———. 1947b. "Dear Member," September 9. BSCP Collection, box 31, folder 2, Chicago History Museum.

——. 1948a. "ABCs of Consumer Cooperatives." *Black Worker,* April, 7.

——. 1948b. "Special Notice." October 15. Mimeograph. A. Philip Randolph Collection, box 75, folder 7, Library of Congress, Washington, D.C.

——. 1949a. Letter to A. Philip Randolph, July 25. A. Philip Randolph Collection, box 75, folder 7, Library of Congress, Washington, D.C.

——. 1949b. "Special Bulletin" to the members, July 11. A. Philip Randolph Collection, box 75, folder 17, Library of Congress, Washington, D.C.

——. 1952. Speech at the 27th anniversary of the Brotherhood of Sleeping Car Porters, August 27. BSCP Collection, box 33, folder 4, Chicago History Museum.

——. 1953. "Special Letter." Mimeograph. BSCP Collection, box 33, folder 4, Chicago History Museum.

——. n.d. [ca. 1941.] "Excerpts from *The Worker as a Consumer.*" C. L. Dellums Papers, carton 24, BANC MSS 72/132, "Ladies Auxiliary, 1940–44" folder, Bancroft Library, University of California, Berkeley.

Wilson, Halena, Minnie A. Lee, and Agnes Thornton. 1947. General letter to the members, September 26. A. Philip Randolph Collection, box 75, folder 7, Library of Congress, Washington, D.C.

Wilson, Halena, and A. Philip Randoph. 1938. "Bulletin of Instruction on Decisions and Orders of the First Convention of Ladies Auxiliary and International Executive Board." Mimeograph. BSCP Collection, box 27, folder 6, Chicago History Museum.

Wilson, Halena, Agnes Thornton, and Minnie A. Lee. 1950. To the members, with enclosed check, February 3. Mimeograph. A. Philip Randolph Collection, box 7, Library of Congress, Washington, D.C.

Winbush, Raymond. 2003. "The Earth Moved: Stealing Black Land in the United States." In *Should America Pay? Slavery and the Raging Debate over Reparations,* ed. Raymond Winbush, 46–56. New York: Harper Collins.

Woods, Clyde. 1998. *Development Arrested: The Blues and Plantation Power in the Mississippi Delta.* London: Verso.

——. 2007. "'Sittin' on Top of the World': The Challenges of Blues and Hip Hop Geography." In *Black Geographies and the Politics of Place,* ed. Katherine McKittrick and Clyde Woods, 46–81. Toronto: Between the Lines.

Woodson, Carter G. 1929. "Insurance Business Among Negroes." *Journal of Negro History* 14 (April): 202–26.

Workers Education Bureau. 1940. "Current Event Publications." Ladies Auxiliary to the Brotherhood of Sleeping Car Porters. BSCP Collection, box 26, folder 2, Chicago History Museum.

YNCL (Young Negroes' Co-operative League). 1932. "Program of the Second National Conference of the Young Negroes' Cooperative League at the Twelfth Street Y.M.C.A., 1816—12th St., NW, Washington, D.C., Sunday, April 3, 1932." Box 2, folder 2, Schomburg Center.

Young, Andrew. 2005. Remarks as recipient of the 2005 FSC/LAF's Estelle Witherspoon Lifetime Achievement Award, August 18. Birmingham Civil Rights Museum, Birmingham, Alabama.

Zippert, John. 2005. Interview by author, Epes, Alabama, June 23.

——. 2012. "History of the Federation of Southern Cooperatives." Presentation given at the CoopEcon2012 conference, Epes, Alabama, July 27.

Index

Page numbers in italics indicate figures and tables.

Leflore County (Mississippi) massacre, 57
legal liability, of corporations vs. coopera-
    tives, 7
legislative advocacy, 223–25. *See also* policy
    advocacy
Leigh, Wilhelmina A., 213
Leikin, Steve, 48, 49
Lemacks, Marcus, 167
lending circles, 90
lessons learned
    from Depression-era cooperatives, 81–82,
        146–47
    from early cooperatives, 28–30, 81–84
Levine, David, 14
Lewis, John, 218
Lexington Savings Bank, 63, 65–66
Liberia, shipping between U.S. and, 68–69
Light of Tyrrell Cooperative, 91
Logue, John, 14
Los Angeles (California)
    school-based youth cooperatives in, 228
    worker sovereignty in, 216–17
Louisiana, agricultural cooperatives in, 195,
    198, 210–11, 261 n. 6
Love, Reverend, 55, 253 n. 4 (ch. 2)
Lusane, Clarence, 190
Lusty Ladies Theater, 217
Lynch, Ruth G., 109–10
lynchings, 101, 256 n. 12
Lyons, A. E., 124

mail fraud, 44, 68, 254 n. 8
Mandela Foods Cooperative, 215–16
Marable, Manning, 107
Marini, M., 251 n. 4
market failures, advantages of cooperatives
    and, 11, 13
marketing cooperatives, 172, 173
Maroons, 33
Marshall, Ray, 172
Marshall, Mrs. Thurgood, 136
Martin, Tony, 66–67, 254 n. 7
Maryland. *See also* Baltimore
    Depression-era cooperatives in, 128
    mutual-aid societies in, 45
Masiero, Attilio, 214
Massachusetts
    communes in, 35–37, 40
    cooperative education in, 95
    women-owned cooperatives in, 166–67
    youth development in, 230–31
Matney, W. C., 75, 105, 213, 254 n. 11, 256 n. 14
MCC. *See* Mondragon Cooperative Corpora-
    tion
McCarthyism, 256 n. 17
McDonald, Joseph A., 255 n. 3

McKnight, Albert J., 195, 198, 199–200, 260
    n. 3 (ch. 9), 261 n. 6
McLanahan, C. J., 159
Measure for Measure, 179, 220
media coverage. *See* press coverage
Melman, Seymour, 220
members, cooperative
    education of. *See* education
    vs. membership in other business forms, 6
    requirements for, 4
Memphis (Tennessee)
    agricultural cooperatives in, 174
    early cooperatives in, 74, 89, 105
Mercantile Cooperative Company, 73
Messenger (magazine). *See also* Randolph,
    A. Philip
    articles on cooperatives in, 17, 94, 102, 255
        n. 10
    on Burroughs, 151
    as competitor of *Crisis*, 256 n. 12
    Schuyler's work on, 112, 115
methodology, 17–20
MFDP. *See* Mississippi Freedom Democratic
    Party
microenterprise, 13
microfinance, 13
microlending, study circles in, 90
migration, Black, 195–96, 198
milk cooperatives, 133, 135–36
Mills, Kay, 182–83, 185, 186
Milwaukee (Wisconsin), late twentieth-
    century cooperatives in, 219
Mississippi
    agricultural cooperatives in, 57, 174, 175,
        178–86, 198, 209–10
    late twentieth-century cooperatives in, 217
    Leflore massacre in, 57
    voting rights in, 178, 180
Mississippi Freedom Democratic Party
    (MFDP), 178–79, 180
Mississippi Union Leagues, 53
Missouri. *See* Kansas City
Modern Cooperative Association, 136–37
Mondragon Cooperative Corporation (MCC)
    credit union of, 225
    definition of, 252 n. 8, 253 n. 5 (ch. 3)
    education programs of, 85, 90, 95, 96
    as example for Black urban redevelopment,
        16, 252 n. 7
    lessons learned from, 235
    origins of, 252 n. 8
    replicable elements of, 16
    solidarity in, 214, 220, 235
    structure of, 252 n. 8
    as system of interlocking cooperatives, 222,
        235